Macroeconomics

MACROECONOMICS

THE STATIC AND DYNAMIC ANALYSIS OF A MONETARY ECONOMY

Rosalind Levačić

Lecturer in Economics, The Open University

First edition 1976
Reprinted 1977, 1978

ELBS edition first published 1978

Published by
THE MACMILLAN PRESS LTD
London and Basingstoke
Associated companies in Delhi Dublin
Hong Kong Johannesburg Lagos Melbourne
New York Singapore and Tokyo

ISBN 0 333 16869 0 (hard cover)
0 333 18704 0 (paper cover)

ISBN 0 333 23993 8 (ELBS paperback edition)

Printed in Hong Kong by
The Hong Kong Printing Press (1977) Limited

Contents

Preface

This book gives a thorough grounding in modern macroeconomic analysis to the level that should be attained by specialist economics undergraduates during their second and third years. A knowledge of basic economic principles is presupposed. This should include the simple goods market Keynesian model of national income determination. It will also be helpful if a basic micro theory and a basic mathematics course are being followed as well. The mathematics in the main text is kept to a minimum, making use only of algebra and basic differential calculus. A fuller mathematical treatment of some topics can be found in appendices.

The basic aims of the book are closely interconnected and are as follows.

(1) To explain how a developed market economy functions. Since such an economy is necessarily a monetary economy the monetary and real aspects of macroeconomic behaviour are interrelated throughout the book.

(2) To show how one can attempt to make predictions about the behaviour of macro variables. This involves the construction and testing of theories. A brief introduction to empirical testing is given in Chapter 1 and summaries of empirical results, with particular emphasis on the U.K. economy, are given where appropriate.

(3) To discuss the policy implications of macro theory. This includes specifying the different views regarding the behaviour of a capitalist economy and the consequent macroeconomic objectives that may be pursued, as well as discussing the means by which such objectives can be attained.

With these aims in mind emphasis is laid on the following points which are crucial to an understanding of macroeconomic behaviour but are nevertheless neglected in most macro texts.

(1) Macroeconomic behaviour depends upon the behaviour of the underlying micro units which make up the economy. The micro foundations of consumption, investment, the demand for money, the supply of money and inflation theory are treated thoroughly. The behaviour of such variables is thus derived from the behaviour of individual decision-units who make choices over a number of time periods. It is only from this basis that one can show how current behaviour is influenced by the past values of variables and by their expected future values. This is essential for understanding how the economy adjusts over time.

(2) Cautious use only is made of comparative static analysis. It is stressed that this mode of analysis is a useful simplification which shows the interdependencies existing amongst variables and allows one to predict the final direction and magnitude of change in a variable on the assumption that it returns to static equilibrium. This text eschews instructing students to perform mechanical tricks with models at the expense of understanding the analysis behind them and appreciating both their usefulness and their limitations. With the same provisos, use is made of dynamic equilibrium analysis of a growing economy.

(3) Therefore, there is explicit treatment of disequilibrium analysis. This is emphasised in the treatment of the individual macro functions which is then related to the wider disequilibrium aspects of macro models. This is discussed with reference to an economy in unemployment disequilibrium (Keynes and the so-called reinterpretation of Keynes), inflation and trade-cycle theory. Trade-cycle theory is explicitly seen as the disequilibrium behaviour of a growing economy. This grounding in disequilibrium analysis enables one to appreciate the problems of devising and applying economic policy measures.

The objectives outlined above are pursued by providing a structure of economic analysis which enables the student to see the macroeconomic system as a whole by relating its constituent parts and seeing their common analytical content. Given this aim I consider it harmful to present economic theory as a boxing match in which each school of thought's theoretical punches are chronicled. Instead I have tried to distill the essential ideas from the various theories on a given subject in order to synthesise and show how these theories contribute to our total understanding of the subject in hand.

In my experience students of economics are too apt to be taken in by the academic game of controversy manufacturing and see theoretical differences where none exist. As a result they often fail to appreciate the essential similarities of approaches which are addressed to the same problem. I have tried, therefore, to counteract this tendency by concentrating on the concepts which are common throughout economic analysis and by showing how models differ because they apply to different economic circumstances, for example full employment or unemployment, and not because they are fundamentally different.

In this third-best world I would be happy to achieve limited objectives, such as banishing the use of the term 'speculative demand for money' to the history of economic thought and discarding the terms cost-push and demand-pull inflation, which are possibly useful for classification but quite redundant in the analysis of inflation.

I would like to express my gratitude to my friends and colleagues, Jock Oliver and Alex Rebmann-Huber, who have encouraged me and helped me to formulate my ideas and who have improved the following chapters by reading them thoroughly and critically before offering their suggestions. Alex has helped me at all stages of production and has contributed a chapter on economic growth. For all this I am extremely grateful. My final thanks go to my secretary, Rosalind Ruzica, for being a veritable *alter ego* and typing an illegible manuscript.

1 Introduction to Macroeconomics

1.1 WHAT MACROECONOMICS IS ABOUT

Macroeconomics is the study of the behaviour of the whole economy. The main body of macro theory applies to a developed, capitalist economy. A capitalist economy is one where wealth is owned by individuals whose independently taken decisions interact to determine the values of variables. Capitalist economies are mixed economies nowadays and differ in the extent to which they allow market forces to operate.

Macroeconomics is concerned with the determination of the broad aggregates in the economy such as national product, employment, the price level and the balance-of-payments position. Aggregates are made up of constituent elements. This means that one cannot investigate economic behaviour at the macro level without inquiring into the behaviour of individual decision units in the economy. The study of macroeconomics therefore must be founded on a thorough understanding of the underlying micro theory, which makes predictions based on maximising behaviour by decision units.

Partial and General Equilibrium Analysis

It is important to relate macro theories to their micro foundations. This process has been a particularly noticeable trend in macro theory over the last twenty years. Micro theory investigates individual behaviour, taking as fixed those variables which the individual cannot alter by himself. It constructs models which determine a limited number of micro variables, such as the price and output of a particular product. It is therefore said to involve partial equilibrium analysis, since all other variables in the economy are assumed to be unaffected by changes in the variables being analysed. Micro theory analyses a single market or a set of closely related markets independently of the rest of the economy.

Macroeconomics considers the interaction of all the individual decision units in the economy and must therefore involve general equilibrium analysis. In micro theory we examine the consumption and saving behaviour of a household in relation to the rate of interest which is exogenously given to that household. At the macro level we look at how households' savings plans and their demands for financial assets interact with the investment and financing plans of firms to determine the level of interest rates in the economy. The essential feature of macroeconomics is that it analyses the interdependencies between variables and the repercussions of a change in one variable upon other variables together with the feedback effects on that variable.

One approach to macroeconomic analysis is to work with all the micro equations of the economy and to determine the prices of commodities and factors of production and the quantities of commodities produced by solving the model for general equilibrium. As each commodity, factor of production and household is represented by its own behavioural equations, such models are difficult to handle.

The alternative, and more widely used approach in macro analysis, is to suppress the individual behavioural relationships and to work with broad aggregates. A common procedure is to derive behavioural relationships at the individual, micro level and to generalise to the aggregate level. For instance one hypothesises that a household's consumption will vary directly with its disposable income and then extends this hypothesis to a relationship between aggregate consumption and national disposable income.

1.2 AGGREGATION

The basic difficulty with aggregation is to ensure that the measure of the aggregate accurately reflects the relative quantities of the constituents of the aggregate. One aspect of the problem involves obtaining an appropriate unit of measurement for the aggregate.

Real and Nominal Quantities

An example of the difficulties attached to using a single unit of measurement is provided by the measurement of national output which consists of millions of heterogeneous goods and services. These cannot be measured using a common physical unit. The only common unit in which they can be measured is money. National output is therefore measured by the sum of the quantity of each good or service times its price. The problem with this measurement is that we are interested in the physical or real quantity of national output, as this gives us some indication of the standard of living of the members of the economy.

The real quantity of national output is inaccurately measured by national output in money terms because this measure of national output may increase in value, not because of an increase in the physical quantity of goods and services produced but because of a general rise in the level of prices. To isolate changes in the physical quantity of output from changes in the price level, output has to be measured at constant money prices. This is done by comparing over time real output levels obtained by measuring national output in all the years in the prices that ruled in one of those years. This is equivalent to deflating national output at current prices by an index of the price level. We thus get the following definitions. The value of a variable measured in current prices is its money or nominal value. The nominal value deflated by an index of the price level is its real value. In this book the following notation is used:

Y is the nominal national output or output measured in current prices, y is the real national output or output measured in constant prices, P is an index of the price level; by our definition $y = Y/P$.

A price index is the weighted average of the prices of a limited number (in relation to total output) of goods and services. The price of each commodity is weighted by the proportion of total expenditure devoted to that commodity. Because the pattern of supply and demand changes, the proportion of expenditure allocated to various goods changes with time. This introduces bias into a price index. Therefore the weights used in constructing a price index are intermittently revised to correct this bias.

Aggregation: Fixed Relative Quantities

Aggregate analysis cannot allow for changes in the composition of the individual items that constitute the aggregate. When we aggregate over all commodities to obtain the aggregate national output its composition in terms of relative quantities of goods and services is assumed fixed. This means that in this type of macro analysis we take relative prices as fixed and treat the sum of all goods and services as if it were a single good. Most macro models which contain aggregate functions are constructed in terms of a single aggregate output.

This makes for a particular problem because of the need to include consumption goods, which are used up for current enjoyment, and capital goods, which are used to produce future consumption, in the same model. If one is assuming a single aggregate output then one is assuming that the price of consumption goods relative to capital goods is fixed and therefore determined outside the model. All the models dealt with formally in this book are of this type.

Capital is an aggregate which is particularly difficult to measure since it consists of heterogeneous goods, differing in age and in the kind of technology that they embody. It is difficult to derive even a monetary measure of the value of the capital stock. The prices at which the existing capital goods were acquired in the past do not reflect their current value. Allowance has to be made for depreciation, which is difficult to calculate accurately, and for the current replacement costs of the capital. There is the further problem of deflating the monetary value of the capital stock by an appropriate price index to obtain its real value.

Problems arise in deriving aggregate relationships between variables by summing over the individual components. For instance one can postulate a particular functional relationship between household consumption and household disposable income for each of N households, but one may not be able to derive the form of the aggregate relationship between total consumption and total income without making further assumptions. In the simple case of linearity

$$C_i = a_i + b_i\, y_{di},$$

where C_i is the consumption of ith household and y_{di} is the disposable income of ith household. The aggregate relationship is

$$C = \sum_{i=1}^{N} C_i = \sum_{i=1}^{N} a_i + \sum_{i=1}^{N} \frac{y_{di}}{y} b_i y.$$

The aggregate marginal propensity to consume (m.p.c.) is the weighted average of the individual m.p.c.s, the weights being each household's income as a proportion of total income. An additional variable, namely the distribution of income, explains aggregate consumption but it is not a determinant of individual household consumption.

It needs to be borne in mind that aggregation does present problems but if we are to do any analysis that goes beyond the level of the individual decision-maker we have to aggregate. Imperfect knowledge of the composition of the aggregates one is working with does not necessarily mean that one cannot produce useful results. Natural science made great progress without knowing the composition of the atom.

1.3 KEYNESIAN AND NEOCLASSICAL MACRO THEORY

The basic macro model of national income determination is constructed in terms of broad aggregates, namely output, consumption and investment. It was developed by economists who attempted to simplify and interpret J. M. Keynes's *The General Theory of Employment, Interest and Money* [1]. *The General Theory* is regarded as a revolutionary work since, therein, Keynes set out to challenge the mainstream (neoclassical) economic thought of his day.

Neoclassical economics grew out of the marginalist school of the latter part of the nineteenth century which developed economic theory on the basis of maximising behaviour. These ideas were elaborated by Alfred Marshall, Leon Walras and others and provide the theoretical underpinning to modern economic theory. Keynes himself used neoclassical theory to develop consumption, investment and labour demand and supply functions.

Keynes criticised neoclassical economics for conceiving of a market economy as being self-regulatory. A main policy conclusion of the neoclassical economists of that period was that government intervention to regulate the economy was unnecessary and brought about distortions. Keynes set out to explain why a market economy does not return easily to full-employment equilibrium once it is disturbed from equilibrium. *The General Theory* is complex and difficult to understand, particularly as it is a non-mathematical analysis of an economy in disequilibrium. Economists attempted to interpret *The General Theory* with simple static models and it is this body of theory which is known as Keynesian economics.

Keynesian economics, which had its heyday in the 1940s, advocates the necessity of government management of the economy by the use of fiscal policy to achieve such objectives as full employment, stability and growth. The Keynesians tended to ignore the influence of money in explaining the behaviour of macro variables and as a result monetary policy was regarded as virtually ineffective during the 1940s and early 1950s.

Since the mid-1950s there has been a resurgence of neoclassical economics, associated with a group of economists centred on the University of Chicago around Milton Friedman. These economists, known as the monetarist school, emphasise the importance of money in explaining macroeconomic behaviour. However, the simple faith of the early Keynesians in government management of the economy has now evaporated. The task is now seen to be far more complex than it had first seemed. In contrast to the Keynesian view of economic policy, the Friedman—monetarist view is that short-run demand management is likely to be unsuccessful, even destabilising, and should not be undertaken.

The debate between Keynesian and neoclassical economists has evolved a common analytical framework for macroeconomic analysis which is known as the Keynesian—neoclassical synthesis. An exposition of this framework is given in the following chapters.

1.4 THE METHODOLOGY OF ECONOMICS

Students should be aware that it is in the interests of academics who wish to make a name for themselves to seek out points of disagreement rather than of agreement. This is the way a subject progresses but in the process it can get side-tracked into debating unimportant issues. Excessive debate on methodology is particularly stultifying as it leaves a profession with little time for developing the main body of its discipline. A newcomer to a subject should not take at face value the claims of rival schools of thought to be so different from each other, without first looking for common elements.

If economics is to be a science it must be capable of explaining economic behaviour. We must therefore judge between contending theories, not on the grounds of how politically or aesthetically pleasing we find them, but on how well they explain real world phenomena. Since the real world is so complex and involves the interaction of so many variables, it is necessary to simplify by constructing theories or models. To further our understanding of the world we need to impose a structure upon the disorganised mass of observed phenomena. It is only when students of a subject work within an agreed structure that they can communicate with each other.

In constructing a theory or model we select those variables which, on the basis of *a priori* reasoning (this is reasoning on the basis of casual observation and intuition, before appealing to factual evidence) we think are important. These variables are then analysed in isolation from all other variables. We make assumptions concerning the behaviour of the variables in the model and from this we derive deductions of a causal nature. If a certain variable, X, changes we predict how other variables will react. It is the predictions of a theory that are important. The assumptions of the theory are irrelevant to our judgements about the theory's explanatory power. We can only distinguish between theories by comparing their predictions. If two theories have different assumptions but the same predictions we have no means of distinguishing between them [2].

The role of assumptions in a theory is to select those elements of behaviour we consider important and to simplify them for the purposes of making predictions. The behaviour assumed is not a detailed description of actuality. If it were it would not serve the purpose of theory which is to derive relatively simple predictions that can be applied quite generally. The maximisation of utility, that is the satisfaction gained from consuming goods and services, is the basic assumption underlying economic theory. We do not require that people actually engage in complex calculations in order to maximise their utility but that their behaviour is the same as if they did so. For instance we require that people with a fixed real income will buy less of a good when its price rises as is predicted by utility maximising behaviour. If we observe that people do behave in this way, the theory that the demand for a good is inversely related to its price is supported. The assumption of utility maximising behaviour has not been tested. All we know is that it is consistent with observed facts.

1.5 MODEL BUILDING AND THE USE OF MODELS FOR ANALYSIS

We take as an example of model building the Keynesian one-sector model of national income determination [3]. This is the main variable with which the model is concerned. National income is an example of a *flow variable* which is one that can only be measured as a rate of flow per period of time. To say that national output is £63 million is meaningless unless one specifies the time period, such as a year, over which it is measured. A *stock variable* has no time period in its measurement as it relates to a particular moment in time. The labour force is a stock variable as it consists of 24 million people at a particular moment.

The Keynesian one-sector model makes a number of simplifying assumptions.* It assumes that both the stock of capital and the labour force, which when fully utilised determine the maximum level of real output the economy can produce, are constant. An underlying behavioural assumption of the model is that firms act as profit maximisers. If demand for their output exceeds the supply firms increase production, providing there are spare resources to put to work. Conversely if supply exceeds demand firms reduce output.

The model is a short-run model and determines the value of real national output for a particular period of time, such as a year. The model solves for the *static equilibrium* level of real output, this being the value of real output (or any other variable) that has no tendency to change once it has been established. Static equilibrium in this model requires that firms wish in aggregate neither to expand nor contract the quantity of output which they are currently producing. This requires that the supply of real national output, y, equals the quantity of national output which people wish to buy, E. *The condition for static equilibrium* in this model is therefore

$$y = E \qquad (1.1)$$

where E is the desired aggregate demand or, alternatively, desired aggregate expenditure.

We then define aggregate demand as being composed of real consumption expenditure, C, and real investment expenditure, I. This is an example of a *definitional relationship* and is written

$$E = C + I. \qquad (1.2)$$

A further behavioural assumption is made, namely that real consumption varies directly with real national income. This *behavioural relationship* is written

$$C = a + by, \qquad (1.3)$$

where $b = dC/dy$ and is known as the marginal propensity to consume.

Another simplifying assumption is that investment is *exogenous*. This

---

* It is assumed that students are already acquainted with the simple Keynesian model and with basic national income accounting to the level achieved in such books as Ford [3].

means that the variable is fixed at some known value and is not deter-mined in the model. This is indicated by writing $I = I_0$. The terms *independent* and *autonomous* are synonymous with exogenous. The coefficients of a model, such as a and b above, and the exogenous variables, all of which are assumed constant, are known as the *param-eters* of the model. The values of the parameters and the form of the relationship which make up the model are referred to as the model's *structure*. Equations (1.1), (1.2) and (1.3) are the *structural equations* of the model.

Consumption and income are *endogenous* variables. The value of an endogenous or dependent variable is determined in the model. To solve the model in order to find the static equilibrium values for consumption and real income we substitute equation (1.3) into (1.2) and the result into (1.1) to obtain

$$y = a + by + I_0 \qquad\qquad (1.4)$$

$$y = \frac{a + I_0}{1 - b} = \frac{A}{1 - b} \qquad\qquad (1.5)$$

where A is the autonomous expenditure and $1/(1 - b)$ is known as a multiplier. By substituting equation (1.5) into (1.3) we obtain

$$C = a + bA/(1 - b). \qquad\qquad (1.6)$$

Equations (1.5) and (1.6) are called the *reduced form* equations of the model as they express each endogenous variable in terms of the exoge-nous variables only.

Comparative Static Analysis

Given the values of the parameters of the model we can predict the values of the endogenous variables. Comparative static analysis is used to predict the impact on the equilibrium values of the endogenous variables of a change in an exogenous variable. This is done by changing the values given to the parameters of the model and comparing the different positions of static equilibrium obtained. For instance if invest-ment increases, given some excess capacity in the economy, real output will be higher at the new equilibrium position.

Static analysis is timeless. An instantaneous change occurs since a static model can only tell us what are the equilibrium values of the endogenous variables. As all variables in a static model are given values for the current period only, such a model can tell us nothing about how the variables adjust when the model is not in equilibrium. Static equilib-rium does not exist in the real world since the values of parameters are constantly changing and instantaneous adjustment does not occur. Comparative static analysis is useful because it allows us to predict the

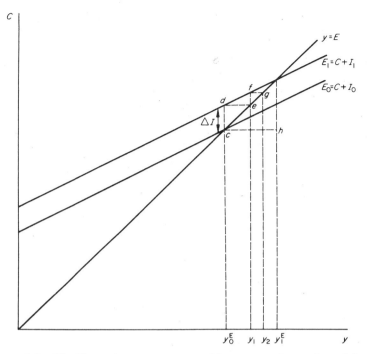

FIGURE 1.1   *The Keynesian one-sector model; comparative static and dynamic analysis*

direction in which a variable will move following a change in its determinants as well as the final magnitude of the change if the system came to rest at equilibrium again.

A static model cannot be used to predict what values a variable takes on as it moves from one position of equilibrium to another. It will tell us, as shown in Figure 1.1, that an increase in investment of $\Delta I = cd$ will, when equilibrium is regained, have caused an increase in real output of ch from y_0^E to y_1^E. The increase in the equilibrium level of output, following an increase in autonomous investment, is given by the long-run multiplier which is $1/(1 - b)$.

Dynamic Analysis

If we wish to trace out a time path of output as we move from one equilibrium position to another, we must construct a dynamic model. Such a model postulates lags in the adjustment of variables, in which the current value of a variable depends upon the past values of either: itself or of other variables. Dynamic models containing separate periods of analysis, say intervals of a quarter of a year, are couched in terms of *discrete time* periods. A dynamic model may alternatively relate the rate of change of a variable to the rates of change of other variables (i.e. first or higher order derivatives). Such a model is constructed in terms of *continuous time*. For example, growth models relate the rate of change of real output to those of the capital stock and the labour force.

The one-sector model of income determination can be made dynamic simply by postulating a lag in the adjustment of consumption to income. Let us assume that if incomes change people do not respond immediately but change their consumption in the next quarter. The consumption function is therefore lagged one period and written

$$C_t = \acute{a} + by_{t-1} \tag{1.7}$$

where the subscript t refers to the time period to which the variable relates, C_t is the consumption in the current period (quarter in this example), and y_{t-1} is income in the previous period. Since static equilibrium requires that income remains unchanged over time this condition is written as

$$y_t = y_{t-1} = y^E.$$

If investment increases we can trace out a time path of income which we could not do in the static model. After one period income rises by the increase in investment, ΔI, which is assumed to be a permanent increase. Consumption in the first quarter does not rise at all as there was no change in output in the previous quarter when the system was in equilibrium. In Figure 1.1 output rises in the first quarter by ΔI which equals *cd* which, in turn, equals *de*. In the second quarter income rises because consumption increases by b times the first quarter's rise in income. The second quarter's increase in income is $b\Delta I$ which equals *ef* which, in turn, equals *fg*. Thus after two quarters income has risen by *de + fg* to y_2. This sequence of income increases is shown in Table 1.1. Each time output increases a fraction, b, of this is injected back into aggregate

TABLE 1.1. The Dynamic Sequences of the Expenditure Multiplier

	Change in I	Change in C	Change in y
After 1 period	ΔI	0	ΔI
After 2 periods	0	$b\Delta I$	$b\Delta I$
After 3 periods	0	$b^2\Delta I$	$b^2\Delta I$
.	.	.	.
.	.	.	.
.	.	.	.
After N periods	0	$b^{N-1}\Delta I$	$b^{N-1}\Delta I$

expenditure via an increase in consumption and becomes next period's increase in output. This analysis shows how a given increase in autonomous expenditure generates over time a greater increase in income. This process is the expenditure multiplier at work.

The final increase in income is obtained by summing the increase for each period, i.e.

$$\Delta y = \Delta I(1 + b + b^2 + \cdots + b^{N-1}). \tag{1.8}$$

Multiply both sides of equation (1.8) by b and substract the result from equation (1.8) so that

$$(1-b)\Delta y = (1-b^N)\Delta I$$

$$\Delta y = \frac{(1-b^N)\,\Delta I}{(1-b)} = \lim_{N \to \infty} \frac{\Delta I}{(1-b)},$$

since if $0 < b < 1$, b^N tends to 0 as N tends to infinity.

In the dynamic model income approaches equilibrium gradually, never quite attaining it since some small change $b^N \Delta I$ is still going on but becomes negligibly small with time. In this case income is said to converge towards equilibrium. The time path for the above model is shown by the stepped adjustment path in Figure 1.2. A continuous time

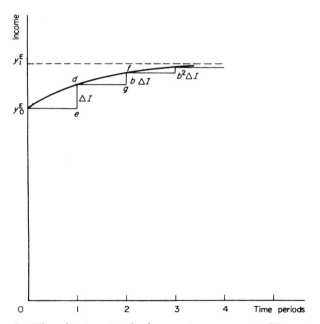

FIGURE 1.2 *The adjustment path of income in a one-sector Keynesian model*

model would give a smooth adjustment path as indicated in Figure 1.2.

If b were equal to or greater than one, equilibrium would be unstable since any change in income would be respectively equal to or greater than the previous period's change in income. Over time output would steadily diverge from its static equilibrium value. So long as b lies between plus and minus one the model has a *stable equilibrium*. This means that when disturbed from equilibrium the model returns towards equilibrium.

The construction of models which specify lags in the adjustment of variables is particularly important for policy purposes. Policy-makers wish to know not only the direction of change and its final magnitude, but also how long it takes to institute a change of a given magnitude. We can therefore distinguish impact multipliers, which give the short-run variation in income consequent upon a change in one of its determinants, from the long-run multiplier which gives the final change in income when all re-adjustments have worked themselves out.

1.6 THE STOCHASTIC NATURE OF ECONOMIC RELATIONSHIPS

Economic variables and relationships between economic variables cannot, by their nature, be precisely quantified. An economic variable is not deterministic as it does not take on a fixed, definite value. For instance we cannot say that consumption is always 90 per cent of disposable income. A variable which is not deterministic but takes on a range of possible values is known as a *random or stochastic variable*. A series of experiments with a random variable will produce a range of values for the variable. For instance if one throws a die several times one will record numbers between one and six, or questioning people with an annual income of £4000 one will find that they have different consumption expenditures.

One cannot give a single numerical value to a random variable but one can quantify the range of values that the random variable can take on, alternatively known as its population, by assigning it a probability distribution. This weights each possible value of the random variable by a number which is a fraction. The sum of the probabilities defined over all the possible values of the random variable is constrained to equal one. For example the probability of each of the numbers one to six appearing on the throw of a die is one-sixth so that the probabilities of all the possible events sum to one.

Two features of a probability distribution are extremely useful in specifying the behaviour of a random variable.

(1) *The expected value of a random variable*. This is obtained by weighting each value of the random variable by its probability and summing over all values. Thus if a random variable, X, takes on values

$X_1, X_2, \ldots, X_i, \ldots, X_N$, each with a probability of $P_1, P_2, \ldots, P_i, \ldots, P_N$, the expected value of X is

$$E(X) = \sum_{i=1}^{N} X_i P_i.$$

Alternatively the expected value can be thought of as the average or mean value for X.

(2) *The dispersion of the random variable about its expected value* is the extent to which values of the random variable lie on either side of the expected value. This dispersion is measured by the *variance* of the variable. Its variance is obtained by subtracting each possible value of X from its expected value and squaring the result so that negative and positive deviations do not cancel out. Each squared deviation about the mean is multiplied by the probability of X_i, P_i, and all the squared deviations are summed. Thus variance of X is given by

$$\text{var } X = \sigma_x^2 = \sum_{i=1}^{N} [X_i - E(X)]^2 P_i.$$

The square root of the variance is called the standard deviation, or σ_x. Thus

$$\sigma_x = \sqrt{\sum_{i=1}^{N} [X_i - E(X)]^2 P_i}.$$

A very useful probability distribution is the bell-shaped normal distribution which is completely specified once its expected value and standard deviation are known. The expected value, standard deviation and other properties of a theoretical probability distribution are known as its parameters and are also referred to as statistics. Any normal distribution can be standardised by subtracting its expected value from every possible value of X and dividing the result by the standard deviation of X. This gives a zero expected value and a standard deviation of one to the normalised distribution, as shown in Figure 1.3.

The normal distribution is symmetric as half the distribution lies on either side of the expected value. 68 per cent of the distribution lies within one standard deviation of the expected value. This means that there is a 0·68 probability that any particular value of X will lie within one standard deviation of its expected value. There is a 0·95 probability that X will lie within two standard deviations of its expected value. The normal distribution is widely used in the statistical testing of economic relationships.

1.7 THE STATISTICAL TESTING OF ECONOMIC RELATIONSHIPS

The parameters of a theoretical probability distribution describe the behaviour of a random variable. If we do not know the values of these parameters we can attempt to estimate them by conducting experiments. These experiments, because they cannot be exhaustive, reveal

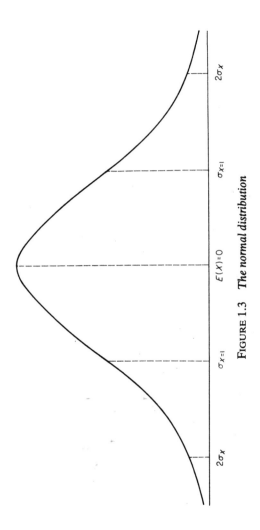

FIGURE 1.3   *The normal distribution*

incomplete information about the population of a random variable and its theoretical probability distribution.

An experiment necessarily involves taking a sample of events concerning the variable X from the population of possible events. Statistical inference is the method of inferring values for the theoretical probability distribution of X from samples taken from the population of X. We must always be careful to distinguish the theoretical statistics, such as expected value and standard deviation, from the corresponding estimated statistics obtained by sampling. In the notation sample statistics are distinguished from their population values by placing a hat over them. For example $E(X)$ equals the theoretical mean and $E(\hat{X})$ equals the sample mean.

Laboratory experiments work on the principle of sampling from the population. For instance if one burns one gramme of magnesium the weight of magnesium oxide obtained will vary slightly from one experiment to another. The average value obtained will be used to infer the expected value of magnesium oxide obtained from one gramme of magnesium.

Confidence Limits

If one could conduct an infinite number of experiments the average weight of magnesium oxide would tend towards the expected weight. Since one is trying to obtain information about the expected weight of the theoretical probability distribution from the average weight of the sample and it is not possible to carry out an infinite number of experiments, one needs to calculate the probability that the average weight is within a certain range of the expected weight. In other words a confidence limit is placed about the average weight, so that we can say that there is, for example, a 0·95 probability that the expected population value equals the sample average value plus or minus some number.

The normal probability distribution is used to establish a confidence limit for the population mean of a variable X. This is usually set at 0·95 or 0·99 because these probabilities encompass respectively two and three standard deviations about the expected value. (We can do this because the central limit theorem tells us that the distribution of the mean of a sample around its expected value tends to a normal distribution as the sample size increases.) Thus we need an estimate of the standard deviation of the theoretical probability distribution of X to establish a confidence limit around the average value of X obtained from experimentation. The estimate of the standard deviation of the theoretical probability distribution of X is obtained from the standard deviation of the sample of X. Thus we can write that there is a 95 per cent probability that $E(X)$ lies within two standard deviations of the average values of X obtained from sampling in the following way:

$$P(E(\hat{X}) - 2\hat{\sigma}_x < E(X) < E(\hat{X}) + 2\hat{\sigma}_x) = 0 \cdot 95.$$

Hypothesis Testing

A hypothesis is a conjecture about a variable which may concern its numerical value or its relationship with other variables. An example is the hypothesis that the expected value of X is some number μ_0. We write this hypothesis as

$$H_0 : E(X) = \mu_0.$$

There is always an alternative or null hypothesis which in this case is

$$H_1 : E(X) \neq \mu_0.$$

To test the hypothesis we draw a sample of X from its population and calculate its average value, $E(\hat{X})$. If μ_0 lies within the range $E(X) = E(\hat{X}) \pm 2\hat{\sigma}_x$ we accept the hypothesis $H_0 : E(X) = \mu_0$ with a 95 per cent probability of being right. There is still a 5 per cent chance that we reject the hypothesis when it is in fact true. If μ_0 does not lie within the range $E(X) = E(\hat{X}) \pm 2\hat{\sigma}_x$ we reject the H_0 hypothesis and accept the null hypothesis, but there is some probability that we have wrongly accepted hypothesis H_1 when H_0 is true. This test is referred to as a significance test. If we accept $H_0 : E(X) = \mu_0$, the expected value of X is said to be not significantly different from μ_0. Thus if evidence supports a theory we do not say that the theory is proven but that it has failed to be rejected.

Economic research is more concerned with testing hypotheses about the relationships between variables rather than with finding values for single variables. The principles which apply to individual random variables also apply, with extensions, to two or more variables considered together. We will limit the discussion to two random variables. Extension to N variables follows the same principles.

Properties of the Relationship between two Random Variables

We now have two random variables, assumed to be consumption, C, and disposable income, Y. When C and Y are considered together we can define a joint theoretical probability distribution over both variables. Each element in the joint probability distribution consists of a particular value of Y, Y_i, associated with a particular value of C, C_j. Thus if Y and C can each take on N values, there are N^2 elements in the joint theoretical probability distribution, each element written as (Y_i, C_j), each with a probability of occurrence of $P(Y_i, C_j)$.

There are a number of types of relationship that can exist between Y and C. They can

(1) be completely unrelated, that is they are independent random variables;

(2) move together in some systematic way in which case they are associated or correlated; or

(3) be causally related. For example C is the dependent variable and depends on Y, the independent variable.

Relationship (1) excludes (2) and (3), while (2) can exist without implying (3). We will examine these relationships in turn.

(1) *Independence: Zero Covariance.* If Y and C are independent they move in relation to each other in an entirely random fashion. This means that the probability, P_i, of any particular value of Y, Y_i, is the same regardless of the value of C. If Y and C are independent random variables and we plotted the Y_iC_j population against the C and Y axes, we would obtain a random collection of points. This is indicated in Figure 1.4, where it has not been possible to show the whole YC population. If we look at a particular value of Y, Y_i, we find it occurs for a wide variety of values of C and is thus independent of C. A useful way of presenting such a scatter diagram is by measuring the deviations of C and Y about their respective expected values along the C and Y axes so that zero deviations about the expected value occur at the origin. This is also shown in Figure 1.4. One measure of the way two or more random variables vary together is their covariance. For each pair of Y_iC_j we take their deviation from their respective expected value, multiply by the probability of their joint occurrence, $P(Y_i, C_j)$, and sum over all Y_iC_j. Hence

$$\text{cov } YC = \sum_{i=1}^{N} \sum_{j=1}^{N} [Y_i - E(Y)] [C_j - E(C)] P(Y_i, C_j).$$

If C and Y are independent random variables the covariance is zero.

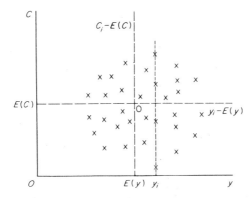

FIGURE 1.4   *The population of two independent random variables*

One would estimate the covariance of the joint CY probability distribution by sampling the CY population to calculate the deviation of each C and Y observation from its sample mean. If this covariance is not significantly different from zero, we conclude that C and Y are independent.

(2) *Association Between Two Random Variables: Correlation.* If C and Y move together in some systematic way, then the probability of Y_i occurring is affected by the value of C. For instance if C and Y move directly together a high value for C is more likely to occur the higher the value of Y. In this case C and Y are not independent of each other but are associated with each other. Their covariance is therefore non-zero. This is illustrated by Figure 1.5, which depicts the CY population expressed as deviations about their respective expected values. (Again it has not been possible to show realistically the whole population.)

From Figure 1.5 we see a clear tendency for deviations of C about its expected value to be positively associated with the deviations of Y about its mean. On the whole positive and negative $[C_i - E(C)]$s, are associated respectively with positive and negative $[Y_i - E(Y)]$s, giving a positive covariance. If the CY relationship were an inverse one, positive (negative) $[C_i - E(C)]$s would be mainly multiplied by negative (positive) $[Y_i - E(Y)]$s to give a negative covariance.

The size of the covariance depends on the number of Y_iC_j values and on the units in which C and Y are measured. A measure of association

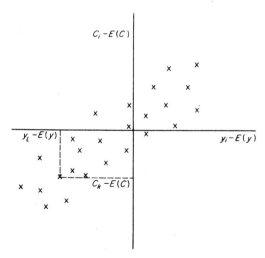

FIGURE 1.5   *The correlation between two random variables*

which is independent of such considerations is the correlation coefficient. This is obtained by dividing the covariance by the standard deviation of C multiplied by the standard deviation of Y:

$$r_{cy} = (\text{cov } CY)/(\sigma_c \cdot \sigma_y).$$

The correlation coefficient will have the same sign as the covariance. Independent variables have a zero correlation while a correlation of plus or minus one means that the two variables are perfectly related. All their values lie on a straight line so that the relationship between C and Y is exactly given by a linear function of the form

$$C = a + bY$$

or

$$Y = -a/b + C/b.$$

Correlation between two variables does not imply causation. C and Y may both be determined by some third variable, Z, and thus move together but be causally unrelated. There can be no common causal link at all and yet an association can be recorded, such as that between the number of storks and the number of human births.

The population correlation, like all the other statistics of a theoretical probability distribution, can be estimated by sampling the population and subjecting it to significance testing. A correlation coefficient significantly different from zero indicates that a causal relationship may exist and further investigation is required to establish whether or not this is the case.

(3) Testing for a Causal Relationship Between Two Variables: Linear Regression. If two variables are functionally related we specify that the dependent variable (C in our example) depends upon the independent variable, Y, restricting ourselves here to linear relationships. An *exact functional relationship* is written

$$C = a + bY. \tag{1.3}$$

Once we know the values of a, b and Y we know exactly what is the value of C. Many functional relationships are not exact because of the influence of other variables which are not included for reasons of simplicity, either because they cannot be quantified or because they are unknown. This means that even if we know the true values for a and b, such as $a = 100$, $b = 0\cdot9$, we cannot definitely say that when $Y = 2000$, $C = 1900$.

In this case the functional relationship between C and Y is a *stochastic* one, so that to each value of C, C_i, predicted from a given value of Y, Y_i, we have to add a random error term u_i, which may be positive or negative. Thus the stochastic form of equation (1.3) is

$$C_i = a + bY_i + u_i. \tag{1.9}$$

Equation (1.9) is a theoretical stochastic consumption function. One thinks of all the possible values of C and Y as a population over which a theoretical probability distribution is defined. The coefficients a and b are therefore the population parameters. We can think of these as the 'true' values of a and b. The theoretical probability distribution gives the expected value of consumption by assuming that the expected value of the error term is zero. This is justified by assuming that, on average, the positive and negative effects on consumption of all the excluded variables cancel each other out. If they do not cancel each other out the average effect would be caught in the value of the parameter a. Thus

$$E(C) = a + bE(Y).$$

Economic theory postulates functional relationships such as that between consumption and income. Statistical testing to see whether or not this hypothesis can be rejected and, if it cannot be rejected, the estimation of the population parameters is the province of that branch of economics known as econometrics.

To test the theoretical consumption function one needs to sample the income–consumption population. We can obtain a cross-section sample by selecting a group of households, which reflects the distribution of income over all households, and collecting data on their disposable income and consumption for a specified period. We can also test the relationship by taking a time series for U.K. aggregate consumption from, say, 1950 to 1973. This is also a sample from the population of all aggregate consumption–national income combinations which could exist if the variables excluded from the equation took on values different from those that actually existed.

Figure 1.6 shows the observed sample values of C plotted against the observed sample values of Y. A line drawn through the scatter of observations will have an intercept $\hat{a}$ and a slope $\hat{b}$ and can be used to estimate the values of C_i given the observed values of income Y_i. Thus we can write that estimated consumption is

$$\hat{C}_i = \hat{a} + \hat{b}Y_i.$$

The residual error between the observed value of C and its estimated value is indicated by e_i:

$$e_i = C_i - \hat{C}_i.$$

Therefore

$$C_i = \hat{a} + \hat{b}Y_i + e_i. \qquad (1.10)$$

The line which gives the best estimates of consumption relative to its observed sample values is that line which minimises the squared sum of errors. (Each error is squared so that positive and negative errors do not cancel out.) This is the line of best fit or the regression line and equation (1.10) is referred to as the regression equation. The estimates of the

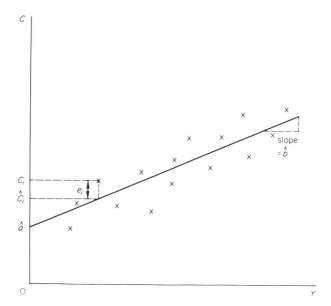

FIGURE 1.6 *The line of best fit*

population parameters a and b are $\hat{a}$ and $\hat{b}$ and are obtained by minimising

$$\sum_{i=1}^{N} e_i^2 = \sum_{i=1}^{N} (C_i - \hat{C}_i)^2 = \sum_{i=1}^{N} (C_i - \hat{a} - \hat{b}Y_i)^2.$$

The equations obtained for $\hat{a}$ and $\hat{b}$ are called the ordinary least squares estimators (O.L.S. for short) and are

$$\hat{b} = \frac{\sum_{i=1}^{N} [C_i - E(\hat{C})][Y_i - E(\hat{Y})]}{\sum_{i=1}^{N} [Y_i - E(\hat{Y})]^2} = \frac{\widehat{\text{cov}}\ CY}{\widehat{\text{var}}\ Y}$$

$$\hat{a} = E(\hat{C}) - \hat{b}E(\hat{Y}).$$

Before we can make any inferences about the true values of a and b from their estimated values we have to test that $\hat{a}$ and $\hat{b}$ are significantly different from zero. This is done by placing a confidence limit around $\hat{a}$ and $\hat{b}$. The latter variable is the important one since if b is not significantly different from zero we must reject the hypothesis that consumption depends on income.

As discussed earlier, to obtain a confidence limit for the estimate we need to know the standard deviation of the estimator. The standard deviation of the estimator, $\hat{b}$, depends on the standard deviation of the random error, u_i. Although we do not know the standard deviation of the random error we can estimate it from the standard deviation of the residual error, e_i. The estimate of the standard deviation of $\hat{b}$ is known as the standard error of the estimate, indicated by s.e.$\hat{b}$. For a large sample we can say that

$$P(\hat{b} - 2\text{s.e.}\hat{b} < b < \hat{b} + 2\text{s.e.}\hat{b}) = 0 \cdot 95.$$

If the sample is small we have to use the t distribution and not the normal distribution to calculate the confidence limit. We then write

$$P(\hat{b} - t \text{ s.e.}\hat{b} < b < \hat{b} + t \text{ s.e.}\hat{b}) = 0 \cdot 95.$$

The value of t depends on the sample size and exceeds two for samples of less than sixty.

The standard presentation of a fitted regression equation gives either the standard error or the t value in parenthesis under the estimate. For example, the standard error as reported in [4] is

$$C_t = 11 \cdot 45 + 0 \cdot 78 \ Y_t \qquad R^2 = 0 \cdot 986.$$
$$(0 \cdot 02)$$

If the standard error is reported we need to look up the appropriate t and multiply it by the standard error. If this number is larger than the estimate of b, then b is not significantly different from zero because there is a $0 \cdot 95$ probability that the true value of b lies within a range which includes zero. For a rough check on the significance of an estimate multiply the standard error by two. If this number is still less than the estimate, the latter is significant. If the t test is reported a rough check for significance is to look for a t value slightly in excess of two.

A regression study also reports the proportion of the variance in the dependent variable that has been explained by the fitted equation. This statistic is known as the coefficient of determination and is

$$R^2 = \sum_{i=1}^{N} [\hat{C}_i - E(C)]^2 \Big/ \sum_{i=1}^{N} [C_i - E(C)]^2.$$

The coefficient of determination is also the square of the correlation between the dependent and independent variables. Multiple regression techniques are used if more than one independent variable is used to explain the dependent variables. The O.L.S. estimators and their sampling properties are derived in basically the same way as for two variable regressions.

Properties of Estimators

It is desirable that an estimator of a population parameter should have certain properties. The most important are:

(1) The estimator should be unbiased. This means that the expected value of the estimator, which one could in principle obtain from its

average over a large number of samples of size N, should equal the true value of the population parameter. When an estimator is biased we no longer know the probability that the confidence limit put around the estimated value of b contains the population parameter, b.

(2) The estimator should have a small variance. The smaller the standard error of the estimator the narrower the range within which we can say the population parameter lies with a given degree of probability. In choosing between estimators we may have to trade off biasedness against small variance.

Under certain conditions, given below, the O.L.S. estimators have the desired properties of unbiasedness and minimum variance. The conditions required are the following assumptions about the theoretical probability distribution defined over the consumption function.

Assumption (1). The expected value of the random error is zero:

$$E(u_i) = 0.$$

Assumption (2). The sample residual errors are drawn from the same population of random errors and therefore have a constant variance:

$$E(u_i)^2 = \text{var } u_i = \sigma_u^2$$

which is a constant.

Assumption (3). The random errors are independent of each other and hence their covariance is zero. This condition is known as the absence of autocorrelation:

$$E(u_i u_j) = \text{cov } u_i u_j = 0.$$

Assumption (4). The exogenous variable, Y in this example, is truly independent and therefore unrelated to any other variable. Hence the covariance between Y and the random error is zero:

$$E(Y_i u_j) = \text{cov } Y_i u_j = 0.$$

We will now consider briefly what effect the failure of any of these assumptions to hold has upon the properties of the estimators.

Assumption (1). If $E(u_i) = \mu \neq 0$, it makes no difference so long as μ is constant. But if the random errors are drawn from different populations with different expected values the estimator b will be biased.

Assumption (2). If var $u_i \neq \sigma_u^2$ because, for example, the error term increases absolutely with the size of income and consumption, the standard error of the estimator will be biased as it is estimated from the residual errors of the regression equation. This means that the significance test is no longer accurate.

Assumption (3). If cov $u_i u_j \neq 0$, autocorrelation is present. Autocorrelation is particularly prevalent in time-series data, when the values of some of the omitted variables are growing over time and exerting a continuous upward or downward pressure on consumption. This is revealed by a sequence of time periods showing residual errors in the same direction. Autocorrelation means that the standard deviation of the residual error underestimates the standard error of the estimator making the significance test inaccurate. If the dependent variable is related to lagged values of itself, autocorrelation also produces biases.

The Durbin–Watson statistic, often presented with results, tests for the presence of autocorrelation. The precise value required to show the absence of autocorrelation depends on the sample size. It needs to be roughly two. A low value for the Durbin–Watson statistic provides a strong indication of positive autocorrelation (cov $u_iu_j > 0$).

Assumption. (4). If cov $Y_iu_i \neq 0$, the estimator will be biased. This cause of biasedness occurs when Y is not completely independent of C but is partly determined by C. This is the case in the consumption function which is only one amongst a number of equations which make up a model of national income determination. Thus C depends on Y, but in turn the level of Y depends on the level of C. This cause of biasedness is likely to occur in single-equation studies which look at one economic relationship in isolation from its interdependence with other relationships. One way of avoiding this bias is to estimate two or more equations together in the form of an economic model. Measurement errors in the independent variables also result in bias.

There are a number of ways of overcoming these estimation problems but nevertheless they still persist in econometric work. Empirical results should be evaluated cautiously, particular attention being paid to the significance tests and, to a lesser extent, to the coefficient of determination. One should also bear in mind that autocorrelation and interdependency between the 'dependent' and 'independent' variables render the results less reliable.

In evaluating the acceptability of a hypothesis and the estimated values of population parameters one must look, not at any single study, but at the whole range of related studies. If they reach a rough consensus one can accept the hypothesis or range of values for the population parameters with a high degree of probability. In the rest of this book, when reference is made to empirical work, these points should be borne in mind. This brief survey is only a guide and is no substitute for a more detailed study of econometrics, such as found in [5], [6], [7].

REFERENCES

[1] J. M. Keynes, *The General Theory of Employment, Interest and Money* (London: Macmillan, 1936).
[2] Milton Friedman, 'The Methodology of Positive Economics', in *Essays in Positive Economics*, (The University of Chicago Press, 1953).

[3] A. G. Ford, *Income, Spending and the Price Level* (London: Fontana, 1971).
[4] T. E. Davis, 'The Consumption Function as a Tool for Prediction', *Review of Economic Statistics*, 34 (1952).
[5] J. J. Thomas, *An Introduction to Statistical Analysis for Economists* (London: Weidenfeld & Nicolson, 1973).
[6] R. J. and T. H. Wonnacott, *Econometrics* (New York: Wiley, 1970).
[7] K. F. Wallis, *Introductory Econometrics* (London: Gray-Mills, 1972).

2 The *ISLM* Model

The one-sector Keynesian model of the economy, which was reviewed in Chapter 1, deals only with the demand for output in the real sector or, as it is alternatively named, the goods market. This sector is concerned with the receipts of the national product by factors of production and the expenditure of this income by households, firms and the government. The model is short-run and solves for static equilibrium for one period of time. The maximum amount of output that the economy can produce is fixed by the quantity of factors of production that exist. When all factors are fully utilised national output is said to be at its full-employment level. In practice full employment is not a unique quantity of output but a range of output levels at which resource limitations are felt by an increasing number of production sectors. In the one-sector Keynesian model, so long as there are idle resources, the volume of output produced depends on the level of aggregate demand. Once all resources are fully employed increased aggregate demand cannot raise real output; it can only increase the general level of prices.

2.1 THE INTERACTION OF REAL AND FINANCIAL SECTORS OF AN ECONOMY

The Role of Money and Financial Assets

The one-sector Keynesian model does not concern itself with how expenditure is financed. In an economy where people are no longer self-sufficient goods and services are exchanged on markets. A barter economy is one where transactions involve the exchange of goods and services directly for other goods or services. Barter is costly in the time it takes for buyers and sellers to be brought together and to agree on a price. The use of a generally accepted medium of exchange, which is called money, makes exchange more efficient. As well as being a medium of exchange money acts as a *numéraire* or unit of account, in which the prices of all commodities are expressed. In analysing the behaviour of a market economy it is essential to investigate the role of money.

In addition to the use of money as a medium of exchange, we need to consider how people obtain the command over resources necessary to finance expenditure. In a monetary economy households receive income in the form of money from hiring out their factor services and they exchange that money for the goods and services they wish to consume.

In any one time period a decision-unit's expenditure may differ from its income. If expenditure is less than income the unit is saving and is said to be surplus unit.* The general rationale for saving is the postponement of consumption from the present into the future. Surplus units require a means by which they can carry forward into the future their claim to purchasing power which they decide not to exercise in the present, but which they wish to enjoy in the future. Such a means is known as a store of value or as an asset. Any commodity which lasts for some considerable time can act as a store of value. This would be the only type of asset in a barter economy. In a monetary economy the store of value function is also performed by money and by paper claims upon other people's income.

Such paper claims, known as financial assets, arise from financing the expenditure of deficit units who currently spend in excess of their income. In order to spend more on resources than they are entitled to by their current income, deficit units take up those resources that surplus units do not wish to consume in the present. In return the deficit units issue paper claims upon themselves, which commit them to repay at some future date the resources that they have borrowed from the surplus units, together with a rate of return. These claims are liabilities to the deficit units who issue them, but are assets to those who own them.

Financial assets take many forms in the real world. A bond is a promise to repay a nominally fixed sum of money at some future date (infinity in the case of perpetuities) and to pay at stated intervals a nominally fixed income which is calculated as a constant rate of interest on the original sum lent. (For example, £100 originally lent for twenty years at an original, or coupon rate, of 5 per cent, pays £5 a year for twenty years plus £100 at the end of the twentieth year.) Marketable financial assets, such as bonds, can be exchanged at a price so that the original lender can obtain cash without waiting twenty years for the bond to be redeemed. Non-marketable claims, such as building society shares and Post Office savings accounts, have to be repaid by the

* Terminology popularised by Gurley and Shaw [1].

borrower before the lender can exchange his store of value of goods and services.

The Distinction Between Expenditure and Portfolio Allocation Decisions

In a monetary economy the process of lending and borrowing results in a stock of financial assets being built up over time. This means that in any one period trading takes place both in newly issued and in existing financial assets. An economic unit has two distinct decisions to make.

(1) It must decide what proportion of its current income to spend. For a household this is its consumption decision and necessarily its saving decision also. For a firm it is a decision about its real investment: which is its demand for real capital goods.

(2) A financing or portfolio decision must also be made. A deficit unit needs to decide what types of liabilities to issue, and a surplus unit what kinds of assets to hold. In any one period of time the unit's portfolio decision involves not only the financing of its current consumption or real investment plans but also the rearranging of its existing portfolio of assets and liabilities.

Flow Equilibrium and Stock Equilibrium

The consumption and real investment decisions directly involve decisions about the values of the flow variables in the economy. Flow equilibrium requires that the amount of output produced must be taken up by willing purchasers. This means that the volume of resources to which surplus units receive a claim that they decide not to exercise in the current period must be transferred, via the operation of the financial system, to deficit units for consumption or real investment. Some of the resources saved by surplus units are transferred to deficit households to be consumed by them. After taking account of this transfer, we are left with the net aggregate saving of the economy.

It must be noted that an individual act of saving does not automatically lead to a corresponding act of planned investment. The resources released by the saver may be lent to another household to finance its consumption, in which case the resources are used. If the saver stores his savings in already existing assets, such as money or bonds issued in the past, the resources he did not wish to use in the current period are not transferred to a firm wishing to finance real investment.

If aggregate desired saving exceeds planned investment aggregate demand will be deficient and real output will decline, whereas there will be inflationary pressures if the planned demand for real investment exceeds aggregate desired saving at a given level of real income. For the real sector to be in equilibrium we therefore require the flow equilibrium condition that investment equals saving.

Stock equilibrium in the financial sector requires that people are willing to hold the existing stock of both real and financial assets at their current prices. If the demand for assets does not equal the supply, the prices of assets will be changing and this will have repercussions on consumption and real investment decisions. Similarly if flow equilibrium does not exist, say investment exceeds saving and firms lower asset prices to borrow more funds, stock equilibrium cannot exist either. Therefore for overall equilibrium of the economy we require both flow and stock equilibrium.

2.2 THE *ISLM* MODEL: THE KEYNESIAN VERSION

A framework for analysing the interrelationship between the real and financial sectors of a market economy is provided by the *ISLM* model. It was originally developed by J. R. Hicks [2] as an interpretation of Keynes's *General Theory of Employment, Interest and Money* and has since been further simplified.

The Goods Market Equations

We start with a closed economy in which there is no government. When there are idle resources the price level is constant and is exogenously determined, so that the price index, P, can be set equal to one. All the variables in the model are in real terms. Since $P = 1$ we do not need to explicitly deflate each variable by the price level.

The following symbols are defined.

y = real national output,
Y = nominal national output,
$y = Y/P = Y$ when there are idle resources and $P = 1$,
E = desired aggregate demand = national expenditure,
C = planned consumption,
I = planned investment,
S = planned saving, and
i = the market rate of interest.

There are two definitions:

$$E = C + I \tag{2.1}$$

and

$$Y = C + S. \tag{2.2}$$

Equation (2.1) states that aggregate demand consists of consumption and investment, and equation (2.2) shows that households can dispose of their income either by consuming or saving. For static flow equilibrium we must have real output equal to the aggregate demand for it. The flow equilibrium condition is given by equation (2.3) or by the alternative version in equation (2.4).

$$y = E. \tag{2.3}$$

Substituting (2.1) and (2.2) into (2.3) we obtain

$$C + S = C + I, \tag{2.4}$$

$$S = I. \tag{2.4}$$

As previously discussed, flow equilibrium necessarily requires that desired saving and investment are equal.

'Ex Ante' and 'Ex Post' Values of Variables

It should be noted that actual saving in the economy will equal the actual amount of investment done by firms. If saving exceeds planned investment (that is real output exceeds aggregate demand) firms will find unsold stocks of goods on their hands which they have to add to their inventories. In such an event firms engage in involuntary inventory investment and will therefore alter their production plans in the next period so that static equilibrium cannot prevail. The values that variables actually take on after the effects of economic decisions have worked themselves out are referred to as being *ex post* values. The planned values of variables are known as their *ex ante* values. The *ex post* value of a variable will differ from its *ex ante* value in disequilibrium. In the example above *ex ante*, or planned investment, is smaller than *ex post* investment. It is the planned or desired values of variables that directly influence the actual values that variables take on. It is firms' planned investment, not their *ex post* investment, that determines their demand for capital goods. Equilibrium requires equality between the *ex ante* and *ex post* quantities of variables.

The Investment Function

The *ISLM* model brings in the connection between the real and financial sectors by postulating that investment is inversely dependent on the rate of interest. Investment is the demand for capital goods that are wanted because they will produce additional goods and services in the future. Thus expectations about the future are a crucial determinant of investment demand. When a firm buys a capital good the costs are incurred in the present but the revenues the firm expects to obtain from the sale of commodities produced using the capital good will accrue in the future. The firm must therefore compare costs and revenues which occur at different time periods. The way of doing this is to bring all future costs and revenues to their value in the current period. This is known as their present value.

If there is a positive market rate of interest, say 10 per cent, then £100 received next year is worth less than £100 received today. This is because £100 received now can be lent at 10 per cent and becomes $£100(1 + 0 \cdot 1) = £110$ next year. The present value of £110 received in one year's time is $£110/(1+0\cdot1) = £100$, since an individual would be indifferent between the prospect of receiving £100 now and lending it at 10 per cent and receiving £110 in a year's time. Similarly £100 lent for two years at 10 per cent would be worth $£100(1+0\cdot1)^2 = £121$ in two years' time. Thus the present value of £121 received in two years' time is $£121/(1+0\cdot1)^2 = £100$. From this it can be seen that a present value calculation is the reverse of a compound interest calculation. In general the present value of £x received in n years' time when the rate of interest is i per cent and is paid at annual intervals is $£x/(1+i)^n$.

The net present value (N.P.V.) of an investment project is the discounted value of all revenues minus the discounted value of all costs, and is given by the following expression where the market rate of interest is called the discount rate:

$$\text{N.P.V.} = -S_0 + \frac{R_1}{(1+i)} + \frac{R_2}{(1+i)^2} + \frac{R_3}{(1+i)^3} + \cdots + \frac{R_n}{(1+i)^n}.$$

The initial cost of the capital equipment is given by S_0 and the net revenue expected in the ith year by R_t. The net revenue is calculated as the revenue from selling the output produced by the capital equipment minus operating costs. These include maintenance and the costs of other factors of production used in the process. Any scrap value that the capital has at the end of its life is included in the net revenue for the final year.

Given that firms have the objective of maximising their overall net present value, which is equivalent to maximising the present value of their future expected profits, they will adopt all investment projects which have a non-negative net present value. If expectations improve so that the estimated net revenue stream increases, or the price of capital goods declines, or the market rate of interest falls, the net present value of any particular investment project will rise. This means that there will be more investment projects with a non-negative net present value and hence a greater demand for investment goods. In the *ISLM* model expectations and the price of capital goods are taken to be constant, whereas the rate of interest is endogenous.* The investment function which enters the *ISLM* model is

$$I = I(i), \qquad \partial I/\partial i < 0. \tag{2.5}$$

It must be remembered that each investment schedule exists for a particular value of the state of expectations and the price of capital goods.

---

* Many expositions of the *ISLM* model assume the supply curve of capital goods fixed, rather than the price, in order to derive, in a somewhat unsatisfactory way, a determinate investment schedule. If the price of investment goods is allowed to vary this conflicts with the assumption of an exogenous price level. The derivation of an investment schedule is discussed further in Chapter 4.

Flow Equilibrium in the Goods Market: Derivation of the IS Function

Savings are assumed to depend directly on the level of income. The savings function, equation (2.6), is the counter part to the consumption function given by equation (1.2),

$$S = -a + sy,\qquad(2.6)$$

where s is the marginal propensity to save.

There are now two endogenous variables to solve in the model, namely the real level of national output and the rate of interest. For the goods market to be in equilibrium planned investment must equal planned saving. Substituting equations (2.5) and (2.6) into equation (2.4) we obtain

$$-a + sy = I(i)\qquad(2.7)$$

$$y = \frac{a + I(i)}{s}.\qquad(2.7a)$$

Equation (2.7a) shows that there are various combinations of the level of real output and of the rate of interest that will make investment and saving equal. A higher interest rate which reduces investment has to be balanced by a lower y which reduces saving. The locus of goods-market equilibrium values of real output and the interest rate is called the *IS* schedule. This is now derived geometrically in Figure 2.1.

Turning to quadrant 1 we see that when income is y_0 the desired amount of saving is S_0, which is transferred on to the verical axis in quadrant 2. The 45° line in quadrant 2 converts any distance along the vertical axis (the ordinate) into an equal distance on the horizontal axis (the abscissa). Investment must equal I_0 for it to equal saving when income is y_0. The investment schedule in quadrant 3 shows that given a particular state of expectations and price of capital goods the rate of interest must be i_0 to result in a level of investment of I_0.

The co-ordinate of i_0 and y_0 is then plotted in quadrant 4. We then have one combination of income y_0 and interest rate i_0 for which saving equals investment. The same process is repeated for income level y_1 to obtain an interest rate of i_1 which makes saving, when income is y_1, equal to the level of investment. In this way we can obtain a large number of interest rates and output levels for which investment equals saving, and by joining them obtain the locus of all such points which is the *IS* schedule. This geometric derivation of the *IS* schedule is identical to the process we went through to obtain the *IS* function algebraically. What we have done here geometrically is to substitute equations (2.5) and (2.6) into (2.4) so as to derive equation (2.7a).

The *IS* schedule alone is insufficient to determine both the level of real income and the interest rate since we have a single equation (2.7a), which is the equation of the *IS* schedule, in two unknown variables, real

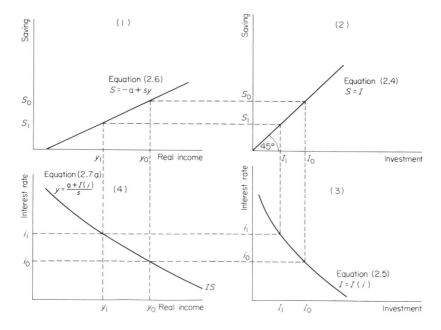

FIGURE 2.1 *Derivation of the IS function*

income and the rate of interest. To solve a model we must obtain determinate and hence equilibrium values for all the endogenous variables. This requires that we have as many independent equations as there are endogenous variables. To solve the *ISLM* model we therefore need another function in addition to the *IS* function. The financial sector is brought into the analysis to obtain a determinate solution.

The Financial Sector

It is assumed in the *ISLM* model that there are only two financial assets; money and bonds. Money has a zero rate of return since the price level is constant and no rate of interest is paid on money. By definition money is any commodity which is generally accepted as a medium of exchange, and, in modern economies, consists of notes and coin in circulation with the public plus bank deposits which are transferrable by cheque.

As well as being a medium of exchange money can be a store of value. Money is defined to be a perfectly liquid asset since a nominal quantity of money, such as one pound, can always be exchanged for the same nominal quantity without fear of loss and without incurring transactions costs. The liquidity of an asset is a concept which embraces the time, the transactions costs and the risk of loss associated with turning an asset into money, (that is liquidating it).

The Inverse Relationship Between the Price of Bonds and the Rate of Interest

A bond is an imperfectly liquid asset since in order to convert it into cash it has to be sold on a market at the risk of making a capital loss if the selling price is less than the price at which the bond was originally bought. The alternative of waiting till the bond matures and the principal is repaid involves time, which is included in the concept of illiquidity. Hence a financial asset is regarded as more illiquid the longer its time to maturity. The price of a bond on a market is the present value of the income stream to which the bond is a claim. This can be expressed as,

$$\text{bond price} = B_p = \frac{A}{(1+i)} + \frac{A}{(1+i)^2} + \cdots + \frac{A+R}{(1+i)^n} \qquad (2.8)$$

where A is the nominally fixed annual income and R is the principal which is repaid after n years. If the bond is a perpetuity, such as the British Government's consolidated fund (consols) the price is

$$B_p = \frac{A}{(1+i)} \sum_{t=0}^{\infty} \left(\frac{1}{1+i}\right)^t. \qquad (2.8)$$

Applying the formula for summing a geometric progression with an infinite number of terms we obtain*

$$B_p = \frac{A}{1+i}\left(\frac{1}{1-1/(1+i)}\right) = \frac{A}{1+i}\left(\frac{1+i}{i}\right) = \frac{A}{i}. \qquad (2.9)$$

From equation (2.9) we see that if the current interest rate rises the price of existing bonds must fall. This happens in order to equalise the rate of return on bonds issued at different dates at different coupon rates. Take the example of a consol issued at £100 with a coupon rate of 2·5 per cent in the 1930s. This bond pays an annual income of £2·50. If currently new bonds worth £100 have a coupon rate of 10 per cent they give an annual income of £10. To make people willing to hold the 1930s consol its price will fall to £25 to give a rate of return of £2·50/25 which gives us 10 per cent.

This example illustrates the inverse relationship between the price of bonds and the current rate of interest. The current interest rate is the yield on bonds, which is defined to be that rate of interest which, used as a discount rate, makes the present value of the future income from a bond equal to its market price. In the case of a perpetuity the yield is

* See Chapter 1. p. 11.

obtained by rearranging equation (2.9):

$$\text{yield} = \frac{\text{annual income}}{\text{current bond price}} = \frac{A}{B_p}. \tag{2.10}$$

Thus if bond prices rise the yield or current interest rate falls. As the ISLM model contains only one interest-bearing financial asset there is only a single rate of interest to be considered. In an economy with a number of financial assets, differing in marketability, riskiness and date to maturity, there exists a whole range of interest rates which is known as the interest rate structure. There is a tendency for interest rates to move in line with one another so that reducing the number of interest rates to one, is a simplification which still allows us to conduct a useful analysis.

The Demand for Money

People wish to hold money in order to finance transactions. This is known as the transactions demand for money and arises from the non-synchronisation of receipts of income and the disbursement of expenditures. If the moment people made expenditures coincided with the receipt of income, and an account was kept which recorded the instantaneous exchange of goods and services between people, money would not have any function as a medium of exchange. The demand for money therefore depends on the money value of transactions which it finances.

A commodity may be exchanged several times in the process of production before it becomes embodied in a final good. An input such as wheat will be sold several times before it is retailed as a loaf of bread. Exchange takes place not only in currently produced goods but also in second-hand goods which were produced in the past. It is for such reasons that the value of transactions in an economy exceeds the value of national income.

Since it is difficult to obtain data on the value of transactions it is more useful to relate the demand for money transactions balances to the level of national income. This is done by assuming a given relationship between the value of transactions and the value of national income. It is therefore assumed that the demand for money for transactions purposes is a function of the level of income.

The demand for money can be expressed either in nominal or in real terms. The nominal value of money, M, is the actual number of currency units, such as pounds, in existence. The real value of money, M/P, is its nominal value deflated by an index of the price level. This gives the purchasing power of a particular stock of money in terms of goods and services it can buy. Equation (2.11) expresses the demand for money in real terms.

$$(M/P)^D = f(y). \tag{2.11}$$

The quantity of nominal money required to finance transactions will depend on the nominal value of national income, Y. Thus if the price level rises, real output remaining constant, a greater amount of nominal money will be demanded. It is assumed that if the price level changes the demand for real money balances will remain unchanged in relation to the level of real income.* Written in money terms equation (2.11) would be

$$M^D = f(yP) = f(Y). \tag{2.11a}$$

In an *ISLM* model which has idle resources the price level is constant at $P = 1$, so we can write

$$M^D = f(y). \tag{2.11}$$

As a unit of money changes hands several times in the course of a year, the quantity of money required to finance transactions is usually between one-half and one-third of the quantity of national output. The relationship between the quantity of real transactions balances demanded and real national income depends on various features of the payments mechanism. The more frequently people are paid per year the smaller is the average value of transactions balances they need to hold. The use of credit cards, and arrangements whereby depositors pay banks annual bills at monthly intervals, reduce the average bank balance people need to keep. All such factors are assumed exogenous to the *ISLM* model and any change in them would alter the relationship given by equation (2.11).

Money is also demanded as an asset. There are substitutes in the form of other financial assets and real assets for the store of value function of money. In the *ISLM* model there is only one financial asset substitute, namely bonds. The advantage of holding a bond is that it bears a rate of interest; the disadvantage is that a bond is imperfectly liquid since a capital loss may be incurred when it is sold. If interest rates rise the price of bonds will fall and the total rate of return from holding bonds may be negative if the capital loss outweighs the interest payment. Keynes[†] hypothesised that the lower is the current rate of interest the more likely are wealth holders to expect the rate of interest to rise and hence the price of bonds to fall. This means that the lower are current interest rates, the greater will be the demand to hold money rather than bonds as an asset.

* The demand for real money balances is said to be homogenous of degree zero in money prices. To ascertain the degree of homogeneity of $y = f(x)$ the dependent and all independent variables are multiplied by a constant, λ, so that $\lambda^n y = f(\lambda x)$. The degree of homogeneity is given by n. In $n = 0$, y is unaffected by multiplying the x variables by λ.

† *The General Theory*, ch. 15.

The asset demand for money is therefore hypothesised to be dependent on expectations about future interest rates and inversely related to the current interest rate. The total amount of wealth to be allocated between money and bonds is also a determinant of the asset demand for money. The state of expectations and the stock of wealth are assumed to be exogenous in the *ISLM* model.* The total demand for real money balances both as a medium of exchange and as a store of value is therefore written as

$$(M/P)^D = \frac{M}{P}(y, i).\qquad(2.12)$$

It is assumed that all the other determinants of the demand for money are exogenous. For the moment it is also assumed that the money supply is exogenously determined by the government.

Stock Equilibrium in the Financial Sector: Derivation of the LM Function

Equilibrium in the financial sector requires that the demand for money equals the stock of money and that the demand to hold bonds also equals the stock of bonds supplied. Since we have only two financial assets it must be the case that if the bond market is in equilibrium so is the money market.† If people were holding excess money balances they would be running these down to buy bonds and bond prices would be rising. This means that it is sufficient to work with money market equilibrium without giving specific consideration to the bond market.

The condition for stock equilibrium in the *ISLM* model is therefore that the demand for money should equal the money supply, M_0^S:

$$\left(\frac{M}{P}\right)^D = \frac{M}{P}(y, i) = \left(\frac{M_0}{P}\right)^S \qquad(2.13)$$

If we wish to depict the demand function for money on a two-dimensional diagram, we need to hold all except one determinant constant. Figure 2.2 shows the demand for money as a function of the rate of interest. Each demand for money schedule holds income as well as the exogenous variables constant.

Demand schedule D_0D_0 is plotted for a level of real national income which is constant at y_0. The supply of money, $(M_0/P)^S$, is given by the vertical line. If the level of output is y_0, the interest rate must be i_0 for the demand and supply of money to be equal. At a higher level of output

* Real wealth is the capital stock which is assumed fixed. Financial wealth is bonds and money. The number of nominal units of money is exogenous, so is the nominal quantity of bonds. This is the number of bond units paying a nominal annual income of one pound.
† The proposition that a model with n market clearing equations solves for $n-1$ independent equations and hence $n-1$ variables, allowing the nth variable to be dropped from explicit consideration, is known as Walras's Law.

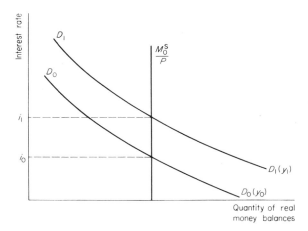

FIGURE 2.2   *The demand for money as a function of the rate of interest, all other variables remaining constant*

y_1 the transactions demand for money is greater, hence a higher interest rate i_1 is required to make the asset demand for money lower so as to still equate the money stock with the demand for money. In Figure 2.3 we plot the various combinations of the level of real income and the rate of interest which, given a particular demand function for money and a certain stock of money, $(M_0/P)^S$, make the demand for money equal to the supply. The locus of such real income and interest rate combinations is known as the *LM* function whose equation is given by (2.13).

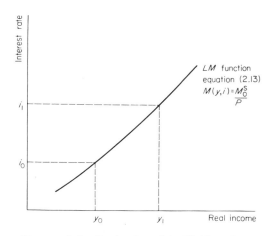

FIGURE 2.3   *Derivation of the LM function*

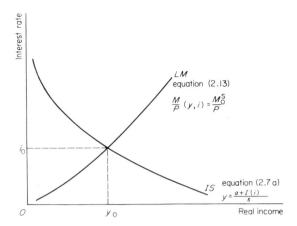

FIGURE 2.4   *Simultaneous equilibrium in the goods and money markets; the Keynesian ISLM model*

Goods and Money Market Equilibrium

Now that we have derived the *IS* and the *LM* functions it becomes possible to solve the model. It is very important to bear in mind that we are talking in terms of real magnitudes. When both the goods and money market are in equilibrium, as indicated by the intersection of the *IS* and *LM* functions in Figure 2.4, we have determined the interest rate and the real level of output for which the aggregate demand for real output equals the aggregate supply of real output and for which the demand for real money balances equals the real quantity of money in existence.

Since the model is concerned with real values, we must not forget the role of the price level in determining real values. At the outset we made a simplifying assumption that the price level is fixed at one. An exogenous price level characterises the Keynesian version of the *ISLM* model. The assumption of a constant price level can be made if we assume there is a considerable degree of unemployed labour and underutilised capacity in the economy. In addition it has to be assumed that the existence of idle resources means that firms' short-run average costs are constant. They can expand or contract output at unchanged average costs and hence the price level remains constant as the volume of output changes. The aggregate supply function is therefore assumed to be perfectly elastic up to the full-employment level of output.

It is very important to understand that the Keynesian *ISLM* model of national income determination is an entirely demand-orientated

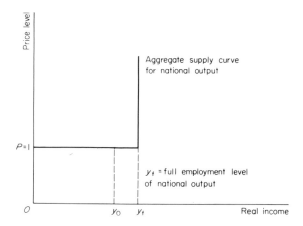

FIGURE 2.5   *The Keynesian ISLM model; demand for output determines the supply of output up to full employment*

theory. It applies to the short-run determination of output when the economy is less than fully employed. In these circumstances the amount of output that is produced is determined by the quantity that is demanded. The quantity demanded in equilibrium is determined by the joint equilibrium of the goods and money markets and is y_0 in Figure 2.4.

If we transpose the equilibrium quantity of real output, y_0, demanded from Figure 2.4 to Figure 2.5, we can see the gap between the actual quantity supplied, y_0, and the maximum quantity the economy could supply if aggregate demand were sufficiently high. The price level, which is exogenous in this model, is determined by the level of firms' short-run costs.

2.3   THE NEOCLASSICAL VERSION OF THE *ISLM* MODEL

In this chapter we have made some simplifying assumptions about the economy's short-run average cost function for output. Average costs and hence the price level are constant up to full employment and then rise as aggregate demand increases. The neoclassical version of the *ISLM* model applies to the case of full employment. Prices and costs are assumed to be flexible and real output is determined exogenously at y_f when all resources are fully employed. In the neoclassical *ISLM* model the price level and the rate of interest are the two endogenous variables determined in the model.

In the neoclassical *ISLM* model, goods market equilibrium, which is

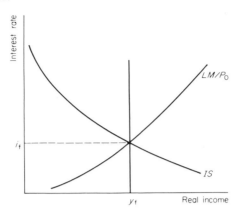

FIGURE 2.6 *The neoclassical ISLM model; the full-employment level of output exogenously determined*

the outcome of investment decisions, determines the rate of interest. This is shown in Figure 2.6 as i_f, which is the rate of interest that makes investment equal to the full employment level of saving. Money market equilibrium establishes the price level. Given the nominal stock of money, M_0^S, the price level must be such that the real value of the money supply, M_0^S/P_0, equals the demand for real money balances, which is already determined by the full-employment level of output and the rate of interest, i_f, required for goods market equilibrium.

2.4 COMPARATIVE STATIC ANALYSIS WITH THE *ISLM* MODEL

Shifts in the IS Function

If any of the parameters in the *IS* equation changes there will be a shift of the *IS* schedule. This is illustrated in Figure 2.7 for an increase in desired investment caused by improved expectations about the future returns from investment. Initially the investment schedule is I_0I_0 and the *IS* schedule is given by IS_0. Due to improved expectations of future earnings desired investment at every rate of interest increases so that we have a new investment schedule I_1I_1. This means that the rate of interest which equates investment to saving at each level of output must rise. At output y_0 we now require an interest rate of i_0' for equilibrium in the goods market. Thus an increased desire to invest shifts the *IS* schedule upwards to the right. The reverse movement in the *IS* curve will result from a decline in investment due to a fall in expectations about future returns.

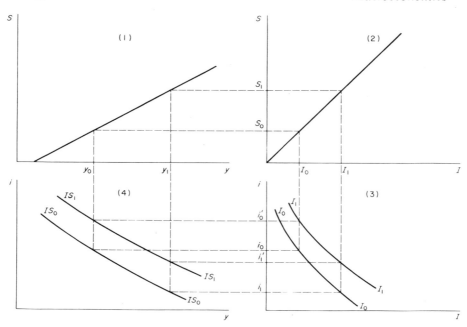

FIGURE 2.7   *Shift in the IS function due to a change in the desire to invest*

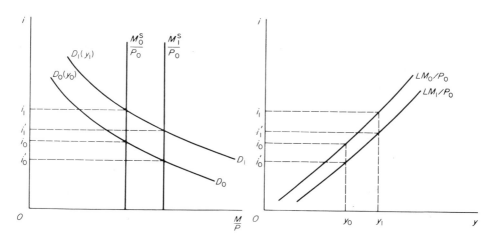

FIGURE 2.8   *Shift in the LM function due to a change in the supply of money*

Shifts in the LM Function

Similarly a change in the parameters of the demand for money or supply of money functions will result in a shift in the *LM* schedule. This is illustrated in Figure 2.8 for an increase in the supply of money, as we normally assume a stable demand function for money in terms of its determinants.

We assume the price level is constant at $P_0 = 1$. The original nominal money supply is M_0^S for which the corresponding *LM* function is LM_0/P_0. The nominal money supply is increased to M_1^S. The real money supply then increases by an equivalent amount since the price level is constant. In order for the demand for money at each level of output to equal the increased supply of money the rate of interest must be lower. Thus, when output is y_0 the interest rate must now be i_0' for monetary equilibrium. The *LM* curve has therefore shifted down to the right. If the money supply were reduced the *LM* function would shift up to the left.

The Size of the Investment Multiplier

Using comparative static equilibrium analysis we can predict that an increase in investment, given idle resources, will cause an increase in real output. There is an increased production of capital goods, which, via increased incomes, leads to greater consumption demand and to a further expansion of output. This is the familiar multiplier effect and is an example of positive feedback. The initial impulse, an increase in aggregate demand, causes changes which move the initiating variable in the same direction.

There will also be monetary effects which can be analysed with the *ISLM* model. The increased level of output results in a greater demand for money to finance transactions. If the money supply is constant this must result in a higher rate of interest if the demand for money is to equal the money supply. This is illustrated in Figure 2.9 where the *IS* schedule shifts from IS_0 to IS_1 and, given a fixed *LM* schedule LM_0, output rises from y_0 to y_1.

As the rate of interest rises from i_0 to i_1 there are repercussions on the level of investment which is consequently lower than it would be had the rate of interest remained unchanged. This is an example where negative feedback effects occur. The initial change in the variable causes changes in other variables which move it in the opposite direction to the initiating impulse. The rate of interest would remain at i_0 if the money supply were increased so that the *LM* schedule shifted to LM_1. In such an event the increase in real output would be greater, rising to y_2 since there are no disincentive effects of a higher interest rate on investment. If the rate of interest remains unchanged the investment multiplier is the same size as it is in the simple one-sector Keynesian model. The multiplier is

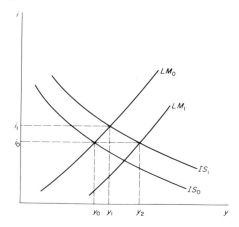

FIGURE 2.9   *The impact of negative feedback from the monetary sector on the size of the expenditure multiplier*

smaller, the more the interest rate changes as a result of the larger transactions demand for money consequent upon the increase in output.

If the economy were already at full employment when the increase in investment demand occurred there could be no increase in real output. Instead excess aggregate demand would emerge causing prices to rise. As the price level rises the real value of the money supply declines and

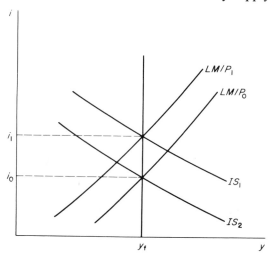

FIGURE 2.10   *The effect of an increase in investment demand when the economy is fully employed*

the interest rate therefore increases. The inflation in this model is brought to an end because the nominal money stock is fixed. This means that eventually monetary and real sector equilibrium are regained at a higher price level and higher interest rate at which the demand and supply of real money balances are once more equal and excess aggregate demand has been eliminated. In the new equilibrium the price level and hence the nominal value of national income have increased, real national income staying unchanged.

2.5 THE *ISLM* MODEL WITH THE GOVERNMENT SECTOR

The analysis of the effect of the government sector on the economy can be readily incorporated into the *ISLM* model. Consumption and saving now become functions of disposable income, yd. Government expenditure, G_0, is assumed exogenous whilst for simplicity the government's tax revenues, T, are assumed to be proportional to national income, the factor of proportionality being the tax rate, t. The savings function is given by equation (2.14):

$$S = -a + syd \qquad (2.14)$$

$$yd = y - T \qquad (2.15)$$

$$T = ty. \qquad (2.16)$$

Substituting (2.16) and (2.15) into (2.14) we obtain

$$S = -a + s(1-t)y. \qquad (2.14a)$$

Aggregate demand now includes government expenditure as well as investment and consumption, so that goods market equilibrium requires

$$y = E = C + I + G_0. \qquad (2.17)$$

Disposable income is divided between saving and consumption,

$$yd = y - T = C + S \qquad (2.18)$$

$$y = C + S + T. \qquad (2.18a)$$

Substituting (2.18a) into (2.17) and removing C from both sides of the equation shows that goods market equilibrium requires

$$S + T = I + G_0. \qquad (2.19)$$

Substituting (2.14a), (2.16) and (2.5) into (2.19) we obtain the equation for the *IS* function

$$I(i) + G_0 = -a + s(1-t)y + ty. \qquad (2.20)$$

The geometrical derivation of the *IS* function (2.20) is shown in Figure 2.11. Quadrant 1 indicates the level of savings plus tax that is associated

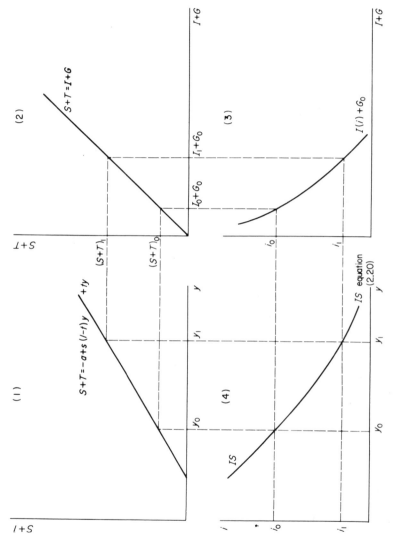

FIGURE 2.11 *Derivation of the IS function when the government sector is included in the model*

with various real income levels. If the level of real output is y_0 the level of savings plus tax would be $(S + T)_0$. Quadrant 2 shows that, to equal $(S + T)_0$, investment plus government expenditure must be $I_0 + G_0$. The rate of interest required to bring this about is i_0. Thus we get one particular combination of interest rate and output level which gives goods market equilibrium.

An increase in the tax rate will cause the $S + T$ function to swing towards the left. This means that for each output level a lower interest rate is required so that investment is increased to compensate for the increase in $(S + T)$ and to preserve goods market equilibrium. Thus the *IS* curve shifts down to the left. A reduction in taxation or an increase in government spending will shift the *IS* schedule to the right. (An equal initial increase in government expenditure and taxation does not leave the *IS* function unchanged but will shift it to the right. This is because an increase in taxation of £x million will raise $S + T$ by less than £x million as savings decline when disposable income falls.)

2.6 FISCAL AND MONETARY POLICY

We can now analyse the impacts of fiscal and monetary policy which governments use in an attempt to regulate the level of aggregate demand. The general desired direction of policy in a closed economy would be to increase aggregate demand if there is unemployment or to reduce it if there is inflationary excess demand. Monetary policy in this model involves the alteration of the money supply by the central bank. Fiscal policy is the management of the government's budget, which consists of its expenditure outflow and tax revenue inflow, in order to affect the level of aggregate demand. The government runs a budget deficit if its expenditure exceeds its tax revenue. Such a deficit can be financed either by the government selling securities (bonds in the *ISLM* model) to the non-bank public or by expanding the money supply. Similarly a budget surplus, arising when tax revenue exceeds expenditure, can be financed by redeeming government securities from the public or by reducing the money supply.

For the purposes of analysis we define a pure fiscal policy to be a budgetary change which leaves the money supply unaltered. In terms of *ISLM* analysis this means that a shift in the *IS* function caused by a change in the government's budget leaves the *LM* schedule unaffected. If the government increases its spending, without increasing taxation, it injects money into the economy as it finances its expenditure. If, simultaneously, bonds of an amount equal to the additional government expenditure are sold to the public, their money balances are drawn down and replaced by bonds. The net effect is that the nominal money supply remains unaltered. A reduction in government spending or an increase in taxation must be financed by buying bonds from the public if the nominal money supply is to be kept constant.*

Assuming that idle resources exist we can now examine the determinants of the impact of fiscal and monetary policy on the level of output.

Fiscal Policy

An expansionary pure fiscal policy, which is shown by a rightward shift in the *IS* function, will cause an increase in the rate of interest. To finance the fiscal expansion the government sells bonds to the public, thus replacing with bonds money that was held as an asset. This money is then used by the government to finance expenditure which employs previously idle resources. As real output and the related transactions demand for money rise, so does the rate of interest.

The increase in the interest rate will be greater the more interest inelastic is the demand for money, since a larger change in the interest rate is required to persuade people to hold a given money stock at a higher level of income. This is shown in Figure 2.12.

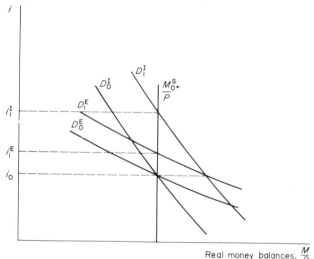

FIGURE 2.12   *The size of the change in the rate of interest consequent upon a change in the demand for money increases as the demand for money becomes more interest inelastic*

* If the money supply remains constant but the quantity of government bonds changes, total wealth will change, unless one assumes the public discounts all future tax payments required to pay interest on government bonds. In this case the public feels no better off in aggregate if the quantity of government bonds they hold increases. Alternatively, if the public feel wealthier, this is assumed negligibly small relative to their total wealth.

The demand and supply of money are initially in equilibrium when output is y_0 at an interest rate of i_0. This holds for both a relatively interest-elastic demand for money function, D_0^E, and for an alternative relatively interest-inelastic function, D_0^I. The demand for money schedule shifts up when output increases to y_1 due to expansionary fiscal policy. Each demand schedule shifts by the same horizontal distance. In the case of the more elastic function the rate of interest rises only to i_1^E to equate the increased demand for money with the constant money stock. If the demand for money is less interest elastic, the rate of interest will rise further to i_1^I.

We have seen from Figure 2.12 that the change in the rate of interest required to maintain monetary equilibrium when output changes is greater the more interest inelastic is the demand for money. This means that the slope of the *LM* function is steeper the more interest inelastic is the demand for money.

Since the increase in the rate of interest following a given expansionary fiscal policy is greater the more interest inelastic is the demand for money, the resulting increase in real output is smaller. This is due to the larger contractionary impact of the interest rate on private investment. This point is illustrated by Figure 2.13. Expansionary fiscal policy shifts the *IS* schedule from IS_0 to IS_1. In the case of a relatively elastic money demand function the *LM* schedule is LM_1^E. The rate of interest rises only to i_2, hence real output increases as far as y_2. The fiscal policy multiplier is larger than if the money demand function is more interest inelastic. The relevant *LM* schedule is then LM_0^I, the interest rate rises further to i_1 and consequently the rise in output to y_1 is smaller.

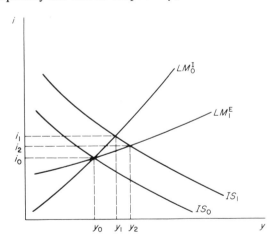

FIGURE 2.13   *The expenditure multiplier increases as the elasticity of the demand for money increases*

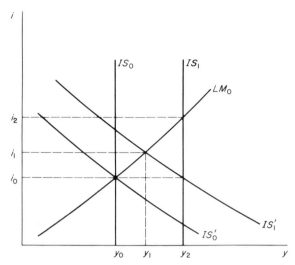

FIGURE 2.14   *Fiscal policy is more effective the less interest elastic is investment*

The effectiveness of fiscal policy would not be impaired at all by an increase in the interest rate if investment were perfectly unresponsive to interest rate changes. If investment is autonomous (unrelated to income or the rate of interest) the *IS* schedule would be vertical. Only one level of income would produce the level of saving equal to the volume of autonomous investment. Figure 2.14 illustrates the case when investment is perfectly interest inelastic, the fiscal policy multiplier is the same size as in the one-sector Keynesian model (output rises by y_0y_2). The multiplier diminishes as the interest elasticity of investment increases. With the same fiscal expansion, output only increases by y_0y_1 when investment is interest responsive.

Monetary Policy

A standard method of changing the money supply is for the central bank to engage in open-market operations in government securities. To increase the money supply the central bank buys bonds from the public. In order to persuade the public to hold fewer bonds and more money the government has to raise the price of bonds, that is to lower the rate of interest. This means that the interest rate falls in the process of monetary expansion and rises if there is monetary contraction.

In the *ISLM* model as constructed here, the transmission mechanism of monetary policy is indirect. An increase in the money supply at the original equilibrium interest rate and output level would cause disequilibrium, since there would be an excess supply of real money balances over the demand for them. In Keynesian analysis such disequilibrium causes a movement into other financial assets. The demand for bonds increases, bond prices rise and the interest rate falls.

As a result of the reduced interest rate, investment (also consumption, particularly the demand for consumer durables, may depend on the interest rate) increases and output rises. This mechanism, by which monetary changes affect real output, is referred to as Keynesian. There are two chains in this link between changes in the money supply and consequent changes in real output that may impair the effectiveness of monetary policy.

First, the interest rate may be very unresponsive to changes in the money supply due to the high interest elasticity of the demand for money. This can be seen by reference to Figure 2.12. If we shift the money supply line to the right, we can see that an increase in the money supply will cause a smaller decline in the interest rate when the demand for money function is more interest elastic. Since the interest rate falls only slightly, there is little stimulus to investment and the expansion of output is consequently small.

A second factor which would render monetary policy ineffective would be the unresponsiveness of investment and consumption to interest rate changes. Even if an increase in the money supply caused a fall in the interest rate, this would have little effect on aggregate demand or, consequently, on output.

The Relative Effectiveness of Fiscal and Monetary Policy

It has therefore been deduced that *monetary policy is more effective* in changing the level of real output *the more interest inelastic is the demand for money* and the *more interest elastic are investment and consumption*. The opposite conclusions hold for *fiscal policy. It is more effective the more interest elastic is the demand for money and the less interest elastic are investment and consumption.*

The debate between the proponents of fiscal and monetary policy has been fought partly on these grounds. The early Keynesians, who were fiscal policy enthusiasts, assumed the demand for money to be fairly interest elastic and investment interest inelastic. The monetarists, who criticise the excessive reliance of the Keynesians on fiscal policy and neglect of monetary factors, maintain that the demand for money is a stable function of its determinants. Their case is strengthened if the demand for money can be shown to be interest inelastic.

Keynesian analysis has been restricted to the substitutability between money and other financial assets. People adjust to any excess demand or supply of money by respectively moving out of or into bonds. The monetarists see the adjustment of actual real money balances towards their desired level as occurring across a much wider range of assets. This adjustment involves not only all financial assets, but real assets as well. The latter includes consumer durable goods, which are regarded as assets because they embody a stock of services which are yielded up over a number of years.* Thus in the monetarist view, a change in the money supply will cause people to adjust via their expenditure on goods as well as on financial assets. This will have a much more diffuse and pervasive impact than an adjustment occurring only via financial assets.

The issues concerning the effectiveness of fiscal and monetary policy can only be settled by an appeal to the empirical evidence. A considerable body of such evidence has now accumulated and is reviewed in the relevant chapters of this book.

It should not be concluded from this discussion that monetary and fiscal policy are mutually exclusive. They can both be used to reinforce each other. It should not be thought that a government uses a pure fiscal policy. This was merely a simplifying theoretical assumption which allowed us to distinguish between the effects of both policies. A government dealing with a depression due to deficient aggregate demand could reinforce the expansionary effects of a budget deficit by financing it with an increase in the money supply.

2.7 COMPARATIVE STATIC ANALYSIS

A warning needs to be sounded regarding the use of comparative static equilibrium analysis. All that we have done is predict that the final equilibrium change in output, resulting from, say an increase in government expenditure, will depend upon the responsiveness of money demand and investment to the rate of interest. Nothing has been said about how the values of the variables change over time when the economy is out of equilibrium.

There are lags in adjustment, which means, for instance, that it takes time for the demand for money to alter in response to interest-rate changes, and further time for investment plans to be revised. In dynamic analysis we also need to consider the repercussions of a change in one variable upon another and the feedback effects on the original variable. Take the example of an increase in the money supply which initially lowers the interest rate. The fall in the interest rate stimulates aggregate demand. Real output increases, the demand for transactions balances increases and the interest rate rises. This has a depressing impact on investment and output, which feeds back to the interest rate. Comparative static analysis has nothing to say about the pattern of repercussions amongst variables; it only predicts the final outcome when equilibrium is re-established.

* See Chapter 3 for a further discussion.

Comparative static analysis is helpful in allowing us to make predictions about the long-run direction and size of a change in a variable, but any assessment of the methods of demand management must include knowledge of the ways in which the economy adjusts to fiscal and monetary measures.

2.8 CONCLUSIONS

The *ISLM* model provides the basic framework for analysing, in terms of broad aggregate variables, the demand side of a market economy. In Chapter 8 it will be extended to analyse an open economy. In its static form the model can be applied to an economy with unemployed resources, in which case it is a Keynesian model. The real value of national output is determined by the level of aggregate demand and the price level is exogenous. If the model is used to analyse an economy in which the real level of output is exogenously fixed by the limited supply of factors of production, it becomes a model in which the quantity of money determines the price level. In such a case it is a neoclassical model.

Keynesian analysis has stressed the impact of real expenditure flows, and particularly the role of autonomous expenditure and the multiplier on the level of national income. Since Keynesian predictions of national-income behaviour rely on the multiplier concept, they require the consumption function to be a stable relationship with respect to its determinants. Monetarists have rectified the Keynesian neglect of money and stress the relationship between the quantity of money and the nominal value of income. This requires a stable demand for money function so that aggregate demand reacts in a predictable manner to money supply changes.

These are not mutually exclusive ways of analysing macro behaviour, and only appear so if excessive attention is paid to very simple models couched either in Keynesian multiplier or in quantity of money terms. These simple models apply to different unemployment conditions. The scope of *ISLM* model analysis is limited because it is short run and because it does not determine both the price level and real output within the model. We need models that explain both the determination of real income and the price level and which distinguish between factors which determine short-run behaviour of variables from those that determine their long-run trends. Such models are developed in later chapters.

To obtain a better understanding of the stable aggregate relationships in the economy and how they interact, and to gain insight into how variables adjust when the economy is out of equilibrium, we need to examine in greater detail the four basic macro functions. These are the consumption, investment, supply of and demand for money functions. They form a basic part of any macro model in which the real and financial sectors interact. This task is accomplished in the next four chapters.

REFERENCES

[1] J. Gurley and E. Shaw, *Money in a Theory of Finance* (Washington, D.C.: The Brookings Institution, 1960).
[2] J. R. Hicks, 'Mr Keynes and the "Classics"; A Suggested Interpretation', *Econometrica*, 5 (April 1937) 147–59.

3 Consumption

It is important at the outset to distinguish the desire to purchase a certain quantity of a commodity per period of time from the enjoyment over the same period of time of the services from a commodity. A commodity is purchased at an instant in time in order to enjoy the services of that commodity over some period of time. It is the satisfaction from the possession of a good that influences the desire to purchase that good, but it is the intended purchases of goods that constitutes effective demand, which is a major determinant of the volume of national income produced.

Goods, whether they be classified as consumer or capital goods, yield services for a varying number of time periods, and have a present value which is the discounted value of the expected future stream of services yielded by the good. Consumer goods vary in the length of time over which they yield services. For some, such as a restaurant meal or a bus journey, the length of time over which the commodity is enjoyed is quite short and occurs around the same instant of time as the purchase. The length of time over which clothes yield utility varies directly with the fashion consciousness of the wearer. Cars, refrigerators and the like, which yield services over a number of years, are commonly known as consumer durables, yet a man may keep his suit longer than his car. All this goes to show the arbitrary nature of classification and that one cannot distinguish a capital good from a consumer good according to the length of the period over which it yields its services. A method used in national income accounting is to distinguish between the two by ownership. Thus a car owned by a company, or a washing machine owned by a launderette are capital goods, but are consumer goods if owned by a household, which is taken to be a non-productive unit, in the sense that it does not use these goods to produce services which are sold on a market. The same is true of goods which yield up their services quickly. Ice-cream in a shop's freezer is a capital good as it is part of the shop's inventory, but once purchased by a customer it becomes a consumer good.

In examining the determinants of the desire to purchase both capital and consumer goods, one must necessarily analyse the relevant decision-unit's behaviour over time. The present value of the expected future services of the good has to be compared to the purchase price of the good, both in deciding whether the good is worth buying in the first place, or, if already possessed, whether it is worth replacing. Thus the existing stock of goods and the type and time profile of the services they are expected to yield will affect current purchases of the good. The value of the existing stock of a good exerts a disincentive effect on the desire to purchase additional units of that good. Thus past decisions to purchase influence current decisions. This will also be the case for habit-forming goods such as drink and tobacco: past enjoyment of the commodity exerts a positive effect on current purchasing plans [1].

Although one cannot distinguish a capital good from a consumer good by the length of time over which the good yields its services, one can use time to distinguish the act of consuming from that of investing. Consuming involves using up the services of a good, whereas investing is purchasing a good which has the capacity to yield an expected flow of services. The term 'investment' is normally reserved for the act, as defined above, when it is done by a 'firm' or productive unit, with the intention of selling future services from the good on a market. Thus the term 'investment' can be applied to an individual when buying an education, if this is done in the expectation of earning a higher income which yields a positive rate of return on the cost of that education. If, on the other hand, the individual buys an education in order to enjoy the experience itself, then it is usually defined as a consumer good. Hence the confused terminology, for we have no distinct word to describe the act of purchasing a consumer good, that is a good expected to yield services which are not to be traded on a market, and this act is commonly called 'consumption'. We therefore need to distinguish consumption, meaning the enjoyment of and using up of the services yielded by a good, from consumption meaning consumer purchases. It is consumer purchases plus investment which make up effective demand, but it is plans to enjoy the future services of goods which play an important part in determining both consumer purchases and investment levels.

Real net national output is the flow of goods and services produced by the economy per period of time (such as a year) which leaves the value of the capital stock unchanged. The act of consuming in that year involves using up the services of goods purchased both in the current and in previous years. It is the current year's planned consumer purchases plus intended investment that determines whether aggregate effective demand exceeds or falls short of the current year's supply of output, and whether firms will revise their production plans upwards or downwards. As we have seen current consumer purchases are undertaken in order to derive satisfaction from consuming the services of goods in the current and future periods, and will be influenced by the existing stock of goods brought forward from past years, as determined by past purchasing and consumption plans. Firms undertake investment in the current period in anticipation of providing goods and services to meet future consumer purchasing plans. Here again, past investment, reflected in the value of the existing capital stock, together with expectations about future consumer purchasing demand are important determinants of current investment decisions.

Households may allocate their current period's income to current or to future consumer purchases, the latter decision being known as saving. The act of saving is simply the act of not consuming current income. The most important motive for saving is the postponement of consumption in order to enjoy it at some future date, either directly oneself or through one's heirs.

The decision to spend current income on current consumer purchases necessarily involves some consideration of one's future consumption plans. Thus Keynes's dictum that 'consumption – to repeat the obvious – is the sole end and object of all economic activity' [2] is the central theme of the interrelationships amongst economic decision-units at the macro level. Consumption plans, saving plans and investment plans all involve economic decision-units in activities which are intended to obtain as much satisfaction as is possible from consuming the services of commodities over some time horizon.

3.2 INTERTEMPORAL CHOICE

The intertemporal nature of consumption choice at the micro level of the household will be treated more formally, using analysis that originated in the work of Irving Fisher [3, 4]. Assuming that consumption is the ultimate purpose of all economic activity, household utility is taken to be a function of the time profile of its consumption, in the sense of the enjoyment of services which commodities provide:

$$U = f(C_0, C_1, C_2, \ldots, C_N). \tag{3.1}$$

The household is assumed to choose that time profile of consumption which maximises its utility, subject to the constraint imposed by the household's wealth, where wealth is the present value of future income from both human and non-human sources. Conceptually, the present value of the future flow of services of goods owned by the household are included in this measure of wealth:

$$W = y_0 + \frac{y_1}{1+i} + \frac{y_2}{(1+i)^2} + \cdots + \frac{y_N}{(1+i)^N} \qquad t = 0, \ldots, N \tag{3.2}$$

where

$$C_t = \text{consumption in period } t$$
$$y_t = \text{income in period } t$$
$$W = \text{wealth}$$
$$i = \text{market rate of interest}$$

in real terms.

In this simple model of household consumption decision-making conditions of certainty are assumed to prevail, that is future income in each of the future years, and the future market rate of interest are assumed to be known with a probability of one. The capital market is assumed to be perfectly competitive so that the household can borrow or lend at the going market rate of interest as much as it wants, without affecting that rate. Transactions costs involved in borrowing and lending activities are taken to be zero.

Given the above assumptions we will start by simplifying even further and will consider the problem of intertemporal choice over two periods, the present and the next period, which can be called the future.[*]

$$U = f(C_0, C_1) \quad \text{utility function} \tag{3.1a}$$

$$W = y_0 + y_1/(1+i) \quad \text{wealth constraint} \tag{3.2a}$$

$$C_0 + C_1/(i+1) = W. \tag{3.3}$$

Equation (3.3) gives the condition that the present value of consumption equals wealth on the assumption that all the income is spent over the two time periods.[†] Equation (3.3) written as

$$C_1 = W(1+i) - C_0(1+i),$$

is the equation of the budget line AB in Figure 3.1, the slope of which is $-(1+i)$. It is the constraint subject to which utility is maximised. For utility to remain constant it is necessary that the first-order total differential of equation (3.1) be set equal to zero, i.e.

$$dU = \frac{\partial U}{\partial C_0} dC_0 + \frac{\partial U}{\partial C_1} dC_1 = 0. \tag{3.4}$$

Equation (3.4) is the equation of movements along a particular indifference curve, for instance U_1, which shows the various combinations of consumption in the present and consumption in the future which yield the same level of utility. In Figure 3.1 we see that U_1, is the highest indifference curve, or level of utility, attainable given wealth constraint AB. Therefore utility is maximised by choosing OC_0^1 consumption for the present and OC_1^1 consumption for the future period.

[*] It is assumed that $\partial U/\partial C_0 > 0$ $\partial U/\partial C_1 > 0$ and that $\partial^2 U/\partial C_0^2 < 0$, $\partial^2 U/\partial^2 C_1 < 0$. This is required to fulfil the second-order conditions for a maximum.
[†] See Appendix, Note 1, for a multi-period model.

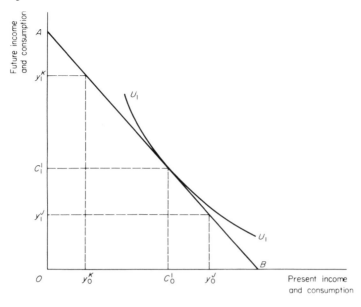

FIGURE 3.1   *Intertemporal consumption choice*

The slope of the indifference curve is given by rearranging (3.4).

$$\frac{dC_1}{dC_0} = -\frac{\delta U}{\delta C_0} \bigg/ \frac{\delta U}{\delta C_1}, \tag{3.4a}$$

that is the marginal rate of substitution between present and future consumption equals the ratio of the marginal utility of future consumption to the marginal utility of present consumption, all along the indifference curve. Utility is maximised subject to the wealth constraint when the marginal rate of substitution of present for future consumption, which is determined by the household's preferences, equals the rate at which future consumption can be transformed into present consumption, which is given by the market rate of interest. This can be seen by differentiating the wealth constraint equation (3.3) so that

$$dC_1/dC_0 = -(1+i). \tag{3.3a}$$

When utility is maximised subject to the wealth constraint (3.3a) is set equal to (3.4a):

$$\frac{dC_1}{dC_0} = -(1+i) = \frac{\delta U}{\delta C_0} \bigg/ \frac{\delta U}{\delta C_1}. \tag{3.5}$$

There are many combinations of present and future income which will give the wealth constraint imposed by budget line *AB*. Two of the combinations y_0^J, y_1^J and y_0^K, y_1^K are shown in Figure 3.1. In the case of income stream y_0^J, y_1^J, utility is maximised by consuming less than current income in the present, and thus by consuming more than the next period's income in the future. This time profile of consumption and income is financed by saving out of current income an amount equal to the distance between C_0^1 and y_0^J, and investing it at the market rate of interest, which converts it into an amount equal to the distance y_1^J, C_1^1, which is exactly equal to the amount by which the future period's consumption exceeds the period's initially given income of y_1^J. In the case of income stream y_0^K, y_1^K, utility is maximised by consuming more than current income in the present, and thus by consuming less than the income which will accrue in the next period. This is financed by borrowing an amount equal to the distance $y_0^K C_0^1$, on which the market rate of interest i must be paid. The sum which must be repaid next period is $y_0^K C_0^1 (1+i)$ which equals the distance $C_1^1 y_1^K$, which is exactly equal to the extent to which next period's income y_1^K exceeds next period's planned consumption C_1^1.

From this analysis one can deduce that, given this type of household behaviour, current household consumption plans depend not only on current income, but also on the future expected income stream, the market rate of interest at which this income stream is discounted and the time preference of the consumer. A further important deduction is that the decision to save is inherently linked with the consumption decision, since the decision to save out of current income is a decision to postpone consumption, whereas dissaving involves consuming in the present at the expense of future consumption. The act of saving in the current period is the execution of a decision to postpone consumption; it does not indicate anything about the household's proposed timing of future consumption. This, as we shall discuss later, will be indicated by the type of assets in which the household chooses to hold its stock of savings. Once we consider a world of uncertainty, the household is no longer sure of the exact timing or volume of its future income stream. Such uncertainty extends to the timing and volume of the future consumption stream. Saving then serves as a means of accumulating assets which will allow the household to release its consumption plans from closely following the time profile of income.

At the aggregate level consumption will be affected by the distribution of households with respect to time preference and also with respect to income if the marginal propensity to consume out of disposable income differs amongst households.

3.3 KEYNES'S AND POST-KEYNESIAN THEORIES OF CONSUMPTION

In *The General Theory*, Keynes discusses the determinants of consumption behaviour with the foregoing theoretical apparatus in mind, but emphasises the importance of income in the argument of a consumption function, relegating the other factors to a secondary role.

The fact that given the general economic situation the expenditure on consumption ... depends in the main on the volume of output and employment is a justification for summing up the other factors in a portmanteau function 'propensity to consume'. For while other factors are capable of varying (and this must not be forgotten) the aggregate income ... is as a rule the principal variable upon which the consumption constituent of the aggregate demand function will depend [5].

Subsequent writers [6] ignored Keynes's provisos, often because they were constructing formal macro models and wrote consumption as an undated function of disposable income. This type of consumption function is known as the absolute income hypothesis and is frequently rather erroneously attributed to Keynes. Keynes hypothesised, on an *a priori* basis, that the marginal propensity to consume is a positive fraction of disposable income and that the average propensity to consume declines both for individuals as their incomes increase, and for the economy as a whole as national income increases.

For the satisfaction of the immediate primary needs of a man and his family is usually a stronger motive than the motives towards accumulation, which only acquire effective sway when a margin of comfort has been attained. These reasons will lead, as a rule, to a greater proportion of income being saved as real income increases [5].

A falling average propensity to consume is consistent with either a non-linear consumption function, for which the m.p.c. also declines with income or with a linear consumption function (constant m.p.c.) which has a positive intercept and is therefore referred to as being non-proportional. The hypothesis that the a.p.c. falls with increases in national income was adopted by Keynesian economists to explain the appearance of chronic unemployment in a mature capitalist economy; as the capacity of the economy to produce output increases over time, so the proportion of that level of aggregate demand necessary to maintain full employment, consisting of consumption expenditure, falls, requiring an increasing proportion to be made up by investment. If investment opportunities fail to increase rapidly enough, the level of aggregate demand will be insufficient to create full employment.

Empirical Evidence

In the decade following the publication of *The General Theory*, various empirical studies of the consumption function were undertaken. Empirical testing and quantification of economic relationships is necessary in order to see whether *a priori* hypotheses about economic behaviour fail to be rejected as explanations of observed economic phenomena. Providing the hypothesis stands up to such testing and yields significant quantified coefficients, one can attempt to predict future behaviour by projecting into the future what is assumed to be a stable behavioural relationship between variables. Thus if econometric research provides a significant relationship for the economy of the form $C_t = a + by_t$ one can attempt to predict future consumption expenditure by feeding into the equation the future expected value of disposable income. For the purposes of economic policy it is desirable to be able to make short-term forecasts. The knowledge that consumption and income move together on average over a long period of time is not particularly helpful to a policy-maker trying to offset fluctuations in economic activity, if consumption behaves erratically in the short run and is not a known stable function in the short run of other variables.

As with most economic relationships two types of data, cross-section and time-series data, are available for testing the consumption function. Cross-section data are provided by sampling households to obtain information for a particular time period on their consumption expenditure, disposable income and other relevant explanatory variables such as family composition by age and sex, and social class. Such budget studies have shown that the average propensity to consume does decline with income and typically that low income households dissave. There is also evidence that consumption functions fitted to budget-study data tend to be non-linear. Results from the U.K. 1952 National Survey of Personal Incomes and Savings are graphed in Figure 3.2 which illustrates the typical features of budget studies.

The first time-series data to become available was that of the United States for the years 1929–41 and the least squares regression on this data gives the following equation [7]:

$$C = 26 \cdot 5 + 0 \cdot 75y$$

where C is the real aggregate consumption, y is the real disposable national income, and the units of measurement are billions of dollars. Short-run time series data have produced linear non-proportional consumption functions. On the basis of such regression equations, American economists at the end of the Second World War attempted to forecast post-war consumption and concluded, that unless a high level of government expenditure continued, aggregate demand would be insufficient to maintain full employment. In the event American post-war consumption was considerably greater than had been predicted by many economists and it appeared that the whole pre-war consumption function must have shifted upwards. Also, if one extends a non-proportional linear consumption function back to the ordinate one would arrive at the nonsensical conclusion that an economy consumed in excess of its income, in the past, when real national income had been much lower. When long-run time

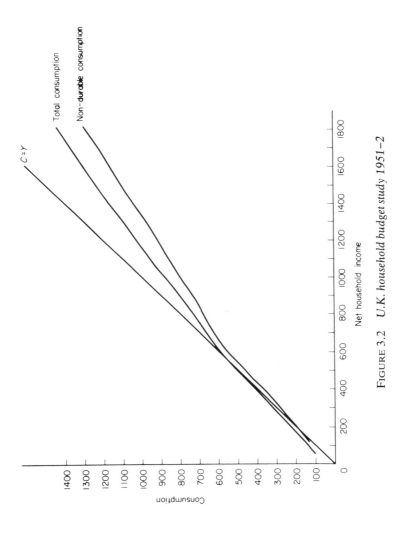

FIGURE 3.2   *U.K. household budget study 1951–2*

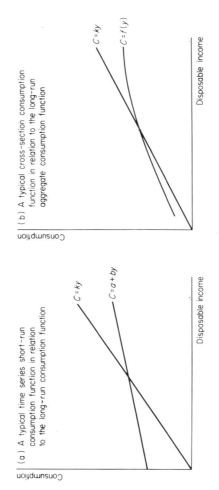

(a) A typical time series short-run consumption function in relation to the long-run consumption function

(b) A typical cross-section consumption function in relation to the long-run aggregate consumption function

FIGURE 3.3   *Proportional and non-proportional consumption functions*

series data for the U.S. economy were published by Simon Kuznets [8], it became evident that the long-run a.p.c. had not fallen as national income had increased, but was on the whole quite stable, and maintained a long-run average of around 0·84–0·89, only rising to above 0·89 when national income fell in the decade 1929–38. From Kuznet's data is obtained a proportional long-run consumption function, since the long-run a.p.c. and m.p.c. are not significantly different.

The history of consumption theory is an example of the process by which economic theory is first formulated on the basis of *a priori* hypothesising about human behaviour, confronted with the empirical facts and then modified when found inadequate in explaining these facts. Post-Keynesian consumption theory has been concerned with reconciling the apparently conflicting observations that the long-run aggregate a.p.c. is constant, while budget studies have shown the size of the a.p.c. and of the m.p.c. of households to be inversely related to household disposable income. A further conflict arises from the observation that the short-run consumption function is non-proportional and has a lower m.p.c. than the long-run aggregate consumption function, and that there is a tendency for the a.p.c. to vary cyclically, rising when income falls. These observations are illustrated in Figure 3.3.

An examination of post-war U.K. data on disposable income and consumption reveal similar observations. The values of the annual a.p.c. for the United Kingdom calculated by dividing annual total consumption expenditure by total disposable income and of the annual m.p.c. calculated as a ratio of annual changes in consumption and income are given in Table 3.1. The a.p.c. is reasonably stable and shows a marked downward trend. This is explained by the high level of consumption occurring in the immediate post-war period following the war years when consumption expenditures had been deliberately restrained. The annual m.p.c: has fluctuated greatly, ranging from −0·49 to 2·27. Further evidence of the erratic behaviour of short-run changes in consumption expenditure relative to changes in total personal disposable income, is obtained from quarterly data for the United Kingdom for the period 1959–72, and is shown in Figure 3.4. The secular trend in consumption is clearly indicated, but the quarter-to-quarter changes in consumption, particularly for the period 1966–7 and 1968–70, are erratic, sometimes occurring in the opposite direction as in the second quarter of 1969 when income declined but consumption rose.

The consumption function fitted to annual data for 1949–70 is

$$C_t = 2412 + 0·915y_t \quad \text{(1963 prices, £ million)}.$$
$$(693) \quad (0·046)$$

whereas the consumption function fitted to quarterly data for 1959–72 is

$$C_t = 3287 + 0·35y_t \quad \text{(1963 prices, £ million)}.$$
$$(1111) \quad (1·98)$$

Table 3.1*

	Annual a.p.c. $\dfrac{Total\ consumer\ expenditure}{Total\ disposable\ income} = \dfrac{C_t}{y_t}$	Annual m.p.c. $\dfrac{Change\ in\ consumer\ expenditure}{Change\ in\ disposable\ income} = \dfrac{C_t - C_{t-1}}{y_t - y_{t-1}}$
1949	0·98	—
1950	0·98	1·03
1951	0·98	0·98
1952	0·94	−0·49
1953	0·95	1·03
1954	0·95	1·26
1955	0·95	0·20
1956	0·93	0·26
1957	0·93	1·23
1958	0·95	2·27
1959	0·95	0·42
1960	0·93	0·65
1961	0·91	0·71
1962	0·92	1·50
1963	0·93	1·05
1964	0·92	0·88
1965	0·92	0·73
1966	0·92	0·87
1967	0·92	1·12
1968	0·93	1·30
1969	0·92	0·30
1970	0·92	0·76

* 1963 prices
Source: National Income and Expenditure.

The m.p.c. of the quarterly consumption function is much lower than that for the annual data and is insignificant. This is not surprising given the erratic short-run behaviour indicated in Figure 3.4. The tendency for the m.p.c. to rise with the length of the time period over which the consumption function is fitted has been noted by Friedman for the U.S. economy. The U.K. results are also consistent with the U.S. observation that the short-run m.p.c. is less than the long-run a.p.c.

The post-war U.K. data provide further evidence that consumption expenditure is not a simple direct function of current disposable income. In seeking an explanation of consumer behaviour, it must be borne in mind that the available statistics give information about consumer expenditure, not about consumption, in the sense of using up goods and services. Also income data do not include the services that could be yielded up by existing consumer goods brought forward from previous years. Earlier in this chapter we examined the theory of intertemporal consumer choice, which leads to the deduction that current income only

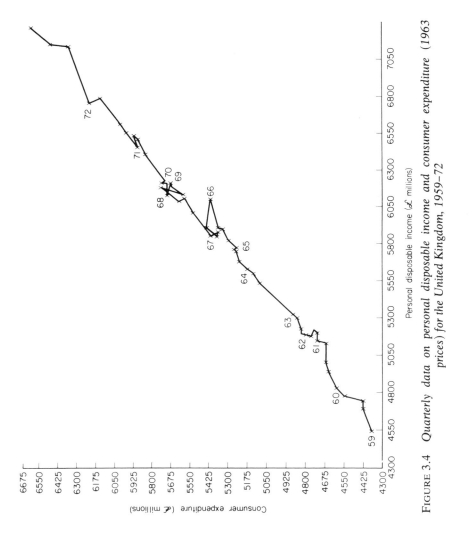

Consumer expenditure (£ millions)

Personal disposable income (£ millions)

FIGURE 3.4 *Quarterly data on personal disposable income and consumer expenditure (1963 prices) for the United Kingdom, 1959–72*

affects current consumption plans to the extent that it influences consumer wealth. This deduction is consistent with a preliminary examination of the data. Post-Keynesian writing on the consumption function has been directed at providing a better explanation of consumer behaviour than that given by the absolute income hypothesis, and from this work have emerged three groups of theories.

3.4   THE RELATIVE INCOME HYPOTHESIS

The first of these to be discussed is the relative income hypothesis (R.I.H.) elaborated by James Duesenberry [10]. The underlying behavioural assumption of Duesenberry's theory is that consumers derive utility, not from an absolute level of consumption but from a level that is judged in relation to both the consumer's own past standards and the consumption standards of others. A household's desired standard of consumption will be influenced by the living standards it sees maintained by other households with whom it has contact. From this Duesenberry deduces that consumption will be determined not by a household's absolute income but by its position in the income scale relative to its reference group, that is by its relative income. In support of this hypothesis Duesenberry cites a comparison of the savings of negroes and whites in New York and Columbus [11], which showed that negroes saved more out of a given absolute income than whites. This supports Duesenberry's argument if one bears in mind that at any given absolute income a negro is higher up his income scale than is a white.

The relative income hypothesis is used to reconcile the two basic conflicts apparent in the data in the following way. It is observed from budget studies that the a.p.c. falls with the size of disposable household income. This is consistent with consumption depending on relative income and the a.p.c. declining the higher is the household's relative income. If over time the absolute level of real national income is rising and a household experiences an increase in its absolute income, while maintaining its relative income position in the income distribution, its a.p.c. remains unchanged. If, on the other hand, a household moves to a higher (lower) income group its a.p.c. will fall (rise) to that of the income group in which the household now finds itself. Thus, if the income distribution is reasonably stable over time, while national income is rising, a constant aggregate long-run a.p.c. is quite consistent with a cross-section a.p.c. which varies inversely with the size of household relative income.

The second part of Duesenberry's reconciliation of consumption theory with empirical fact is his explanation of the observation that the short-run m.p.c. is less than the long-run m.p.c., and that the short-run a.p.c. and m.p.c. vary over the trade cycle. This is because households become accustomed to their existing consumption standards and are reluctant to reduce them. Thus in a depression although households are often forced to reduce consumption when their incomes fall, they consume a higher proportion of their income than they do in times of prosperity (i.e. their a.p.c. rises).

When economic activity increases and incomes rise, households build up their assets, which had been depleted during the depression, and consumption does not therefore immediately adjust to the higher level of income. Thus the short-run m.p.c. is lower than the long-run m.p.c. because in the short run consumption adjusts proportionally less than income.

Duesenberry captures this behaviour by assuming that consumption depends on the previous peak level of income as well as on current income. He writes the consumption function as

$$C_t = b_0 y_t - b_1(y_t^2/y_0) \tag{3.6}$$

where y_0 is the previous peak income. When expressed as an equation for the a.p.c. it becomes

$$(C_t/y_t) = b_0 - b_1(y_t/y_0). \tag{3.7}$$

Duesenberry fitted equation (3.7) to U.S. data for the period 1929–40 and obtained*

$$(C_t/y_t) = 1 \cdot 196 - 0 \cdot 25(y_t/y_0). \tag{3.7a}$$

In the long run when income is growing at a steady rate, g, current income is always higher than previous peak income. Thus we have

$$y_t = (1+g)y_{t-1} = (1+g)y_0. \tag{3.8}$$

This means that the economy is moving along the long-run consumption function *OB* in Figure 3.5. Substituting y_0 in equation (3.7) by $y_0 = y_t/(1+g)$ derived from equation (3.8), we obtain an expression for the long-run a.p.c. which shows it to be constant. Thus

$$\text{the long-run a.p.c.} = C_t/y_t = b_0 - b_1(1+g). \tag{3.9}$$

Assuming a growth of $0 \cdot 03$ and using Duesenberry's estimates of b_0 and b_1, we obtain a long-run a.p.c. of $0 \cdot 94$ which is consistent with Kuznet's findings. The long-run m.p.c. is of course the same as the long-run a.p.c.

In the short run the m.p.c. and the a.p.c. differ from their long-run or average values over time. In a severe depression previous peak income will be higher than current income and its influence causes consumption to be reduced by less than income. The economy moves down a short-run consumption function as indicated by Figure 3.5. The intersection of the

---

* Duesenberry's data are put on a *per capita* basis and deflated by the Bureau of Labour Statistics consumer price index. He reports a correlation of $0 \cdot 9$ but no significance tests.

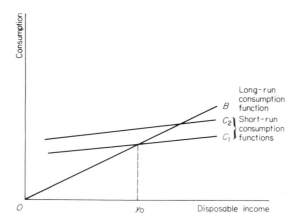

FIGURE 3.5   *The relative income hypothesis: the time-series reconciliation*

operative short-run consumption function with the long-run consumption function is determined by the level of previous peak income. Once income has recovered to y_0 consumption proceeds to expand along the long-run consumption function, OB, until interrupted by another depression. It then contracts along the short-run consumption function, such as C_2C_2, which is operative at that time.

The same short-run adjustment behaviour is explained by equation (3.7). In a depression, as peak income exceeds current income, y_t/y_0 is less than one in contrast to a period of expansion when it is more than one. Thus the a.p.c. is higher in the depression than in the boom. The short-run m.p.c. is obtained by differentiating equation (3.6) with respect to y_t:

$$\text{the short-run m.p.c.} = \frac{dC_t}{dy_t} = b_0 - 2b_1 \frac{y_t}{y_0}. \qquad (3.10)$$

This compares with the long-run m.p.c.:

$$\text{the long-run m.p.c.} = b_0 - b_1(1 + g). \qquad (3.9)$$

Therefore, even in the expansion when y_t/y_0 is greater than one and equals $(1 + g)$, the short-run m.p.c. is smaller than the long-run m.p.c. Using Duesenberry's estimates for b_0 and b_1 and assuming y_t and y_0 are approximately equal, we obtain a short-run m.p.c. of $0 \cdot 69$ [12].

The smaller size of short-run reactions compared to longer-run responses derives from the gradual nature of people's adjustment to changed circumstances. This type of response applies to many economic relationships. Here it is illustrated by the difference between the short-run and long-run consumption functions which is common to all approaches to consumption theory.

3.5 THE PERMANENT INCOME HYPOTHESIS

The permanent income hypothesis (P.I.H.) of Milton Friedman [13] is based explicitly on the theory of intertemporal choice discussed at the beginning of this chapter. On the assumption that consumers take account of future income and future consumption possibilities when planning current consumption, changes in current income which Friedman terms measured income, will only affect current consumption by way of resulting changes in wealth. In a world of certainty, permanent income is the return on the household's human and non-human wealth. The household's wealth is the present value of the future flow of income, which is expected by the household to be variable from year to year. Permanent income can be thought of as being that constant yearly annuity (given the symbol A) which, if paid out over each of the future years of the expected income stream, would have the same present value as that future income stream (see equation (3.12)):

$$W = \sum_{t=1}^{N} \frac{y_t}{(1+i)^t} \quad \text{(wealth constraint)} \tag{3.2}$$

where W is wealth, y_t is the income in year t and i is the rate of interest.

$$W = \sum_{t=1}^{N} \frac{A}{(1+i)^t} \tag{3.11}$$

$$= \frac{A}{i}\left[1 - \left(\frac{1}{1+i}\right)^N\right]$$

$$\therefore \quad A = iW\left[1 - \left(\frac{1}{1+i}\right)^N\right]^{-1} \tag{3.12}$$

$$\lim_{N \to \infty} A = iW. \tag{3.13}$$

Assuming an infinite time horizon, permanent income, A, is the stock of wealth multiplied by the interest rate, or annual return on wealth. Thus permanent income is the amount that can be consumed annually while leaving the stock of wealth intact.

Once uncertainty is introduced into the analysis, both the household future income stream and future interest rate depend on the household's expectations and the concept of permanent income is less clearly defined. We think of it as that part of a household's measured income which is regarded as stable and as reflecting the household's income expectations. The difference between measured and permanent income, which may be positive or negative, is called by Friedman transitory income and occurs due to temporary and unanticipated changes in current income. Similarly current or measured consumption is split into permanent and transitory components:

$$y_m = y_p + y_T \tag{3.14}$$

and

$$C_m = C_p + C_T \qquad (3.15)$$

where y_m is measured income, y_p is permanent income, y_T is transitory income, C_m is measured consumption, C_p is permanent consumption and C_T is transitory consumption. Friedman assumes that permanent consumption, defined to mean the act of consuming the services of goods, is planned on the basis of permanent income and that the relationship between the two variables is proportional, i.e.

$$C_p = Ky_p. \qquad (3.16)$$

The coefficient of proportionality, K, which is the 'true' underlying m.p.c. and a.p.c. is assumed to depend on those factors which affect the household's saving decision. These factors are household preferences, the nature of the uncertainties facing the household (an example of which is the extent of state welfare provisions), the rate of interest and the ratio of human to non-human wealth. Human wealth is the present value of future income that people expect to earn by using their personal skills and labour. Non-human wealth is the present value of income obtained from financial and capital assets. The particular uncertainties attached to labour income make it more difficult to borrow using human than non-human wealth as security. Thus the higher the ratio of human to non-human wealth the greater is the incentive to save and acquire non-human wealth.

Since the permanent and transitory components of income and consumption are unobservable, the proportionality hypothesis cannot be refuted by an appeal to the facts unless the model is further specified. It is therefore assumed that zero correlations hold between y_p and y_T, C_p and C_T, and y_T and C_T. The last assumption means any positive transitory income is not spent on consumption but is saved. Saving is defined to include investment in consumer durables as well as in financial assets and capital goods. Thus, consumption refers purely to the using up of goods by enjoying their services. *These assumptions mean that any changes in measured income will only affect current consumption if they cause the household to alter its estimate of permanent income.*

Cross-Section Analysis

Friedman's proportionality hypothesis, $C_p = Ky_p$, applies both to aggregate time series and household consumption functions. We will first discuss how the P.I.H. reconciles the constancy of the long-run aggregate a.p.c. with the decline of the cross-section a.p.c. with household income. Cross-section studies regress measured household consumption on to measured household income using the following type of regression equation:

$$C_m = a + by_m \qquad (3.17)$$

where b is an estimate of the cross-section m.p.c. According to the P.I.H. changes in consumption are due only to changes in permanent income, hence consumption will only change in response to changes in measured income, to the extent that previously unanticipated changes in measured income are regarded as permanent and cause estimates of permanent income to be revised. The more that changes in measured income are due to the random transitory components of income, the less will permanent income be revised when measured income changes. Thus, the greater the variability of a household's income, the greater will be the proportion of the variability in measured income which is attributed to transitory income, and the smaller the proportion of the variability in measured income attributed to permanent income. The latter measure is symbolised by P_y, which, as it is a proportion, must be between 0 and 1. Thus, Friedman shows* that b is an estimate of the true m.p.c., K, which is biased downwards, i.e.

$$b = KP_y. \tag{3.18}$$

If $P_y = 1$, that is all of the variability in measured income is caused by permanent income, $b = K$.

The P.I.H. leads us to expect that income earners with more variable incomes would have a lower m.p.c. when this is estimated by regressing measured consumption on measured income. The 1941 budget study carried out in the United States which showed that farm families had on average an a.p.c. of $0\cdot83$ and an m.p.c. of $0\cdot57$, and that urban families had an a.p.c. of $0\cdot92$ and an m.p.c. of $0\cdot79$, is consistent with the P.I.H. One should note also that this observation is not inconsistent with the R.I.H., which would explain the lower a.p.c. of farm families caused by their socially determined consumption habits.

The downward bias imparted to the m.p.c. by cross-section regression of measured consumption on measured income can be illustrated by Figure 3.6.

The non-proportional consumption function AC_m is obtained by regressing measured consumption on measured income for a group of households (for example, non-farm families in 1950 or wage-earner families for 1888–90). Friedman notes that the average a.p.c. calculated for a particular group of households by dividing average group consumption by average group income lies on the proportional long-run consumption function $C_p = Ky_p$ where $K = 0\cdot9$. This observation supports Friedman's assumption that the average measured income for the group is also the group's average permanent income, shown as $\bar{y}_p$ in Figure 3.6. y_{mi} is the measured income of household i which is observed to consume C_i. Consumption expenditure of C_i is planned on the basis of household i's permanent income, y_{pi}. This is obtained by drawing a straight line from B

* See Appendix, Note 2. Reported in Friedman [9], p. 16.

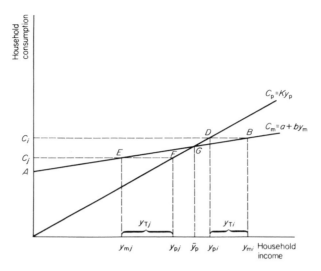

FIGURE 3.6   *The permanent income hypothesis: the cross-section consumption*
function

to C_i. This line cuts the underlying 'true' consumption function OC_p at D.
By extending a perpendicular from D to cut the abscissa at y_{pi}, the ith
household's permanent income is found. Given a permanent income of
y_{pi}, the proportional consumption function, $C_p = Ky_p$ tells us that household i will consume C_i. The ith household's measured income is y_{mi}, so
that point relating the household's consumption to its measured income
appears on the non-proportional consumption function, $C_m = a + by_m$.
The difference between household i's measured income and its permanent income is its transitory income shown as y_{Ti}, which for household i is
positive. We can repeat the same exercise for household j, whose measured income is y_{mj}, and whose permanent income, y_{pj}, is below the group
average. This household therefore has a negative transitory income for
this year. If instead the cross-section regression had produced an estimated consumption function $Z\hat{C}_m$, shown in Figure 3.7, household i with
a measured income of y_{mi} would now have a permanent income of $\hat{y}_{pi}$ and
consequently a smaller transitory income equal to $y_{mi} - \hat{y}_{pi}$. This result
applies to all households in the group. Therefore, we can see that as the
proportion of the variability in measured income which is attributable to
transitory income falls (measured and permanent income approach each
other and P_y rises) so the estimated m.p.c., b, rises and approaches K.
    Friedman cites the negro–white consumer survey, used by Duesen-
berry to support the R.I.H., as evidence in favour of the P.I.H. Since
average measured income is lower for negroes, so is their average

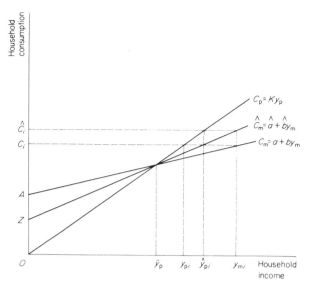

FIGURE 3.7   *The permanent income hypothesis: the bias of the estimated m.p.c.*
is greater the larger is the transitory component of measured income

permanent income. Any given level of measured income implies a lower permanent income for a negro than for a white, and explains their observed lower consumption.

Time-Series Analysis

The P.I.H. can also be used to reconcile the time-series observations on short- and long-run consumption functions over the trade cycle. Transitory income will be negative in the recession and positive at the peak, thus the higher a.p.c.s recorded in the depression years of the 1930s relative to the secular a.p.c. for the United States can be explained by relating consumption in that period to a level of permanent income which was larger than measured income. Similarly, the lower a.p.c.s of the Second World War years can be explained in terms of positive transitory income and negative transitory consumption then existing.

The shorter the time period over which data are taken, the greater one would expect to be the variability in aggregate measured income attributable to transitory income, and thus the greater the downward bias found in estimates of the m.p.c., obtained by regressing measured consumption on measured income. The tendency for the estimated m.p.c. to be smaller, the shorter the time period of the regression is confirmed by an examination of the U.S. data ([9] p. 16). and is consistent with the results obtained for post-war U.K. data ([9] p. 12).

Since permanent income is unobservable, a proxy, based on the assumption that future expected income depends on past experiences of the level and rate of growth of income, can be substituted. Friedman adopts the adaptive expectations hypothesis. This hypothesis assumes that estimates of the expected variable (permanent income in this case) are revised when differences are observed between the expectations that were held about the variable and the actual value that the variable takes on, i.e.

$$y_{pt} - y_{pt-1} = \lambda(y_t - y_{pt-1}). \tag{3.19}$$

Equation (3.19) shows that estimates of permanent income are changed when a discrepancy occurs between measured income, y_t, and the permanent income which was expected in the previous period to exist in the present period, y_{pt-1}. The coefficient of adjustment, λ, lies between 0 and 1, since the proportion of the difference between permanent and measured income which is due to transitory income will not cause ideas about permanent income to be adjusted.

Rearranging equation (3.19) we obtain

$$y_{pt} = (1-\lambda)y_{pt-1} + \lambda y_t. \tag{3.20}$$

If we iterate equation (3.20) backwards in time we obtain current permanent income as a distributed function of past values of measured income. This type of equation is known as a distributed lag function.

$$y_{pt-1} = (1-\lambda)y_{pt-2} + \lambda y_{t-1} \tag{3.20.1}$$

$$y_{pt-2} = (1-\lambda)y_{pt-3} + \lambda y_{t-2} \tag{3.20.2}$$

$$\vdots \qquad \vdots \qquad \vdots \qquad \vdots \qquad \qquad \vdots$$

$$y_{pt-N} = (1-\lambda)y_{pt-N-1} + \lambda y_{t-N}. \tag{3.20.N}$$

Substitute equation (3.20.1) into equation (3.20) to obtain

$$y_{pt} = (1-\lambda)[(1-\lambda)y_{pt-2} + \lambda y_{t-1}] + \lambda y_t \tag{3.21}$$

Then substitute (3.20.2) into (3.21) to obtain

$$y_{pt} = (1-\lambda)^2[(1-\lambda)y_{pt-3} + \lambda y_{t-2}] + \lambda(1-\lambda)y_{t-1} + \lambda y_t. \tag{3.22}$$

The process is repeated by successively substituting equation (3.20.N) into (3.20.N − 1) and so on until we obtain

$$y_{pt} = (1-\lambda)^{N+1}y_{pt-N-1} + \lambda \sum_{n=0}^{N} (1-\lambda)^n y_{t-n}. \tag{3.23}$$

As $N \to \infty$, $(1-\lambda)^N \to 0$, and the term $(1-\lambda)^{N+1}y_{pt-N-1}$ approaches zero and drops out of equation (3.23).

Equation (3.23) is an example of a geometrically declining distributed lag function since the weight $(1-\lambda)^n$ gets smaller with time as n gets larger. This means that past income has less influence on permanent income as time is extended backwards.

Using Friedman's proportionality hypothesis

$$C_{pt} = Ky_{pt}. \tag{3.16}$$

Substituting equation (3.23) into equation (3.16) we obtain

$$C_{pt} = K\lambda \sum_{n=0}^{\infty} (1-\lambda)^n y_{t-n}. \tag{3.24}$$

A distributed lag function, such as equation (3.24), presents estimating problems because it contains many past values of the dependent variable which will be related to each other. The Koyck [14] transformation is a well-known method of simplifying geometrically declining distributed lag functions. This is done by first lagging equation (3.24) by one period, i.e.

$$C_{pt-1} = K\lambda \sum_{n=0}^{\infty} (1-\lambda)^n y_{t-n-1} \tag{3.25}$$

Equation (3.25) is then multiplied by $(1-\lambda)$ to give

$$(1-\lambda)C_{pt-1} = K\lambda \sum_{n=0}^{\infty} (1-\lambda)^{n+1} y_{t-n-1}. \tag{3.26}$$

Equation (3.26) is subtracted from equation (3.24)

$$C_{pt} = K\lambda[y_t + (1-\lambda)y_{t-1} + (1-\lambda)^2 y_{t-2} + \cdots + (1-\lambda)^N y_{t-N}] \tag{3.24}$$

$$(1-\lambda)C_{pt-1} = K\lambda[(1-\lambda)y_{t-1} + (1-\lambda)^2 y_{t-2} + \cdots + (1-\lambda)^N y_{t-N}] \tag{3.26}$$

$$C_{pt} - (1-\lambda)C_{pt-1} = K\lambda y_t \tag{3.27}$$

$$C_{pt} = K\lambda y_t + (1-\lambda)C_{pt-1}. \tag{3.28}$$

The dependent variable, C_{pt}, is a function of the independent variable and of itself lagged one period. The short-run marginal propensity to consume is obtained by differentiating consumption with respect to current income. Hence

the short-run m.p.c. $= dC_{pt}/dy_t = K\lambda$.

In the long run consumption will be fully adjusted to permanent income and in static equilibrium will maintain the same value from one period to another. This condition gives

$$C_{pt} = C_{pt-1} = C_p. \tag{3.29}$$

Substituting equation (3.29) into (3.28) we obtain the long-run consumption function with the long-run m.p.c. equal to K, i.e.

$$C_p = Ky_p. \tag{3.16}$$

Since λ is less than one, the short-run m.p.c. is smaller than the long-run m.p.c. The size of the short-run m.p.c. relative to the long-run m.p.c. depends on the speed with which permanent income, and hence consumption, adjusts to a change in current income. The lower the value of λ the longer it takes permanent income to adjust to a change in current income.

When estimating the expectations model discussed above, Friedman truncated the permanent income equation (3.23) after seventeen periods because, thereafter, the coefficients fell to $0\cdot001$. He estimated λ to be $0\cdot33$ which, given a long-run m.p.c. of about $0\cdot9$, produces a short-run m.p.c. in the region of $0\cdot3$, in line with the short-run quarterly U.K. consumption function reported on p. 65.

3.6 THE LIFE-CYCLE HYPOTHESIS

The life-cycle hypothesis (L.C.H.) developed by Ando, Brumberg and Modigliani [15, 16, 17], is, like the P.I.H., based on household utility maximising behaviour. Given that the household has a known life span and intends to leave no legacies and given certainty, the motive for saving is to rearrange lifetime consumption in relation to the expected future income stream. The L.C.H. stresses the accumulation of non-human wealth as the means of achieving this aim. Uncertainty provides an additional, related motive for saving, that of protecting consumption plans from the effects of unexpected falls in income.

The typical time profile of a lifetime income stream is one that rises in the early working years, reaches a plateau in middle years and is followed by a sudden decline upon retirement. Thus, the household's saving ratio and the relationship between its current consumption and its accumulated assets will depend upon its age. There is no simple, direct relationship between saving and net wealth. Although a high level of household consumption accompanied by a large stock of assets is likely to be observed, this does not mean that the high level of assets causes the high rate of consumption. In the L.C.H., which abstracts from inheritancies, it is a high lifetime income stream that results in a related high level of consumption and associated asset accumulation.

It is assumed that the household's current consumption (defined as non-durable consumption plus the rental value of consumer durables) is proportional to its total resources, the factor of proportionality depending on the interest rate used to discount future income, tastes and age of household. Total resources are subdivided into current income, y_t, the present value of future income from human sources, y^E, and accumulated assets A_{t-1} brought forward from the previous period. Total resources are the same as Friedman's present value of all future income expected from human and non-human sources, which forms the basis for estimating permanent income.

The difference between the L.C.H. and P.I.H. is one of emphasis in that the L.C.H. is concerned explicitly with the role of asset accumulation and the effect of age on household consumption. The L.C.H. is similar to the P.I.H., in that it assumes that any change in total resources, due to any of the three components, will cause a proportional change in planned consumption in all future periods. The a.p.c. for a given age group is therefore deduced to be the same for all levels of income, to fall with middle age and rise again upon retirement. The middle years are a period when income is relatively high, consumer durables have been acquired and there is a need to accumulate assets with which to finance consumption upon retirement.

The result of a change in current income on consumption depends on the effect of that change upon the household's total resources. If the change is regarded as only temporary it will have very little effect on current consumption. If the change is considered permanent it will cause expectations of income to be revised in the same direction. The younger is the household the more its current consumption will be affected by a change in current income regarded as permanent, since there is a longer period over which the changed level of expected income will be discounted and hence a larger impact on total resources.

Cross-Section Analysis

The L.C.H. reconciles the non-proportional consumption function produced by budget studies with the constancy of the long-run aggregate a.p.c., in a manner very similar to that of the P.I.H. Cross-section regression of current consumption on current income will produce non-proportional consumption functions because the higher-income

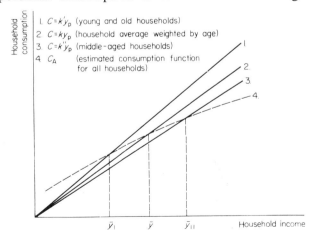

FIGURE 3.8 *The life cycle hypothesis: the cross-section consumption function*

households contain a larger proportion of people who have recently experienced an increase in income than do the lower-income households. To the extent that such increases are regarded as temporary there will be no corresponding increase in consumption and the household's observed a.p.c. will be lower than for a low-income household experiencing a temporary decrease in income.

One would also expect to be able to stratify budget studies by age, so that the estimated consumption function for middle-aged households would lie below those for young and old households. According to the L.C.H. each age group has a proportional relationship between its consumption and total resources, the coefficient of proportionality, K, being lower for middle-aged households than for the young and old. The proportional relationship is shown in Figure 3.8 as one between consumption and permanent income, which is the flow variable equivalent of total resources. The proportional consumption function for old and young households lies above that for middle-aged households, the average for all age groups lying in between. Out of a given income the a.p.c. for the middle-aged is less than that of the young or old. The estimated consumption function for each group is non-proportional and cuts the group's underlying proportional consumption function at average group income. ($\bar{y}_1$ = average income of young and old households which is less than the average of all age groups $\bar{y}$, and of the middle-aged households $\bar{y}_{11}$.) There is evidence, such as that of the U.K. 1952 National Survey of Personal Incomes and Saving, which is used by Ando and Modigliani, that the saving ratio does vary with age in the manner assumed by the L.C.H.

The consumption function for each age group is assumed to be

$$C_t^T = K^T(V_t^T) \qquad (3.30)$$

where V_t is the total resources at time t and T indicates the age group to which the function applies.

$$V_t^T = f(y_t^T, y^{TE}, A_{t-1}^T) \qquad (3.31)$$

where y_t is the current income, y^E is the present value of future expected labour income, and A_{t-1} are assets. Making equation (3.31) linear and substituting into equation (3.30) we obtain

$$C_t^T = \alpha_1^T y_t^T + \alpha_2^T y^{TE} + \alpha_3^T A_{t-1}^T. \qquad (3.32)$$

Aggregate consumption will be a weighted average (the weight W^T attached to each C_0^T being the proportion of households in age group T) of the various age groups' consumption levels. If the economy was stationary (income and population constant over time) and certainty allowed people to fulfil their plans of consuming all their assets before death, the net saving of the working population would be exactly offset by the dissaving of the retired, given that the age structure of the population was constant. Goods and services not consumed in the current period by the savers would be transferred for consumption to the retired, who would finance this by selling their assets to the savers. Net saving would be zero, as would be net investment in a stationary economy. If national output is growing over time and the age structure of the population is constant, the savings of the working population would also be growing, since savings are a constant proportion of income. If the retired are living off fixed interest securities, they are not sharing in the growth of national income and their dissaving is less than the saving of the working population. Net aggregate saving is positive and provides the resources needed for positive net investment, which is required to sustain growth.

The aggregate consumption function is a weighted average of equation (3.32) and is written

$$C_t = a_1 y_t + a_2 y^E + a_3 A_{t-1}. \tag{3.33}$$

The aggregate a.p.c. is

$$\frac{C_t}{y_t} = a_1 + a_2 \frac{y^E}{y_t} + a_3 \frac{A_{t-1}}{y_t} \tag{3.34}$$

and is constant if, over time, future income is proportional to current income (steady growth or a stationary economy), and the net wealth–income ratio remains constant. Equation (3.33) can be simplified by assuming expected income is a function of current income, i.e.

$$y^E = \beta y_t \tag{3.35}$$

$$C_t = (a_1 + \beta a_2) y_t + a_3 A_{t-1} \tag{3.36}$$

$$= \alpha y_t + a_3 A_{t-1} \tag{3.36a}$$

where $\alpha = a_1 + \beta a_2$. Ando and Modigliani estimate α to be in the region of $0 \cdot 52$–$0 \cdot 60$. The estimated m.p.c. rises to around $0 \cdot 68$–$0 \cdot 71$ when another variable is added, which extends the expectations hypothesis to make y^E depend on the proportion of the labour force employed. The coefficient on wealth, a_3, is estimated to be in the region of $0 \cdot 072$ to $0 \cdot 1$.

Time-Series Analysis

The L.C.H. reconciles short- and long-run time-series data in a similar manner to the R.I.H. The short-run consumption function, given by equation (3.36a) is non-proportional, the intercept term being given by $a_3 A_{t-1}$. As net wealth increases in a growing economy, so the short-run consumption function shifts up over time as shown in Figure 3.9.

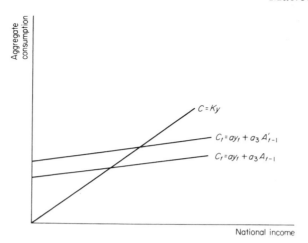

FIGURE 3.9   *The life cycle hypothesis: the time-series consumption function*

Cyclical variations in the a.p.c. are explained in the following way. In a recession, although current income falls, expected income is not much affected and assets can be used to sustain consumption; thus the a.p.c. rises. In the recovery, the savings ratio rises as assets are built up to the level required to match the growth trend of income.

3.7   CONCLUSION

The P.I.H. and L.C.H. are based explicitly on intertemporal utility maximising behaviour on the part of households. The R.I.H. is not so based but its assumption that households are influenced by the consumption standards of surrounding households is not inconsistent with the planning of consumption over some time horizon. Both the P.I.H. and L.C.H. assume that the underlying cross-section relationship between consumption and the permanent income component is a proportional one, whereas the R.I.H. assumes that the a.p.c. declines as household relative income rises. The cross-section proportionality postulate is not an essential element of the L.C.H. or P.I.H. whose main achievement is to relate current consumption to that part of income which is basically stable and not directly observable from income data. Both the L.C.H. and P.I.H. relate aggregate permanent or expected income to past income, and thus join the R.I.H. in emphasising the role of lagged values of income in determining current consumption.

The post-Keynesian theories of consumption have assisted our understanding of the difficulties that exist in making short-run predictions of consumption purchases from data on current income. First, it is not consumer purchases that households are concerned with directly when planning enjoyment from consuming the services of goods. The purchase of consumer durables is in effect the acquisition of an asset, which will yield services over a number of time periods. Secondly, current consumption plans are not related simply to current income which is subject to unforseen fluctuations but to a more stable, but unobservable, component of income. The fluctuations in the variation between quarterly income and quarterly consumer expenditure and the large variations of the annual m.p.c. for the United Kingdom indicate how difficult it is to predict future consumption purchases without a thorough knowledge of the underlying lag structure between income and consumption, and an awareness of the impact of changes in expected future income and asset values.

APPENDIX

Note 1. Intertemporal Consumption Choice Over N Periods

$$U = U(C_0, C_1, \ldots, C_t, \ldots, C_N) \qquad t = 0 \cdots N \tag{3.1}$$

$$W = \sum_{t=0}^{N} \frac{y_t}{(1+i)^t} = \sum_{t=0}^{N} \frac{C_t}{(1+i)^t}. \tag{3.2}$$

Equation (3.1) is maximised subject to equation (3.2) by forming the Lagrangean

$$U^* = U(C_0, \ldots, C_t, \ldots, C_N) - \lambda \left(\sum_{t=0}^{N} \frac{C_t}{(1+i)^t} - W \right) \tag{3.3}$$

$$\frac{\partial U^*}{\partial C_0} = \frac{\partial U}{\partial C_0} - \lambda = 0 \tag{3.4}$$

$$\frac{\partial U^*}{\partial C_1} = \frac{\partial U}{\partial C_1} - \frac{\lambda}{1+i} = 0 \tag{3.4.1}$$

$$\frac{\partial U^*}{\partial C_2} = \frac{\partial U}{\partial C_2} - \frac{\lambda}{(1+i)^2} = 0 \tag{3.4.2}$$

$$\cdots \cdots \cdots \cdots$$

$$\frac{\partial U^*}{\partial C_N} = \frac{\partial U}{\partial C_N} - \frac{\lambda}{(1+i)^N} = 0. \tag{3.4.N}$$

From equation (3.4)

$$\partial U / \partial C_0 = \lambda. \tag{3.5}$$

From equations (3.4) and (3.4.1)

$$\frac{\partial U}{\partial C_1} \Big/ \frac{\partial U}{\partial C_0} = \frac{1}{1+i} \tag{3.5.1}$$

$$\cdot \qquad \cdot \qquad \cdot$$
$$\cdot \qquad \cdot \qquad \cdot$$
and
$$\cdot \qquad \cdot \qquad \cdot$$

$$\frac{\partial U}{\partial C_2} \Big/ \frac{\partial U}{\partial C_1} = \frac{1}{1+i} \tag{3.5.2}$$

and

$$\frac{\partial U}{\partial C_N} \Big/ \frac{\partial U}{\partial C_{N-1}} = \frac{1}{1+i}. \tag{3.5.N-1}$$

Therefore, the marginal rate of substitution between consumption in period t and consumption in period $t-1$ equals $1/(1+i_t)$ and given a constant expected interest rate, is the same between all periods.

If the interest rate is known to be different in the future, the marginal rate of transformation between consumption in period t and consumption in period $t-1$ will equal $1/(1+i_t)$ where i_t is the market interest rate expected to rule in the tth period.

Note 2. The Relationship Between Measured Consumption and Measured Income, Showing that the Estimator, b, of the m.p.c. is Biased Downwards

$$C_1 = \alpha + KY + U \tag{3.37}$$

Equation (3.37) is the theoretical consumption function.

$$C_m = a + bY_m \tag{3.38}$$

Equation (3.38) is the estimated consumption function. The least squares estimates of α and K are a and b and are given by

$$b = \frac{\sum (C_m - \bar{C}_m)(Y_m - \bar{Y}_m)}{\sum (Y_m - \bar{Y}_m)^2} \tag{3.39}$$

$$a = \bar{C}_m - b\bar{Y}_m \tag{3.40}$$

(the bar over a variable indicates its mean).
Since

$$Y_m = Y_p + Y_T \tag{3.14}$$

$$C_m = C_p + C_T. \tag{3.15}$$

Substituting equation (3.14) and (3.15) into equation (3.39) gives

$$\begin{aligned}
\sum (C_m - \bar{C}_m)(Y_m - \bar{Y}_m) &= \sum (C_p + C_T - \bar{C}_p - \bar{C}_T)(Y_p + Y_T - \bar{Y}_p - \bar{Y}_T) \\
&= \sum (C_p - \bar{C}_p)(Y_p - \bar{Y}_p) + \sum (C_p - \bar{C}_p)(Y_T - \bar{Y}_T) \\
&\quad + \sum (C_T - \bar{C}_T)(Y_p - \bar{Y}_p) + \sum (C_T - \bar{C}_T)(Y_T - \bar{Y}_T).
\end{aligned} \tag{3.41}$$

$$C_p = KY_p \qquad (3.16)$$

Substituting equation (3.16) into equation (3.41) gives

$$\sum (C_m - \bar{C}_m)(Y_m - \bar{Y}_m) = K \sum (Y_p - \bar{Y}_p)^2 + K \sum (Y_p - \bar{Y}_p)(Y_T - \bar{Y}_T)$$

$$+ \frac{1}{K} \sum (C_T - \bar{C}_T)(C_p - \bar{C}_p) + \sum (C_T - \bar{C}_T)$$

$$\times (Y_T - \bar{Y}_T). \qquad (3.42)$$

Since it is assumed that the correlations between C_p and C_T, Y_p and Y_T, C_T and Y_T are zero, all terms except the first drop out of equation (3.42) to give

$$b = \frac{K \sum (Y_p - \bar{Y}_p)^2}{\sum (Y_m - \bar{Y}_m)^2} = KP_y$$

where

$$P_y = \frac{\sum (Y_p - \bar{Y}_p)^2}{\sum (Y_m - \bar{Y}_m)^2}$$

which is the proportion of the variance in measured income which is attributable to variations in permanent income. If $P_y = 1$, $b = K$, and if $P_y < 1$, $b < K$ and is therefore biased downwards.

REFERENCES

[1] H. Houthakker and L. Taylor, *Consumer Demand in the U.S.A.* (Harvard University Press, 1966).
[2] J. M. Keynes, *The General Theory of Employment, Interest and Money* (London: Macmillan, 1936) p. 104.
[3] I. Fisher, *The Rate of Interest* (New York: Macmillan, 1907).
[4] I. Fisher, *The Theory of Interest* (New York: Macmillan, 1930).
[5] J. M. Keynes, *The General Theory*, pp. 96–7.
[6] J. R. Hicks, 'Mr Keynes and the Classics: A Suggested Interpretation', *Econometrica* (1937).
[7] G. Ackley, *Macroeconomic Theory* (New York: Macmillan, 1961) ch. 10.
[8] S. Kuznets, *The National Product Since 1869* (National Bureau of Economic Research, 1946).
[9] M. Friedman, *A Theory of the Consumption Function* (Princeton University Press, 1957) ch. 5.
[10] J. Duesenberry, *Income, Saving and the Theory of Consumer Behaviour* (Cambridge, Mass.: Harvard University Press, 1949).
[11] H. Menderhausen, 'Differences in Family Savings Between Cities of Different Sizes and Location, Whites and Negroes', *Review of Economics and Statistics* (August 1940).

[12] M. Bruce Johnson, *Household Behaviour, Consumption, Income and Wealth* (Harmondsworth: Penguin, 1971).

[13] M. Friedman, *A Theory of the Consumption Function.*

[14] L. M. Koyck, *Distributed Lags and Investment Analysis* (Amsterdam: North-Holland, 1954).

[15] F. Modigliani and R. Brumberg, 'Utility Analysis and the Consumption Function: An Interpretation of Cross Section Data', in *Post-Keynesian Economics*, ed. K. Kurihara (London: Allen & Unwin, 1955).

[16] A. Ando and F. Modigliani, 'Tests of the Life Cycle Hypothesis of Savings: Comments and Suggestions', *Bulletin of the Oxford University Institute of Statistics*, 19 (1957).

[17] A. Ando and F. Modigliani, 'The Life Cycle Hypothesis of Saving: Aggregate Implications and Taste', *American Economic Review*, 53,1 (1963).

4 Capital and Investment Theory

Capital is a stock of man-made resources yielding services which are combined with labour to produce a flow of output. The essential feature of capital is that its accumulation requires the sacrifice of labour and resources that could have been devoted to present consumption. The return to capital is the additional future consumption goods that can be produced as a result of using the services of capital. The choice of the size of capital stock to hold is an intertemporal choice problem since it involves comparing future benefits with present costs.

Once the decision as to what quantity of resources to devote to capital goods production is made, capital takes on specific forms as various types of goods. It is necessary to distinguish liquid capital, which is money or financial assets, from real capital goods, into which liquid capital can be converted. This chapter is concerned with analysing the demand for real capital goods, whose services are used in production processes. Real capital can be subdivided into two types. Fixed capital is such items as plant, machinery and transport infrastructures that keep their particular physical form throughout their working life. Working capital consists of stocks of raw materials, manufactured inputs and final goods awaiting distribution and retailing. Each unit of working capital changes its form as it passes through the production process to the point of final consumption.

An economy can only produce additional output over time by either acquiring greater quantities of factors of production, or, through technical progress, increasing the amount of output a given combination of factors can produce, or by both methods. The accumulation of capital is therefore a vital element in economic growth. This has two aspects; with a positive rate of return on capital and a given state of technical knowledge, the acquisition of capital enables the economy to produce more goods and services in the future; when technical progress occurs, and is embodied in particular types of capital equipment, the acquisition of new capital is essential to the utilisation of such technical progress.

From the theoretical standpoint, a stationary economy is one in which technical progress is absent and the capital stock is constant. As capital is used up in the production of goods and services, it must be replaced by new equipment. Thus, in a stationary economy, the amount of replacement investment is identical to the amount by which the capital stock depreciates. In such an economy in long-run equilibrium, all net national output will consist of consumption and net saving will be zero.

If the capital stock grows larger over time, the increase in capital stock per period of time is known as net investment. Gross investment is then made up of replacement investment and net investment. If the capital stock declines over time, disinvestment occurs since depreciation exceeds replacement. By saving, the community as a whole is releasing from present consumption resources which can be converted into capital goods, and hence into additional future consumption. Thus the process of capital accumulation, or net investment, involves net saving in aggregate by members of the community.* This may be done either by the government allocating resources to both consumption and capital accumulation in a centrally planned economy, or by the interaction of individual saving and investment decisions in a market economy. In a mixed economy a combination of both methods is possible.

It must be stressed that investment is a flow variable which is undertaken to eliminate the discrepancy between the desired and actual capital stock. This adjustment process has been termed the capital stock adjustment principle. Once a discrepancy between the desired and actual capital stock has been noted, it takes time for firms to adjust. There is a lag between making the appropriations for capital equipment, and its delivery and installation. Investment expenditure occurs at the time of delivery and installation. This means that investment expenditure in any one time period is related to decisions to adjust the capital stock to its desired level made several periods ago. Investigation of the determinants of investment involves consideration of

(1) the factors that affect the desired capital stock, and
(2) the process of adjusting the actual capital stock to its desired level.

4.1 THE CHOICE OF THE CAPITAL STOCK AS THE CHOICE OF DATED CONSUMPTION STREAMS

Production Sector Only: No Capital Market

We start by considering the determination of the optimal stock of capital by a decision-maker whose objective it is to maximise utility from

* An open economy can import capital goods, financing this by borrowing from abroad.

consumption over time [1, 2]. This problem differs from that of Chapter 3 because the decision-maker is both a producer as well as a consumer. The analysis is conducted in the context of an economy in which there is a single good that serves as both a capital good and a consumption good. This assumption allows us to measure both goods in terms of a common physical unit, which means that the relative price of capital goods to consumer goods is exogenously given as one.* Using this assumption enables a simple model to be constructed which gives insights into the process of capital accumulation and which yields testable predictions.

Take the example of Robinson Crusoe, endowed with a sack of potatoes, deciding on consumption for two periods, the present and the future. He knows with certainty at what rate potatoes planted this year will yield potatoes next year. This information is contained in the production function which assumes the quantity of other factors is fixed. The production relationship between the quantity of potatoes planted this year and next year's output is shown by the production possibility curve AB in Figure 4.1, where OB is Crusoe's initial endowment of potatoes. As we move from B towards the origin we obtain the quantity of potatoes that are not consumed this year, but become capital and are planted. The production function is of the form

$$C_1 = f(-C_0). \tag{4.1}$$

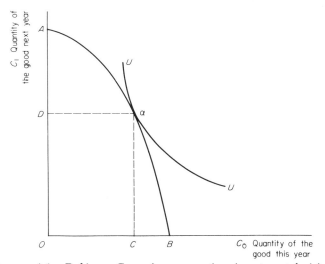

FIGURE 4.1   *Robinson Crusoe's consumption–investment decision*

* The considerable difficulties involved in measuring capital have been raised by Joan Robinson [31].

The negative sign appears in front of C_0 because it is the amount of consumption sacrificed in the present, which is also the stock of capital in the same period. Diminishing marginal productivity of capital is assumed.* The marginal product of capital is

$$-\frac{dC_1}{dC_0} > 0 \quad \text{and} \quad \frac{d^2C_1}{dC_0^2} < 0$$

(note: from equation (4.1) dC_1/dC_0 is negative).

Crusoe's utility depends upon the quantity of potatoes consumed both this year and next, i.e.

$$U = f(C_0, C_1). \tag{4.2}$$

The equation of movements along each indifference curve is

$$dU = \frac{\partial U}{\partial C_0} dC_0 + \frac{\partial U}{\partial C_1} dC_1 = 0. \tag{4.3}$$

Therefore the slope of each indifference curve is given by

$$\frac{dC_1}{dC_0} = \frac{-\partial U}{\partial C_0} \Big/ \frac{\partial U}{\partial C_1}. \tag{4.4}$$

Expression (4.4) is the marginal rate of time preference. It is the rate at which consumption this year must be substituted for consumption next year to maintain the individual at the same level of utility.†

Crusoe is assumed to maximise his utility subject to the constraint of his production function. To do this he will choose that stock of capital which will get him on the highest attainable indifference curve, which is point α in Figure 4.1. As the stock of capital increases from B towards the origin, the marginal product of capital declines, while the rate at which consumption this year can be substituted for by consumption next year to maintain the same level of utility increases. His optimal plan involves consuming OC potatoes this year, saving CB, which becomes the stock of capital which is converted into OD potatoes which is consumed next year. The desired stock of capital is that stock for which the marginal product of capital equals the marginal rate of time preference.

The Crusoe model applies to intertemporal decision-making in a centralised economy where the utility function is that of the planning agency. It is a useful theoretical device in that it shows clearly that the *opportunity cost of capital acquisition is forgone present consumption, and that the basic choice is between consumption at different periods of time.*

* The production possibility curve is assumed convex to the origin to ensure a unique optimum.
† See Chapter 3, p. 59.

Introduction of the Capital Market

We can apply the same analysis to individual choice in a decentralised, market economy. The individual's consumption preferences and production opportunities are defined as before. In addition the individual can borrow or lend the good on a perfectly competitive capital market at an exogenously given rate of interest, i. This market opportunity is represented by any straight net present value line parallel to GF in Figure 4.2. OG of the good can be lent in the present period to obtain OF in the next period. The present value of OF is $OF/(1+i) = OG$. Along FG we are given various combinations of the good received this year and received next year, which have the same net present value or wealth. Therefore we can write

$$W = C_0 + C_1/(1+i). \tag{4.5}$$

Rearranging we obtain the equation for the net present value line

$$C_1 = (1+i)(W - C_0) \tag{4.6}$$

$$dC_1/dC_0 = -(1+i). \tag{4.7}$$

The slope of the net present value line is given by equation (4.7) and its position depends on the total wealth it represents.

The individual can now dispose of the non-consumed portion of his endowment in two ways, either by investing it in his own productive process or by lending it to somebody else at the market rate of interest.

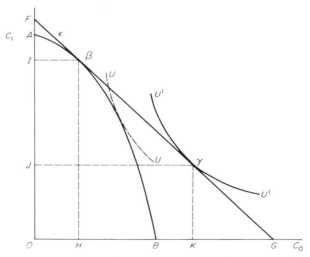

FIGURE 4.2   *The separation of the consumption and investment decisions in the presence of a perfect capital market*

Alternatively, by borrowing, he can consume more in the present than that part of the endowment which remains after investing in his capital stock.

The individual is endowed with *OB* of the good in the present. If the market lending and borrowing opportunities were not available the individual would maximise his utility at α as in Figure 4.1. Now that these market opportunities are open to him, the individual can decide what production solution will maximise his wealth, and then proceed to allocate that wealth between present and future consumption so as to repay the debt plus interest payments incurred in the first period. This leaves *OJ* for consumption in the future period.

If the individual had different preferences and maximised his utility at ε in Figure 4.2, his optimal plan would involve holding a capital stock greater than *HB*. But any addition to the capital stock used in the productive process would yield a marginal rate of return on capital which is less than the market rate of interest. (The slope of the production opportunity curve is less than that of the wealth line.) Any capital stock that the individual holds in excess of *HB* will be lent on the capital market at the market rate of interest.

The Separation of Net Present Value Maximisation from Utility Maximisation

The interesting result that emerges from this model is that in a world of certainty and a perfect capital market, the decision concerning the desired quantity of capital to place in the production process, which is the investment decision, is separate from the consumption decision. To determine the optimal amount of investment in production we do not need to know the individual's utility function. It is sufficient to aim at maximising wealth from investment in production, to arrive at the optimal capital stock. It should be noted that, in this model, the quantity of consumption forgone and converted into the capital stock, is the same as the amount of net investment in the current period. This is because we start with a zero capital stock and then decide what proportion of the endowment to place (invest) in the production process.

The analysis extends to a firm owned by many individuals, which is run to maximise the owners' utility from a time stream of consumption. To achieve this objective, the firm has only to maximise its net present value. If the firm issues shares this corresponds to maximising the market value of its shares. Given zero transactions costs, each shareholder can buy and sell financial assets so as to achieve his desired time profile of consumption.

For the firm to maximise its wealth in the two-period model, it must acquire capital until

$$-(\mathrm{d}C_1/\mathrm{d}C_0) = 1 + i. \tag{4.8}$$

That is until the marginal rate of productivity on the addition to the capital stock equals the market rate of interest. Alternatively equation (4.8) can be written as

$$dC_0 + dC_1/(1+i) = 0. \qquad (4.9)$$

In equation (4.9) dC_0 represents the cost of capital goods in terms of forgone marginal consumption and is negative since it represents a reduction in current consumption. The marginal unit of capital is just worth acquiring since the additional cost currently incurred, dC_0, is equal to the present value of the net returns, $dC_1/1 + i$, from that unit of capital. Given certainty and a perfect capital market, the market rate of interest is the appropriate discount rate to use to calculate the net present value of future returns. This is because the market rate of interest in a perfect capital market correctly measures the opportunity cost, in terms of a forgone rate of return, of the resources placed in the firm's capital stock. The marginal cost of capital to the firm is that rate of return it could have earned by placing resources in the next best investment alternative, which in this model is lending at the market rate of interest. The marginal cost of capital is always the appropriate discount rate to use in calculating the net present value of a capital project.

A firm wishing to maximise its wealth would adopt each additional capital project for which the net present value is positive. (In a two-period world the net present value equals $dC_0 + dC_1/(1+i) \geq 0$.) The marginal project will have a net present value of zero.

The Internal Rate of Return

An alternative decision rule to the net present value criterion outlined above, is to calculate the internal rate of return on a capital project and compare it to the market rate of interest. If the internal rate of return is greater or equal to the rate of interest the project will be adopted. The internal rate of return is that rate of discount, ρ, which makes the net present value of an addition (that is capital project) to the capital stock equal to zero, i.e.

$$dC_0 + dC_1/(1+\rho) = 0. \qquad (4.10)$$

Equation (4.10) tells us that an investment of dC_0 in the production process is equivalent to investing dC_0 at a rate of interest of ρ, since $dC_1 = -dC_0(1+\rho)$.

The internal rate of return is alternatively known as the yield and was termed the marginal efficiency of capital by Keynes [3]. In a two-period world of certainty, a firm using either criterion will select the same stock of capital (*HB* in Figure 4.2).* As we have seen above, with a stock of

* This depends on the convexity of the production opportunity curve. If it is non-convex, i.e. has bumps, the internal rate of return will have more than one value, only one of which will select the capital stock with the highest net present value.

capital of *HB*, an additional small unit of capital adds nothing to the net present value of the firm (equation (4.9)). Applying equation (4.10), the internal rate of return will equal the market rate of interest when the stock of capital is *HB* in Figure 4.2

Multiperiod Analysis

We now extend this analysis to the selection of capital projects which yield returns over a number of years, moving away from the model in which consumer and capital goods are the same good. For a firm the initial cost of a capital project is the market price of the required capital goods. Keynes called this the supply price of capital and is here given the symbol S_0. The future net returns from the project are the revenues from selling the goods and services produced, minus the costs of maintaining the capital equipment and the costs of other factors of production used. R_t indicates the net revenue expected in year t. The life of the capital needs to be estimated and any scrap value that the equipment has must be included in the net revenue of the last year. Once we drop the assumption of certainty we must estimate the expected value of the net revenue stream.* This depends on the firm's expectations about such factors as future product demand, factor prices and new technological developments. The net present value (N.P.V.) of a capital project is given by equation (4.11):

$$\text{N.P.V.} = -S_0 + \frac{R_1}{(1+i_1)} + \frac{R_2}{(1+i_1)(1+i_2)} + \cdots + \frac{R_N}{(1+i_1)(1+i_2)\cdots(1+i_N)}.$$

$$(4.11)$$

The interest rate expected to rule in year t is given by i_t and the cost and net revenue stream $-S_0, R_1, R_2, \ldots, R_N$ is known as the project's cash flow.

Alternatively firms may calculate the internal rate of return on each project being considered:

$$0 = -S_0 + \frac{R_1}{(1+\rho)} + \frac{R_2}{(1+\rho)^2} + \cdots + \frac{R_N}{(1+\rho)^N}. \qquad (4.12)$$

Equation (4.12) tells us that if S_0 were invested for N years at a compound interest rate of ρ, one would obtain the same sum of money after N years as if one invested S_0 and as a result obtained R_1 in the first year, which was reinvested at the rate ρ for $N-1$ years, received R_2 in the second year

---

* Once we introduce uncertainty, the question as to what is the appropriate discount rate arises. Two methods have been pursued. One is to discount by a higher rate of interest to take account of risk, the other is to reduce the net revenue stream to a certainty equivalent and to discount by the riskless rate of interest, i.e. the interest rate that would be returned by a riskless security.

which was reinvested at rate ρ for $N-2$ years, and so on until R_N was received in the last year.

Once we progress to more than two periods, the internal rate of return criterion may not select the capital stock which maximises net present value, unless we stipulate a constant rate of interest and net revenue streams which give a unique solution to the internal rate of return.* Nevertheless much use is made of the concept of the marginal efficiency of capital in macro theory.

Determination of the Desired Stock of Capital

On the assumption that firms select a capital stock which will maximise their net present value, we can make deductions about the determinants of the capital stock. From equation (4.11) we can see that the net present value of any capital project will be greater the lower is the price of capital goods, the lower is the discount rate i, and the higher are expected net revenues. A change in any variable which increases the net present value of capital projects will increase the size of the capital stock for which the marginal addition has a zero net present value. Thus we can predict that firms' desired stock of capital will vary inversely with the price of capital goods and with the cost of capital, or discount rate, and will depend directly on the level of expected net revenues. These relationships are then assumed to apply at the aggregate level.†

If we hold the price of capital goods and the expected net revenue stream from capital constant, we will derive, on the basis of assuming that

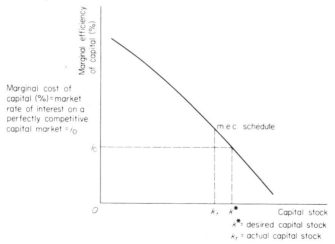

FIGURE 4.3   *The marginal efficiency of capital schedule*

* See [2] and the Appendix to this chapter.
† See the discussion on aggregation problems in Chapter 1.

the marginal rate of productivity of capital decreases with the size of the capital stock, a declining marginal efficiency of capital schedule for the economy, as shown in Figure 4.3. For each additional unit of capital stock the marginal efficiency of capital declines, since the expected net revenues decline, due to the diminishing marginal productivity of capital.

If the supply price of capital goods or the expected net revenues from the capital stock change, the whole m.e.c. schedule will shift. The desired stock of capital will be that which equates the marginal efficiency of capital with the marginal cost of capital, which, with a perfectly competitive capital market, is the market rate of interest.

4.2 CAPITAL STOCK ADJUSTMENT

So far we have discussed the determination of the desired stock of capital and have seen that if this exceeds the actual capital stock net investment will take place. The theory dealt with above tells us nothing about the speed at which this adjustment occurs. If the adjustment were instantaneous the rate of investment would be infinite [4]. Several approaches to this problem have been developed. These can be subdivided into those approaches stressing factors internal to the capital-using firm and those emphasising factors that are attributable to the capital-supplying firms.

The latter approach regards the rate of investment as being determined by the capital goods-supplying industries [5]. The demand price of capital is the present value of the existing capital stock divided by the number of units of capital, as is shown in Figure 4.4 (Note that the existing stock of

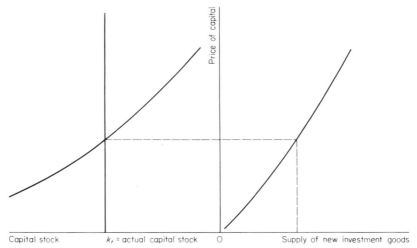

FIGURE 4.4   *The rate of investment determined by the quantity of new investment goods supplied at the demand price of capital goods*

capital is large relative to investment.) The demand for the stock of capital depends, as already discussed, on the interest rate and the expected future net revenues. If the demand price of capital exceeds the supply price, the capital goods-supplying industries will wish to produce additional investment goods. On the assumption that the capital goods industry has a rising supply curve, a determinate rate of investment will exist which equates the demand and supply price of capital. Any additional investment goods are not wanted in this period by capital goods-using firms as they would have a negative marginal net present value.

That the capital goods industry has such a rising supply curve is a dubious proposition since firms frequently ration limited supply not by raising price but by lengthening order books. If capital-using firms cannot obtain immediate delivery of the capital goods they order, capital stock adjustment will not be instantaneous.

Another approach to obtaining a determinate rate of investment has been suggested by Eisner and Strotz [6]. The advantage to the firm of speedy adjustment to attain the desired capital stock is that profits are brought forward in time. If the marginal costs of adjustment, due to such internal factors as reorganising production within the firm or due to paying higher capital goods prices to ensure speedy delivery, are rising the firm will not adjust immediately. It will choose a path of adjustment which maximises net present value. Therefore the rate of interest enters as a determinant of net investment by affecting the optimal adjustment rate as well as the desired stock of capital.*

4.3 THE MARGINAL COST OF CAPITAL

It has been deduced on the basis of utility maximising behaviour that, given certainty and a perfect capital market, the desired stock of capital is inversely related to the market rate of interest. In these circumstances the rate of interest correctly measures the opportunity cost of placing capital in a particular production process. We have also seen that given these conditions optimal investment decisions are taken independently of the decision regarding the financing of investment.

These deductions must be modified when the simplifying assumptions upon which they are based are changed. Once we move into an uncertain world, the firm is not necessarily indifferent to the methods used to finance investment. Funds can be secured from internal sources which are retained profits and depreciation,† or from external sources. These are raising debt by borrowing from banks or selling bonds, or issuing equity. The capital structure of the firm is the division of its money capital sources between various types of debt and equity. An unlevered firm is one whose entire capital structure is made up of equity.

* See ([7] ch. 4) for a more detailed outline of this approach.
† See Appendix, Note 2.

The market value of a firm is the present value of the future income expected from the firm. If we simplify by assuming that the firm is expected to earn a constant annual net income, A, for an infinite time horizon then we can write

$$V = A/\rho \qquad (4.13)$$

where V is the market value of the firm and ρ is the internal rate of return of the existing assets. Since ρ is the minimum rate of return that any additional investment project must yield if the shareholders are not to be made worse off because of a reduction in the firm's market value, ρ is the marginal cost of capital. The higher is a firm's business risk, given its expected annual income, the greater is its cost of capital, since share-holders require compensation for risk bearing.

The value of the firm, V, must also equal the sum of the market value of its debt, L, and equity, E. The market value of a firm's shares is the present value of the stream of dividends the shares are expected to yield. The rate of return on equity, r^e, which is the cost of equity capital to the firm, is that rate of discount which makes the present value of the expected dividend stream, D, equal to the current market valuation of the shares, E:

$$E = D/r^e. \qquad (4.14)$$

Thus in practice the cost of equity capital is often calculated on a rule of thumb basis as the ratio of current dividend per share to share price. The cost of capital to the firm depends on the proportions in which the various sources of finance are used to fund an investment project. Given that a rate of interest, i, is paid on the firm's debt, we have the firm's income divided up between dividends and interest payments on debt:*

$$A = D + iL \qquad (4.15)$$

$$= r^e E + iL \qquad (4.16)$$

$$V = \frac{A}{\rho} = \frac{r^e E + iL}{\rho}. \qquad (4.17)$$

Therefore

$$\rho = \frac{r^e E}{V} + \frac{iL}{V}. \qquad (4.18)$$

The firm's cost of capital is a weighted average of its equity capital cost and the market rate of interest.

There is a long-standing hypothesis that the firm's cost of capital

* If part of a firm's income is retained to finance investment, this is not included in A since this would be double counting. We should not include both the supply price of a capital project (retained earnings) and the present value of its future expected returns in the firm's market value.

depends on its leverage (its debt–equity ratio). As the firm increases the proportion of debt in its capital structure and so long as the marginal rate paid on debt is less than the return on equity, the proportion of the firm's earnings that each share receives as dividends increases. Shareholders are better off in the sense that their expected return has increased with leverage. On the other hand increased leverage involves the shareholders in greater risk. This is because as the firm's total interest payments on debt rise, the likelihood of the firm being unable to meet these commitments and thus being declared bankrupt increases. If risk increases, *ceteris paribus*, shareholders demand a higher return on equity in compensation. In this view as leverage rises from zero the expected return from leverage first outweighs the increased risk, so the shareholders' required return declines, causing the firm's cost of capital to fall. This is reversed as leverage rises further, resulting in the cost of capital rising with the debt–equity ratio.

This hypothesis has been disputed by Miller and Modigliani [9], who maintain that the firm's cost of capital is independent of leverage and is equal to the shareholders' required rate of return in an unlevered company in the same risk class. This means that the cost of capital is exogenous to the individual firm as determined by market forces and cannot be affected by the source of finance used. Retained earnings will have an opportunity cost of ρ. This is the minimum rate of return a project must earn if shareholders are not to be worse off by forgoing the opportunity of receiving dividends which they could have reinvested at ρ.

If one is undertaking an investigation of investment behaviour at a higher level of aggregation, a problem arises in selecting an appropriate cost of capital. A higher risk class of firm will have a higher cost of capital to compensate shareholders for the greater risk. If one is looking for a single rate of return to put in a macro equation, one would select the riskless rate which provides the base upon which the risky rates are calculated by the addition of a risk premium. The nearest one can get to such a rate in practice is the long-term rate on government bonds or on high-class corporate bonds. At a less aggregated level, the cost of equity capital, or the price of shares, has been used by investigators in attempts to include the effects of externally determined financing costs on investment. Stock prices have an additional role in investment determination because they are observable indicators about expected future returns from investment.

If the capital market is imperfectly competitive, the proposition that the cost of capital to the firm is externally determined may not be valid. Capital market imperfections result from any of the following conditions. Lending and borrowing rates differ. Some borrowers face a rising marginal cost of borrowing schedule. Positive transactions costs mean that households are no longer indifferent to the timing of dividends. They cannot borrow and lend to arrange for the time profile of consumption to differ from that of income without incurring transactions costs. Taxation has differential effects on the various participants in the capital market and creates distortions.

There are features of the tax structure which complicate the calculation of an appropriate opportunity cost for retained earnings. If the firm retains earnings and uses them to finance projects which have a rate of return oelow that of the market rate, shareholders may nevertheless gain when they pay a h:gher marginal tax rate on income than on capital gains. In such a case the opportunity cost of retained earnings is lower than the market rate of return. This does not mean firms can retain all profits at the expense of dividends without raising their cost of capital. Shareholders use current dividends as an indicator of future expected dividends, so that firms are constrained to pay out a certain level of dividends to maintain the value of their shares and thus prevent their cost of capital from rising.

Those who consider that firms can affect the cost of capital by manipulating their capital structure would include internal financial variables such as the debt–equity ratio, profits, retained earnings and liquid assets, as determinants of investment.

Financial variables which influence the marginal cost of capital will influence net investment only through their impact on the desired stock of capital. Thus, it would take some time for the change, in say the rate of interest, to affect current investment. It has also been hypothesised that changes in the marginal cost of capital will have asymmetrical effects. It is possible to cancel projects that are in the pipeline if the marginal cost of capital rises, but not so easy to speed up new projects that become viable if the marginal cost of capital falls. This argument leads to the conclusion that monetary policy is more effective in contracting than in expanding the economy.*

4.4 CAPITAL THEORY RELATED TO THE NEOCLASSICAL THEORY OF THE FIRM

In analysing investment we must consider firms making production decisions which involve future time periods as well as the present, and we have concentrated entirely on the decision regarding the quantity of capital to hold and have not considered labour specifically. Capital is analysed differently from labour because, in modern societies, labour services are typically hired. Labour services are a flow input for which a price is paid for services given per period of time. Firms typically buy a stock of capital which will yield services over a number of time periods and for which an initial lump sum is paid. This difference should not be overstressed as the decisions firms take with regard to maintaining a labour force do have a time dimension.

* Readers should refer to [8] for a more detailed exposition of financial theory.

The production function is generally written as $y = f(L, K)$, where output, y, and labour, L, are unequivocally flows. If K stands for the capital stock, it is being assumed that capital services are proportional to the capital stock. It is a well-known proposition of neoclassical theory that profit-maximising firms will select that ratio of labour to capital which minimises the costs of producing a given level of output. The selection of a technique of production is usually presented as a single-period decision problem. To do this one has to convert the cost of the capital stock, which consists of a lump sum supply price plus the opportunity cost of holding the capital stock in each period (this is the rate of interest that could have been earned elsewhere had not the capital been tied up in the specific production process), into a cost per period of a unit of capital services. This cost will consist of the depreciation of the capital per period of time, plus the rate of interest, minus the real rate of appreciation of the capital stock.

This expression for the cost of capital services is derived by Jorgenson [10–13], who has developed a neoclassical model of capital accumulation by the firm, in which the intertemporal choice problem reduces to single-period analysis. In each period the profit-maximising firm selects that ratio of labour to capital which maximises profits. Thus, the relative price of capital to labour and the price of the product determine the optimal capital stock in each period. If factor prices change over time, so will the optimal capital stock, so that a time path of investment can be derived.*

4.5 THE ACCELERATOR THEORY OF INVESTMENT†

The accelerator theory of investment emphasises the relationship between the capital stock and the flow of output, which is known as the capital–output ratio. The optimal capital–output ratio occurs when the capital stock is operated at a level of capacity utilisation which maximises profits. When the actual and optimal capital–output ratios are equal, the rate of profit on capital is such that firms' investment policies lead them in aggregate neither to increase nor decrease the ratio of capital to output.

The desired stock of capital, K^*, is therefore related to the volume of output firms plan to produce by means of v, the optimal capital–output ratio. This relationship is given by equation (4.19):

$$K^* = vy. \qquad (4.19)$$

In a growing economy firms will add to the capital stock in order to produce more output and thus maximise profits. The desired capital stock, K_t^*, which firms wish to have by the end of the current period, in

* See ([7] ch. 5), for a summary of the Jorgenson approach.
† The accelerator theory predates Keynes; see [14].

order to produce next period's output optimally, is related to the expected volume of future output, y_t^e. Thus

$$K_t^* = vy_t^e. \qquad (4.20)$$

If the discrepancy between the actual capital stock, K_{t-1}, with which firms start the period, and the desired capital stock is entirely made up within the period, net investment is given by

$$I_t^n = K_t^* - K_{t-1} = v(y_t^e - y_{t-1}). \qquad (4.21)$$

Equation (4.21) is the basic version of the accelerator theory which relates net investment to the expected increase in output times the optimal capital–output ratio or accelerator coefficient as it is known. For simplicity the accelerator relationship is assumed here to be linear. The incremental optimal capital–output ratio, dK/dy, which indicates how many additional units of capital are required by profit-maximising firms to produce an additional unit of output, is assumed to be constant. It is assumed not to vary with the economy's capital stock and is therefore equal to the average capital–output ratio.

Expected output cannot be observed directly so it is assumed to be related to past levels of output. The simplest expectations hypothesis is that which takes the current change in output to be the future expected change. This gives

$$I_t^n = v(y_t - y_{t-1}). \qquad (4.22)$$

If the existing capital stock is not being fully utilised, net investment will be correspondingly smaller, and equation (4.22) is modified by subtracting that portion, β, of the capital stock that is currently underutilised:

$$I_t^n = v(y_t - y_{t-1}) - \beta K_t. \qquad (4.23)$$

This simple version of the accelerator relationship failed to perform adequately when tested and the value of v estimated in investment equations was considerably lower than the average capital–output ratio [15]. This failure is probably due to neglecting the lags that occur in adjusting the capital stock. These are taken account of in flexible accelerator models of investment, originally developed by Chenery [16] and Koyck [17].

If it is assumed that expected future output is a function of past output levels, where geometrically declining weights, μ^i, are attached to previous outputs, the capital stock in existence in any time period depends on past values of output:

$$K_t = v(1-\mu) \sum_{i=0}^{\infty} \mu^i y_{t-i} \qquad (0 < \mu < 1). \qquad (4.24)$$

Using the Koyck transformation we obtain*

$$K_t - \mu K_{t-1} = v(1-\mu)y_t. \qquad (4.25)$$

* See Chapter 3, p. 77.

Subtracting $(1 - \mu)K_{t-1}$ from both sides,

$$K_t - K_{t-1} = I_t^n = v(1 - \mu)y_t - (1 - \mu)K_{t-1}. \tag{4.26}$$

The expression for gross investment includes an item for replacement investment, which is usually assumed proportional to the existing capital stock:

$$I_t^G = I_t^n + \partial K_{t-1} = v(1 - \mu)y_t - (1 - \mu - \partial)K_{t-1}. \tag{4.27}$$

Thus, we have the hypothesis that investment is related positively to the level of current output and negatively (providing $0 < \partial + \mu < 1$) to the existing capital stock. The flexible accelerator coefficient, $v(1 - \mu)$, is lower than the average capital–output ratio.

The accelerator theory is often treated without specific reference to a firm's profit-maximising behaviour, as an *ad hoc* relationship in a world of uncertainty, imperfect information and continual change, which would be capable of providing short-run predictions of the level of investment. The neoclassical theory, in which relative factor prices are determinants of the optimum stock of capital, has been developed in formal models that usually assume certainty. The accelerator model provides an expectations hypothesis which makes the level of expected future output depend on current and past values of output. If we consider a firm maximising its profits from the production of a given planned output level, relative factor prices would determine the capital intensity of the production technique selected and hence influence the capital–output ratio. In a growing economy with constant expectations, firms would expand capital in relation to the expected increase in output, while the capital–output ratio would be affected by relative factor prices. In growth models the accelerator theory provides the investment function while, in line with neoclassical thinking, relative factor prices determine the equilibrium capital–output ratio.

4.6 EMPIRICAL EVIDENCE*

Theorising and empirical investigation are closely related. Empirical work requires the specification of hypotheses to be tested. Some of these are carefully based on optimising choice behaviour, others are *ad hoc* relationships. When the latter give good empirical results the framework of theory is redeveloped to provide a choice theoretic basis for such relationships. This process has been at work in the theory and testing of investment.

The general form of investment functions is based upon the capital adjustment principle

$$I_t^n = \omega(\rho)(K_t^* - K_{t-1}) \tag{4.28}$$

where $\omega(\rho)$ is a distributed lag function which specifies the time lags in

* A number of good surveys of empirical work on investment have been published, to which the reader is referred [18–20].

the adjustment process. The desired stock of capital in these investment functions is expressed as a function of its hypothesised determinants, Z:

$$K_t^* = f(Z). \tag{4.29}$$

The distributed lag function may take various forms. The geometric distributed lag function in which the weights decline steadily with time has already been mentioned.* A more likely distributed lag function for investment is one where the weights at first rise with time, reach a peak and then decline. Of particular interest is the length of time it takes for a determinant to have its peak effect, the average lag (the time taken for 50 per cent of the effect of a change in a determinant to be felt) and the total length of time for such a change to work out its impact on investment.

It can be reasonably concluded from looking at a broad range of investment studies that the average lag is about six quarters. It is useful to compare estimates produced by econometric studies of lags, which are of dubious reliability, with lag estimates obtained by questionnaire and interview studies. Mayer's study [22, 23] of new industrial plant and plant additions started in the United States in 1954 and 1955 obtained an average lag from the investment decision to completion of seven quarters. Nobay [24] has calculated an average lag between ordering and delivery of engineering goods in the United Kingdom in 1965 of about four quarters. Addition of a planning period of one quarter gives an average five quarter lag between appropriations and point of expenditure. Econometric studies frequently select that lag structure which gives an estimation equation with the highest correlation coefficient. A number of U.S. econometric studies have obtained average lags in the region of six to seven quarters.†

There appears to be broad agreement that the capital stock adjustment principle combined with a distributed lag function is a satisfactory specification of the investment function. Econometric studies differ in the variables chosen to be tested as determinants of the desired capital stock and hence of investment. Accelerator models feature output (sales or profits are alternatives) and capacity utilisation. Jorgenson's neoclassical model contains output and the price of capital services which depends on the price of capital goods, the interest rate and the tax rate. One can further distinguish models by whether they consider external or internal financing variables. External financing variables are the cost of capital, which depends on the interest rate on corporate debt and on the cost of equity capital. The latter variable may not be calculated exactly but is approximated by considering share prices or the firm's market value. Thus the Jorgenson model tests external financial variables as determinants of investment. 'Internal liquidity' models are those that

* See Chapter 3, p. 76.
† Reference [20] contains references to [10, 22, 23, 25].

test the importance of internal financial variables, such as the firm's cash flow, retained earnings and liquid assets.

The finding of U.S. studies are that real output is the most important single determinant of investment. Financing variables also appear to be significant and there is now considerable body of evidence that the long-term rate of interest is a determinant of investment, though the elasticity of investment with respect to the rate of interest is less than that with respect to output. Also it seems that investment takes longer to respond to interest rate changes than to variations in the level of output. The role of internal financial variables in investment determination has not been established satisfactorily. Profits tend to be statistically insignificant when included with output, suggesting that their role is as a proxy for output rather than as a financing variable.

This overview is generally supported by U.K. investment studies which are far less numerous than their American counterparts. Lund's study [21] of investment in industrial buildings and machine tools obtained evidence favouring a capital stock adjustment model in which the desired capital stock depends on output. He found interest rates significant in determining investment in industrial buildings, and profits and stock prices used as an expectations proxy were significant for the machine tools industry.

Hines and Catephores [28], using quarterly data for U.K. manufacturing 1956–67, tested a flexible accelerator model and a simplified Jorgenson neoclassical model. They found both output and the interest rate to be significant variables, the output elasticity being larger than that for the rate of interest. The estimated average lag between a change in the interest rate and its impact on investment was nine quarters, while the average lag for output was six quarters.

Burman [29] also tested both the flexible accelerator and neoclassical models for U.K. manufacturing, 1957–68, and found that capacity utilisation explained most of the variation in investment. He obtained an average lag of seven to eight quarters between output and investment expenditure changes. Profits, cash flow and interest rates were not found to be significant for individual industries. The neoclassical model performed badly.

Nobay [24] allowed for supply lags by including a waiting time for capital goods as an independent variable. He found capacity utilisation to be the most important explanatory variable. The actual change in output, used as a proxy for expectations, performed better than alternative measures. Interest costs, though significant, did not contribute much to explaining investment.

4.7 INVESTMENT AND SAVING IN A CAPITALIST ECONOMY

The neoclassical approach assumes people save in order to postpone consumption into the future. Investment is also the postponement of consumption in order to create capital goods which will produce additional goods and services in the future. A single objective underlies both saving and investment decisions, that of maximising utility from consumption over time. The rate of interest is determined by the interaction of saving and investment plans. In equilibrium the rate of interest is the rate of return on capital. It is known as the real rate of interest, since it is the rate at which goods in the present can be transformed into future goods. The rate of return on capital is referred to by some writers as the rate of profit.

In a capitalist economy saving and investment decisions are taken by different sets of people. Many households are passive holders of wealth and allow the resources to which they own claims to be used by entrepreneurs. The entrepreneur makes real investment decisions and in a dynamic economy seeks out new investment opportunities. The entrepreneurial function is increasingly undertaken by salaried management rather than by individuals who own and run their own businesses. This does not alter the separation of real investment decisions from the decision of households regarding what proportion of their income to save and how to allocate their existing stock of wealth amongst various types of financial assets. The portfolio allocation decision is further separated, as many small savers hold their wealth in the liabilities of financial institutions such as unit trusts or assurance companies, who in turn decide what assets to hold in their portfolios.

This separation of the savings and investment decisions is common to all modern schools of economic thought. The neo-Keynesians* emphasise the functional distribution of income between wages and profits. The majority of households receive their income in the form of wages and do very little saving. Most of the resources necessary for capital accumulation are released from current consumption by those households who receive their income mainly from profits and by firms, who by retaining profits, undertake saving and portfolio decisions as well as investment decisions. The neo-Keynesians lay stress on a further motive for the accumulation of wealth than the rearrangement of consumption over time. This is the utility derived from the power and influence that the ownership of wealth confers.

A feature of neo-Keynesian macroeconomic models is that the marginal propensity to consume is much higher for wage earners than for profit receivers. This can be reconciled with the Friedman view that the proportion of permanent income consumed by households of all income levels is the same. If wage earners have more stable measured incomes

* A group of economists centred on Cambridge, England, who are critics of neoclassical economics. Their revival of Ricardian and Marxian economics and their different methodological emphasis place them outside the mainstream of contemporary economics.

than profit receivers, the observation that their short-run estimated marginal propensity to consume is higher than that of profit receivers is consistent with Friedman's hypothesis. If we are talking in the context of dynamic equilibrium growth paths, where expectations are continually being realised, the neoclassical and neo-Keynesian approaches conflict over the question of income groups' marginal propensities to save.

The neoclassical view that Keynes set out to attack in *The General Theory* recognised that investment and saving are done by different decision units, but was mistaken in considering that a household's saving is automatically transferred into a voluntary act of investment. Alfred Marshall expressed this view: 'But it is a familiar axiom that a man purchases labour and commodities with that portion of his income which he saves just as much as he does with that which he is said to spend' [30]. This is only correct when the economy is in equilibrium. In the classical view the required equality between investment and saving is brought about by adjustments in the rate of interest. Real forces, which underlie the productivity of capital and the time preference for consumption, were regarded as the determinants of the rate of interest.

Keynes emphasised the disequilibrium tendencies of a capitalist economy. Investment, since it depends on expectations about an uncertain future, is volatile. Saving depends on the level of income, the rate of interest being an unimportant determinant. Therefore saving and investment plans are likely to diverge. When they do it is not easy to regain equilibrium, since the capital market has difficulty in establishing a rate of interest on financial assets which reflects the real rate of return on capital necessary for full-employment equilibrium. The level of real national output therefore changes in response to any divergence between investment and saving.

Here we have the key elements in Keynes's analysis of instability in a capitalist economy; an uncertain future, changing expectations, the importance of considering time rather than analysing timeless states and the effect of introducing money into the analysis. The question of how a model which contains only real variables differs from one which also includes money and other financial assets is of vital importance in analysing a capitalist economy. To get a better understanding of this problem we will now turn to a consideration of the demand and supply of money.

APPENDIX

Note 1. Internal Rate of Return and Net Present Value Criteria

The internal rate of return calculation cannot take account of the variation of the present value of £x received in t years time, due to changes in the discount rate. In the two-period case the internal rate of return is the same for the marginal unit of capital as the marginal product of capital minus one $(-dC_1/dC_0 - 1)$. The marginal product of capital in a two-period world can be unambiguously defined as the change in output that results from a change in the capital stock. Once we consider multiperiod analysis, an additional unit of capital results in additional output in many future periods. The marginal product of capital is generally used to refer to the additional flow of current output in a single period that results from an additional unit of capital. The marginal rate of transformation of goods in period t into goods in period $t + s$ is given by the production function and is the quantity of goods received in s period's time from a given sacrifice of consumer goods in period t and is dC_{t+s}/dC_t. The capital stock is of optimal size when a marginal addition of capital has a zero net present value;

$$0 = dC_0 + \frac{dC_1}{(1+i_1)} + \frac{dC_2}{(1+i_1)(1+i_2)} + \frac{dC_N}{(1+i_1)(1+i_2)\cdots(1+i_N)}.$$

The marginal rate of transformation of goods in period t into goods in period $t + 1$ is

$$\frac{dC_{t+1}}{dC_t} = -\frac{(1+i_1)(1+i_2)\cdots(1+i_t)(1+i_{t+1})}{(1+i_1)(1+i_2)\cdots(1+i_t)} = -(1+i_{t+1}).$$

The internal rate of return is a single number. Generally it does not equal the marginal rate of transformation of goods between every two periods. If the marginal rate of transformation differs from period to period, the internal rate of return cannot reflect actual economic opportunities since its calculation assumes each period's returns can be reinvested at ρ. This is not possible if the market rate of interest or the marginal rate of transformation differ from ρ.

Therefore if one is selecting one out of several mutually exclusive investment projects, the internal rate of return may select a project which does not maximise net present value, as it may not be possible to reinvest the net cash flows at the internal rate of return, ρ.

An additional problem is that there may be multiple solutions for the internal rate of return, in which case one does not know which value to apply. Multiple solutions occur when the cash flow stream changes sign more than once.

Note 2. Depreciation

In principle depreciation is the decline in the value of a capital good that occurs over a given period of time. Given the uncertainty of future net revenue from capital and the difficulty of calculating the proportion of the firm's net present value attributable to a particular item of capital, and that recourse to second-hand market values is not available in many cases, firms use rule-of-thumb methods of calculating depreciation. The straight-line method depreciates capital at $1/n$ of its initial price each year, where n is the expected life of the capital good. The declining balance method depreciates, by a fixed proportion, the remaining value of the capital each year. Internal rate of return and net present value calculations take into account depreciation by including the initial cost of the capital equipment. The estimated amount of depreciation is subtracted from a firm's revenues when net profit is calculated and is thus a source of internal finance for new capital projects.

REFERENCES

[1] Irving Fisher, *The Theory of Interest* (New York: Macmillan, 1930).
[2] J. Hirschleifer, 'On the Theory of Optimal Investment Decision', *Journal of Political Economy*, 66 (1958) 329–72.
[3] J. M. Keynes, *The General Theory of Employment, Interest and Money* (London: Macmillan, 1936) ch. 11.
[4] Trygve Haavelmo, *A Study in the Theory of Investment* (The University of Chicago Press, 1960) pp. 162–5.
[5] J. G. Witte, 'The Microfoundations of the Social Investment Function', *Journal of Political Economy*, 71 (1963) 441–56.
[6] R. Eisner and R. Strotz, 'Determinants of Business Investment', in commission on Money and Credit, *Impacts of Monetary Policy* (Englewood Cliffs, New Jersey: Prentice-Hall, 1963).
[7] P. N. Junankar, *Investment: Theories and Evidence* (London: Macmillan, 1972).
[8] A. A. Robichek and S. C. Myers, *Optimal Financing Decisions* (Englewood Cliffs, New Jersey: Prentice-Hall, 1965).
[9] F. Modigliani and M. Miller, 'The Cost of Capital, Corporation Finance and the Theory of Investment', *American Economic Review*, 48, 3 (1958) 261–97.
[10] D. Jorgenson, 'Capital Theory and Investment Behaviour', *American Economic Review*, Papers and Proceedings, 52 (May 1963).
[11] D. Jorgenson, 'The Theory of Investment Behaviour', in *Determinants of Investment Behaviour*, ed. R. Ferber (New York: National Bureau of Economic Research, 1967).
[12] D. Jorgenson, 'Anticipations and Investment Behaviour', in *The Brookings Quarterly Econometric Model of the U.S.A.* ed. J. Duesenberry *et al.* (Chicago: Rand McNally & Co., 1965).
[13] D. Jorgenson, *et al.*, 'A Comparison of Alternative Econometric Models of Quarterly Investment Behaviour', *Econometrica* (March 1970).
[14] J. M. Clark, 'Business Acceleration and the Law of Demand', *Journal of Political Economy*, 25, 1 (March 1917).

[15] S. Kuznets, 'Relation between Capital Goods and Finished Products in the Business Cycle', *Economic Essays in Honour of Wesley Clair Mitchell* (New York: Columbia University Press, 1935).

[16] H. B. Chenery, 'Overcapacity and the Acceleration Principle', *Econometrica*, 20 (January 1952).

[17] L. M. Koyck, *Distributed Lags and Investment Analysis* (Amsterdam: North-Holland, 1954).

[18] M. K. Evans, *Macroeconomic Activity* (New York: Harper & Row, 1969) chs. 4 and 5.

[19] R. Eisner and R. Strotz, 'Research Study Two: Determinants of Business Investment', in Commission on Money and Credit, *Impacts of Monetary Policy* (Englewood Cliffs, New Jersey: Prentice-Hall, 1963).

[20] D. W. Jorgenson, 'Econometric Studies of Investment Behaviour: A Survey', *Journal of Economic Literature* (1971).

[21] P. Lund, *Investment: the Study of an Economic Aggregate* (Edinburgh: Oliver & Boyd, 1971).

[22] T. Mayer, 'Plant and Equipment Lead Times', *Journal of Business*, 33 (1960).

[23] T. Mayer, 'Inflexibility of Monetary Policy', *Review of Economics and Statistics*, 42 (1960).

[24] A. R. Nobay, 'Forecasting Manufacturing Investment 1959–67: Some Preliminary Results', *National Institute Economic Review*, 52 (May 1970).

[25] S. Almon, 'The Distributed Lag Between Capital Appropriations and Expenditures', *Econometrica*, 33, 3 (August 1955).

[26] R. M. Sachs and A. G. Hart, 'Anticipations and Investment Behaviour: an Econometric Study of Quarterly Time Series for Large Firms in Durable Goods Manufacturing', in *Determinants of Investment Behaviour*, ed. Ferber (National Bureau of Economic Research, 1967).

[27] W. H. Locke Anderson, *Corporate Finance and Fixed Investment and Econometric Study* (Boston: Harvard University Press, 1964).

[28] A. G. Hines and G. Catephores, 'Investment in U.K. Manufacturing Industry 1956–67', in *The Econometric Study of the U.K. Economy*, ed. K. Hilton and D. Heathfield (London: Macmillan, 1970).

[29] J. P. Burman, 'Capacity Utilisation and the Determination of Fixed Investment', in *Econometric Study of the U.K. Economy*, ed. Hilton and Heathfield.

[30] A. Marshall, *Pure Theory of Domestic Values*, reprinted in Scarce Tract Series (London: London School of Economics, 1930) p. 34.

[31] J. Robinson, 'The Production Function and the Theory of Capital', *Collected Economic Papers*, 2 (1965).

5 The Money Supply

Money is defined to be any object which is generally accepted as a means of payment when an exchange of goods or services occurs. Therefore the objects which constitute money in an economy are those widely accepted as a medium of exchange. Commodity money is a good which has an intrinsic value of its own, independent of its function as a medium of exchange, gold being the best known example. Fiat money, which may be issued by the government or by private sector banks, has a value greatly in excess of its worth as a non-monetary commodity. This excess value is due entirely to the commodity being accepted as a means of payment. Nowadays coins have a metallic content which, if melted down, is worth less than the face value of the coin. Paper notes have a value stemming from their acceptability as a medium of exchange which is much greater than their production costs. A U.K. one pound bank note declaims its promise to pay the bearer on demand the sum of one pound. This promise relates to the days before the First World War, when gold coins circulated internally, and a paper pound note could be exchanged at a bank for a gold sovereign. Nowadays all this promise indicates is that notes, as well as coins, are legal tender and regarded by law as an acceptable means of payment. General public confidence in sterling as an acceptable medium of exchange for domestic transactions makes one pound note equal to one pound's worth of goods and services.

The Bank of England can set the nominal value of notes and coin as one pound or ten pence, but cannot determine their real value independently of the other forces in the economy. The price level refers to the quantity of goods and services for which a pound note can be exchanged, and is an endogenous variable in the economic system. The determination of the price level is discussed in later chapters but it should be borne in mind at this stage, that even if the government can control the nominal quantity of money, it can only influence the real value of the money supply, not determine it independently of other sectors in the economy.

Notes and coins issued by the Bank of England or the central bank of any economy, are known as cash or currency. In modern economies private sector bank deposits which are transferrable by cheque are also generally acceptable as a medium of exchange, and thus constitute part of the money supply. The money supply is a stock variable, worth £x million at any particular moment. It consists of notes and coin in circulation with the public (more accurately the non-bank domestic sector) plus bank deposits.

The decision as to which type of bank deposit to include in the money supply is not clear cut. An exclusive, tight definition of the money supply includes only current account deposits, since these are held primarily for the purpose of financing current transactions and are directly transferrable by cheque. Deposit accounts are held by the public more as a stock of assets which can be easily and quickly turned into a medium of exchange, than to be used frequently as a medium of exchange, as are deposits held in current accounts. This difference is borne out by the fact that deposit accounts in the United Kingdom earn a rate of interest which is forgone for seven days if a week's notice is not given of intent to withdraw cash from these accounts. Also banks charge for operating a current account, basing these charges directly on the number of transactions occurring per period of time, and inversely on the average balance. A more inclusive definition of the money supply embraces deposit accounts since they can be so easily transferred into current accounts and used to finance transactions. The U.K. official statistics [1, 2] employ two definitions of the money supply. M_1 consists of notes and coin in circulation with the public plus sterling current account bank deposits. M_3* includes notes and coin in circulation together with the total sterling and non-sterling deposits of the domestic sector with the banks and discount houses† (since 1968 Giro deposits are included).

Many writers have been concerned with the effect of people's ability to finance expenditure from their holdings of so-called 'near-monies', such as building society deposits, which can be transferred easily into money. Since money is distinguished from other objects by its medium of exchange property, any asset which first has to be converted into money to serve as a means of payment, cannot itself be money. There have also been suggestions that trade credit, which is used by firms to finance transactions both between each other and with their final customers,

* M_2, which is a commonly used abbreviation for the inclusive definition of the money supply, has been discontinued in official U.K. statistics.
† To be discussed later in the chapter.

should be included in the money supply [3]. Trade credit serves to extend the length of time between which goods and services are finally exchanged for money, and although some transactions financed with trade credit may cancel out, net debts have ultimately to be settled by a payment of money. Thus, although the extension of trade credit does affect the volume of transactions that, in any period of time, can be financed by a given stock of money, it is not money, since it is only an intermediate, not a final means of payment.

5.2 FINANCIAL INTERMEDIATION

In examining the determinants of the money supply we need to consider the relationship between the currency provided by the government, or central authorities, and the volume of deposits created by the banking system. A bank, like a building society, insurance company, or unit trust is a financial intermediary. A financial intermediary is an institution which mediates in the process whereby surplus units in the economy transfer the current resources, to which they have a claim, over to deficit units, who wish to spend on resources in excess of their current income. In return for transferring his claim to current resources to a deficit unit, the lender obtains a paper claim on the borrower, making some promise of repayment and an associated rate of return. These paper claims are an asset to the lender who holds them, but are a liability to the borrower who issues them. Primary claims are those issued by firms borrowing to finance real investment or by households to finance consumption expenditure. Such economic units are referred to as ultimate borrowers.

Claims differ with respect to expected return and riskiness. A general term used to distinguish assets is the extent of their liquidity. Liquidity refers to the ease of exchanging an asset into cash, and hence involves the asset's marketability, and the costs and risk of loss associated with encashing the asset. Therefore the term embraces the riskiness of an asset. Money is the perfectly liquid asset in the sense that it can immediately, without risk or cost be transferred into itself. Although the real value of money, as of all nominally fixed assets, such as bonds, varies inversely with the price level, it is nevertheless defined to be perfectly liquid as it completely preserves its nominal value in terms of convertability into goods, which involves zero transaction costs.

A primary borrower issues a relatively illiquid asset. It may not keep its nominal value as the firm may default. Transactions costs are incurred when the lender eventually wishes to exercise his claim to the consumption of resources and converts the asset into cash, so as to switch into goods and services. Financial intermediaries intervene in the lending transactions between surplus and deficit units. They borrow from ultimate lenders to whom they issue claims. The claims issued by financial intermediaries are known as secondary claims and are assets to

households that own them, but are liabilities to the financial intermediaries who have issued them. The financial intermediaries transfer
the resources lent to them by surplus units to the deficit units who are
the ultimate borrowers. The financial institutions do this by taking up
the primary claims issued by the ultimate borrowers.

Because financial intermediaries are specialist institutions, engaging
in large-scale borrowing and lending, they can take advantage of
economies of scale. They make a profit by paying out a lower rate of
return on the secondary claims they issue than thay obtain on their
holdings of primary claims. The greater liquidity and lower risk offered
by financial intermediary claims makes households willing to hold such
claims, rather than put their entire stock of savings into primary claims
which have a higher expected rate of return. By providing households
with a great variety of assets, some of which are extremely liquid,
financial intermediaries encourage saving and can thereby contribute to
a higher rate of growth in a market economy.

In such an economy a stock of claims, which vary in riskiness,
marketability and expected rate of return, is built up over time and
offers wealth holders a wide range of assets in which to hold their
accumulated stock of savings. To calculate the net wealth of the private
sector one would net out all claims which are both assets to some
persons in the private sector but are liabilities to other members of the
private sector. The process of cancelling out such private sector claims is
known as consolidating balance sheets, since the balance sheet is an
account showing an economic unit's stock of assets and liabilities. (The
concept of net wealth is discussed in Chapter 7, Section 7.3.)

5.3   DETERMINATION OF THE VOLUME OF BANK DEPOSITS

A commercial bank acts as a financial intermediary. It borrows from
households who deposit currency with the bank and get in return a bank
deposit, which is repayable in cash on demand and which can be
transferred by cheque. Whenever a bank receives a deposit of cash, the
asset side of its balance sheet rises by the amount of the additional cash
and the liabilities side rises also by the amount of the bank deposit,
issued in return for the customer's cash. Thus the assets and liabilities
sides of a bank's balance sheet are always equal. An individual bank can
increase its cash assets by receiving a deposit transferred to it by a
customer from another bank. Since the bank can rely on only a small
proportion of its customers making net withdrawals of cash from their
deposits, the bank need hold only a small proportion of its assets in the
form of non-interest bearing cash. The proportion of total deposits
which is matched or backed by the asset cash is known as the cash ratio

or reserve ratio.* In most countries the government imposes a requirement on banks to hold a certain minimum proportion of their assets in the form of reserve assets, and this is called the required reserve ratio. Banks may choose, for reasons of their own preferred liquidity position, to keep a reserve ratio in excess of that required by the government.

If the bank, which for simplicity we assume for the time being to be a monopoly, keeps a minimum cash ratio of 0·1 and receives a new deposit of cash of £100, it will keep £10 of this in the form of cash and acquire interest bearing assets with the other £90. The bank is acting as a financial intermediary by lending out cash deposited with it. The alternative, given no bank, would be for the depositor to lend directly to the borrower, but in such a case the lender would obtain a far more illiquid asset than a bank deposit. The act of depositing cash will cause the following changes in the bank's balance sheet, starting from the original equilibrium.

Position 1:

Liabilities		Assets	
Deposits		Cash	£10,000
		Loans	£90,000
Total	£100,000		£100,000
		Cash ratio: 0·10	

Position 2:

Additional cash deposits of 100

Liabilities		Assets	
Deposits		Cash	£10,100
		Loans	£90,000
Total	£100,100		£100,100
		Cash ratio: 0·101	

Position 3:

Additional loans of £90 out of cash deposit of £100

Liabilities		Assets	
Deposits		Cash	£10,010
		Loans	£90,090
Total	£100,100		£100,100
		Cash ratio: 0·10	

If the total currency in circulation had originally been £20,000, the total money supply would have been £120,000. One must be careful to distinguish currency in circulation, which forms part of the money supply (£20,000 in this example) from currency with the banking system (£10,000 in this example) which forms bank reserves which are held to back bank deposits. Bank deposits are part of the money supply, but the

---

* In the United Kingdom, as is discussed later in the chapter, other liquid assets are included in reserve assets as well as cash.

reserves which back them are not, or one would be double counting. Currency in circulation together with bank reserves are known as 'high-powered' money (£30,000 in this example).

In the above example an increase in 'high-powered' money of £100 occurred. This could have been created by the government to finance a budget deficit or earned by way of a balance-of-payments surplus. If this £100 is placed in the monopoly bank, £10 kept in reserves and £90 loaned out, the money supply rises to £120,100, the extra £100 consisting entirely of bank deposits. The borrowers of the £90 use it to finance transactions. These may be financed either by the transfer of bank deposits or by cash withdrawals from the bank. But the bank does not lose the cash that is withdrawn because we assume that the people who ultimately receive any cash originating from the payments made by the bank's borrowers do not wish to hold any additional currency and therefore deposit it in the bank. To develop the most simple form of deposit and hence money supply equation, we will assume initially that any cash lent out by the bank is redeposited with it. Therefore position 3 is only an interim position not an equilibrium one. Position 4 is recorded when the £90 loaned out at stage 1 is all redeposited with the bank.

Position 4:

Liabilities		*Assets*	
Deposits £100,100 + 90		Cash	£10,100
		Loans	£90,090
Total	£100,190		£100,190

Cash ratio: 0·1008

To return to its minimum 0·1 cash ratio the bank retains £9 of the £90 additional deposits (this is the £90 of the original £100 addition to the bank reserves which, if it leaves the bank, finds its way back to the bank) and extends loans by a further £81. This is recorded in position 5.

Position 5:

Liabilities		*Assets*	
Deposits		Cash	£10,019
		Loans	£90,171
Total £100,190			£100,190

Cash ratio: 0·10

The money supply has now risen by £190, all of which is held in the form of bank deposits and this increase has occurred on the basis of an original increase of £100 in high-powered money. It is evident that on the basis of our assumption that any cash lent out by the bank is redeposited with it, Position 5 is only temporary. The £81 of loans granted at stage 2 of this credit creation process will be redeposited with the bank and provide the basis for further expansion of loans, which can continue until deposits have expanded by £1000 to £101,000, at which level the whole of the additional £100 of cash, which is held entirely by the bank, is needed to maintain its 10 per cent reserve ratio.

Banks differ from other financial intermediaries in that their liabilities, bank deposits, serve as a medium of exchange. This means that, when banks make loans, they give their borrowers bank deposits which are accepted in payment for goods and services. In the case of a monopoly bank, when currency holdings of the public are fixed, no cash will ultimately leave the bank and all transactions financed by bank loans will be settled by a transfer of bank deposits from the bank's borrowers to those from whom they buy goods and services. Thus a monopoly bank, knowing this, can straightaway expand deposits by the full amount of £1000 in the example above.

The foregoing process of credit expansion by a monopoly bank is consistent with our view of a bank as a firm making profits out of financial intermediation and can be shown to correspond to profit-maximising behaviour by the bank. Some formal models of money supply determination based on explicit simplifying assumptions will now be discussed and the following symbols will be used:

C = currency in circulation with the public,
R = currency held by the banking system as reserve assets,
H = high-powered money,
D = bank deposits (assumed to be current accounts unless otherwise stated),
M = money supply,
L = earning assets (assumed to be in the form of bank loans),
i_L = bank lending rate,
r = minimum reserve ratio held by bank,
d = currency – deposit ratio,
k = currency – money supply ratio,
T = total bank costs,
π = bank profits, and
ρ = central bank discount rate (e.g. minimum lending rate of the Bank of England).

Basic definitions:

$$H = C + R \tag{5.1}$$

$$M = C + D \tag{5.2}$$

$$L = D - R \tag{5.3}$$

$$r = R/D \tag{5.4}$$

$$d = C/D \tag{5.5}$$
$$k = C/M \tag{5.6}$$
$$d = k/(1-k) \tag{5.7}$$
$$\pi = L(i_L) - T. \tag{5.8}$$

Model 1: Perfect Competition, Public's Currency Holdings Constant

Model 1 examines money supply determination under a perfectly competitive banking system. All bank deposits are assumed to be current account deposits so that banks do not pay a rate of interest to induce households to deposit currency with them. It is assumed that when the total money supply changes, the total amount of currency held by the public does not change (i.e. $\Delta C/\Delta M = 0$). This is the same as the previous assumption that all cash lent out by the banking system is redeposited with it by the public. Given that the banking system does not pay interest to the public on their deposits, it does not matter in principle, given the stringent assumptions of the models, whether we specify a monopoly bank or a perfectly competitive banking industry. We can obtain the same results as far as the credit creation process is concerned so long as all banks in the industry expand or contract credit together.

In the example above, if one bank receives a £100 new deposit of cash (that is to say one that has come from outside the banking system, not merely a transfer of cash from one bank to another) and loans out £90, that £90 is redeposited in many of the other banks in the industry, who proceed to expand credit, by loaning out a total of £81 at the second stage of the process. When a perfectly competitive banking system is specified each bank can lend as much as it wishes without affecting the loan rate it charges. The banking industry as a whole may reasonably be expected to face a downward sloping demand schedule for loans with respect to its lending rate, but each bank is a price taker, and faces the market determined lending rate. The total costs of each bank are assumed to be directly related to the level of deposits, as administrative and clerical costs will rise with the volume of transactions undertaken by the bank for its customers, i.e.

$$T = T(D) \tag{5.9}$$

where $dT/dD > 0$, i.e. marginal cost is positive and may be assumed to be constant or increasing. The bank's total revenue

$$V = L(i_L) \tag{5.10}$$
$$= (D - R)i_L \tag{5.10}$$

therefore

$$\pi = (D - R)i_L - T(D). \tag{5.11}$$

Substituting equation (5.4) into (5.11) we obtain

$$\pi = D(1-r)i_L - T(D). \tag{5.11a}$$

Profits are maximised by setting the first derivative of profits with respect to deposits equal to zero:

$$d\pi/dD = (1-r)i_L - (dT/dD) \tag{5.12}$$
$$= 0$$

or

$$(1-r)i_L = dT/dD. \tag{5.13}$$
$$(\text{marginal revenue}) = (\text{marginal cost})$$

But we must remember that profits are maximised subject to a constraint that the required minimum reserve ratio be met (equation (5.4)). If expanding deposits until marginal revenue equals marginal cost involves falling below the required reserve ratio, this constraint will be binding and marginal revenue will be in excess of marginal cost (as shown in Figure 5.1). In this case if the banks receive additional cash reserves they will expand deposits by the process already discussed so long as marginal revenue exceeds marginal cost. The deposit supply equation is then given by the constraint expressed in equation (5.4).

$$D = R/r \tag{5.4a}$$

and

$$M = D + C \tag{5.2}$$

$$M = (R/r) + C \tag{5.2a}$$

where R, r and C are all exogenously determined.

Instead of looking at a position of static equilibrium to derive this result, we can obtain it by consideration of the banking system's dynamic behaviour when adjusting to a change in the level of its reserves. This has already been discussed in terms of a numerical example. It is assumed that a new deposit of cash, ΔR, has been received by the banking system. In model 1, since the amount of currency held by the public is assumed to be constant, any increase in high powered money, even if initially in the form of currency with the public, ends up in the banking system as reserves. Therefore, $\Delta H = \Delta R$ in this model because of the assumption that $\Delta C/\Delta M = 0$.

Table 5.1 traces out the stages of credit creation as banks expand loads, lending out their excess reserves, which are then redeposited with the banking system to provide the reserve base for a further expansion of loans.

Following row (1) we see that an additional deposit of cash, ΔH, increases required reserves by $r\Delta H$ leaving excess reserves of $(1-r)\Delta H$ which are lent out in order to increase profits, so long as marginal

TABLE 5.1

	(1) Increase in bank assets Increase in deposits	(2) Increase in required reserves	(3) Increase in bank loans	(4) Redeposition of cash lent out Increase in deposits at the next stage
(1)	ΔH	$r\Delta H$	$(1-r)\Delta H$	$(1-r)\Delta H$
(2)	$(1-r)\Delta H$	$r(1-r)\Delta H$	$(1-r)^2\Delta H$	$(1-r)^2\Delta H$
(3)	$(1-r)^2\Delta H$	$r(1-r)^2\Delta H$	$(1-r)^3\Delta H$	$(1-r)^3\Delta H$
.	.	.	.	.
.	.	.	.	.
.	.	.	.	.
(N)	$(1-r)^{N-1}\Delta H$	$r(1-r)^{N-1}\Delta H$	$(1-r)^N\Delta H$	$(1-r)^N\Delta H$

revenue exceeds marginal cost. Given the assumption that the public holds a constant amount of currency, the $(1-r)\Delta H$ which is lent out by the banks is redeposited with them to provide the basis for a further expansion of deposits at stage 2. Since $(1-r)$ is a positive fraction, $(1-r)^t$ becomes smaller as t increases. Therefore the amount by which deposits expand at each round of the credit creation process diminishes and approaches zero as t tends to infinity. The total expansion of deposits based on an increase in high-powered money of ΔH, and thus the consequent expansion of the money supply, is obtained by adding up all the rows in column 1:

$$\Delta M = \Delta D$$

$$= \Delta H[1 + (1-r) + (1-r)^2 + (1-r)^3 + \cdots + (1-r)^{N-1}] \quad (5.14)$$

$$= \Delta H\left[\frac{1-(1-r)^N}{r}\right]$$

therefore

$$\lim_{N\to\infty} \Delta M = \lim_{N\to\infty} \Delta D$$

$$= \Delta H[1/r] \quad (5.15)$$

therefore

$$\Delta D/\Delta H = 1/r.$$

So long as the marginal revenue from deposit expansion exceeds the marginal cost, and the rate of increase of deposits, given an increase in reserves, $dD/dR = dD/dH$ (this has previously been written in terms of Δs indicating discrete changes) is constant, we can integrate to obtain

TABLE 5.2

	(1) Decrease in bank assets Decrease in bank deposits	(2) Decrease in required reserves	(3) Deficiency in reserves	(4) Decrease in deposits Decrease in assets at next stage
(1)	$-\Delta H$	$-r\Delta H$	$(1-r)\Delta H$	$-(1-r)\Delta H$
(2)	$-(1-r)\Delta H$	$-r(1-r)\Delta H$	$(1-r)^2\Delta H$	$-(1-r)^2\Delta H$
(3)	$-(1-r)^2\Delta H$	$-r(1-r)^2\Delta H$	$(1-r)^3\Delta H$	$-(1-r)^3\Delta H$
.	.	.	.	.
.	.	.	.	.
.	.	.	.	.
(N)	$-(1-r)^{N-1}\Delta H$	$-r(1-r)^{N-1}\Delta H$	$(1-r)^N\Delta H$	$-(1-r)^N\Delta H$

equation (5.4a), which is the deposit supply equation:

$$D = \int_0^R dD = \int_0^R \frac{dR}{r} = \frac{R}{r}. \qquad (5.4a)$$

The expression $1/r$ is known as bank multiplier, since it shows the level of deposits as a multiple of the level of bank reserves.

The process outlined above works in reverse for a decrease in bank reserves, given the same set of assumptions. If banks are profit-maximising institutions, and marginal revenue exceeds marginal cost, they will be at their required minimum reserve ratio before the contraction in reserves occurs.

From Table 5.2 we see that following a decrease in reserves of ΔH, bank deposits must also decline by ΔH, so that banks need to hold rH fewer cash reserves, but are deficient in reserves by $(1-r)H$. Banks therefore recall $(1-r)H$ loans to get back to the required reserve ratio.* This means that bank deposits fall by a further $(1-r)H$, so that in these circumstances banks have to reduce deposits in total by $\Delta H/r$, given again by summing up all rows in column (1) to infinity. The lower level of reserves is now just adequate to support the new level of deposits, to give a restored cash ratio of r.

Model 2: Monopoly Bank, Public's Currency Holdings Constant

In model 2 we keep the same assumptions except that we deal with the case of a monopoly bank, which therefore can only expand loans by lowering its lending rate. This is expressed in equation (5.16) as

$$i_L = f(D) \qquad (5.16)$$

* This assumes that the banks cannot borrow from the government or from abroad. These effects are discussed later.

where $di_L/dD < 0$. Bank profits are written again as

$$\pi = D(1-r)i_L - T(D) \qquad (5.11a)$$

therefore

$$\frac{d\pi}{dD} = (1-r)i_L + D(1-r)\frac{di_L}{dD} - \frac{dT}{dD} = 0. \qquad (5.17)$$

Marginal revenue equals $(1-r)i_L + D(1-r)\, di_L/dD$ which since di_L/dD is negative is, as one would suppose, less than the average revenue $(1-r)i_L$. It is also the case under monopoly that profits are maximised subject to the constraint of equation (5.4) that $r = R/D$. Since marginal revenue under monopoly is less than it is under perfect competition, given that the reserve constraint is not binding and that the same cost function applies, deposits will be expanded to a lower level by a monopoly bank. This is illustrated in Figure 5.1 where D_c is the profit-maximising level of deposit creation by a perfectly competitive banking industry, given reserves do not provide a constraint, D_M is the profit-maximising level of deposit creation by a monopoly, given the reserves do not provide a constraint, and D^1 is the level of deposit creation for both monopoly and perfectly competitive industry, given reserves do act as a constraint.

We can see from Figure 5.1 that the reserve constraint, which must bite in order for deposits to be determined by the bank multiplier formula, comes into effect at a lower level of deposits for a monopoly bank. So long as all accounts are current accounts and the reserve constraint is operative, the bank multiplier formula for deposit determination applies both to profit-maximising perfectly competitive and to monopoly banks.

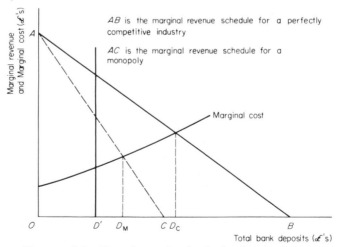

FIGURE 5.1   *Deposit creation by the banking industry*

Model 3: *Constant Currency–Deposit Ratio*

We will now modify models 1 and 2 and assume that instead of holding a fixed amount of currency, the public maintains a desired ratio of currency to deposits. The desired currency–deposit ratio, $d = C/D$, is given by equation (5.5). Alternatively one can conduct the analysis in terms of the desired currency–money supply ratio, $k = C/M$, equation (5.5), where since

$$C/M = k \tag{5.6}$$

and

$$D/M = 1 - k \tag{5.6a}$$

we have

$$C/D = d = k/(1-k). \tag{5.7}$$

Factors that determine the public's desired currency–money supply ratio have been examined by Cagan [4] for the United States. The demand to hold bank deposits, as opposed to currency stems from their convenience and safety in transferring larger sums of money. Changes in banking techniques, such as the introduction of bank and credit cards, encourage the use of bank deposits as a medium of exchange, whereas the desire to avoid paying tax through engaging in non-recordable cash transactions, and bank charges on current accounts, discourage the holding of bank deposits. Long-term factors, such as urbanisation and the growth of income, which stimulate banking, are thought by Cagan to explain the secular decline in the U.S. currency ratio, which has been interrupted by upturns in the 1930s and during the Second World War. Lack of confidence in the banking system, like that which occurred in the United States in the early 1930s, causes a short-term increase in the preference for currency, and the increased mobility of people during the war can explain the upturn then experienced in the currency ratio. Similar factors may be expected to apply to the U.K. currency ratio which is plotted for the years 1881 to 1962 in Figure 5.5 (p. 134).

In model 3, it is assumed that the public have a fixed desired currency–money supply ratio, k, which is determined by such factors as mentioned above. We assume either a perfectly competitive or monopoly banking system, operating within its reserve constraint. The other assumptions are maintained.

If there is an increase in high-powered money of ΔH, a fraction k of this kept by the public as currency and $(1 - k)$ is deposited in the banking system in order to maintain the desired currency ratio. Thus bank reserves rise initially by $\Delta R = (1 - k)\Delta H$. A fraction r is retained by the banking system as required reserves, leaving $(1 - r)(1 - k)\Delta H$ to be lent out. Unlike models 1 and 2, not all of the loans made by the banks are redeposited with them by the public, since to maintain the desired currency ratio the public always retain k of any increase in

Table 5.3

	(1) Increase in bank assets / Increase in bank deposits	(2) Increase in required reserves	(3) Increase in bank loans	(4) Redeposition of cash lent out / Increase in deposits in next stage
1	$(1-k)\Delta H$	$r(1-k)\Delta H$	$(1-r)(1-k)\Delta H$	$(1-r)(1-k)^2\Delta H$
2	$(1-r)(1-k)^2\Delta H$	$(1-r)(1-k)^2\Delta H$	$(1-r)^2(1-k)^2\Delta H$	$(1-r)^2(1-k)^3\Delta H$
3	$(1-r)^2(1-k)^3\Delta H$	$r(1-r)^2(1-k)^3\Delta H$	$(1-r)^3(1-k)^3\Delta H$	$(1-r)^3(1-k)^4\Delta H$
.	.	.	.	.
.	.	.	.	.
.	.	.	.	.
N	$(1-r)^{N-1}(1-k)^N\Delta H$	$r(1-r)^{N-1}(1-k)^N\Delta H$	$(1-r)^N(1-k)^N\Delta H$	$(1-r)^N(1-k)^{N+1}\Delta H$

deposits as currency and only redeposit $(1-k)$ with the banking system. This is shown in Table 5.3.

Therefore as the credit creation process continues, the banking system now loses reserves as it expands its deposits. Every time the banking system expands deposits by an amount ΔD, it loses $k\Delta D$ in reserves because the public demand that the increased deposits they are holding are matched by an increase in currency, which they obtain from the banks. The total additional deposits now created on the basis of an addition to high-powered money is obtained by summing all rows in column 1 of Table 5.4.

$$\Delta D = (1-k)\Delta H[1+(1-r)(1-k)+(1-r)^2(1-k)^2$$
$$+\cdots+(1-r)^{N-1}(1-k)^{N-1}] \tag{5.18}$$
$$= (1-k)\Delta H\left[\frac{1-\{(1-r)(1-k)\}^N}{1-(1-r)(1-k)}\right]$$

therefore

$$\lim_{N\to\infty}\Delta D = \frac{(1-k)\Delta H}{k+r(1-k)}. \tag{5.19}$$

The increase in currency in circulation with the public is obtained by summing up k times the rows in column 3 (k times each row entry is the increase in currency in circulation at that round of the credit creation process) and adding to this sum the initial increase in currency in circulation which is $k\Delta H$:

$$\Delta C = k\,\Delta H[1+(1-r)(1-k)+(1-r)^2(1-k)^2$$
$$+\cdots+(1-r)^{N-1}(1-k)^{N-1}] \tag{5.20}$$
$$= k\Delta H\left[\frac{1-\{(1-r)(1-k)\}^N}{1-(1-r)(1-k)}\right]$$
$$\lim_{N\to\infty}\Delta C = \frac{k\Delta H}{k+r(1-k)} \tag{5.21}$$

$$\Delta M = \Delta C + \Delta D = \frac{\Delta H[k + (1-k)]}{k + r(1-k)}$$

$$= \frac{\Delta H}{k + r(1-k)} \qquad (5.22)^*$$

therefore

$$\frac{\Delta M}{\Delta H} = \frac{1}{k + r(1-k)}$$

which for very small changes in the variables is written

$$\frac{dM}{dH} = \frac{1}{k + r(1-k)}. \qquad (5.22a)$$

Thus, on integrating we can obtain an expression for the money stock as a function of the stock of high-powered money, the currency ratio and the reserve ratio:

$$M = \int_0^H dM = \int_0^H \frac{1}{k + r(1-k)} \, dH = \frac{H}{k + r(1-k)}. \qquad (5.23)$$

Alternatively equation (5.23) can be derived from a comparative static exercise, using definitions (5.1) to (5.7) as equilibrium relationships that must hold. From equation (5.1)

$$C = H - R \qquad (5.1a)$$

$$R = rD \qquad (5.4)$$

$$C/M = k \qquad (5.6)$$

$$D/M = 1 - k. \qquad (5.7a)$$

Substitute equations (5.1a) and (5.4) into equation (5.6) to obtain

$$H - rD = kM. \qquad (5.24)$$

---

* Equation (5.22) can also be obtained by noting that the currency–deposit ratio $d = k/(1-k)$ must be maintained

$$\frac{\Delta C}{\Delta D} = d = \frac{k}{1-k} \qquad (5.7)$$

therefore

$$\Delta C = \frac{k}{1-k} \Delta D = \frac{k}{1-k} \left(\frac{(1-k)\Delta H}{k + r(1-k)} \right)$$

$$= \frac{k\Delta H}{k + r(1-k)} \qquad (5.22)$$

Substituting for ΔD from equation (5.19)

$$\Delta M = \Delta C + \Delta D = \frac{k\Delta H}{k + r(1-k)} + \frac{(1-k)\Delta H}{k + r(1-k)} = \frac{\Delta H}{k + r(1-k)}.$$

Substitute equation (5.7a) into equation (5.24)

$$H - r(1 - k)M = kM \qquad (5.25)$$

therefore

$$M = \frac{H}{k + r(1 - k)}. \qquad (5.23)$$

Given that $k = d/(1 + d)$ from equation (5.7), an alternative way of writing the money supply equation, (5.23), is

$$M = \frac{H(1 + d)}{d + r}. \qquad (5.23a)$$

$1/\{k + r(1 - k)\}$, or its equivalent $(1 + d)/(d + r)$, is a bank multiplier which, because of the presence of the currency ratio, is considerably smaller than that of models 1 and 2. High-powered money, the reserve ratio and the currency ratio have been termed the proximate determinants of the money supply [5].

5.4   FACTORS INFLUENCING THE PROXIMATE DETERMINANTS OF THE MONEY STOCK

From the money supply equation (5.23) we can see that the money stock is not solely under the control of the government through its requirement that banks maintain a minimum reserve ratio. Even if high-powered money were under government control, the lending policies of the banks determine whether they maintain a reserve ratio in excess of that required by the government. Also the public's desire to hold currency *vis-à-vis* bank deposits is a determinant of the money supply which is entirely outside the government's direct control. The term proximate determinants indicates that these three variables are not the sole determinants of the money supply. Underlying the reduced form equation (5.23) are variables which influence the values of the proximate determinants. Some of the variables which are likely to affect the currency ratio have already been discussed and we now turn to consider other variables which may influence the values of the proximate determinants. In doing so we will introduce some additional institutional features of the banking system which so far has been of an extremely simple form.

Discount Rate

The central bank, which, in the United Kingdom, is the Bank of England, has various functions in relation to the banking system. It is usually responsible for the issuing of currency, acts as banker to the government and to the rest of the banking system. In its function as banker to the banking system, the central bank holds deposits of the private banks, which form part of their cash reserves. In order to preserve financial stability by maintaining public confidence in the private banks' ability to repay deposits in cash on demand, the central bank has taken on the responsibility of acting as lender of last resort to the banking system. If the private banks run short of cash reserves, these can be borrowed from the central bank, which charges a rate of interest, known as discount rate,* on these borrowings. It may be central bank policy to charge a discount rate which is in excess of the private bank's lending rate, thus encouraging the banks to repay their central bank loans as soon as possible. The ability to borrow reserves from the central bank, albeit at a discount rate, provides the banking system with an avenue for deposit expansion. The cost of expanding deposits becomes a function of the central bank's discount rate. In terms of the analysis in Figure 5.1, the marginal cost curve of deposit expansion will shift upwards with increases in the central bank discount rate, assuming this rate to be exogenous. The amount of reserves that the banking system holds now depends first on the volume provided by the government in the form of high-powered money deposited with the banks by the public, and secondly on the extent that banks can borrow reserves at discount rate from the central bank.

The effect of including the ability to borrow reserves has been analysed in terms of the effect on the banks' desired reserve ratio. It is assumed that the desired reserve ratio is inversely related to the central bank discount rate, it being presumed that banks are willing to hold smaller reserve ratios and are more prepared to take the risk of running short of reserves, which incurs the penalty of borrowing from the central bank, the lower is the discount rate [6].

Central bank lending policy may be so lax as to allow banks to borrow reserves and expand deposits until the marginal cost of doing so equals the marginal revenue. On the other hand, the central bank may limit its lending to the banking system so that marginal revenue remains above marginal cost. In the latter case equation (5.23) still determines the money supply, with the provision that high powered money and the reserve ratio vary inversely with the central bank discount rate. In either case, a change in high-powered money, provided free by the government, will cause a corresponding change in bank deposits. For instance an increase in such high-powered money provides banks with reserves on which they previously had to pay a discount rate. This both shifts down the marginal cost curve in Figure 5.1 and moves the reserve constraint to the right, causing a multiple increase in bank deposits.

* Known as Bank Rate in the United Kingdom until October 1972. Since called the Bank of England's minimum lending rate.

Commercial Banks' Lending Rate

Several writers have assumed that the supply of bank deposits varies directly with the bank lending rate, on the grounds that the higher the interest rate the more willing are banks to create deposits by lending to the public. This supposition requires careful analysis. A glance at Figure 5.1 shows that the increased lending rate must take the form of an upward shift in the demand curve for loans. If banks were constrained by their reserve position to the extent that marginal revenue exceeded marginal cost, banks would still be unable to expand loans. The level of deposits would remain at OD^1 and bank profits would increase. If, on the other hand, the level of reserves were more than sufficient to provide a basis for expanding deposits until marginal revenue equalled marginal cost, then the increased demand for bank loans, by increasing marginal revenue, would allow banks to expand credit and the level of bank deposits would be directly related to the market rate of interest. Cagan's [4] examination of the U.S. data leads him to conclude that there is little evidence of a long-term relationship between the bank's usable reserve ratio (usable reserves = total reserves − required reserves) and the interest rate, although he does not rule out the possibility that interest rates may have a cyclical influence.

Teigen [6] develops a model of money supply determination, which, in terms of the equations used here, assumes that the bank's desired reserve ratio is directly related to the market rate of interest and inversely related to the discount rate. He gives no theoretical basis for, or direct empirical test of, the structural equations of his model. Teigen tests a jointly determined demand and supply of money model and obtains a significant, positive money supply elasticity with respect to the interest rate and a negative supply elasticity with respect to the discount rate.

The Rate of Interest on Deposit Accounts

So far we have assumed that the only bank deposits issued by the banking system are current account deposits. We will consider now the effect of deposit accounts (time deposits in the United States) on the determination of the money supply. Banks pay a rate of interest to depositors willing to place with them deposits on which notice must be given of withdrawal or interest payments are forfeit. If the currency ratio is a function of the deposit rate, the banks can induce the public to lower its currency ratio and hold a greater proportion of the money supply as bank deposits. Given this assumption, the banking system can increase the proportion of high-powered money that is held as bank reserves, by raising the deposit rate. Increasing the deposit rate may be expected to cause the public to shift from current accounts to deposit accounts, which will only give banks an incentive to expand credit if they can hold a lower level of reserves against deposit accounts as against current accounts. In the U.S. system the required reserve ratio against time deposits is lower than that against current accounts. One can only hypothesise that, in the United Kingdom where this is not the case, banks may desire to hold a smaller usable reserve ratio when the proportion of deposits held as deposit accounts increases. Therefore a higher deposit rate, *ceteris paribus*, provides the basis for bank deposit expansion if it reduces the currency ratio or causes the desired reserve ratio to fall due to a shift from current to deposit accounts.

The introduction of deposit accounts means that the bank deposit expansion costs are directly related to the deposit rate, which is itself a function of the level of bank deposits created. In a perfectly competitive banking system, individual banks whose marginal revenue is greater than their marginal cost, but who are prevented from further deposit expansion by lack of reserves, will bid up the deposit rate in an attempt to attract more reserves, until marginal cost is brought into equality with marginal revenue, and the banking system as a whole is earning normal profits.

This is illustrated in Figure 5.2 where OD' is the level of bank deposits that the banking system creates on the basis of its reserves, which depend on H, k and r, given there are no deposit accounts. If deposit accounts exist, and as a result bank reserves rise or the desired reserve ratio declines, deposits can be expanded further to OD''. The consequent bidding up of the deposit rate by competitive banks shifts up the marginal cost curve so that abnormal profits disappear.

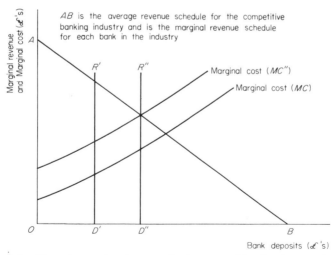

FIGURE 5.2 *Deposit creation by a perfectly competitive banking industry with and without interest-paying deposit accounts*

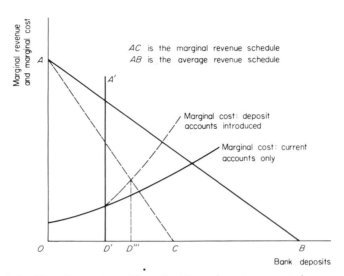

FIGURE 5.3   *Deposit creation with and without deposit accounts by a monopoly bank*

Any increase in reserves upon which banks do not have to pay a rate of interest, will lower both the bank lending and borrowing rates. The acquisition of additional low cost reserves means that the banks can maintain the level of deposits OD'' at a lower marginal cost than before. Since marginal revenue now lies above marginal cost, the banks will expand lending, so that lending and borrowing rates must fall until marginal revenue and cost are again brought into equality.

In the case of a monopoly bank, its marginal revenue $(1-r)i_L + D(1-r)\,di_L/dD$ lies below its average revenue $(1-r)i_L$ as indicated in Figure 5.3.

Without the existence of deposit accounts and constrained by lack of reserves, the bank creates OD' deposits. If deposit accounts are introduced, the monopoly bank will acquire more reserves by charging a deposit rate such that its marginal cost equals its marginal revenue. The new marginal cost curve will diverge from the old at Z, since for deposit levels less than OD' there is no need for the bank to hold deposit accounts. The bank will create deposits of OD''' such that marginal cost equals marginal revenue, and will be earning abnormal profits, unlike the case of the perfectly competitive industry. Following an increase in reserves for which the bank does not have to pay an interest rate, there will be a multiple expansion of credit, since marginal revenue exceeds marginal cost and the bank can expand deposits on the basis of its additional low cost reserves until marginal revenue and cost are once more equal.

Given that the existing banking system in the United Kingdom is an oligopoly, that the Bank of England exerts some restraint on the amount of reserves borrowed from it by the banking system, the proximate determinants of the money supply provide good indicators of the factors that are important in influencing the stock of money.

The Sources of High-Powered Money

Changes in high-powered money come from either the government or foreign sectors.* Increases in high powered money will occur if the government runs a budget deficit and does not finance it entirely by borrowing from the private sector by selling it securities. The remaining deficit must be ultimately financed by issuing currency or bank reserves. Government securities sold to the Bank of England, merely result in the creation of Bank of England deposits which the government uses to finance its expenditures and which pass into the hands of the public to be held as currency or private bank deposits. If the private banks are holding excess reserves and buy up government securities, they are acting as financial intermediaries, transferring deposits loaned to them by the non-bank private sector to the government, which is ultimately borrowing from the public. If, on the other hand, the private banks are at their minimum reserve ratio, to induce them to take up additional government securities, the government must provide them with additional reserves, thus increasing high-powered money.

The government alternatively may finance part of its budget deficit by borrowing from abroad by selling its securities to foreign residents. Under a fixed exchange system such transactions lead to an inflow of foreign exchange which is transferred into domestic currency for the government to finance its expenditure. This causes an increase in high-powered money. Thus, any proportion of the budget deficit which is not financed ultimately by borrowing from the domestic private sector, must cause an increase in high powered money. The reverse is true of a budget surplus which is not financed by redeeming government securities from the private sector.

The government can cause changes in high-powered money by engaging in open-market operations in its securities which may occur independently of the financing of budget deficits or surpluses. Open-market sales of government securities to the non-bank private sector will cause a reduction in bank reserves and bank deposits, as the public will exchange these for government securities. The reverse will occur if the government purchases securities from the public.

High-powered money will increase under a fixed exchange rate system if a surplus is earned on the balance of payments. This is alternatively

* There are also changes arising from the private sector if gold is mined domestically and becomes either currency or reserves.

termed a positive total currency flow and will correspond to a net inflow of foreign exchange. The U.K. holders of the net inflow of foreign exchange transfer it into sterling, and either keep it as currency in circulation or deposit it with a bank. Either action will be an increase in high-powered money. Similarly a balance-of-payments deficit, or negative total currency flow, will create a reduction in high-powered money and will be a force for decreasing the money supply.

The two sources of high-powered money are therefore:

(1) The quantity of government bonds held by the central bank minus central bank holdings of government deposits. This equals the amount of high-powered money that the government has issued in the past to finance its net budget deficit over the years.*

(2) Foreign exchange reserves. Under a regime of fixed exchange rates the balance of payments is not necessarily in equilibrium. If it is

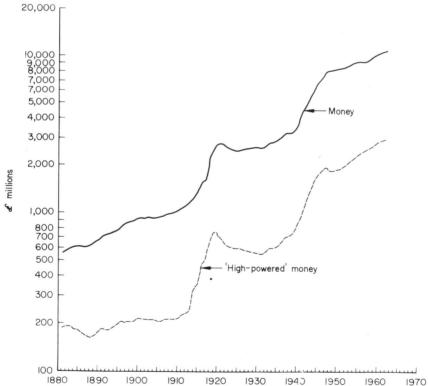

FIGURE 5.4   *Money and 'high-powered' money stocks outstanding in the United Kingdom 1881–1962*

* Of lesser importance is central bank lending or advances to the banking sector.

TABLE 5.4   Contribution of Selected Determinants of the Money Stock United Kingdom and United States 1881–1962 and 1881–1960

Period	Change in M (£ millions)	Impact of ΔH (per cent)	Impact of Δr (per cent)	Impact of Δk (per cent)	Interaction (per cent)
			United Kingdom		
1881–1962	+10,367	92·1	−1·2	+9·6	−0·6
1881–1960	+9942	91·4	−1·1	+9·9	−0·6
1881–1913	+607	32·5	−4·4	+77·0	−5·0
1913–20	+1727	120·5	−3·4	−17·8	−0·6
1913–18	+1062	147·5	−18·6	−33·4	+4·4
1921–29	−152	319·3	−105·5	−105·2	−8·8
1921–39	+503	60·7	+20·2	+17·9	+0·8
1929–33	+188	80·8	−30·6	+50·0	−1·4
1933–39	+467	146·4	−4·6	−42·1	+0·4
1939–46	+4124	111·2	+5·1	--15·5	−0·8
1948–62	+2747	160·4	−7·2	−54·6	+1·4
1948–60	+2322	160·6	−6·3	−59·4	+1·2
	($ milliards)		United States		
1881–1960	+206·0	+85·7	+2·8	+8·8	+2·7
1881–1913	+13·1	+62·4	+6·4	+23·8	+7·4
1913–20	+19·0	+93·1	+11·9	−4·4	−0·6
1913–18	+11·0	+107·8	+5·8	−12·3	−0·5
1921–39	+16·2	+239·7	−144·9	+1·0	−0·6
1921–29	+13·7	+24·1	+14·6	+57·0	−0·4
1929–33	−16·0	−33·4	+58·0	+95·5	−20·5
1933–39	+18·5	+163·0	−84·5	+31·0	−14·1
1939–46	+90·0	+89·4	+31·4	−12·3	−6·8
1948–60	+60·7	+18·5	+42·5	+31·2	+7·7

Source: Sheppard, *Growth and Role of U.K. Financial Institutions.*

not, the quantity of foreign exchange reserves is changing. Thus the equilibrium quantity of high-powered money is not exogenous and the government cannot determine the equilibrium quantity of the nominal money supply. (For further explanation see Chapter 8.)

The two uses of high-powered money are, as previously defined, currency in circulation and commercial bank reserves.

Contributions of the Proximate Determinants to Money Supply Changes

Figure 5.4 shows the movements in high-powered money and the money supply (defined to include deposit accounts) that have occurred in the United Kingdom for the period 1881–1962. High-powered money has been estimated to have contributed 92 per cent of the variation in the

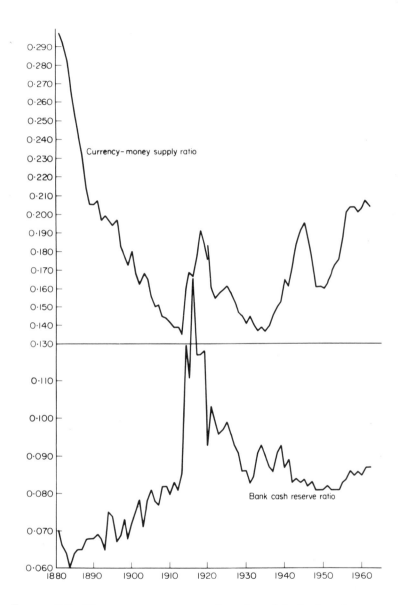

FIGURE 5.5   *The currency–money supply ratio and the bank cash reserve ratio in*
the United Kingdom 1881–1962

money supply [7]. This finding corresponds to those made by Friedman and Schwartz for the United States. The movements of the reserve ratio, r, and currency ratio, k, in the United Kingdom do not correspond as closely to U.S. experience. The U.K. ratios are graphed in Figure 5.5. There are some similarities, the currency ratio in each country fell fairly steadily in the pre-1914 period. The movements in both r and k were in the same general direction in the 1930s and 1950s. There are no further similarities, since in the post-1920 period movements in the U.S. ratios have been considerably larger and their trends were frequently in the opposite direction to those in the United Kingdom.

The contributions of the three proximate determinants of the money stock to changes in the money supply are shown for both countries in Table 5.4. Each entry shows the contribution of a given determinant had the other two determinants remained constant. We can see that for the United Kingdom in the period 1948–62, the rising reserve and currency ratios were forces operating to reduce the impact of increasing quantities of high-powered money on the money supply. The currency ratio can be seen to have a greater impact on the U.K. money supply than is the case in the United States, whereas the reverse is true of the reserve ratio. This indicates the greater stability of the reserve ratio of the British oligopolistic branch banking system where it has been official policy to keep the banks' cash ratio around 8 per cent.

5.5   U.K. BANKING INSTITUTIONS

The U.K. banking system consists of three major types of institutions, the central bank, which is the Bank of England, the discount houses and the banks. The banks can be subdivided into clearing or deposit banks who borrow largely in the form of deposits repayable on demand and who are the major operators of the payments system. These banks are sometimes referred to as primary banks to distinguish them from the secondary banking system [8] which includes merchant banks and overseas banks, which tend to borrow in the form of longer-term deposits, both in the United Kingdom and abroad, and engage in more specialist lending to industry and overseas. At the end of the banking spectrum appear finance houses which accept longer-term deposits than clearing banks and engage in hire-purchase finance.

The Bank of England, established in 1694 and nationalised in 1946, functions in several ways. It is responsible for the note issue being the only bank in the United Kingdom which can issue notes, and sees that the economy is supplied with the necessary cash to finance transactions. Since the Bank Charter Act of 1844 the Bank of England has been divided into two departments for accounting purposes. The note issue is recorded in the balance sheet of the Issue Department of the Bank of England.

Balance Sheet of Issue Department of Bank of England:

Liabilities	Assets	
Notes issued:	Government Securities	
In circulation with	Other securities ⎤	
public	Gold ⎬ very small amounts	
In Banking Department of	Coin ⎦	
Bank of England		

(Note that both sides of any balance sheet will be equal).

From this balance sheet it can be seen that the note issue is no longer backed by gold, but for accounting purposes is backed by government securities, since in return for issuing notes to the Exchequer the Bank of England receives government securities.

The Bank of England acts as banker to the government, conducting the government's ordinary banking business by managing the government's deposits or public deposits, which are recorded as a liability in the balance sheet of the Banking Department. The Bank of England is also banker to the rest of the banking system, which keeps Bankers' Deposits with the Bank of England in order to settle net inter-bank payments and as part of their reserves (cash at the Bank of England). The clearing banks are now required to keep at least 1·5 per cent of their reserves as cash at the Bank of England.

Balance Sheet of Banking Department:

Liabilities	Assets
Public Deposits	Government Securities
Bankers' Deposits	Discounts and advances
Other accounts	Other securities
Special Deposits	Notes and coin

The Bank is the agent of government internal monetary policy. In this role it manages the marketable securities which form part of the outstanding national debt.* It regulates the redemption of maturing debt and the issue of new securities, so as to preserve an orderly market in which undue fluctuations in interest rates on government securities are avoided. Since 1969 the Bank of England has been prepared to allow greater interest rate movements than previously. Government international monetary policy is administered by the Bank's operating the Exchange Equalisation Account through which foreign exchange is bought and sold.

In the models of deposit determination developed above, the commercial banks were assumed to hold only two types of assets, cash reserves and interest-bearing loans. In practice the U.K. clearing banks hold a variety of interest-earning assets, which differ in liquidity and some of which are counted as reserve assets by the Bank of England. It had been the practice

---

* The national debt is the marketable and non-marketable liabilities of the government.

of the U.K. clearing banks, which are few in number and hence form an oligopolistic industry, to agree on common rates to pay on deposit accounts and to charge on loans. This and other features of U.K. banking practice were altered in September 1971 following publication by the Bank of England of new proposals in *Competition and Credit Control* (C.C.C.) in May 1971. As a result of the Bank's desire for greater competition in banking, the banks have abandoned interest rate conformity and are beginning to apply independent interest rate policies. In C.C.C. the Bank of England abandoned the previous cash and liquidity ratios which applied only to the London clearing banks, and set a single 12·5 per cent reserve ratio for all banks, including the secondary banking system, with a 10 per cent reserve ratio for finance houses. The actual reserve ratios adopted are shown in Table 5.5.

It was felt that the previous reserve ratio system had discriminated against the clearing banks in competing for banking business and had thus contributed to inefficiency in the banking industry. This may have been a factor causing the much slower rate of growth of the primary as compared to the secondary banking system in the 1960s.

The assets which count as reserve assets are indicated in the clearing bank balance sheet presented below. The assets are arranged in decreasing order of liquidity. Money at call and short notice is clearing bank loans to the discount houses. Special Deposits are those held at the Bank of England at its request. Sterling certificates of deposit are bank deposits loaned at interest for a specific length of time and are a method of transferring deposits from one bank to another through the interbank loan market. Investments are government securities with between one year and usually up to five years to run to maturity.

Clearing Bank Balance Sheet:

Liabilities	Assets	
Bank Deposits:	Notes and coin in vaults and till of bank	
Current Accounts	Deposits at the Bank of England	⎫
Deposit Accounts	Money at call and short notice	⎪
Sterling certificates	Treasury Bills	⎪
of deposit	British government securities with	⎬ Reserve
	less than a year to maturity	Assets
	Local authority bills eligible	⎪
	for rediscount at the Bank of	⎪
	England	
	Eligible commercial bills	⎭
	Special Deposits	
	Sterling certificates of deposit	
	Investments	
	Advances	

TABLE 5.5. Bank and Finance House Reserve
            Ratios

Date	Banks	Finance houses
20.10.71	15·9	1·7
8.12.71	17·4	2·9
15. 3.72	15·4	4·2
21. 6.72	14·5	7·7
20. 9.72	14·9	10·1
13.12.72	15·7	10·9
21. 3.73	14·1	13·4

Source: Bank of England Quarterly Bulletin.

Discount houses, which form the London Discount Market Association, are specialised institutions dealing in short-term lending and borrowing. Their chief source of borrowing is in the form of money at call and short notice from clearing banks and from large firms. Their main channel of lending is to the government from whom they buy Treasury bills.* The discount houses are unique to the British banking system and intermediate between the banks and the Bank of England. The banks do not take up Treasury bills directly from the Bank of England but buy them from the discount houses when the bills have about two months to run to maturity. The government invites tenders for its weekly Treasury bill issue. Since September 1971 the London Discount Market Association no longer tenders at a commonly agreed price, but is still committed to covering any of the weekly tender otherwise not sold.

When the banks run short of cash, they do not borrow directly from the central bank in the United Kingdom as in other countries, but receive assistance via the discount houses. Clearing banks, if in need of cash, recall money lent to the discount houses who, in turn, borrow, if necessary, from the Bank of England at the Bank of England's minimum lending rate. Until October 1972 this was known as Bank Rate. The Bank of England's minimum lending rate, which is published weekly, is the average rate of discount for Treasury bills at the most recent tender plus an additional 0·5 per cent rounded up to the nearest 0·25 per cent. In lending to the Discount Market the Bank of England is acting as lender of last resort, and may choose to lend at the minimum lending rate, which is a penal rate, since it is above the rate received by discount houses on Treasury bills. Alternatively the Bank

---

* A bill of exchange, such as a Treasury bill, is a debtor's promise to pay a fixed sum at a future date (maturity) which is usually three months hence, to whoever then holds the bill. This sum is greater than the amount lent, therefore the creditor earns a rate of return on the bill, known as the discount rate.

may choose to lend at the market Treasury bill rate. The choice depends on whether the Bank is operating an easy or a tight monetary policy. In the latter event it would lend at a penal rate.

5.6 MONETARY POLICY

Monetary policy is the government's regulation of the supply of money and credit, and the level and structure of interest rates in the pursuit of its economic objectives. There are various means or instruments of monetary policy which the government may use to implement changes in the money supply and consequent changes in the level of interest rates. Since the demand for money is interest responsive, it is not possible to alter the money supply, *ceteris paribus*, without altering interest rates in the opposite direction. This point is illustrated in Figure 5.6, which assumes that the money supply is interest inelastic. This analysis has also been discussed in relation to the *ISLM* model in Chapter 2.

If the money supply is increased from M_1^S to M_2^S, the rate of interest must fall to induce people to hold the additional money supply. The reverse is true of a decrease in the money supply from M_1^S to M_0^S. It must be remembered that Figure 5.6 shows only one sector of the economy, the money market, which is linked to other sectors, for instance the goods market in *ISLM* analysis. Positions C and B are not final equilibrium positions, because as a result of a change in the money supply, and

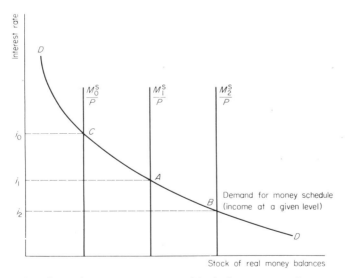

FIGURE 5.6   *The authorities cannot control both the quantity of money and the interest rate*

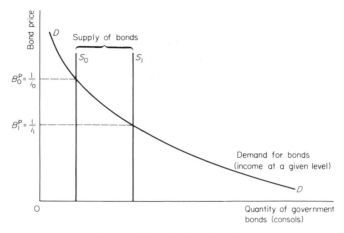

FIGURE 5.7   *The bond market*

consequent interest rate changes, there will be an impact on national income which will shift the money demand schedule.

One method of implementing monetary policy is through open-market operations, which have already been mentioned as a way of affecting the volume of high powered money. To reduce the quantity of bank reserves and thus trigger off some multiple reduction in bank deposits, the government would engage in open-market sales of its bonds to members of the non-bank private sector.

The demand for bonds will depend on people's total wealth, the yield on bonds and expectations about future bond prices.* A demand schedule is drawn in Figure 5.7, along which wealth and expectations are held constant. The demand to hold bonds is directly related to their yield and hence inversely related to their price. In order to sell additional securities the government must lower their price, that is raise the yield, to persuade the public to take up additional bonds. Figure 5.7 is the counterpart to Figure 5.6. Open-market sales, to reduce the money supply, will drive up interest rates, because the government must accept lower bond prices to persuade wealth holders to take up more bonds.

The Bank of England, as reported to the Radcliffe Committee [9], has been afraid that the demand schedule for government securities behaves perversely and that lower bond prices will not stimulate demand but reduce it, since investors may think a decline in bond prices, brought about by deliberate policy action, presages further falls. The Bank of England has the objective of maximising the sales of government securities, and has been afraid that any aggressive selling on its part would diminish the

* To be discussed in the next chapter.

number of holders of government securities. For this reason the Bank has in the past adopted a policy of 'sailing with the wind', that is selling securities on a rising market and buying back securities to maintain their price on a falling market.

This reluctance to allow any large fluctuations, especially upwards, in interest rates has had consequences for the control of the money supply. As Figure 5.6 illustrates, it is impossible for the central authorities to control both the level of interest rates and the money supply. Together with the Bank's apprehension about the impact on government security markets of forcing up interest rates, has been associated a concern with the interest rate level, rather than the money stock, as the key indicator of monetary policy. The desire to hold back increases in the rate of interest means that the Bank of England inevitably loses control of the money supply. Open-market sales of government securities will only cause a multiple contraction of bank credit if banks are not allowed to replenish their lost cash reserves by borrowing from the Bank of England.

For open-market sales to be effective the following process must operate. After open-market sales of government securities to the public the banks, being short of cash, recall money at call from the discount houses who, in turn, borrow from the Bank of England at a penal minimum lending rate. This induces the discount houses to repay the Bank speedily and find cash either by borrowing from the non-bank private sector or by selling Treasury bills to the public. Either action again reduces bank cash reserves and deposits and the process repeats itself until bank deposits have fallen sufficiently to match the lower level of reserve assets. The sale of government securities by the banking system, in order to replenish its cash reserves, will help to drive up interest rates on such securities. If the Bank of England then intervenes in the market to support government security prices by buying securities from the banking system, it provides the banks with the reserves they are seeking and prevents any multiple contraction of credit. Since this is basically the policy pursued by the Bank of England in the 1950s and 1960s, it has not used open-market operations to regulate the money supply. Since September 1969 the Bank has been more willing to see government security yields rise and in C.C.C. it announced its intention of offering the gilt-edged market less support.

In C.C.C. the Bank proposed to rely on Special Deposits, applied to all types of bank, as the method of controlling bank deposits. Special Deposits, introduced in 1960, are deposits that the Bank of England requests banks to place with it. These deposits earn a rate of interest equivalent to the Treasury bill rate, but do not count as reserve assets. A call for Special Deposits has an immediate impact on bank reserves. To be effective in reducing bank deposits, the banks must be brought below their minimum reserve ratio by the call. They will seek then to replenish their reserves by selling off government securities, which will force up their yields. For the policy to be effective the Bank of England must allow yields to rise, as any support for government security prices will just provide banks with the reserves required to maintain their existing level of deposits.

Because of its reluctance to use open-market operations vigorously, the Bank of England came to rely increasingly upon direct controls and requests. These include restrictions on hire-purchase down-payments and repayment periods, and directives or requests to the clearing banks concerning both the nature and volume of their lending. Such policies have been criticised for being discriminatory. The hire-purchase regulations affect consumer goods industries and the directives were aimed solely at the clearing banks, thus harming their competitive position *vis-à-vis* the secondary banking system. In C.C.C. the Bank proposed a reduced reliance on direct controls and requests, in favour of a broad call for Special Deposits which would affect the entire banking system.

5.7   CONCLUSION. THE MONEY SUPPLY: EXOGENOUS
      OR ENDOGENOUS?

The main issue concerning the determination of the money supply is the extent to which it is independent of the major endogenous variables in the economy, namely income and the rate of interest. It is the degree of emphasis which is in dispute since very few would argue that the money supply is entirely exogenous or completely endogenous. The issue is of importance since the money supply exerts a greater influence on the level of aggregate demand the less closely related it is to income and interest rates.

Monetary policy will be more effective the less responsive is the supply of money to changes in the interest rate and in income. Take the case of restrictive monetary policy which will cause interest rates to rise. If the money supply is positively related to the level of interest rates, the restrictive monetary policy will, via higher interest rates, produce a negative feedback to the money supply. The more interest responsive the money supply is, the less it will in fact fall if the government tries to operate a restrictive monetary policy and the less effective this policy will be.

Conversely, fiscal policy is more effective the more interest elastic is the money supply. Interest rates rise (fall) with an expansionary (contractionary) fiscal policy and induce an increase (decrease) in the money supply which in turn reinforces the fiscal policy. (These arguments can be conducted in terms of *ISLM* analysis as in the discussion in Chapter 2 of the relative effectiveness of fiscal and monetary policy. A more interest-elastic money supply is reflected in a more interest-elastic *LM* schedule.)

The money supply can be inherently exogenous but can be made endogenous in practice if the monetary authorities pursue a policy of stabilising interest rates. This policy will make the money supply respond directly to movements in income and interest rates. A rising level of national income, by causing a greater demand for money, will increase interest rates. If the authorities wish to keep down interest rates they will expand the money supply. By and large this has been the policy of the U.K. monetary authorities, although it has been accompanied by intermittent periods of monetary stringency. The growth in the U.K. money supply has therefore been somewhat erratic particularly in recent years.

Whether the money supply is inherently more exogenous than endogenous depends on the extent to which the proximate determinants of the money supply are behaviourally related to income and the rate of interest. The greater the strength of any positive relationship between the currency–deposit and bank reserve ratios on the one hand and income and interest rates on the other, then the more endogenous the money supply becomes.

Monetarist do not deny the feedback effects of income and interest rates on the money supply but do not regard them as important. Their opponents emphasise these factors which they regard as sufficiently important to characterise the money supply as a passive variable, moving directly with income.

These issues can only be settled by empirical work of which little is available for the U.K. economy.* The issue is more complex here because the United Kingdom is an open economy. To the extent that the sterling exchange rate is kept fixed, the government does not have control over the equilibrium quantity of money since the money supply is influenced by movements in the foreign exchange reserves.

REFERENCES

[1] *Bank of England Quarterly Bulletin.*
[2] *Financial Statistics.*
[3] R. W. Clower, 'Theoretical Foundations of Monetary Policy', in *Monetary Theory and Monetary Policy in the 1970's*, ed. G. Clayton, J. Gilbert and R. Sedgwick (Oxford University Press, 1971).
[4] P. Cagan, *Determinants and Effects of Changes in the Stock of Money*, (New York: Columbia University Press, 1965).
[5] M. Friedman and A. J. Schwarz, *A Monetary History of the United States, 1867–1960* (Princeton University Press, 1963).
[6] R. L. Teigen, 'Demand and Supply Functions for Money in the U.S.A.: Some Structural Estimates', *Econometrica* (October 1964).
[7] D. K. Sheppard, *The Growth and Role of U.K. Financial Institutions 1880–1962* (London: Methuen, 1971).

* See [10] as an example.

[8] J. Revell, 'A Secondary Banking System', *The Banker* (September 1968).

[9] *The Radcliffe Report on the Working of the Monetary System*, Cmnd. 837 (London: H.M.S.O., 1959).

[10] R. L. Crouch, 'A Model of the U.K.'s Monetary Sector', *Econometrica*, 35, 3–4 (1967).

6 The Demand for Money

Chapters 3 and 4 dealt with decision-units' flow decisions, which concern the proportion of current resources to be used for consumption and investment, whereas in this chapter we will consider the portfolio decision. If a decision-unit's spending per period of time differs from its income in that period, it has to finance the difference between income and spending. Because of past saving, or dissaving, an economic unit holds a stock of net wealth (assets minus liabilities) and has to decide in what types of assets and liabilities to hold its net wealth. The portfolio decision is the decision concerning the allocation of one's stock of net wealth amongst various types of assets and liabilities, and involves both the allocation of an existing stock of net wealth and the current financing of the difference between income and spending. In this chapter particular attention is paid to the decision to hold wealth in the form of money.

If a household earns its income from hiring out labour services and plans to consume its income exactly in each period, it would have no need to hold assets or liabilities over from one period to another. All we need to consider in this case is how the household finances its spending plans during the period for which income is received.

To see why money is held as a medium of exchange in order to finance current period expenditure plans we will envisage situations in which no money would be held. Obviously in a barter economy transactions are carried out without using a generally accepted medium of exchange. In practice a barter economy would be one which was not at all developed as a market economy. Once households cease to be completely self-sufficient and engage regularly in trade, a medium of exchange comes into existence to reduce the costs of barter. These are incurred through the time devoted to search and information gathering [1].

6.1 MONEY AS A UNIT OF ACCOUNT

Instead of an economy in which money does not exist we can envisage one in which money acts only as a unit of account or *numéraire*, but is never held by transactors. The prices of all goods and services are expressed in terms of the unit of account, so that the relative prices of goods can easily be calculated. Without a unit of account one would have to know a number of exchange ratios in order to calculate any one relative price. For example to calculate the price of good *A* relative to good *C* one might have the following information:

2 units of good *A* trade for 3 units of good *B*
1 unit of good *B* trades for 6 units of good *C*
therefore 1 unit of good *A* trades for 9 units of good *C*.

Thus the relative price of *A* to *C* is one:nine. If one knows that the price of *A* is £9 and that of *C* £1, the calculation is direct.

Imagine that each household receives its income as a book-entry credit. Instantaneously upon receiving income it registers on the debit side of the account book its consumption demands for the period and immediately obtains the required goods and services. At no point in time is the book entry either positive or negative. Thus no money, even of the book-entry type such as bank deposits, is actually held, though it serves as a unit of account.

6.2   THE TRANSACTIONS DEMAND FOR MONEY IN THE ABSENCE OF UNCERTAINTY

It is the perfect synchronisation of receipts of income with the financing of expenditure that accounts for there being no need to hold money. Once the timing of income and expenditure is no longer coincident, money is held in order to bridge the gap. A typical household receives income in the form of money at regular, discrete intervals of time and makes payments throughout the income period. To abstract from uncertainty we assume the exact timing of payments and receipts is known. In any sub-period such as a day, the household is holding a stock of money which serves as a temporary abode of purchasing power. At the beginning of the income period the stock of money balances equals the period's income and dwindles to nothing by the next pay-day.

The quantity of money an individual is said to demand is the average money balance held throughout the income period. This is an average of the amount held on each day. If a household as depicted in Figure 6.1.a spends most of its income at the beginning of the period it will have a lower average cash balance than the household who spends a small proportion of its income at the beginning, doing the bulk of its spending towards the end of the period. If the household spends exactly $1/t$ of its income each day, when there are t days in the period, it will hold an average money balance equal to half the period's income (see Figure 6.1.b).

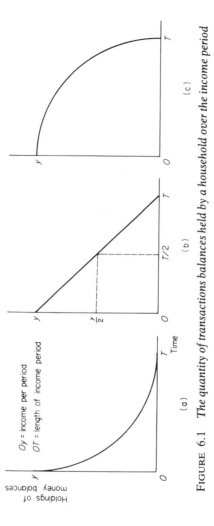

FIGURE 6.1 *The quantity of transactions balances held by a household over the income period*

If there exists an asset other than money, which earns a higher pecuniary rate of return than money, households will forgo that rate of return if they hold their temporary reserve of purchasing power in the form of money. For simplicity we assume that there are two assets, money which has no rate of interest paid on it, and bonds which have a rate of return which is known with certainty. If there are no transactions costs involved in the buying and selling of bonds, no rational household or firm would hold money. The money received at the beginning of the income period would be put into bonds straight away. As the household or firm needs money to finance expenditure it would sell bonds and immediately purchase goods and services. Therefore in the absence of uncertainty and given the existence of bonds, the holding of money is explained by the transactions costs of moving from money into bonds and vice versa. These transactions costs include the brokerage fees paid when assets are bought and sold, telephone and other communication costs, the wages firms pay to employees administering their liquid assets and the time spent by private individuals in trying to economise on their money balances. A rational household or firm will hold the average money balance that makes the marginal asset transactions cost equal to the interest received from the marginal bond holding.

Money held by firms is analogous to any other type of working capital. The holding of an inventory of money balances reduces costs, but also ties up capital that could alternatively be invested at the market rate of interest. This concept can be extended to the demand for money balances by households. Such an inventory theoretic approach to the demand for money was developed separately by Tobin [2] and Baumol [3].

It is assumed that the household's expenditure plans are known exactly and that payments by the household are made evenly throughout the income period. This means that the average holding of assets for transactions purposes is half the period's income. If the household or firm receive an income of y for the period of t days, it will engage in two asset transactions if it uses part of its income to buy bonds and some days later sells them to finance the rest of the period's expenditure. Holding one pound in bonds for the entire period would earn a rate of return of i. Thus if one pound is held in bonds for a fraction x of the period the return is $£(1/x)i$. The individual will maximise his return by buying bonds at the start of the income period and holding them until he runs out of money and has to sell more bonds to finance further expenditure.

If the individual plans to make only two asset transactions, he will obtain the maximum revenue by putting half his income into bonds and holding these until he has run out of money half way through the income period. The bonds are thus sold to provide money to finance the second half of the period's transactions. From Figure 6.2.a we can see that the

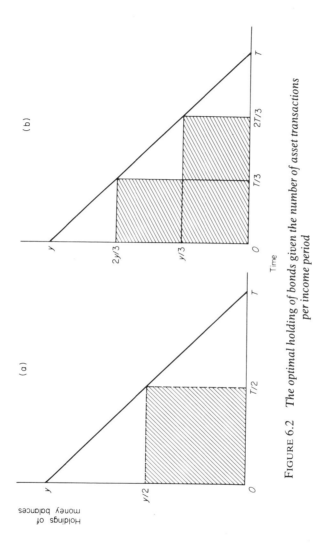

FIGURE 6.2 *The optimal holding of bonds given the number of asset transactions per income period*

shaded rectangle is the largest that can be drawn within the triangle OyT. The revenue from holding bonds equals $(1/2)yi/2$.

If three asset transactions are planned, the maximum revenue would be obtained by putting two-thirds of the period's income into bonds at the start, selling half of that one-third of the way through the period and selling the rest two-thirds of the way through the period. This sequence is illustrated in Figure 6.2.b. In general if n asset transactions are planned $[(n-1)/n]y$ should be placed in bonds at the start of the period and sold off $n-1$ times in equal blocks of y/n at equidistant intervals.

Since payments are made out evenly throughout the period, the average bond holding is $[(n-1)/(2n)]y$. Thus, the revenue from bond holding, R, is $[(n-1)/2n]yi$.

We assume each asset transactions has a fixed cost equal to a. This makes the total transactions costs for the period equal to na. The decision unit aims to maximise the net revenue from bond holding which is NR, given by equation (6.1). We therefore differentiate equation (6.1) with respect to the number of transactions n, to obtain the optimal number of such asset transactions:

$$NR = \frac{n-1}{2n}\, yi - na \tag{6.1}$$

$$\frac{\mathrm{d}NR}{\mathrm{d}n} = \frac{yi}{2n^2} - a = 0 \tag{6.2}$$

$$n^* = \left(\frac{yi}{2a}\right)^{1/2} = \text{optimal number of bond transactions.} \tag{6.3}$$

The marginal revenue from bond holding is $(yi)/(2n^2)$ and is positive but declines with the number of transactions:

$$\frac{\mathrm{d}}{\mathrm{d}n}\left(\frac{yi}{2n^2}\right) = -\frac{yi}{n^3}. \tag{6.4}$$

The solution to equation (6.3) is illustrated by Figure 6.3, which shows n^* as the number of asset transactions that equates the marginal revenue and marginal cost of bond holding. It should be noted that n^* is restricted to being an integer. If it worked out as a number such as 3·5 only three transactions would be made.

From equation (6.3) we see that as the rate of interest rises or transactions costs decrease, the number of asset transactions increases; that is, the demand for money at a given level of income is reduced. The number of asset transactions will also vary with the level of income, although it will rise in discrete jumps as n^* must be an integer. This formulation suggests that the demand for money rises less than proportionately with income, as there are economies of scale associated with

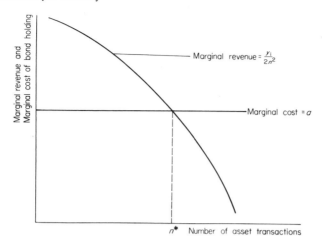

FIGURE 6.3   *The optimal number of asset transactions*

holding money balances. This is consistent with the conclusion that at low levels of income, particularly when variable transactions costs[†] are taken into account, n^* is less than two and it is not worth while to hold bonds at all.

The average cash balance will depend also on various institutional factors which affect the timing of receipts and disbursements of money as well as the costs of making transactions. The lengthening of the interval between the receipts of income will increase the average cash balance held, although annual income has remained unchanged. The vertical integration of industry, whereby several stages of production are conducted by one firm, reduces the volume of market transactions and hence the demand for money balances. Innovations in the payments mechanism, such as the payment by banks of annual bills on a monthly basis, and the extension of trade credit, reduce transactions costs. Since a given level of transactions can be financed at the same level of costs by

---

[†] Variable transactions costs depend directly on the value of bonds bought and sold. If this cost is equal to b, each pound's worth of bond holding will involve a cost of $2b$, as each bond is both bought and sold. This means that it is only worth buying a bond if it is held long enough for the interest earnings to exceed $2b$. The holding period, x, must be such that $i/x \geq 2b$, or $x \geq i/2b$. The effect of such a variable cost is to increase the amount of cash held in the first sub-period of the income period if $1/n < i/2b$. Since the size of n^* depends on the value of income it will not be worth while at low income levels to engage in any asset transactions.

a smaller quantity of money, such innovations reduce the demand for money.*

6.3   THE DEMAND FOR MONEY GIVEN UNCERTAINTY AND NO TRANSACTIONS COSTS

We will now remove the assumption that the decision-unit spends all of its current income in the current period. This means that assets are held over for more than one time period. As discussed in Chapter 3, a household's consumption plans can be thought of as extending over its lifetime and to be constrained by the household's wealth. This is the present value of future expected income from human and non-human sources plus money balances held. Such consumption plans will involve saving in some years and dissaving in others.

A household stores up its claim to future consumption in various types of assets. The only asset which can directly produce future goods and services is real capital. In a capitalist economy households can own indirect, marketable claims to real capital in the form of equity and bonds. As discussed in Chapter 5, the process of financial intermediation brings about a whole range of secondary assets which are claims upon the financial intermediaries, who themselves own primary paper claims to real capital.

The portfolio decision of the household concerns the allocation of its non-human wealth amongst the various types of assets, including

---

* In Tobin's model the timing of expenditure is an exogenous variable and assumed for ease of computation to be spread evenly throughout the period. The inventory choice model can be extended to analyse people's choice of the timing of their expenditures. In our one-period analysis a household is at any moment of time holding an inventory of bonds, money and commodities. If the household holds a large stock of commodities it avoids the costs of frequent shopping trips. This has to be compared to the costs of holding commodities. These include storage, depreciation and forgone interest costs on the capital locked up in commodity inventories.

If there were no costs involved in exchanging bonds for money the household would select that inventory of commodities for which the marginal saving in shopping costs minus marginal storage and depreciation costs per period equalised the rate of interest per period on bonds. If this stock requires replacing x times in the course of an income period, the household would make $x - 1$ bond sales and would only hold money during the time interval between bond sales and commodity purchases. We now consider the cost of exchanging money for bonds which is sufficiently large to make $x - 1$ bond sales cost more than the interest rate earned on the average bond holding. Money balances will now be held between shopping trips. In such circumstances the timing of expenditure, as well as the average cash balance held, are simultaneously determined by comparing at the margin the transactions costs saved by holding inventories of commodities and money with the costs that are involved.

money. We initially simplify the analysis by assuming that there are two types of financial assets, non-interest-bearing money and default-free bonds. The future interest rate on bonds is not known with certainty. Therefore a wealth owner may make a capital gain or loss by holding bonds, depending upon whether the interest rate falls or rises respectively. If the individual knows definitely that he wants to make a purchase of £x in three years' time and can buy bonds which mature three years hence at a terminal value of £x, there would be no risk involved in bond holding as the future sum of money is certain.

Holding bonds is risky when the holder is uncertain when he wants to undertake future consumption. Money is riskless in the sense that it is perfectly liquid because its price in terms of nominal money units does not change. If the price level changes the value of money (and of bonds) will alter in real terms. So long as any change in the price level is thought to be fully anticipated, the real value of money in the future is known with certainty. For the time being we will assume that the price level is not expected to change, so that money is expected with certainty to maintain its real value.

Uncertainty

To describe a variable as being uncertain or random means that its value is not definitely known. Such a variable may be assigned a probability distribution by which each value that the variable may take on is given a probability such that the sum of all the probabilities is one. A variable may be assigned an objective probability function if one has observed the past frequency with which various values of the variable have occurred. Alternatively the random variable can be assigned subjective probabilities, based on the decision-maker's own view as to the likelihood of the various values occurring in the future. A risky situation is one for which a probability distribution can be assigned. If no probabilities can be assigned conditions are said to be those of complete uncertainty.*

Keynes's Analysis of the Demand for Money

Keynes† attributed the asset demand for money to the absence of any risk in holding money. He assumed a two-asset world of money and perpetual bonds, in which the price level is not expected to change. Each wealth owner has his own idea of what the future interest rate will be, to

---

* Uncertainty is also a general term used to cover both risky and uncertain situations.
† *The General Theory*, Ch. 13.

which he attaches a probability of one. To examine Keynes's analysis we use the following definitions:

R_t = the expected rate of return per period of time on holding a bond with a fixed income per period of i_t.

i_t = the interest rate on a bond costing £1 at the beginning of the holding period. It is the nominally fixed income on a bond expressed as the percentage of a pound.

P^e_{t+1} = the expected price of the bond at the end of the holding period.

i^e_{t+1} = the yield or interest rate on bonds expected to rule at the end of the holding period ($i^e_{t+1} = i_t/P^e_{t+1}$).

g_t = the capital gain or loss expected per pound invested in bonds over the holding period.

$$g_t = \frac{P^e_{t+1} - P_t}{P_t} = \frac{i_t}{i^e_{t+1}} - 1 \tag{6.5}$$

$$R_t = i_t + g_t = i_t + \frac{i_t}{i^e_{t+1}} - 1. \tag{6.6}$$

From equation (6.6) we see that the expected return on holding a bond yielding a nominal income of i_t per period is the current rate of interest plus the capital gain or loss. When the capital loss, $-g_t$, equals the current rate of interest, this rate is called the critical rate of interest and is given the symbol i^c_t.

$$i^c_t = -g_t = -\frac{i^c_t}{i^e_{t+1}} + 1 \tag{6.7}$$

$$i^c_t = \frac{i^e_{t+1}}{1 + i^e_{t+1}}. \tag{6.8}$$

If the current rate of interest exceeds the critical rate, the expected return on bonds is positive and the individual will hold his entire portfolio in bonds. Conversely, if the current rate lies below the critical rate, the expected return from bond holding is negative and the wealth holder will only hold money in his portfolio. He will be completely indifferent between holding money and bonds if the current and critical rates of interest are equal.

With a given level of wealth the individual's demand for money function with respect to the rate of interest is discontinuous, since at rates above i^c_t he demands no money and at rates below i^c_t he wishes to hold all his financial wealth in money.

Keynes obtained a continuous aggregate demand for money function by assuming that each wealth owner has a different expected interest rate and hence a different critical rate. Thus, as the interest rate falls, a greater number of financial investors find that their critical rate is above the current rate of interest and consequently wish to hold money.

Keynes based the expected rate of interest on its past and current values. He envisaged each financial investor conceiving of a normal rate of interest determined by his past experience of market interest rates. Expectations about next period's interest rate are formed by assuming that the current rate will move towards the normal rate. Ideas about the normal rate are only revised slowly. Expectations are assumed to be inelastic. If the current rate falls the normal rate and hence the expected rate fall by a smaller proportion. Keynes blamed financial investors' inelastic expectations, which were influenced by the higher interest rate of the 1920s, for keeping the interest rate above its equilibrium level.

The rate of interest may fluctuate for decades about a level which is chronically too high for full employment: particularly if it is the prevailing opinion that the rate of interest is self-adjusting, so that the level established by convention is thought to be rooted in objective grounds much stronger than convention, the failure of employment to attain an optimum level being in no way associated in the minds of either the public or of the authority, with the prevalence of an inappropriate range of rates of interest.*

Keynes's approach to the demand for money emphasises the role of expectations. If these fluctuate, as Keynes supposed, the demand for money function is not a stable function of its determinants, wealth, income and the interest rate. Knowledge of the values of these determinants will not enable one to predict the demand for money if it is also highly dependent on unknown changes in expectations.

Keynes's concern with the effect of expectations in preventing the rate of interest from falling in the short run to a sufficiently low level to bring about the full-employment level of investment was interpreted by Keynesian economists in static terms.† If the current rate of interest has fallen to such a low level that it equals the critical rate for a large number of financial investors they become indifferent between holding bonds and money, since both assets have a zero expected return. The aggregate demand for money function would then be perfectly elastic with respect to the rate of interest. This section of the money demand function is known as the 'liquidity trap'. It is a theoretical possibility, there being no empirical evidence of its having existed even in the 1930s.

Keynes ascribed the interest determined demand for money to the speculative motive. Financial investors act as speculators since they think that they know better than others which way the interest rate will move. A speculator who thinks the rate of interest will rise would sell bonds and hold money in the anticipation of moving back into bonds when their price has fallen. He thus holds money in the anticipation of making a capital gain by doing so.

* *The General Theory*, p. 204. † See Ch. 7.

This theory does not explain why speculators hold money if there are other short-term assets, such as building society shares, which have a certain nominal capital value but earn a higher rate of interest than money. The speculative motive would then explain the holding of such assets but not of money.

The speculative motive for holding short-term assets is a very specialised one and is not an apt description of the reasons that lead the vast majority of people to hold short-term assets. It is unfortunate that this term has come to be so widely used in textbooks as a synonym for the general asset demand to hold money. (It is not used in this way in this text.) As discussed below, the asset demand for money can be ascribed more readily to the desire to hold a low risk asset, or to the precautionary motive.

A further drawback to Keynes's theory is that it does not explain the holding of a diversified portfolio, which is one containing a variety of different assets. Portfolio diversification can be explained by the precautionary motive.

The Portfolio Theory of Asset Holding*

Holding a number of different assets reduces the overall risk of a portfolio by the well-known principle of not putting all one's eggs into the same basket. An asset is risky when one is not sure what its future value will be. In Keynes's formulation of asset choice each wealth owner is only concerned with the expected return from his portfolio. By assuming that each wealth owner attaches a probability of one to his anticipation of the future interest rate, Keynes avoids any formal consideration of risk.

An asset is generally thought to be riskier the greater the likelihood of its actual return diverging from its expected return. Asset A, which has an expected return of 10 per cent that may turn out to be anywhere between −10 per cent and +20 per cent, is riskier than asset B with an expected return of 5 per cent, which may lie between −1 per cent and +11 per cent. So long as the returns of assets A and B are not perfectly and positively correlated (that is, they do not move directly together so that when the rate of return on A is 20 per cent, that on B is 11 per cent, or when the rate of return on A is −10 per cent that on B is −1 per cent) a financial investor can reduce the overall risk of his portfolio by holding both assets. If events turn out badly for asset A, so that its actual return is below its expected return, this is partially offset by the return obtained from asset B.

Thus a wealth owner will have less risk if he holds both assets A and B than if he holds only one of these assets. The higher the amount of asset A held the greater will be the expected return, but the overall risk of the

* For a simple but useful account of this topic see [4].

portfolio will be larger. A risk averter is a person who will only accept additional risk if compensated by a higher expected rate of return and therefore has a trade-off between expected return and risk. The theory of portfolio balance deduces that a risk-averting owner of wealth will hold that combination of assets which gives him his preferred combination of expected return and risk.

The rationale for the demand for money as an asset because of its role in reducing the riskiness of a general portfolio of assets was developed by Tobin [5]. In a simplified version of his model there are two assets, money which is riskless as it has a zero certain return, and a risky asset, perpetual bonds, which has a positive expected rate of return. By holding money in his portfolio, the wealth holder can reduce his portfolio risk but at the expense of sacrificing some expected return.

Each financial investor has a probability distribution assigned to the next period's rate of interest. The mean of this probability distribution, which is the same concept as the expected value of the future rate of interest, is the current interest rate. In other words the individual thinks that a rise or fall in the rate of interest is equally likely. This means that the expected capital gain or loss of holding a bond is zero, thus the expected rate of return is identical to the current interest rate. (Assuming a non-zero expected capital gain or loss complicates the computation but makes no essential difference to the argument.)

The risk of holding a bond is measured by the dispersion of the possible future interest rate about the expected future interest rate. This measure is the standard deviation of the probability distribution defined over the future interest rate.

The larger the standard deviation the greater is the risk of bond holding. As shown in Figure 6.4, probability distribution (b) has a greater dispersion about the mean than probability distribution (a) and thus indicates that greater risk is attached to bond holding (b).*

The following symbols are used:

R = the return per £1 held in the entire portfolio of assets over the holding period.

---

* Readers who have done elementary statistics will recognise the expected value of a variable x, $E(x)$ as the mean of its frequency distribution, which tells us the value x_i of x is observed f_i times. (f_i is the probability of x_i occurring if we talk in terms of a discrete probability distribution.) If we have a frequency function for x where x_i occurs with a frequency of f_i, then the mean or expected value is

$$E(x) = \frac{1}{n} \sum_{i}^{n} x_i f_i$$

and the standard deviation is

$$\sigma_x = \left\{ \frac{1}{n} \sum_{i=1}^{n} (x_i - E(x))^2 f_i \right\}^{1/2}.$$

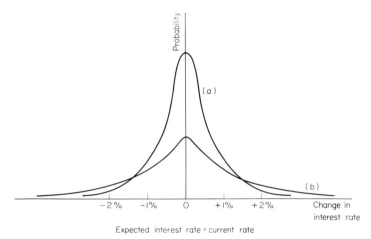

FIGURE 6.4   *The risk of an asset or portfolio of assets depends on the standard deviation of its rate of return*

A_2 = the proportion of the portfolio held in bonds.
A_1 = the proportion of the portfolio held in money.
i = the current rate interest on a bond for the holding period.
g = the capital gain or loss on a bond over the holding period.
μ_R = the expected return on £1 held in the portfolio.
σ_g = the standard deviation of the probability distribution defined over future values of the interest rate. It is the measure of the risk of holding £1 in the bond.
σ_R = the standard deviation of the return on the whole portfolio. It is the measure of the risk of holding £1 in the portfolio.

It is assumed that the portfolio is held for one period and is then reviewed. The wealth holder is therefore concerned with the expected return and risk on each pound invested in the portfolio for one period of time. The expected return, μ_R, on each pound invested in the portfolio is the expected return on a pound held in a bond times the proportion of the portfolio held in bonds and is given by equation (6.9).

$$\mu_R = A_2 i. \tag{6.9}$$

Since the expected capital gain from holding a bond is zero, the rate of interest, i, is the expected rate of return of a pound invested in a bond. The expected return on holding money is zero and therefore does not enter the calculation. The risk of one pound held in the portfolio is the risk of holding one pound in a bond, weighted by the proportion of the portfolio held in bonds, i.e.

$$\sigma_R = A_2 \sigma_g \qquad (6.10)$$

$$A_2 = \sigma_R / \sigma_g. \qquad (6.11)$$

Substituting equation (6.11) into equation (6.9) we obtain equation (6.12), which gives the market trade-off between expected return and risk available to the wealth owner by having different proportions of money and bonds in his portfolio such that

$$\mu_R = (i/\sigma_g)\sigma_R. \qquad (6.12)$$

This is the equation of the opportunity locus *OC* shown in Figure 6.5. The slope of *OC* is given by i/σ_g, so that if either the interest rate or risk changes the market trade-off between expected return and risk will also alter.

The combinations of expected return and risk that the wealth owner will choose depends on his preferences. The individual's utility function is assumed to depend on the expected return and risk of his portfolio.* A risk averter will have the shape of indifference curve depicted in Figure 6.5 since he requires additional expected return to compensate for taking on extra risk. From Figure 6.5 we can see the highest level of utility attainable given the market opportunity locus *OC*. The individual will maximise his utility by choosing a portfolio which has an expected return of μ_{R_1} associated with a risk of σ_{R_1}.

We now need to determine what mix of money and bonds will give an expected return of μ_{R_1} and an associated risk of σ_{R_1}. The bond risk per pound is σ_g and the desired amount of portfolio risk per pound is σ_{R_1}. Equation (6.11) gives the means to work out that proportion of bonds in the portfolio, A_2^1, which will be held in an optimal portfolio since $A_2 = \sigma_R / \sigma_g$. This solution is shown in the lower half of Figure 6.5. Equation (6.11) gives the slope of line *OB* which is $A_2/\sigma_R = 1/\sigma_g$ and thus depends only on bond riskiness. Since we know σ_R and σ_g we can work out A_2. If the desired portfolio risk is σ_{R_1}, we obtain the proportion of the portfolio held in bonds by drawing a perpendicular line to cut *OB* at *D* and then extending a horizontal line from *D* to A_2^1. Correspondingly A_1^1 is held in money.

---

* By postulating that utility depends on portfolio return, $U = f(R)$, and by assuming the probability distribution of portfolio return is normally distributed, one can obtain an expected utility function which is a function only of the expected return and the standard deviation of return. These two parameters completely specify any normal probability distribution. (Expected utility is obtained from the usual utility function by weighting the utility of each possible return by its probability.) We obtain the indifference curves in Figure 6.5 from this expected utility function. For further reference to this problem see [5].

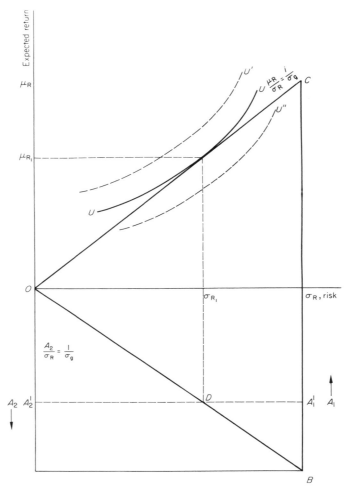

FIGURE 6.5   *To show the optimal combination of portfolio expected return and risk and the resulting apportionment of the portfolio between bonds and money*

The Effect of a Change in the Interest Rate

If the interest rate rises a greater expected return can be obtained from the same degree of portfolio risk (that is σ_g remains unchanged). Thus the *OC* locus swivels to the left. There is no unambiguous effect on the demand for money. It may rise or fall depending on the individual's preferences as in Figure 6.6.

An increase in the rate of interest makes bonds relatively more

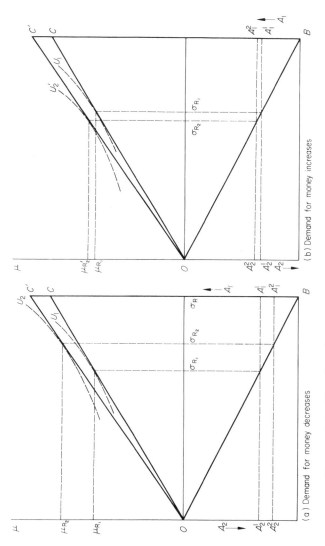

FIGURE 6.6 *The effect of an increase in the rate of interest on the demand for money*

attractive. This substitution effect causes an increase in the demand to hold bonds. On the other hand there is also an income effect in that the return from a pound invested in bonds has increased. The wealth holder may choose to take this additional utility in the form of lower risk since he now has the opportunity of the same expected return combined with lower portfolio risk. If the individual chooses to have less portfolio risk his holdings of money will increase as the result of an increase in the rate of interest. So long as the substitution effect outweighs any negative income effect on the demand to hold bonds, the demand for money will decrease when the interest rate rises. As long as the majority of wealth owners behave in this way the aggregate demand for money will be inversely related to the rate of interest.*

Tobin's analysis can be extended to the selection of a large number of risky assets. Wealth owners first decide in which proportions the risky assets should be held. Each wealth owner then decides what proportion of his portfolio to hold in money, the remaining fraction being held in the optimal combination of risky assets.

The above analysis rationalises the demand to hold money in a world in which money is the only riskless asset and there are no transactions costs involved in buying and selling the risky assets. There exist short-term assets, such as Trustee Savings Bank deposits and building society accounts, which share with money the characteristic of having a nominally fixed capital value but earn a rate of interest. If owners of such assets are certain of being able to withdraw from the financial intermediaries the amount of money that they deposited and there are no transactions costs involved in holding such assets, there is no rational motive for holding currency and bank deposits. (In this event other riskless assets would completely replace currency and bank deposits as money.)

6.4   THE PRECAUTIONARY MOTIVE

It is therefore apparent that uncertainty by itself is insufficient to explain the holding of currency and bank deposits when other riskless assets are available. The demand to hold money is ultimately attributable to

---

* This analysis assumes that the individual starts the period with a constant value of wealth which he has to allocate between money and bonds. Therefore a change in the interest rate has no effect on the amount of wealth the individual starts out with. If we considered people already holding their wealth in bonds, the present value or price of their bonds would move in the opposite direction to any change in the interest rate. We have that the wealth in bonds equals B/i, where B is the number of perpetual one pound nominal income claims owned. Thus a rise in the interest rate would reduce bond holders' wealth and cause a reduction in the demand for money. This effect would reinforce the substitution effect of an increase in the rate of interest.

money's function as a medium of exchange. This characteristic is possessed by those commodities which minimise the transactions costs of financing expenditures.

It is observed that people do hold money balances in excess of those needed to finance current transactions within the income period. This behaviour can be attributed to uncertainty about the timing of future expenditure and about the capital value of marketable assets, combined with the transactions costs involved in moving out of money into other assets and back again when consumption has to be financed.

If a household were certain about the timing of its future flow of expenditure, it could buy bonds the maturity of which was timed to coincide with future consumption expenditure. Thus, capital uncertainty in nominal terms would be avoided while a higher rate of return would be obtained than if money were held. This rate of return would have to exceed the transactions costs of moving in and out of bonds to make such bond holding an attractive proposition. Uncertainty about the timing of future expenditures, combined with no fear of capital loss from bond holding, would also result in no rational person holding money as an asset unless this was warranted by the saving in asset transactions costs. The combined uncertainty about the future capital value of marketable assets and the timing of future expenditure explains the holding of lower return financial assets which have nominally fixed capital values. Only fear of default by financial intermediaries and the transactions costs of moving from money into close money substitutes, which are not themselves generally acceptable as a medium of exchange, explain the holding of money by a rational person.

The desire to hold money or near-money substitutes in asset port-folios in order to reduce risk is known as the precautionary motive. It is this motive that underlies the demand to hold money in Tobin's portfolio approach. The precautionary motive explains liquidity preference, which is the willingness of people to hold assets which are more liquid at a lower rate of return than that obtainable on less liquid assets.

6.5   THE EFFECT OF INFLATION
       ON THE DEMAND FOR ASSETS*

The analysis so far has not dealt with changes in the general price level. Real assets, including equities, have their income denominated in real terms. As the general level of prices rises so do the prices of houses, pictures and capital goods used in production. Since the nominal value of dividends rises with secular increases in the price level, shares are claims to uncertain real-income streams.

Other types of financial assets have their income, price, or both, fixed in

* See [6, 7, 8].

nominal terms. The income yielded by all types of fixed-interest securities, such as bonds, bills of exchange, building-society shares, is fixed in money terms. The market price or capital value of marketable assets is variable, whereas the capital value of non-marketable assets, such as premium bonds, building-society shares or money is fixed in nominal terms. Variations in the price level cause movements in the opposite direction in the real value of a given nominal return from a nominally fixed asset.

If lenders consider equities and bonds to be equally risky, then in a world with a constant expected general price level market forces will equalise the rates of return on both assets.* The rate of return on equities is then the real rate of return on capital, which for capital market equilibrium must equal the rate of interest on bonds.

If instead of expecting the price level to remain stable, asset holders anticipate a positive rate of inflation, then the real rate of return on bonds will be the market rate of interest on bonds minus the expected rate of inflation. For example, if the market rate of interest on bonds is 7 per cent and the anticipated rate of inflation is 3 per cent, the real rate of return from holding bonds is 4 per cent. If the real rate of return on capital is 7 per cent no asset holder will wish to hold bonds and will hold equity instead. This means that the price of bonds will fall until bonds offer a money or nominal interest rate of 10 per cent, making the real rate of return on bonds equal to 7 per cent. We thus obtain in equilibrium, when full adjustments have been made for expected inflation, that†

$$r = i + \left[\frac{dP}{dt} \frac{1}{P} \right]^e \qquad (6.13)$$

where r is the nominal rate of interest, i is the real rate of interest, and $\{(dP/dt)(1/P)\}^e$ is the expected rate of inflation.

Thus, the real rate of return on assets with a nominally fixed income can be kept independent of the rate of inflation by market adjustments which reduce bond prices and thus raise the nominal interest rate to account for expected inflation.

If money pays no rate of interest, the opportunity cost of holding money is the rate of return forgone by not holding alternative assets such as bonds or real capital. In a period of stable prices this opportunity cost is the real rate of interest. If inflation is expected there will be an additional element in the anticipated opportunity cost of holding money. This is the

* If equities are considered more risky, there will be a risk premium established so that the equity rate of return exceeds the bond yield. This in no way alters the analysis with respect to inflation.

† There is an additional term on the right-hand side of the equation which is $i(dP/dtP)^e$. This term decreases as the discounting period diminishes and tends to zero when discounting becomes continuous.

loss in the real value of money due to the expected increase in the price level. Thus *the opportunity cost of holding money consists of the real rate of interest forgone plus the expected loss in the purchasing power of money due to the rate of inflation.* This opportunity cost equals the nominal rate of interest. Of course in the case of expected deflation, the nominal rate of interest will lie below the real rate of interest since nominally fixed assets enjoy an increase in their real value.

6.6 THE DEMAND FOR MONEY AS PART OF CAPITAL THEORY

Money competes for a place in the portfolios of firms and households with all other assets. Thus the demand for money is determined by the attractiveness of holding money relative to that of other assets. Money balances can be thought of as giving their holders utility and hence entering as an argument in the utility function. This utility stems from the convenience of holding money to finance transactions and from the reduction in portfolio risk. Assuming that the marginal utility of money declines with the quantity of money balances held, one deduces that a utility-maximising economic unit will hold that quantity of money which equates the marginal utility of money balances to the marginal utility forgone by not holding some alternative asset. This way of analysing money considers money to be analogous to a consumer durable good.

An alternative approach is to regard money balances as leading to a saving on transactions costs by providing convenience and liquidity. We then analyse money as a producer good, that is as an input into the process by which goods and services are produced. Money is then analogous to working capital. Each household or firm uses money in such a way as to minimise costs. The optimal amount of money to hold is the quantity for which the marginal saving in transactions costs equals the expected rate of return forgone by not holding some alternative asset.*

Viewing money as either a consumer's good or as a producer's good, we can obtain a general form of the demand for money function. This approach subsumes both the transactions and the asset demands for money discussed earlier. In this the demand for real money balances depends on the level of real income, the real interest rates obtainable on other assets and the expected rate of change of the price level.

We can thus write the demand for real money balances as

$$\left(\frac{M}{P}\right)^{\mathrm{d}} = v\left[y, i^{\mathrm{B}}, i^{\mathrm{E}}, \left(\frac{\mathrm{d}P}{\mathrm{d}t}\frac{1}{P}\right)^{\mathrm{e}}\right] \qquad (6.14)\dagger$$

* For a representative treatment of this approach see [9].
† For a fuller discussion of this formulation of the demand for money function see [10].

where i^B and i^E are the real rates of interest on bonds and equities respectively.

Equation (6.14) can be expressed alternatively as the demand for nominal money balances. In this case the nominal value of national income is a determinant of the volume of nominal money balances demanded. The price level will also enter as an argument in this form of the demand for money function since the volume of services provided by one pound depends on the purchasing power of a nominal unit of money. The demand for nominal money balances is therefore

$$M^d = v\left[Y, P, i^B, i^E, \left(\frac{dP}{dt}\frac{1}{P}\right)^e \right]. \tag{6.15}$$

Velocity

The ratio of the nominal value of income to the nominal money stock is known as the income velocity of the circulation of money. (It is the same as the ratio of real income to the stock of real money balances.) Thus

$$V = Y/M. \tag{6.16}$$

Velocity generally lies between two and three in the United Kingdom. If velocity equals three this means that the stock of money required to finance all the transactions that are incurred in producing and distributing the annual national product is one-third of the value of national income. The money stock is a fraction of the value of national income because a unit of money passes from person to person several times in the course of a year and can therefore finance several income generating transactions.

The velocity of circulation can be derived from the demand to hold money. The higher is velocity the more rapidly are people passing on money. Therefore the lower is the average stock of money balances, relative to income, which households and firms wish to hold. We need to distinguish the actual velocity of circulation, which is an *ex post* concept, from the *ex ante*, desired velocity. Actual velocity is the ratio of income to the money stock in existence (equation (6.16b)). It can readily be calculated from income and money supply data. The desired velocity of circulation is the ratio of income to the money stock that people wish to keep (equation (6.16a)). It is determined by the values of the arguments in the demand for money function.

The desired velocity can be derived from equation (6.15). It is necessary to assume that the demand for money is a demand couched in real terms. If nominal income and the price level rise by the same proportion, the other variables remaining constant, the demand for nominal money balances rises by the same proportion. This means that the ratio between real income and real money balances stays the same.* Therefore we can

* The technical expression for this is that the demand for real money balances is assumed to be homogeneous of degree zero in money income and prices (i.e. the nominal demand for money is homogeneous of degree one). See Chapter 2, p. 36.

divide all the nominal variables in equation (6.15) by nominal income and leave the form of the relationship unchanged:

$$\frac{M^{d}}{Y} = \frac{1}{V^{d}} = v\left[1, \frac{P}{Y}, i^{B}, i^{E}, \left(\frac{dP}{dt}\frac{1}{P}\right)^{e}\right] \qquad (6.17)$$

$$V^{d} = \phi\left[y, i^{B}, i^{E}, \left(\frac{dP}{dt}\frac{1}{P}\right)^{e}\right]. \qquad (6.18)$$

Equation (6.18) states that desired velocity depends on real income, real interest rates and the expected rate of price change. Since

$$V^{d} = Y/M^{d} \qquad (6.16a)$$

and

$$V^{a} = Y/M^{s} \qquad (6.16b)$$

therefore desired velocity, V^{d}, and actual velocity, V^{a}, are only equal in monetary equilibrium when the demand and supply of money are equal. If actual velocity is less than desired velocity, people must be holding more money than they wish to. They will rectify this disequilibrium by reducing their holdings of money. This involves attempting to exchange money for commodities and other financial assets and thus increasing velocity.

6.7   THE QUANTITY THEORY OF MONEY

If equation (6.16a) is rearranged it again becomes a demand for money equation:·

$$M^{d} = \frac{1}{V^{d}} Y = \frac{1}{V^{d}} yP. \qquad (6.19)$$

In this form it stresses the relationship between the demand for money and national income, suppressing the other determinants of the demand for money.

This type of money demand function is known as the quantity theory of money.* If V is treated as a constant and if real output is at full employment and hence fixed, we obtain the prediction that an increase in the money supply must lead to a proportionate increase in the price level.

---

* The quantity theory of money can be found in the writings of David Hume. It was developed in this century by Irving Fisher [11], who by concentrating on the institutional factors determining velocity, interpreted it as subject only to slow changes. Equation (6.16b), written as $MV = Py$, is known as the Fisher equation. Written as $M^{d} = Y/V = kY$ it is known as the Cambridge equation, which was developed by Marshall and Pigou for whom k depended on the interest rate. Keynes, by emphasising the rate of interest as a determinant of money demand, stressed the variability of velocity.

Interpreted this way the quantity theory of money is a long standing theory of inflation.

The Stability of Velocity

The modern restatement of the quantity theory by Friedman, which is a more complex version of equations (6.14) to (6.18), contains the same type of variables as a Keynesian formulation of the demand for money function. The difference revolves around the question of whether velocity is a stable or unstable function of its determinants. In Keynesian theory, asset-holder expectations are thought to be volatile, causing the demand for money schedule with respect to the level of interest rates to shift. Thus velocity cannot be predicted from a knowledge of the values of the arguments of equation (6.18). In contrast, the monetarist approach emphasises the stability of velocity and maintains that the demand for money can be predicted from the values of the arguments in equation (6.18).

The quantity theory, according to Friedman, is a theory of the demand to hold money. As such it does not differ in its specifications of variables from a Keynesian demand for money function. The quantity theory gains its distinctive characteristics when combined with other assumptions. The most important of these is that the money supply is an exogenous variable and not an endogenous variable which passively responds to changes in national income.

If a change in the money supply is exogenous, it will cause a discrepancy between the demand to hold money and the existing money stock. Thus an increase in the money supply causes portfolio imbalance. The marginal utility of a pound held in money balances falls below the marginal utility of a pound allocated to other uses, such as buying commodities or other financial assets (see [8]). People therefore adjust their portfolios by spending the excess money balances on goods and financial assets. In the quantity theory view such portfolio adjustment occurs over a wider range of variables and is much more diffuse than in Keynesian analysis, where it is restricted to financial markets.

Given that the money supply is exogenous, the quantity theory is interpreted by monetarists as a theory of the determination of the nominal value of national income. Rewriting equation (6.19) as

$$Y = V^d M^d \qquad (6.20)$$

and substituting into equation (6.20) the condition for monetary equilibrium,

$$M^d = M^s \qquad (6.21)$$

we obtain a relationship between nominal income and the stock of nominal money, i.e.

$$Y = V^d M^s. \qquad (6.22)$$

Looking at equation (6.22) we can see that *the vital link between nominal national income and the money stock is velocity.* If velocity is highly variable, then the link will break down and one will not be able to predict changes in nominal income that are caused by changes in the money stock. Monetarists therefore stress the stability of velocity, and the ability to predict it from a knowledge of the values of its determinants. If the level of interest rates changes when the money stock is altered, velocity also changes. One would therefore need to specify the structural relationships in the economy, particularly the demand for money function, in order to know how changes in the money supply affect velocity, and hence nominal income.

The monetarist approach is criticised for not specifying a determinate model, in which velocity is solved for. Instead monetarists rely on institutional and preference factors, which determine velocity, changing only slowly. Also they see the real interest component of the market rate of interest remaining fairly stable. On the basis of taking desired velocity to be relatively constant monetarists explain changes in nominal income as arising from changes in the money stock. Critics of this approach consider velocity to be subject to short-run fluctuations which make it impossible to accurately predict changes in nominal income arising from changes in the money stock.

All schools of thought agree that any increase in nominal income due to an increase in the nominal money stock is, in the short run, divided between a rise in real income and a rise in the price level. How the change in nominal income is divided between real and nominal changes is not yet satisfactorily explained and is the subject of current analytical work. In the long run real income is seen as determined by real forces, such as the productivity of factors of production, the rate of technical progress and the propensity to save. This means that in the long run, increases in the nominal money stock only cause increases in the price level without affecting real output. If additional nominal money balances are provided, each individual thinks he can obtain more goods and services, now or in the future, by spending his excess money balances on current consumption or the acquisition of financial assets. But it is impossible in aggregate for individuals to do this, if resources are already fully utilised so that no additional real output can be produced. The ensuing excess aggregate demand causes the price level to rise in the long run.

In the context of long-run growth the quantity theory of nominal income determination deduces the following. If the rate of growth of the nominal money supply exceeds the rate of growth of real national income, there will be a rate of inflation equal to the difference between the growth rate of the money supply and that of real income, given an income elasticity of the demand for money equal to one.*

6.8 EMPIRICAL WORK ON THE DEMAND FOR MONEY†

Theoretical work on the demand for money has given rise to a number of questions that have been subject to considerable empirical testing. These are as follows.

(1) Is the demand for money correctly specified in real terms? If it is, one would expect the nominal demand for money to rise with the price level in the long run.

(2) Is the demand for money better expressed as a function of income or of wealth? Transactions demand for money suggests income, whereas in the asset demand for money approach it is wealth that places a constraint upon the size of the individual's portfolio. Friedman uses permanent income in place of current income and wealth. This is consistent with a long-run equilibrium view of the demand for money which does not attempt to distinguish various motives for holding money. A household allocates its permanent income so that a pound spent on holding money balances yields the same marginal utility as a pound spent on consumption or on other financial assets (that is on future consumption).

(3) How responsive is the demand for money to interest rates, and what evidence is there of instability in the demand for money function?

(4) Is the narrow definition of money, which includes only currency and demand deposits, a better specification of what is money than a broader definition, inclusive of time deposits?

Specification of Regression Equations

The data available are on the quantity of money in existence and not on the quantity demanded. In the short run there is likely to have been insufficient time for people to adjust their actual money holdings to the desired level. This needs to be taken account of in econometric tests of the demand for money function. It is therefore necessary to distinguish the long-run equilibrium demand for money, which holds when the individual is fully adjusted to all past changes in the determinants of desired money holdings, from the short-run demand for money. In the short run the individual is not fully adjusted and is therefore not holding his

---

* If $y = y_0 e^{gt}$, $m = ky^b$, where g is the rate of growth of real output and b is the income elasticity of the demand for real balances, m, then the rate of growth of the demand for money is bg. The rate of inflation is the rate of growth of the nominal money supply minus bg.
† See [12] for a more extensive summary.

long-run equilibrium quantity of money balances. By fitting short-run demand for money functions one can attempt to measure these adjustment lags.

The standard model used to estimate the demand for money function is now presented. The long-run demand for real money balances $(M/P)^*$, is assumed linearly or log linearly related to its determinants, such as real permanent income and the rate of interest, i.e.

$$\left(\frac{M}{P}\right)^*_t = a_0 + a_1 y_{pt} + a_2 i_t. \tag{6.23}$$

Equation (6.23) and its variants, which include current income, wealth, long or short-rates of interest and which may be expressed in first differences, is the sole equation of many studies ([14, 15, 16, 17]).† Other studies have proceeded to specify a long-run adjustment of desired to actual money balances. The partial stock adjustment hypothesis has already been discussed in relation to investment. Equation (6.24) postulates that a fraction, θ, of the difference between the desired and actual stock of real money balances is adjusted in each period. A lower value of θ means a slower adjustment, i.e.

$$\left(\frac{M}{P}\right)_t - \left(\frac{M}{P}\right)_{t-1} = \theta\left[\left(\frac{M}{P}\right)^*_t - \left(\frac{M}{P}\right)_{t-1}\right] \tag{6.24}$$

where $(M/P)^*$ is the desired stock of real balances. Adding $(M/P)_{t-1}$ to both sides we obtain

$$\left(\frac{M}{P}\right)_t = \theta\left(\frac{M}{P}\right)^*_t + (1-\theta)\left(\frac{M}{P}\right)_{t-1}. \tag{6.24a}$$

Substituting equation (6.23) into equation (6.24a) we obtain

$$\left(\frac{M}{P}\right)_t = \theta a_0 + \theta a_1 y_{pt} + \theta a_2 i_t + (1-\theta)\left(\frac{M}{P}\right)_{t-1}. \tag{6.26}$$

The reduced form equation (6.26) can be written as

$$\left(\frac{M}{P}\right)_t = b_0 + b_1 y_{pt} + b_2 i_t + b_3 \left(\frac{M}{P}\right)_{t-1} \tag{6.26a}$$

where the bs are the coefficients which are estimated. The structural

---

† All single-equation studies are particularly prone to the identification problem. A money supply equation or some hybrid equation may be estimated rather than a demand function. Some two-equation studies have been done [23, 24]. As they have produced estimates of income and interest rate elasticities similar to those of single-equation studies, it is thought that the identification problem is not serious. See Laidler [12] p. 95.

coefficients can be calculated from the reduced form coefficients as follows:*

$$b_0 = \theta a_0, \qquad b_1 = \theta a_1, \qquad b_2 = \theta a_2, \qquad b_3 = 1 - \theta.$$

This type of model is used in studies [19, 20, 21, 22, 23].

Empirical Results

(1) The evidence supports the specification of the demand for money in real terms. Meltzer[14] obtained a proportional relationship between the price level and nominal money balances. The factor of proportionality tends to be less than one in some cases which use short-run time-series data [19, 25].

(2) Measures of non-human wealth and permanent income have performed better than measured income. As indicated in Table 6.1, the permanent income and wealth elasticities tend to be slightly above one. Chow obtains short-run measured income elasticities that over time tend towards the long-run permanent income elasticity of one. Friedman obtained a measure of $1 \cdot 8$ for income elasticity, and claims that there is a secular decline in velocity. As real income rises, the demand for money rises proportionately more, so that velocity falls. Laidler's studies[16, 17] of long-run annual data, which split the period into three sub-periods, show a decline over time in permanent income elasticity.

(3) The studies show conclusively that the demand for money is stable and inversely related to interest rate, there being no empirical support for the liquidity trap hypothesis. The narrow definition of money appears to be more interest elastic than the broad definition. This can be explained by the fact that interest rate changes, which will include changes in the time deposit rate, cause shifts between non-interest-bearing and interest-bearing money, which are not picked up by a regression of M_2 on interest rates. Studies in the United States show no clear grounds for preferring short- to long-term interest rates. Theorists who see money as a close substitute for near-monies would, *a priori*, expect short interest rates to perform better. Those who consider money as an asset for which all other assets are equally good substitutes, would not expect to find differences between the explanatory power of different interest rates [14, 27]. The elasticity of the long-term rate of interest is higher than that of the short-term. This is to be expected, given that the long-term interest rate fluctuates less than the short-term rate. From Table 6.1 we see that the

---

* If permanent income is used rather than current income, an expectations lag is introduced when, following Friedman, permanent income is measured as a distributed lag function of past measured income, $y_{pt} = \lambda \sum_{i=0}^{n} (1-\lambda)^i y_{t-1}$. There are then difficulties in distinguishing the stock adjustment lag from the expectations lag. See [12, 19, 22].

long-term interest rate elasticity tends to lie between -0.5 and -0.7, whereas the short-term interest rate elasticity is lower at around -0.15. Quarterly studies of U.K. data have found difficulty in obtaining a significant estimate of interest rate elasticity, particularly for the short-term rate.

Less work has been done on testing whether the expected rate of inflation is a determinant of the demand to hold money. It has appeared insignificant in a number of U.S. studies. This can be attributed to the inclusion in the regression equation of nominal interest rates, which incorporate the effects of anticipated inflation, and to the fact that the rate of inflation was low in the United States, except for the Korean war, until the late 1960s. Studies of the demand for money during hyperinflations [28] indicate that the expected rate of inflation is then a determinant of the demand to hold money.

(4) No conclusions have been reached as to whether M_1 or M_2 is a better specification of the money supply. It appears that the income elasticity of M_2 is greater than that of M_1. Laidler's work leads him to conclude that more stable demand functions can be estimated using M_2 as the dependent variable.

(5) The evidence regarding the lag in the adjustment of the demand for money in response to changes in its determinants is less conclusive. This is due to the estimation problems involved. Chow obtains estimates of θ in the 0.4 to 0.01 range. The higher estimate means that about 75 per cent of the adjustment of actual to desired money balances would have occurred after three quarters.* Hamburger [27] obtains an estimate of 75–90 per cent of the adjustment to a change in the bond rate occurring

---

* The adjustment in the first period is

$$M_t - M_{t-1} = \theta(M^* - M_{t-1}). \tag{6.24}$$

The adjustment in the second period is

$$M_{t+1} - M_t = \theta(M^* - M_t) \tag{6.24a}$$

now,

$$M_t = M_{t-1} + \theta(M^* - M_{t-1})$$

Therefore

$$M_{t+1} - M_t = \theta[M^* - (M_{t-1} + \theta(M^* - M_{t-1}))]$$
$$= \theta(1-\theta)[M^* - M_{t-1}].$$

The adjustment after two periods is

$$M_{t+1} - M_{t-1} = [\theta + \theta(1-\theta)](M^* - M_{t-1})$$

Therefore the adjustment after n periods is

$$\theta \sum_{i=0}^{n} (1-\theta)^i (M^* - M_0).$$

TABLE 6.1. Summary of Some Studies on the Elasticity of Demand for Money

Study	Data	Definition of money	Determinant variables (elasticities)					lag on y or W	lag on r
			y_c	y_P	W	r_L	r_s		
Chow [19]	U.S. annual 1897–1958 (short-run demand for money depends on y_c and r_s; long-run demand on y_P and r_L)	M_1	after 1 yr 0·36 2 yr 0·58 3 yr 0·72 4 yr 0·80 5 yr 0·93	1·00	y_P does better than W	−0·75	after 1 yr −0·31 2 yr −0·5 3 yr −0·61 4 yr −0·68 5 yr −0·79		
Heller [18]	U.S. quarterly 1947–58	M_1 M_1 M_2 time deposits	1·076(0·056)* −2·348 (0·808)*		0·9–0·8 1·229(0·07)* 4·32(0·718)*	insig. insig. insig.	−0·104(0·03)* insig. −0·106(0·039)* insig.		
Hamburger [27]	U.S. quarterly 1952(1)–60(4).	M_1 of consumers and non-profit organisations	insig.	insig.	insig.	bond r, −0·15; equity r, −0·14 −0·13			θ <1. 80 per cent of adjustment in 1 yr
Laidler [17]	U.S. annual 1900–65 omitting 1917–18, 1941–5 1946–65	M_2 M_2 {M_2 {M_2	0·55(0·24)*	1·26(0·022)* 1·31(0·045)* 0·65(0·029)*		−0·39(0·073)*	−0·186(0·01)* −0·168(0·04)* −0·18(0·046)*		
Laidler [16]	U.S. annual 1919–60 U.S. annual 1892–1960	{M_1 {M_1 {M_2 {M_2		1·53(0·05)* 1·15(0·06)* 1·39(0·02)* 1·51(0·04)*		−0·72(0·06)* −0·25(0·067)*	−0·21(0·017)* −0·14(0·01)*		
Friedman [13]	U.S. annual 1870–1954, average values over reference cycles	M_2		1·8					

Reference	Data period	Money	Income	Interest rate	Interest rate	θ	λ
Meltzer [14]	U.S. annual 1900–58	M_1	1·11(42)	−0·95(21·8)			
		M_2	1·32(53·2)	−0·50(10·8)			
		M_2 (per cap.)	1·41(34·1)	−0·37(7·3)			
Kavanagh and Walters [26]	U.K. annual 1880–1961 first differences	M_1	1·15(0·021)*	−0·31(0·086)*			
		$\{\Delta M_1$	0·655(0·074)*	−0·02(0·068)*			
		$\{\Delta M_2$	0·619(0·073)*	−0·026(0·03)*			
Laidler [17]	U.K. annual 1900–65, (omitting 1914–18, 1939–45)	M_2	0·66(0·053)*	−0·57(0·053)*			
		M_2	0·795(0·056)*	−0·147(0·013)*			
		M_2	0·63(0·052)*	−0·569(0·055)*			
		M_2	0·75(0·056)*	−0·148(0·014)*			
	1946–65	M_2	0·68(0·31)*	−0·74(0·129)*			
		M_2	0·67(0·26)*	−0·76(0·122)*			
Laidler and Parkin [20]	U.K. quarterly 1955(3)–1967(4).	M_2	0·54(2·12)	−0·16(0·25)		0·203(2·03)	0·803(4·3)
		M_2	0·54(2·47)	−0·006(0·4)		0·794(4·2)	0·204(2·6)
		M_2	0·34(9·01)	0·048(2·4)		(θ)	(λ)
Bank of England [22]	U.K. quarterly 1955–69	M_1	l.r. 1·2 −1·1	l.r. −0·8 s.r. −0·09	l.r. −1·05 s.r. −0·04		
		M_2	l.r. 1·5 −1·2	l.r. −0·5 s.r. −0·06	l.r. −0·81 s.r. −0·03		
Fisher [21]	U.K. quarterly 1951–67	M_1 (s.r.)	0·21(4·19) 0·19(3·69)	−0·1(2·4)	−0·1(2·28)		
		M_2 (s.r.)	0·24(4·24) 0·25(3·6)	insig.	insig.		
		M_1 (l.r.)	0·33(2·07) 1·2(2·15)	insig.	insig.		
		M_2 (l.r.)	0·59(2·37) 1·85(2·37)	insig.	insig.		

M_1 = money supply excluding time deposits,
M_2 = money supply including time deposits,
( ) gives t statistic,
y_c = current income,
y_p = permanent income,

( )* gives standard error of estimate,
s.r. indicates short-run demand for money function,
W = wealth (non-human),
r_L = long-term interest rate,
r_s = short-term interest rate,

l.r. indicates long-run demand for money function,
θ = coefficient of adjustment lag, and
λ = coefficient of expectations lag.

within one year. Fisher's [21] lag coefficient, θ, is approximately 0·3, which means that only 0·62 of the adjustment has occurred after one year. One of Laidler and Parkin's estimates [20] of θ corresponds to Feige's [23] estimate of a year to adjust fully to a new equilibrium level of real money balances. The Bank of England study [22] obtained very low values for θ of approximately 0·1. It is likely that the usual procedures used tend to produce longer lags and this should be taken into account.

6.9 CONCLUSION

It has been established quite conclusively that the demand for money is a stable function of the interest rate and of permanent income or wealth. The results are, not surprisingly, better for long-run time-series data than for short-run data. We can be reasonably confident that there is a long-run stable demand for money function. It is less clear how the demand for money adjusts in the short run to changes in its determinants.

REFERENCES

[1] K. Brunner and A. Meltzer, 'The Uses of Money: Money in the Theory of an Exchange Economy', *American Economic Review*, 61, 6 (December 1971).

[2] J. Tobin, 'The Interest Elasticity of the Transactions Demand for Cash', *Review of Economics and Statistics*, 38 (August 1956).

[3] W. J. Baumol, 'The Transactions Demand for Cash: An Inventory Theoretic Approach', *Quarterly Journal of Economics*, 66 (November 1952).

[4] W. J. Baumol, *Portfolio Theory, the Selection of Asset Combinations* (New York: McCaleb-Seiber Publishing Co., 1970).

[5] J. Tobin, 'Liquidity Preference as Behavior Towards Risk', *Review of Economic Studies*, 25 (February 1958).

[6] Irving Fisher, *The Rate of Interest* (New York: Macmillan, 1907).

[7] Irving Fisher, *The Theory of Interest* (New York: Macmillan, 1930).

[8] M. Friedman, *The Optimum Quantity of Money* (London: Macmillan 1969).

[9] T. R. Saving, 'Transactions Costs and the Demand for Money', *American Economic Review*, 61, 3 (June 1971).

[10] M. Friedman, 'The Quantity Theory of Money: A Restatement', in *Studies in the Quantity Theory of Money*, ed. M. Friedman (Chicago University Press, 1956).

[11] I. Fisher, *The Purchasing Power of Money*, 2nd edn (New York: Macmillan, 1913).

[12] D. Laidler, *The Demand for Money: Theories and Evidence* (Pennsylvania: International Textbook Company, 1969).

[13] M. Friedman, 'The Demand for Money: Some Theoretical and Empirical Results', *Journal of Political Economy*, 67 (August 1959), reprinted in A.E.A., *Readings in Business Cycles*.

[14] A. H. Meltzer, 'The Demand for Money: Evidence from the Time Series', *Journal of Political Economy*, 71 (1963).

[15] D. Laidler, 'Some Evidence on the Demand for Money', *Journal of Political Economy*, 74 (February 1966).

[16] D. Laidler, 'The Rate of Interest and the Demand for Money', *Journal of Political Economy*, 74 (December 1966).

[17] D. Laidler, 'The Influence of Money on Economic Activity – A Survey of some Current Problems', in *Monetary Theory and Monetary Policy in the 1970's*, ed. G. Clayton, J. C. Gilbert and R. Sedgwick (Oxford University Press, 1971).

[18] H. R. Heller, 'The Demand for Money: The Evidence from the Short-Run Data', *Quarterly Journal of Economics*, 79 (June 1963).

[19] G. C. Chow, 'On the Long-Run and Short-Run Demand for Money', *Journal of Political Economy*, 74 (1966).

[20] D. Laidler and M. Parkin, 'The Demand for Money in the U.K. 1956–67, Preliminary Estimates', *Manchester School*, 38 (September 1970), reprinted in *Readings in British Monetary Economics*, ed. H. G. Johnson (Oxford: Clarendon Press, 1972).

[21] D. Fisher, 'The Demand for Money in Britain, Quarterly Results, 1951–67', *Manchester School*, 36 (December 1968).

[22] The Bank of England, 'The Importance of Money', *Bank of England Quarterly Bulletin*, 10, 3 (June 1970), reprinted in *Readings in British Monetary Economics*, ed. Johnson.

[23] E. Feige, 'Expectations and Adjustments in the Monetary Sector', *American Economic Review*, 57 (May 1967).

[24] K. Brunner and A. Meltzer, 'Some Further Evidence on Supply and Demand Functions for Money', *Journal of Finance*, 19 (May 1964).

[25] R. Teigen, 'Demand and Supply Functions for Money in the U.S.', *Econometrica*, 32, 4 (October 1964).

[26] N. J. Kavanagh and A. A. Walters, 'The Demand for Money in the U.K. 1877–1961: Preliminary Findings', *Bulletin of Oxford Institute of Economics and Statistics*, 28, 2 (May 1966), reprinted in *Readings in British Monetary Economics*, ed. Johnson.

[27] M. Hamburger, 'The Demand for Money by Households, Money Substitutes and Monetary Policy', *Journal of Political Economy*, 74 (December 1966).

[28] P. Cagan, 'The Monetary Dynamics of Hyperinflation', in *Studies in the Quantity Theory of Money*, ed. Friedman.

7 The General Macro Model

In discussing the *ISLM* model and its constituent functions we have been concerned only with the demand side of the economy. The factors determining the quantity of output firms wish to supply have been hidden from view so far. We have seen that there are two simplified approaches to the supply side of the economy. Up till now in discussing the Keynesian *ISLM* model we have assumed that the supply of real output is perfectly elastic and that the actual quantity of output produced is therefore determined solely by the level of aggregate demand. Once the volume of output has reached the upper limit set by the supply of resources we move into the neoclassical *ISLM* model in which the full-employment level of real output is determined exogenously.

7.1 THE NEOCLASSICAL MODEL

We will now examine the production sector that is embodied in neoclassical models of the economy. This is done at a highly aggregated level where both labour and capital are assumed to be homogeneous factors of production. Other factors of production do not enter the analysis at this level of aggregation since net national product is defined to be final output. Intermediate stages of production are netted out in the aggregation procedure and in an open economy imports of raw materials and intermediate goods are subtracted from the value of firms' production. Thus net national output is calculated as the value added by the application of labour and capital to raw materials. We can therefore think in terms of an aggregate production of the form

$$y = f(L, K, T) \tag{7.1}$$

where y is the real output per period of time, L is the flow of labour services used per period of time, K is the capital stock which yields a proportionate flow of capital services per period of time, and T is the state of technical knowledge which, as we are conducting short-run analysis, is assumed fixed.

In neoclassical theory labour and capital are assumed to be substitutable *ex ante*. This means that there is a whole range of possible techniques, each representing a particular combination of labour and capital, available to produce a given level of output. Once a particular technique is chosen as being the least-cost technique at that time, capital becomes embodied in specific types of goods. We are then in an *ex post* situation in which there is a smaller degree of substitutability between labour and capital.

Neoclassical analysis has largely concentrated on equilibrium solutions. General equilibrium in the economy requires that demand and supply are equal in all markets. On the supply side of the economy we require factor markets to be cleared. This is made possible by the ability of firms to substitute labour for capital in response to price incentives. If one factor is in excess supply its price will fall and it is then substituted for other factors until demand and supply are brought into equality. If the economy is in equilibrium there will exist a particular ratio of labour to capital together with an associated relative price of labour to capital such that firms' demand for labour equals the quantity of labour supplied, while the existing stock of capital is being optimally utilised.

For the purpose of short-run analysis the stock of capital is assumed fixed and determined by past decisions. These decisions were based on expectations, held in the past, about the future values of relevant variables, such as the level of demand for output. When we move from the past into the current period the values variables were expected to have may diverge from their actual current values. Long-run equilibrium requires that expectations are fully realised so that capacity that was planned in period $t - n$ to operate in period t is in fact working at its optimal level in period t. This may not actually occur in which case we use short-run analysis. This analyses the economy when it is not in long-run equilibrium. If we are in long-run stationary equilibrium then this state is merely a repetition of identical short-run periods.

The Demand for Labour

Since the stock of capital is regarded as fixed in the short run output will vary with the quantity of labour employed. The short-run aggregate production function is therefore written as

$$y = f(L, \bar{K}, \bar{T},) \qquad (7.2)$$

where $\bar{K}, \bar{T},$ are constants. Assuming the law of variable proportions holds in the region in which the economy is operating, we obtain the result that the marginal product of labour is positive but declining:

$$\frac{dy}{dL} > 0, \qquad \frac{d^2y}{dL^2} < 0. \tag{7.2'}$$

Firms are assumed to be profit maximisers operating in perfectly competitive product and factor markets. A firm's profit function will be

$$\pi = Py - WL - TFC \tag{7.3}$$

where π is profits, P is the price of output (on aggregation this is a price index) W is the wage rate in money terms, y is the quantity of output, and TFC is the total fixed costs. Substituting the micro version of equation (7.2) into the first term on the right-hand side of equation (7.3) and differentiating with respect to the quantity of labour employed, L, we obtain the first order condition for a profit maximum:

$$\frac{d\pi}{dL} = P\frac{dy}{dL} - W = 0 \tag{7.4}$$

therefore

$$\frac{dy}{dL} = \frac{W}{P}. \tag{7.5}$$

Equation (7.5) shows that profit-maximising firms will hire that quantity of labour for which the marginal product of labour, dy/dL, equals the real wage, W/P. The marginal labour unit is just worth acquiring since the addition to total cost, which is the money wage rate, just equals the addition to total revenue. (This is the marginal revenue product which is equal to the price times the marginal product of labour, $P \times dy/dL$.) Thus, given pure competition in the product and labour markets, the marginal product of labour schedule is viewed as the demand function for labour with respect to the real wage rate* (see

---

* If the product market is imperfectly competitive, a firm's demand function being $P = P(y)$, a profit-maximising firm will equate the marginal product of labour to the ratio of the money wage to the marginal revenue, i.e.

$$\pi = P(y)y(L) - WL - TFC$$

$$\frac{d\pi}{dL} = P\frac{dy}{dL} + y\frac{dP}{dy} \cdot \frac{dy}{dL} - W = 0$$

$$P\frac{dy}{dL}\left[1 + \frac{y}{P}\frac{dP}{dy}\right] = W$$

$$\frac{dy}{dL} = \frac{W}{P\left(1 + \frac{dP}{dy} \cdot \frac{y}{P}\right)} = \frac{W}{P(1 + 1/e)}$$

or

$$\frac{W}{P} = (1 + 1/e)\frac{dy}{dL} = (1 - k)\frac{dy}{dL}$$

Figure (7.1.a) on page 184). If we assume the law of variable proportions (i.e. diminishing marginal returns) the marginal product of labour declines with the amount of labour employed. Profit-maximising firms will only be induced to hire additional labour and produce more output if the real wage falls. The demand for labour is assumed to be a decreasing function of the real wage rate, as expressed in equation (7.6), given the technical conditions of production and the degree of market competitiveness is held constant:

$$L^d = g\left(\frac{W}{P}\right), \qquad \frac{dL^d}{d(W/P)} < 0. \tag{7.6}$$

The Supply of Labour

The neoclassical theory of labour supply also has a choice theoretic basis. A household is assumed to obtain utility both from leisure time and from real income. In this type of utility function real income is an aggregate variable that embraces both current consumption and future consumption in the form of current saving. The utility function of the ith household which obtains its income from selling labour services is

$$U_i = f(y_i, R_i) \tag{7.7}$$

where y_i is real income and R_i is the number of 'hours' leisure. Utility is maximised subject to the constraint on the total number of 'hours' available:

$$R_i = H_i - S_i \tag{7.8}$$

where H_i is the total number of 'hours' available and S_i is the total number of 'hours' worked. A further constraint is

$$y_i = S_i w \tag{7.9}$$

---

where k is the degree of monopoly in the Lerner sense, i.e.

$$k = \frac{P - \text{marginal cost}}{P}.$$

If the factor market is also imperfectly competitive so that the wage rate the firm pays is $W = W(L)$, the result of profit maximisation will be

$$\frac{dy}{dL} = \frac{W}{P}\left[1 + 1 \Big/ \frac{dL}{dW}\frac{W}{L}\right] \Big/ (1 - k)$$

where $(dL/dW)W/L$ is the elasticity of the supply of labour. Therefore the assumption of imperfect competition does not alter the deduction that if firms are profit maximisers the demand for labour depends on the real wage rate.

where w is the real wage rate per 'hour'. Real income may also include income from non-human wealth but this will be unaffected by the number of hours currently worked, though it will influence how many hours the household decides to work. It is assumed that real income and leisure have positive marginal utility,

$$\frac{\partial U_i}{\partial y_i}, \qquad \frac{\partial U_i}{\partial R_i} > 0. \qquad (7.10)$$

The household maximises the utility it obtains from real income and leisure, subject to the constraints (7.8) and (7.9). The first order condition for this maximum is obtained by differentiating the utility function (7.7) with respect to the number of 'hours' worked and setting the first derivative equal to zero, i.e.

$$\frac{dU_i}{dS_i} = \frac{\partial U_i}{\partial y_i}\frac{dy_i}{dS_i} + \frac{\partial U_i}{\partial R_i}\frac{dR_i}{dS_i} = 0. \qquad (7.11)$$

From equation (7.9) $dy_i/dS_i = w$, and from equation (7.8) $dR_i/dS_i = -1$, therefore

$$\frac{\partial U_i}{\partial y_i} w = \frac{\partial U_i}{\partial R_i}. \qquad (7.12)$$

Equation (7.12) expresses the equilibrium condition for a household. It will choose to work that number of 'hours' per period of time which equates the marginal utility of real income from an 'hour's' work to the marginal disutility of that 'hour's' work. (This is the marginal utility forgone by not devoting that 'hour' to leisure.)

An increase in the real wage rate may cause the household to work either more or less hours depending on its preferences. A higher real wage rate means an increased price of leisure. The substitution effect causes the household to have less of the relatively more expensive commodity, leisure. The increase in the real wage rate means an addition to hourly income which can be spent on extra leisure as well as on goods and services bought on the market. So long as the increased demand for leisure caused by the income effect does not outweigh the substitution effect, the household will work more hours as a result of a higher real wage rate.

Neoclassical analysis of the labour market assumes that the quantity of labour supplied in aggregate is a positive function of the real wage rate, i.e.

$$L^s = h\left(\frac{W}{P}\right), \qquad \frac{dL^s}{d(W/P)} > 0. \qquad (7.13)$$

The hypothesis that more labour is willing to supply itself as real wages rise is applicable in the short run, particularly to marginal participants who enter the labour force in response to higher real wages. The aggregate labour supply function also takes into account the behaviour of individuals who have a reservation real wage below which they are unwilling to take a job. They prefer to remain unemployed and continue searching until they obtain a job at their reservation real wage.

Labour Market Equilibrium

In the neoclassical model the real wage is determined by the equality of the demand for labour and the supply of labour as shown in Figure 7.1.a. When the equilibrium real wage rate, $(W/P)_f$, is determined so is the level of employment, L_f. By definition this is full employment since all labour which is willing to work at or below the equilibrium real wage rate can find employment. Workers seeking jobs above the equilibrium real wage are said to be voluntarily unemployed. Involuntary unemployment would arise in disequilibrium when labour which is willing to work at or below the going real wage rate is unable to find jobs. Full employment of labour is compatible with frictional unemployment which occurs because instantaneous transfer from one job to another is not possible. It takes time for unemployed workers to search for and secure another job, during which time they can choose to remain unemployed by refusing to take up jobs offering inferior terms to those they are seeking.

Given that the labour market solves for the equilibrium real wage and thus for full employment of the labour force, the full-employment level of output is determined from the short-run aggregate production function as shown in Figure 7.1.b. Since both the demand for and supply of labour are defined in real terms the equilibrium real wage rate and the level of employment will be unaffected by any changes in the price level. If both the money wage rate and price level double the real wage rate remains unaltered. Hence the full employment level of real output is invariant with respect to the price level and is depicted as a vertical aggregate supply schedule in Figure 7.1.c. By introducing the production sector we have derived the full-employment level of real output that was exogenously given in the neoclassical version of the *ISLM* model.

The Complete Neoclassical Model

As discussed in Chapter 2, the goods market in a static neoclassical model determines the real rate of interest which will equate investment to the full-employment level of saving. This leaves the quantity of money to determine the price level.*

---

* Classical dichotomy is a term referring to the determination in equilibrium of the real variables in the real sector independently of the monetary sector in which the nominal quantity of money determines the price level independently of the real sector.

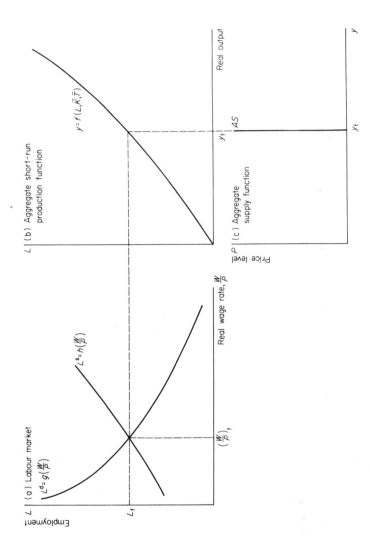

FIGURE 7.1   *The neoclassical model: aggregate supply*

The determination of the price level in the neoclassical model is illustrated in Figure 7.2 in which is derived a so-called aggregate demand schedule for real output as a function of the price level. This is the locus of real output and price levels for which both the money market and the goods market are in equilibrium.

In Figure 7.2.a we see that with a fixed nominal money stock the *LM* schedule shifts up towards the left as the quantity of real money balances diminishes with an increased price level. Thus a higher price level is associated with a lower level of real output that is consistent with both goods and money market equilibrium. The higher the price level the lower is the quantity of real money balances and hence the higher is the rate of interest required to make the demand for real money balances equal to the supply. A higher rate of interest causes a lower level of investment, so that a smaller volume of real output is required to bring saving into equality with investment. The locus of real output and price levels necessary for joint equilibrium in the goods and money markets is transferred to Figure 7.2.b as the aggregate demand schedule, *AD*.

The full-employment level of output has already been determined at y_f in the production sector. The price level is determined at P_f in Figure 7.2.b by the intersection of the aggregate demand and supply schedules. The price level must be such that it makes the real value of the money stock equal to the demand for real money balances which is determined by the full-employment equilibrium values of output, y_f, and the interest rate, i_f. The equations of the three sector neoclassical model are set out below.

The goods market:

Savings function
$$S/P = s(1-t)y \tag{7.14}$$

Investment function
$$I/P = I(i)/P \tag{7.15}$$

Government expenditure
$$G/P = G_0/P \tag{7.16}$$

Tax function
$$T/P = t(y) \tag{7.17}$$

Goods market equilibrium
$$\frac{S}{P} + \frac{T}{P} = \frac{I}{P} + \frac{G}{P} \tag{7.18}$$

Therefore the equation of the *IS* function is
$$[s(1-t)+t]y = I(i)/P + G_0/P. \tag{7.19}$$

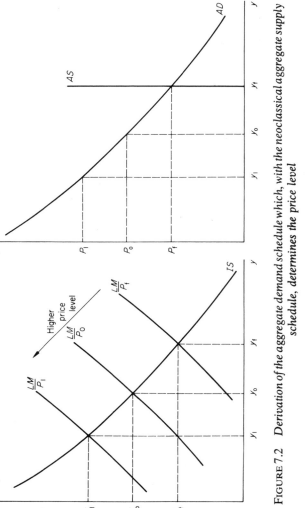

FIGURE 7.2   Derivation of the aggregate demand schedule which, with the neoclassical aggregate supply schedule, determines the price level

The money market:

Demand for money function

$$\left(\frac{M}{P}\right)^d = \frac{M}{P}(y, i) \qquad (7.20)$$

Exogenous supply of money

$$M^s = M_0^s \qquad (7.21)$$

Money market equilibrium

$$\left(\frac{M}{P}\right)^d = \left(\frac{M}{P}\right)^s \qquad (7.22)$$

Equation of *LM* function

$$\left(\frac{M_0}{P}\right)^s = \frac{M}{P}(y, i). \qquad (7.23)$$

Production sector:

Short-run production function

$$y = f(L, \bar{K}, \bar{T}) \qquad (7.2)$$

Demand for labour function

$$L^d = g(W/P) \qquad (7.6)$$

Supply of labour function

$$L^s = h(W/P) \qquad (7.13)$$

Labour market equilibrium

$$L^s = L^d = L_f \qquad (7.24)$$

Substituting equation (7.24) into equation (7.2)

$$y_f = f(L_f). \qquad (7.25)$$

The model has twelve endogenous variables, namely real output, real saving, real government expenditure, real tax revenue, real investment, the real wage rate, the demand for real money balances, the supply of real money balances, the demand for labour, the supply of labour, the real rate of interest and the price level. There are twelve independent equations (7.14, 7.15, 7.16, 7.17, 7.18), (7.20, 7.21, 7.22) and (7.2, 7.6, 7.13, 7.24). These twelve equations collapse into three independent equations in three variables, real output, the interest rate and the price level. Equations (7.14 to 7.18) give the IS function, (7.19). Equations (7.20 to 7.22) give the LM function, (7.23). Equations (7.2, 7.6, 7.13 and 7.24) give the aggregate supply function, (7.25).

A further reduction is made by setting the *IS* function equal to the *LM* equation to obtain the aggregate demand schedule. We obtain the various values of real income and the price level that give equilibrium in both the goods market and the money market. Thus in Figure 7.2 we have reduced the system to two equations in two unknowns, real income and the price level.

If the nominal stock of money is increased the locus of *IS* and *LM* equilibria, depicted in Figure 7.2.a, will change, causing the *AD* schedule to shift up to the right. The price level will be proportionately higher. This is the standard neoclassical result that a change in the nominal money stock, *ceteris paribus*, will leave the static equilibrium values of the real variables unchanged. This property of money is referred to as the neutrality of money.* Thus we get the conclusion that, given the constancy of the institutional factors which influence the demand for money, which is a stable function of its determinants, the nominal quantity of money determines the price level and has no long-run effect on the real variables.

This static equilibrium analysis of the role of money in a neoclassical model is identical to the notion of money as a veil which could be lifted to reveal the workings of the real forces of the economic system, unaffected in any significant way by monetary factors. This concept has caused considerable confusion in economic thinking which is avoided if we keep reminding ourselves that comparative static analysis is only a simplifying mode of thought which guides our predictions about directions and magnitudes of change in a stable economy. The nominal quantity of money may not affect static equilibrium states but the story is quite different when we analyse the economy in disequilibrium. Then the quantity of money does affect real values as both Keynesian and monetarist schools accept.

Adjustment in a Neoclassical Model

It would be wrong to receive the impression that pre-Keynesian economists paid no attention to the adjustment of the economy towards equilibrium. They emphasised the role of flexible money wages and prices in this process. If there were unemployment the cause was diagnosed as excessively high real wages. Unemployed workers would bid down the money wage rate and, providing prices fell less rapidly, the real wage rate would fall causing an increase in the demand for labour and consequently in output.

Keynes pointed out that this adjustment process does not occur in such a simple fashion if prices fall as rapidly as money wages leaving real wages unchanged. He reasoned that this would occur because of a lack

---

* For further reading on this topic see [1, 2].

FIGURE 7.3   *The Keynes effect*

of sufficient aggregate demand to take up the additional output produced. When money wages and hence real wages fall, inducing firms to produce more output, the income equivalent to the increased production is paid out to factors of production. If the marginal propensity to spend out of this additional income is less than one, the resulting increase in aggregate demand will be less than the increase in output. The excess supply of output will cause prices to fall further and real wages will again rise unless money wages continue to fall.

Keynes thought that any stimulus to aggregate demand caused by falling money wages would have to come through the monetary sector. As prices fall so the real value of a fixed nominal money supply would rise causing the interest rate to fall. Investment would therefore increase and, via the multiplier effect, cause a further rise in real output. This process of adjustment, summarised in Figure 7.3, is known as the Keynes effect.

7.2   THE KEYNESIAN THEORY OF INCOME, EMPLOYMENT AND THE PRICE LEVEL

Keynes criticised the neoclassical* economic thinking of his day for its failure to see that the predictions of static, certainty models cannot be applied directly to short-run analysis of a world in which the future is uncertain and in which equilibrium is a state towards which an economy, if stable, is gradually adjusting. *The General Theory* attempts to explain why a capitalist economy, disturbed from full-employment equilibrium, will not adjust smoothly by means of downward price movements as had

---

* Keynes referred to what is commonly called the neoclassical school of economic thought as classical, thus giving rise to some confusion. In common usage classical thinkers, who predate the neoclassicists, are Adam Smith, David Ricardo, Thomas Malthus and James Mill. In this book, what Keynes called classical is referred to as neoclassical in an attempt to minimise confusion. Neoclassical economic thought is associated with the marginalist revolution of the mid-nineteenth century and in the United Kingdom was developed in the works of W. S. Jevons, A. Marshall and A. Pigou which provide the main theoretical underpinning to contemporary theory.

been supposed by neoclassical analysis. The book is a complex work which was hailed as a revolution in economic theory. It required interpretation and simplification. Keynesian economists propagated the ideas they found in *The General Theory* in terms of comparative static analysis. This type of analysis has already been met in the *ISLM* model. Neoclassical ideas have also been reformulated within the same analytical framework to give the neoclassical–Keynesian synthesis which was discussed in Section 7.1. Such precisely formulated models are not to be found in *The General Theory* itself but were developed subsequently.

The Keynesian Three-Sector Model

We will now develop the standard version of the Keynesian three-sector model which has evolved out of the work of Hicks [3], Hansen [4] and Modigliani [5], keeping as closely as possible to Keynes's exposition. The Keynesian three-sector model differs from the neoclassical model in assuming that money wages in a depression are inflexible downwards. Keynes* agreed with neoclassical theory that labour is concerned with the real wage rate it obtains from employment and that in equilibrium the marginal utility from the real wage received for an hour's work is equal to the marginal disutility of that hour's work. This means that more labour is only willing to supply itself at a higher real wage. Keynes disagreed that the above conclusions of neoclassical analysis applied when the economy was in unemployment disequilibrium. In such a situation some workers were involuntarily unemployed since they were willing to work at or below the equilibrium real wage but could not find jobs. In disequilibrium the economy is off the aggregate supply function of labour since more labour than is actually employed is willing to supply itself without there being any increase in the real wage.

Keynes further argued that there is an asymmetry in labour's behaviour. This stems from the fact that in a monetary economy labour can only bargain with employers for a money wage. It cannot directly determine its real wage since the price level is not in labour's sole control. Keynes postulated that workers are more willing to accept a cut in real wages caused by a rise in the price level than a cut in real wages due to a reduction in money wages. The reason for this behaviour is that a rising price level affects all workers more or less equally but a cut in money wages occurs in a piecemeal fashion at the firm or industry level. The latter action is resisted since workers fear a decline in their real wage relative to others. In a depression, therefore, money wages will only fall slowly. In the static interpretation of the Keynesian model the money wage is assumed to be fixed. It is exogenous to the model and explained by institutional factors and past history. If the economy is below full-employment equilibrium, the neoclassical labour supply

* *The General Theory*, ch. 2.

function, equation (7.3), is suspended and replaced by the exogenously determined money wage rate:

$$W = W_0 \quad \text{for} \quad W_0/P > k$$
$$L^s = h(W_0/P) \quad \text{for} \quad W_0/P \leq k$$

(7.14a)

where k is the full-employment equilibrium real wage rate. Given the money wage rate, W_0, the real wage rate varies inversely with the price level as shown in Figure 7.4.d.

As the price level falls the real wage rate rises and, turning to Figure 7.4.a the demand for labour falls along the marginal product of labour schedule, DD. For instance if the price level is P_1, the real wage is $(W/P)_1$ and the demand for labour is L_1. Involuntary unemployment is given by the difference between the amount of labour willing to work at the equilibrium real wage, $(W/P)_f$, and the number finding work at the actual real wage of $(W/P)_1$. When L_1 labour is employed real output is shown in Figure 7.4.b as y_1. Thus the aggregate supply schedule of the Keynesian model is a positive function of the aggregate price level. As the price level rises, with a fixed money wage, the real wage falls and the output firms are willing to supply increases. Once the price level is at least equal to P_f the real wage is $(W/P)_f$, at which the demand and supply of labour are equal. Turning to the production function in Figure 7.4.b we see that the full-employment level of real output is y_f. Since the Keynesian model is applied to conditions of unemployment, the fixed money wage assumption is only relevant to price levels below P_f. If prices rise above P_f money wages rise proportionately leaving the real wage rate unchanged at $(W/P)_f$. We have then reverted to the neoclassical model so that the aggregate supply function is vertical at price levels in excess of P_f.

Determinants of the Price Level in a Keynesian Model

In the Keynesian model real output and the price level are determined by the interaction of the aggregate demand for output with the aggregate supply of output. This is shown in Figure 7.5, the price level and the volume of real output being determined by the intersection of the aggregate demand and supply schedules. The price level in the short run is determined by two sets of factors. The price at which firms are willing to supply real output depends on the productivity of labour and the money wage rate, which both determine firms' average and marginal costs, and on the profit mark-up used between average cost and the price of output.* The upward sloping aggregate supply curve is derived

* See Chapter 9, p. 234 for a discussion of pricing and the relationship between average and marginal cost.

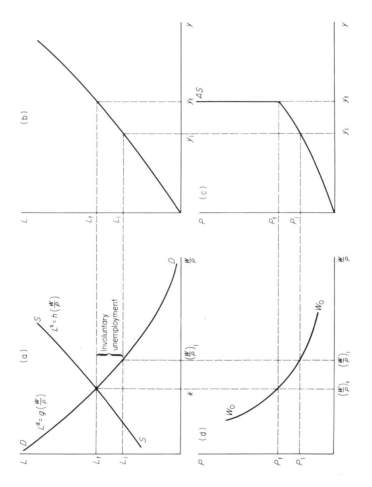

FIGURE 7.4   *The Keynesian model: derivation of the aggregate supply function*

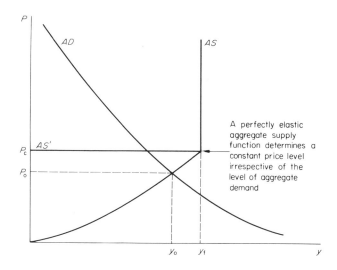

FIGURE 7.5   *The Keynesian three-sector model*

on the assumption that the marginal product of labour declines with output in the short run. Also there may exist costs of using capital which rise with the level of production. Both factors cause firms' marginal cost curves to slope upwards so that profit-maximising firms will only produce additional output if price rises.

If there were constant short-run marginal and average costs due to labour and capital being used in fixed proportions up to full employment, the aggregate short-run demand schedule for labour would be perfectly elastic with respect to the equilibrium real wage rate up to full employment. To this would correspond a perfectly elastic (horizontal) aggregate supply schedule until full employment is reached. In the case, given the average product of labour and the profit mark-up, the price level is determined by the money wage rate. Changes in aggregate demand would have no effect on the price level except when full employment is reached.

This is the assumption underlying the Keynesian *ISLM* model of Chapter 2, where the price level is assumed constant. The neo-Keynesians echo this assumption by emphasising the role of institutional factors which govern wage bargaining in the determination of the price level. Keynes assumed the aggregate supply function to be upward sloping so that the level of aggregate demand, as well as supply conditions, determine the price level. He analysed an increase in effective demand as causing an increase in nominal income which may be divided between a rise in real output and a rise in the price level.

Keynesian Analysis of Wage and Price Flexibility as a Mechanism of Adjustment

Keynes argued that even if money wages and prices were flexible downwards in a depression this flexibility is unlikely to be stabilising. He saw the only likely adjustment mechanism to be the increase in the real value of the money supply consequent upon a falling price level. This would cause interest rates to fall and investment to rise. He thought that the expected return from investment had become so depressed that a low interest was required to create the full-employment level of investment. He doubted whether the rate of interest would fall fast enough or far enough to increase investment by the required amount.

This difficulty was attributed to the activities of speculators on the capital market. As discussed in Chapter 6, if speculators think that the equilibrium interest rate is higher than it really is, they will continue to sell bonds and move into money when the interest rate falls below the level they consider normal. This is because they fear capital losses from holding bonds as they expect the interest rate to rise, when it should fall, if full employment equilibrium is to be restored. These speculative activities prevent the interest rate from falling to its full employment equilibrium level. Keynes viewed the demand for money function as being unstable so that it was continually shifted up by speculators' expectations and thus preventing the interest rate from falling to the low level required for full employment.

The acuteness and the peculiarity of our contemporary problem arises, therefore, out of the possibility that the average rate of interest which will allow a reasonable average level of employment is one so unacceptable to wealth owners that it cannot be readily established merely by manipulating the quantity of money.*

Keynesian economists interpreted this argument in static terms by hypothesising the possibility of a very interest elastic demand for money function. In the extreme case money demand would be perfectly interest elastic. (The lower section of demand for money schedule would become horizontal at some low rate of interest.) As the real money supply expanded, people would hold their additional real money balances without any fall in the interest rate. Investment therefore would not increase so that aggregate demand would not rise as the price level declines. The aggregate demand schedule is therefore invariant to changes in the price level as shown in Figure 7.6 and it is impossible to attain the full-employment level of output, y_f.

Another strand in Keynes's argument regarding the ineffectiveness of money wage flexibility to restore full-employment equilibrium is that, even if the interest rate falls, investment will be slow to react and the

* *The General Theory*, ch. 21, p. 309.

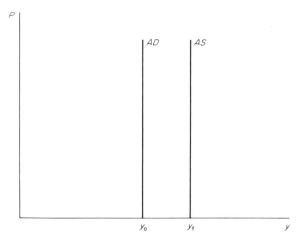

FIGURE 7.6   *The extreme Keynesian case: the impossibility of full-employment output at any price level*

total response will be small: '... moderate changes in the prospective yield of capital or in the rate of interest will not be associated with very great changes in the rate of investment'.*

Keynesian economists interpreteted this argument for static analysis in terms of totally interest-inelastic investment. This would also cause aggregate demand to be invariant with respect to the price level since a falling price level, even if it lowered the interest rate, would leave effective demand unaltered. Figure 7.6 also illustrates this argument in which again no equilibrium solution is possible. Even a fairly interest-inelastic investment schedule could lead to a similar result.

7.3   THE NET WEALTH EFFECT OF CHANGES
IN THE PRICE LEVEL

The Keynesians attempted to show that the neoclassical model with flexible money wages and prices would not have a static equilibrium solution. This occurs if the interest rate mechanism fails to equate investment with the full-employment level of saving, either because investment is perfectly interest inelastic or because wealth holders' demand for money is such that it prevents the interest rate from falling to a sufficiently low level. Pigou [6] subsequently showed that this analysis is incorrect if one considers the impact of a lower price level on real wealth and hence on the incentive to save. If a household's real wealth is increased, the need to sacrifice present consumption in order

* *The General Theory*, ch. 18, p. 250.

to accumulate the means to finance future consumption is lessened. In terms of the permanent income hypothesis, an increase in wealth will cause an upward adjustment of permanent income and thus an increase in consumption.

The real value of assets which are fixed in nominal terms will vary inversely with the price level. When the price level falls the real value of money and of fixed interest assets rises, since they are worth more in terms of goods and services. The owners of such assets consequently have an increased claim to goods and services. On the other hand the issuers of nominally fixed debt feel worse off as the real value of their debt has risen.

It is a standard practice in macro analysis to set the real value of private sector liabilities against the real value of private sector assets so they are netted out against each other. This is known as consolidating balance sheets. Thus if holders of private sector bonds feel better off when the price level falls and consequently save less, this is assumed to be exactly offset by the issuers of these liabilities feeling worse off and reducing their consumption. The net wealth or net worth of the economy is the real value of all assets held less the real value of all liabilities. We are concerned here with analysing the effect of changes in the price level on the real net wealth of the economy.

Holders of commercial bank deposits experience an increase in their real wealth due to a fall in the price level. These deposits, D, are equal to the sum of bank loans to the private sector, L, plus bank reserves, R (i.e. $D = L + R$). When the price level falls the increase in the real value of bank loans partially offsets the increase in the value of bank deposits. This leaves an increase in net wealth equal to the rise in the real value of bank reserves. The net wealth of the private sector rises because bank reserves are an asset to the private sector but not a liability.

Currency holdings similarly increase in real value when the price level falls and are not offset by any liability since the government has no obligation to transform currency into any other medium. Thus when the price level falls the private sector has a net increase in its real wealth, since the real value of high-powered money increases. This type of money has been given the term 'outside money' [7].* As it is not backed by private sector debt its presence causes an increase in net wealth when the price level falls.

* 'Inside money' is money backed by private sector debt. That portion of bank deposits which is matched by private loans on the asset side of banks' balance sheets is inside money. A fall in the price level increases the real value of both the inside money and its corresponding liabilities, so that there is no net wealth effect. It has been pointed out by Pesek and Saving [8], whose analysis has been refined by Patinkin [9], that inside money may have a net wealth effect when the price level changes. A monopoly banking system, which is restricted by

Differing assumptions can be made regarding the effect of changes in the real value of government interest-bearing debt on net wealth. It is argued that since the government can always finance its expenditure by taxing or issuing debt or money, it feels no worse off when the real value of its debt is increased by a fall in the price level [1, 10]. Thus the real value of government interest-bearing debt held by the private sector is included in net wealth. Alternatively it may be assumed that the public discounts the real value of the future tax payments they must make in order to service the government debt [11]. In this case an increase in the real wealth of government debt holders will be exactly offset by the increased present value of taxpayers' liabilities. (This assumes that the same rate of interest is used to discount income from human and non-human sources of wealth.)

The net worth of the economy therefore consists of the stock of real capital goods plus the real value of the outside money stock. Government debt may be included if the appropriate assumptions are made. As it is assumed that the stock of real capital is measured in physical units and that the relative price of consumption to capital goods is fixed, the real value of the capital stock is unchanged when the price level varies. Thus a fall in the price level will increase real net worth by increasing the real value of outside money. An additional impact on real net worth may also come through the increased value of government debt.

The effect of a decline in the price level, which increases real net wealth and thus causes an increase in consumption, is known as the 'Pigou effect'. An increase in net wealth due only to a net increase in the value of the money supply is known as the real balance effect. By making explicit the dependency of consumption on real net wealth as well as on current income and the interest rate, Pigou showed that a static full-employment equilibrium solution must exist in a model in

government policy from producing the real stock of deposits which maximises its profits, may be able to increase its real stock of deposits when the price level falls. This will increase its profits and thus the real net wealth (capitalised profits) of its equity holders. This net wealth effect is independent of the increase in real assets experienced by the banks' deposit holders which is offset by the increased real value of the liabilities of its borrowers. The effect is likely to be small and only reinforces any net wealth effect due to the increase in the real value of outside money brought about by a lower price level. Patinkin's analysis shows that net wealth effects due to a fall in the price level arise from money whose real value rises proportionately more than the costs of maintaining that stock when the price level falls. In a banking system producing the profit-maximising level of real deposits for which marginal revenue and cost are equalised, this can only occur for 'outside money' (i.e. high-powered money). This is because the real value of outside money, which is government fiat money, rises when the price level falls by more than the costs of maintaining the increased real stock of money. There is therefore an increase in net wealth.

which both the money wage rate and the price level are endogenous and some form of outside money exists.

Suppose we have a disequilibrium situation, as shown by Figure 7.6, in which the interest rate mechanism fails to bring about the full employment level of aggregate demand. Once we allow for the Pigou effect, such a level of aggregate demand can exist providing the price level is low enough to create a sufficiently high level of real net wealth.

The Pigou effect would be incorporated into the neoclassical system outlined on p. 187 by including real net wealth in the savings function:

$$\frac{S}{P} = f\left(y, i, \frac{NW}{P}\right). \tag{7.14a}$$

Real net wealth is defined as

$$\frac{NW}{P} = \frac{H_0}{P} + \frac{B_0^G}{Pi} + K_0 \tag{7.26}$$

where H_0 is the nominally fixed stock of high-powered money. The money supply function would therefore be amended to depend on the stock of high-powered money:

$$M^s = H_0 \times (\text{bank multiplier}). \tag{7.21a}$$

B_0^G is the nominally fixed annual income received from government bonds. Hence B_0^G/i is the total market value of government bonds. When deflated by the price level, P, we obtain its real value. (It is being assumed that taxpayers are not discounting the higher real level of taxation brought about by a fall in the price level.) K_0 is the real capital stock which is constant.

We can work with macro models that do not contain income and wealth as separate variables, replacing these variables by permanent income. Since permanent income is the return on the economy's total wealth ($Y_p = iW$)* any change in wealth can be converted into a change in permanent income by multiplying W by the rate of return on wealth, i.

The Pigou effect is designed to show that static full employment equilibrium exists if money wages are flexible. It states little about the dynamics of wage flexibility as a mechanism for attaining full employment. For this mechanism to work we require that the process of a falling price level does not set off other reactions which nullify the effect of increased net wealth on the level of aggregate demand.

The dynamics of the Pigou effect require that a falling price level continually increases aggregate consumption by increasing real net wealth. In terms of the *ISLM* model this would be shown by a rightward shift in the *IS* function as the price level falls, until it intersects the *LM*

---

* See Chapter 3, p.71.

schedule at the full-employment level of real output. This would consequently shift the aggregate demand schedule. Even when the interest rate equilibrating mechanism has broken down, as depicted in Figure 7.6, the aggregate demand schedule would shift rightwards to coincide with the aggregate supply schedule and thus full employment would be attained. It is generally agreed that even if the dynamics of the Pigou effect will return the economy to full-employment equilibrium, it is too slow to be relied upon.

Furthermore the stability of an equilibrium relying upon the Pigou effect has also been questioned. The destabilising effects of a falling price level were analysed by Keynes and further discussed by Patinkin [12]. The Pigou effect, by assumption, ignores the change in the distribution of real wealth that is likely to result from the decline in the price level. Such a redistribution has unpredictable effects on aggregate demand. One likely outcome of a falling price level is that, since it increases the real value of nominally fixed debt, firms become insolvent and go out of business. This disruption reduces aggregate production and employment. A declining price level generates expectations of further falls. Such expectations will cause people to postpone purchases until prices have fallen further. Thus, consumption and investment are further reduced. Keynes thought it likely that a high degree of wage flexibility would be destabilising. If this is the case the downward rigidity of money wages is not a barrier to equilibrium, as in a static world, but a check to destabilising price and output movements.

The chief result of this policy (flexible money wages) would be to cause a great instability of prices, so violent perhaps as to make business calculations futile in an economic society functioning after the manner of that in which we live. To suppose that flexible wage policy is a right and proper adjunct to a system which on the whole is one of laissez-faire, is the opposite of the truth. It is only in a highly authoritarian society, where sudden, substantial, all-round changes could be decreed, that a flexible wage policy could function with success.*

7.4 DYNAMIC PROBLEMS†

It has become increasingly apparent that excessive concentration on comparative static equilibrium results can provide misleading views of problems that require dynamic methods of analysis. This is accentuated by the fact that mathematical techniques, particularly those that are in the economist's standard tool kit, are much less developed for application to dynamic analysis than to comparative static analysis. This problem lies at the heart of the difficulties economists have experienced

---

* *The General Theory*, ch.19 p. 269.
† This section may be omitted on first reading without loss of continuity.

in understanding and developing the ideas of *The General Theory*. Keynes, who wrote of his 'long struggle to escape from habitual modes of thought and expression', not surprisingly found it impossible to present an easily comprehended dynamic analysis of a capitalist economy.

After nearly thirty years of Keynesian economics some economists began to question received doctrine regarding the contents of Keynes's theoretical work. The first major statement of such misgivings about the accepted version of the Keynesian revolution was made by Clower [13]. These have been extended by Leijonhufvud [14] who, as the title of his book proclaims, distinguishes the economics of Keynes, as presented in Keynes's written works, from Keynesian economics. The latter is the static equilibrium framework for aggregate macro analysis that emerged from other people's extensions of Keynes's ideas.

Leijonhfvud's book has not had as much impact on current economics as might have been expected from its generally enthusiastic reception. This can be attributed to two factors. First, the book is, in part, an examination of past economic thought and therefore not of direct relevance to current theory. Secondly, the central theme, that the interpretation of Keynes's dynamic economics within the confines of static analysis has resulted in a fundamental misunderstanding of the theoretical basis of the Keynesian revolution, presents us with analytical problems that are not readily amenable to the current techniques of economic analysis. We attempt here a brief survey of this issue.

The neoclassical economics, which Keynes criticised as being a special theoretical case inapplicable to actual economic society, is now understood as referring to the Walrasian [15] system of general equilibrium.

Walrasian General Equilibrium

This system takes account of the interaction of all transactors in an economy, each of whom acts independently of the others. It shows the existence of a set of prices which will result in equilibrium in all the markets of a competitive economy. The economy consists of households and firms. The aim of households is to maximise the utility received from consumption subject to an income constraint. This income constraint depends upon the household's factor endowment and the prices that factors can obtain on the market. Firms aim to maximise their net present value constrained by the technological factors which govern the transformation of factors of production into output, and also by the market demand for output and the market prices of factors.

We thus obtain a supply function for each factor of production in which its own price and the prices of consumption goods that the owners of factors of production wish to purchase enter as arguments. Each factor of production also has a demand function in which its own price, the price of substitute factors and the prices of the commodities that the factor is used to produce enter as arguments. Each produced commodity has a demand function containing all commodity prices and household incomes. The latter depend on the quantity of factors households can sell and the prices at which they can sell. A supply function, dependent on commodity prices and factor prices, exists for each commodity.

An excess demand function is obtained by subtracting the demand function for a factor or commodity from its supply function. For an individual commodity, q_i, this is written as

$$E^d q_i = D_i(p_1, \ldots, p_i, \ldots, p_m, p_1^f, \ldots, p_j^f, \ldots, p_n^f)$$
$$- S_i(p_1, \ldots, p_i, \ldots, p_m, p_1^f, \ldots, p_j^f, \ldots, p_n^f). \quad (7.27)$$

There are m commodities with prices $p_1 \cdots p_m$ and n factors of production with prices $p_1^f \cdots p_n^f$. There are therefore $m + n$ excess demand equations containing $m + n$ endogenous variables. Other determinants of excess demand, such as household preferences and the technological factors embodied in the production functions, are exogenous to the system.

In equilibrium all markets will be cleared which means all excess demand equations will equal zero. As mentioned in Chapter 2, one of these equations is redundant since if $n + m - 1$ markets are in equilibrium so must be the final, mth, market. This means that the system only solves for $n + m - 1$ commodity and factor prices. It is relative prices that are solved when the system is in equilibrium, not absolute prices which can take on any value. For instance in a two-good world, if the markets for goods A and B are both in equilibrium at a price ratio P_A/P_B of two to one, it does not matter what the absolute prices are in terms of pounds so long as the two to one ratio is preserved.

Every price in a general equilibrium model can be expressed in terms of the price of one particular good. This good is known as a *numéraire*. In the two-good example, if we let good B be the *numéraire*, the price of good A is $2B$. In a system of $n + m$ commodities and factors one of these could serve as a *numéraire*, with its price fixed at one, while all the other $n + m - 1$ prices are expressed relative to the *numéraire*. Money is generally the *numéraire* good and prices are expressed in nominal terms as so many units of money.

The above is an outline of neoclassical value theory. The equilibrium solution of relative values is worked out without direct reference to money. It is relative prices, which are real values, that influence the actions of rational decision-makers. On to this construct neoclassical theorists appended a monetary theory of price level determination. It is assumed that money is held to finance transactions and that the quantity of money is a certain proportion, k, of the money value of transactions. (This is the expression in brackets in equation (7.28).) This is the quantity theory approach to the demand for money:

$$M^d = k\left[\sum_{i=1}^{m} p_i q_i + \sum_{j=1}^{n} p_j^f f_j\right] \qquad (7.28)$$

where q_i is the quantity of the ith commodity and f_j is the quantity of the jth factor of production. If the nominal money stock is fixed at M_0^s, monetary equilibrium requires that

$$M_0^s = k\left[\sum_{i=1}^{m} p_i q_i + \sum_{j=1}^{n} p_j^f f_j\right]. \qquad (7.29)$$

The relative prices p_i/p_1, p_j^f/p_1 are determined by the solution of the $n + m$ excess demand equations. The introduction of a fixed nominal money stock determines a unique price level. There is just one level of money prices which make the demand and supply of money equal. A change in the money stock changes the price level while leaving the real values of relative prices and quantities unchanged.*

How equilibrium is achieved in a system of independently acting decision-units is a difficult problem which continues to exercise economic theorists. Walras imagined a process of *tâtonnement* or groping towards equilibrium. A fictional auctioneer exists who takes no part in exchange. He calls out a set of prices and registers the quantities the transactors wish to buy and sell. If some markets remain uncleared, the auctioneer calls out another set of prices. The process continues until the auctioneer has found that set of prices which clears all markets. Trade then takes place at equilibrium prices.

The neoclassical system of general equilibrium exchange is essentially a barter system and does not satisfactorily explain the role of money in a monetary economy. As discussed in Chapter 6, if there is certainty and no transactions costs, there is no need to hold money. In the Walrasian system market participants have no need of money. Providing they all know that they can conduct the desired amount of exchange at the equilibrium prices, these transactions can occur without money changing hands.

The neoclassical system of Walrasian exchange is a special theoretical case. All transactors have perfect information at zero cost since they are told what is the equilibrium set of prices. Perfect information involves knowledge of current as well as future equilibrium prices. The lack of a properly defined role for money is due to the existence of perfect information and certainty.

The Attainment of Equilibrium with Imperfect Information

Keynes's work is important in providing a major advance in the integration of monetary theory and value theory. Keynes was critical of neoclassical

* See [2] for a fuller discussion.

theory for concentrating on the determination of relative values, while assuming that total output was fixed. He was concerned to provide a theory which would explain the aggregate level of production in the short run. The reinterpretation of Keynes by Clower and Leijonhufvud stresses the importance of Keynes's disequilibrium analysis. They contend that Keynes accepted the neoclassical assumptions of rational choice by decision-makers in response to price incentives but rejected the ability of the equilibrating process of *tâtonnement* to make predictions applicable to the real world.

In practice trade does take place at non-equilibrium prices. This is referred to as 'false' trading. When this occurs we need to distinguish between a household's notional demand for commodities, which is what it would like to buy at equilibrium prices could it also sell its factors of production at equilibrium prices, from its actual demand for commodities. Similarly firms have a notional demand for factors of production based on what the market demand for their product would be if households could sell their factor services at equilibrium prices. Once the economy has moved into disequilibrium and involuntary unemployment appears, households cannot sell all the labour they wish to sell at the current price. Their actual or effective demand for commodities is constrained by the incomes they can obtain in disequilibrium and not by those they would receive were the economy in equilibrium.

Communication between transactors is hampered in a market economy that lacks a Walrasian auctioneer. Without this market clearing device households cannot signal to firms that they would like to buy additional commodities if only they could sell more of their factor services. The Walrasian auctioneer would see excess notional supply in the labour market and excess notional demand in the goods market and would alter prices accordingly.

Neoclassical economists extended this analysis to real world disequilibrium situations where they viewed price adjustments as the means of restoring equilibrium. The reappraisal of Keynes views him as having reversed the neoclassical ordering of adjustment, which was largely via price changes rather than output changes. Keynes's analysis was that once the economy has been disturbed into unemployment disequilibrium, the dynamics of adjustment involve output rather than price reductions. Once households cannot sell their desired quantity of factor services, their effective demand is curtailed. This causes a further reduction in the demand for factors. Thus the Keynesian multiplier is seen as a deviation amplifying mechanism that magnifies an initial disturbance. So long as the marginal propensity to spend is less than one, the multiplier is of finite size, so that the economy is not explosively unstable.

Adjustment in unemployment disequilibrium by quantity rather than by price reductions and the destabilising effects of falling prices are due to the difficulties of obtaining information in an uncertain world. Uncertain future events affect the outcome of decisions taken in the present. Often one cannot even attach probabilities to such events. People deal with such circumstances by assuming that

the present is a much more serviceable guide to the future than a candid examination of past experience would show it to have been hitherto . . . (and) assume that the existing state of opinion as expressed in prices and the character of existing output is based on a correct summing up of future prospects so that we can accept it as such unless and until something new and relevant comes into the picture [16].

It is particularly difficult for the price system in a monetary economy to convey correct intertemporal information to transactors, so that saving and investment decisions are likely to be unco-ordinated and are thus a source of disequilibrium. By saving, households indicate that they wish to consume in the future but, because of uncertainty they do not commit themselves to specified future purchases of goods and services. Hence this future demand is not communicated directly to firms. An increased desire to save is translated into the desire to hold a larger portfolio of assets. In a monetary economy wealth owners can hold financial as well as real assets. To the extent that they translate their increased desire to save into a demand for more financial assets, the signal for firms to invest and produce more goods and services for future consumption becomes muted. It is transmitted via an increase in asset prices which results in a fall in the interest rate and this provides firms with an incentive to invest.

The role of money is of key importance in understanding the functioning of a market economy under conditions of uncertainty. Holding money and other short-term financial assets forms a means of linking the present with the future which allays people's fears of the uncertain future by giving them liquidity. The cost of holding money has to be increased, as it is by a higher real rate of return on capital goods or by inflation, before people will part with liquidity. The desire for safety makes people forgo the higher rate of return on capital in order to hold assets which are more liquid. This problem is at the crux of Keynes's concern with the role of investment, saving and portfolio decisions in explaining the disequilibrium tendencies of the economy.

In the Walrasian system transactions are made in perfectly certain real terms. The lack of perfect information in a monetary economy means that people cannot in general make contracts to exchange goods and services in terms of certainly realisable relative prices. A worker and employer agree on a money wage, both making their decision to buy or sell labour on their estimation of the real wage involved. If the price level changes un-expectedly the actual real wage will differ from the estimated real wage.

For this reason falling prices can be destabilising and increase rather than reduce the volume of unemployment. An unemployed worker is willing to work at or above his reservation real wage. His idea of what money wage is an acceptable real wage depends on his previous experience of money wages and prices which influences his expectations about their future values. If prices are falling, he may not be aware that his reservation money wage is in fact higher than the one required to give him his reservation real wage. Such job seekers lengthen their period of search as they only gradually revise their opinion of their acceptable money wage. Meanwhile their effective demand has fallen, causing labour to be laid off elsewhere in the economy.

Involuntary unemployment appears with workers being unable to find jobs although they are willing to work at the going real wage rate. Once in disequilibrium we are off both the aggregate demand and supply functions of labour. The actual real wage may be lower than the equilibrium real wage. In disequilibrium the demand for labour at the equilibrium real wage is less than it would be in full-employment equilibrium because of the lower level of effective demand.* It is only in static analysis that the actual real wage appears greater when there is unemployment than when there is full-employment equilibrium.

If Keynes is interpreted in static equilibrium terms, he is attributed with having pointed out that wage and price rigidities exist and hence price flexibility will not restore equilibrium because prices will not fall. If such is the case he would have said nothing at odds with neoclassical thinking. Keynes's argument is quite different. Price and wage flexibility are unlikely to return the economy to equilibrium in a dynamic world as they are destabilising. He saw wage rigidity as a factor preventing large, destabilising falls in the price level, rather than as hindering a return to equilibrium. In Keynesian analysis reducing money wages or increasing the money supply work through the same transmission mechanism of falling interest rates stimulating aggregate demand. The latter method has the advantage of not inducing destabilising price expectations. The following passage summarises Keynes's conclusions:

There is therefore, no ground for the belief that a flexible wage policy is capable of maintaining a state of continuous full employment:– any more than for the belief that an open market monetary policy is capable, unaided of achieving the same result. The economic system cannot be made self-adjusting along these lines.†

7.5 CONCLUSION: KEYNESIANS AND MONETARISTS

It is in the interest of academics, who wish to contribute to academic debate, to emphasise and even create points of disagreement that do not exist in the extreme forms in which they may be expressed. This has

* See [17] for the construction of this type of model.
† *The General Theory*, p. 267.

occurred in macroeconomics by concentrating on extremely simple models, which differ by virtue of their simplifying assumptions and hence produce different results. The neoclassical *ISLM* model, or even more simplified quantity theory, is posited against a Keynesian one-sector or *ISLM* model, and thus differences are exaggerated.

The neoclassical three-sector model that has emerged from the Keynesian–neoclassical debate over *The General Theory* shows those factors that influence the behaviour of macro variables in the long run. The real rate of interest is determined by the interaction of the productivity of real capital, which is maintained by continual technical change, and by the desire to save. There is a full-employment region of output determined by the constraints imposed by the limited availability of resources. The supply of output can be expressed in terms of an aggregate production function. Underlying the aggregate production function are the micro equations of the economy expressing the excess demand functions for commodities and factors of production. Thus, neoclassical economists see the Walrasian system of general equilibrium equations as determining the full-employment level of national output. Over the long run the quantity of money is the major determinant of the price level.

Keynesian macro model building has been very much concerned with the short-run determination of variables, particularly with the determination of real output below its full-employment level. Keynesian thought is characterised by a belief, acquired from the history of the 1930s, that capitalist economies tend to a state of chronic unemployment. It stresses the impact of monetary phenomena upon the rate of interest and the resulting divergence of the actual rate from the real rate required for full-employment equilibrium. The price level is seen in the short run as being determined by two sets of forces, those coming from the supply side of the economy, namely labour productivity and the money wage rate, and those embodied in the level of aggregate demand.

Keynesian economists have been concerned with detailed macro model building. They have developed large-scale econometric models of the economy which are disaggregated versions of the basic three-sector model. These are used in attempts to forecast the values of macro variables. Keynesian methodology is concerned with the detailed investigation of the structure of macro models. This involves the desire to disaggregate and include more variables as well as the examination of the transmission mechanism by which variables react upon one another.

The monetarist school of thought has now rectified the early-Keynesians' neglect of monetary theory, though monetary analysis was an important element of Keynes's work. The monetarist methodology believes in the virtue of extremely simple models. So long as the model predicts well, for instance in correlating nominal income and the money supply, monetarists have not been greatly concerned with the details of how money affects economic activity. Friedman has responded to criticism of this neglect by providing 'A Framework for Monetary Analysis' [18, 19] which is based on the *ISLM* model. This is a good indication that many of the contested issues in the Keynesian–monetarist debate are more apparent than real.

REFERENCES

[1] L. A. Metzler, 'Wealth, Saving and the Rate of Interest', *Journal of Political Economy*, 59 (April 1951).

[2] D. Patinkin, *Money, Interest and Prices*, 2nd edn. (New York: Harper & Row, 1965).

[3] J. R. Hicks, 'Mr Keynes and the Classics: A Suggested Interpretation', *Econometrica*, 5, 2 (1937).

[4] A. Hansen, *A Guide to Keynes* (New York: McGraw-Hill, 1953).

[5] F. Modigliani, 'Liquidity Preference and the Theory of Interest and Money,' *Econometrica*, 12 (1944).

[6] A. C. Pigou, 'The Classical Stationary State', *Economic Journal*, 53 (December 1943).

[7] J. G. Gurley and E. S. Shaw, *Money in a Theory of Finance* (Washington, D.C.: The Brookings Institution, 1960).

[8] B. P. Pesek and T. R. Saving, *Money, Wealth and Economic Theory*, (New York: Macmillan, 1967).

[9] D. Patinkin, 'Money and Wealth: A Review Article', *Journal of Economic Literature*, 7 (1969).

[10] W. Smith, 'Current Issues in Monetary Economics', *Journal of Economic Literature*, 8, 3 (September 1970).

[11] R. A. Mundell, 'The Public Debt, Corporate Income Taxes and the Rate of Interest', *Journal of Political Economy*, 60 (1960).

[12] D. Patinkin, 'Price Flexibility and Full Employment', originally published in *American Economic Review*, 38 (1948) revised version in *Readings in Monetary Theory*, American Economic Association (New York: Blackistone, 1962).

[13] R. W. Clower, 'The Keynesian Counter-Revolution: A Theoretical Appraisal', in *The Theory of Interest Rates*, ed. F. H. Hahn and F. Brechling (London: Macmillan, 1965).

[14] A. Leijonhufvud, *On Keynesian Economics and the Economics of Keynes* (Oxford University Press, 1968).

[15] L. Walras, *Elements of Pure Economics* (1874) translated by W. Jaffé (Illinois: Homewood, 1954).

[16] J. M. Keynes, 'The General Theory of Employment', *Quarterly Journal of Economics*, 51 (1937) p. 212.

[17] R. J. Barro and H. I. Grossman, 'A General Disequilibrium Model of

Income and Employment', *American Economic Review*, 61 (March 1971).
[18] M. Friedman, 'A Theoretical Framework for Monetary Analysis', *Journal of Political Economy*, 78 (1970).
[19] M. Friedman, 'A Monetary Theory of Nominal Income', *Journal of Political Economy*, 79 (1971).

8 The Open Economy

The analysis of macroeconomic behaviour has so far been conducted within a closed economy. We now extend the analysis to an economy which is engaged in foreign trade. The formal models of an open economy that are presented here assume that the domestic economy is small relative to the rest of the world. This obviates the need to take account of the effect of the domestic economy, which is referred to as the United Kingdom, upon the rest of the world and the resulting feedback effects from the rest of the world to the home economy.

8.1 THE BALANCE OF PAYMENTS

The money flows arising from the transactions in goods, services and assets between the United Kingdom and foreign residents that occur over a given period of time is summarised in the balance-of-payments accounts.* The balance-of-payments accounts can be subdivided into the balance of payments on current account, the balance on capital account and official financing. The balance of payments on current account is the value of exported goods and services net of imported goods and services. A subdivision of the balance of payments on current account is the balance of trade which is the difference between the value of exported and imported goods. The capital account records both the borrowing and lending of funds abroad by residents. The difference between non-official borrowing and lending abroad is the net capital flow to or from the domestic country. If borrowing exceeds lending there is a net capital inflow.

The export of U.K. goods and services and borrowing from abroad (sales of U.K. assets to foreigners) give rise to an equivalent supply of foreign currency by foreigners who demand sterling in exchange. This they use to

---

* A more detailed treatment can be found at an elementary level in [1] and at a more advanced level in [2].

TABLE 8.1 The Balance-of-Payments Account

Exports of goods and services − imports of goods and services	
	Balance on current account $(X-F)$
Non-official borrowing − lending abroad	+
	Net capital flow (N.K.)
	=
	Total currency flow (T.C.F.)
	+
Official financing =	− Total currency flow
	= Zero

finance their purchases of U.K. goods, services and assets. Correspondingly, the import of foreign goods and services and lending abroad (buying foreign assets) give rise to a supply of sterling by U.K. residents, who demand an equivalent amount of foreign exchange to finance their foreign purchases. To summarise we have:

exports + non-official borrowing abroad = demand for sterling = supply of foreign exchange;
imports + non-official lending abroad = supply of sterling = demand for foreign exchange.

The balance of payments is in equilibrium if exports + borrowing abroad = imports + lending abroad, i.e. if (exports − imports) + (borrowing − lending abroad) = 0, i.e. if balance on current account + net capital flow = 0. In the United Kingdom the balance on current account plus the net capital flow is known as the total currency flow. If this is negative the balance of payments is in overall deficit and if the total currency flow is positive the balance of payments is in surplus.

The final part of the balance-of-payments account shows how the deficit or surplus is officially financed. The official financing item by definition equals, and is opposite in sign to, the total currency flow. A deficit is financed by running down the country's gold and foreign exchange reserves or by official borrowing from foreign central banks or the International Monetary Fund. A surplus allows a country either to reduce its official liabilities or to increase its foreign exchange reserves. The total currency flow plus official financing necessarily sum to zero, as shown in Table 8.1.

8.2 THE EXCHANGE RATE

The exchange rate is the price of the domestic currency in terms of foreign currency. It is the number of units of foreign exchange, Q, that one unit of

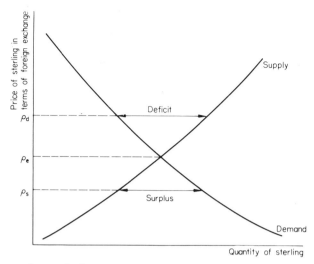

FIGURE 8.1   *The foreign exchange market and the balance of payments*

the domestic currency will buy. The exchange rate is in equilibrium when demand equals the supply of the domestic currency on the world's foreign exchange markets. This state corresponds to balance-of-payments equilibrium, or a zero total currency flow. If the supply of sterling exceeds the demand for sterling on the foreign exchange market there will be a tendency under free, stable market conditions, for the exchange rate of sterling to fall.

The demand and supply of sterling on the foreign exchange market will bear the usual relationship to the price of sterling. The demand for sterling increases as the exchange rate for sterling depreciates. Depreciation lowers the foreign exchange price of U.K. exports and, assuming that foreign demand is negatively related to price, it will increase the demand for U.K. exports and thus the demand for sterling. The sterling price of imports is increased by a depreciation of sterling and, given a normal demand function, will reduce the demand for imports. Providing import demand is price elastic, this will reduce the supply of sterling.*

A flexible or floating exchange rate is one that is allowed to find its own level as determined by the market forces of supply and demand. (This would be exchange rate ρ_e in Figure 8.1.) A country may, at the other

* The sum of the elasticities of demand for imports and exports must exceed one for depreciation to cause a net reduction in the excess supply of sterling. This assumes an infinitely elastic supply function for both imports and exports. The demand and supply functions for sterling each hold all other variables except the exchange rate constant. This means that they assume, among other things, a constant rate of domestic expenditure (absorption).

extreme, maintain a fixed exchange rate, which can differ from its equilibrium exchange rate. If the fixed exchange rate exceeds the equilibrium rate, the country will run a balance-of-payments deficit, as shown in Figure 8.1. To prevent the exchange rate from falling, the central bank must intervene in the foreign exchange market and buy up the excess supply of the domestic currency by selling foreign exchange reserves. A surplus country prevents its exchange rate from appreciating by selling its domestic currency to satisfy the excess demand for that currency. Foreign exchange is bought with the domestic currency and reserves are accumulated.

8.3 A MODEL OF THE OPEN ECONOMY

Following from the assumption that the domestic economy is too small to affect the rest of the world, it can be assumed that foreign real output, interest rates and price levels are fixed. The reader should be particularly aware, when studying open economy models, that the conclusions depend crucially on the underlying assumptions, and should bear in mind that only a limited number of variables are included in the following analysis. When the economy is opened to international transactions three equilibrium conditions have to be met if the economy is to be in overall equilibrium. These are goods market equilibrium, money market equilibrium and foreign exchange market equilibrium. Each of these equilibrium conditions is discussed in turn.

Goods Market Equilibrium

For goods market equilibrium desired aggregate demand for the domestic product, E, must equal the amount supplied, y. All the variables are measured in constant U.K. prices.

$$y = E \quad \text{(equilibrium condition)} \tag{8.1}$$

$$y = C + S + T \quad \text{(ways of disposing of income)} \tag{8.2}$$

$$E = C + I + G + X - F \quad \text{(components of aggregate demand).} \tag{8.3}$$

Using these equations we can express the equilibrium condition for the goods market in the form of either equation (8.4) or (8.4a).

$$y - (C + I + G) = X - F \quad \text{(where } A = C + I + G\text{)} \tag{8.4}$$

$$(S - I) + (T - G) = X - F \quad \text{(current account balance).} \tag{8.4a}$$

The sum of consumption, investment and government expenditure is known as absorption, and is given the symbol A. Absorption is the demand by domestic residents for goods and services, including their demand for imports. Absorption is quite distinct from aggregate expenditure, E, which is the demand by residents and foreigners for goods and services produced by U.K. firms.

If absorption is less than U.K. national output, then the left-hand side of both equations (8.4) and (8.4a) is positive. An excess of U.K. output over absorption corresponds in equation (8.4a) to the sum of net saving by the U.K. private sector $(S - I)$, and net saving by the government $(T - G)$, being positive. For goods market equilibrium, the surplus of absorption over U.K. output must be sold to foreigners. This gives a surplus on the current account ($X - F$ is positive and equals $y - A$). If absorption exceeds the U.K.'s G.D.P., the excess demand for goods and services by U.K. residents must be bought from foreigners in order to equate aggregate demand and supply. In this event the balance on current account will be in deficit.

A positive balance on current account means that the economy as a whole is engaged in net saving. The difference between the volume of output produced and the volume of U.K. and foreign output bought by U.K. residents is accumulated in foreign assets. Thus net aggregate saving can equally well be regarded as net financial investment by the country. A positive current account balance is financed by net lending abroad. Under a regime of fixed exchange rates the acquisition of foreign exchange finances any excess of exports minus imports over the net capital flow.

Conversely, a negative balance on current account means that the economy is using more resources than are made available by its national product. This excess is obtained from abroad and is financed by net borrowing from abroad. (This includes the sale of existing assets held by U.K. residents.) Under a regime of fixed exchange rates, any current account deficit which exceeds the net private capital flow is financed by selling foreign exchange reserves.

We assume that the demand for U.K. exports depends on the size of the foreign national product and on the relative price of U.K. goods with respect to foreign goods. For the purposes of this analysis it is assumed that the rest of the world's real output and price level are fixed. Given the latter assumption the relative price of U.K. goods to foreign goods depends on the U.K. price level, P, and on the exchange rate, ρ. Imports depend on the U.K. national income, the U.K. price level and the exchange rate. The export and import demand functions are given below:

$$X^d = X(\rho, P) \tag{8.5}$$

$$F^d = F(\rho, P, y). \tag{8.6}$$

For given values of ρ and P we can derive the IS function for an open economy. This shows the various levels of the interest rate and real output for which the goods market is in equilibrium. A change in ρ or P, taxation, government expenditure and other items of autonomous expenditure shift the *IS* function.

Money Market Equilibrium

In this model there are three types of financial assets that the private sector can hold, money, domestic bonds and foreign bonds. Foreigners hold domestic bonds but, unless the domestic currency serves as a reserve currency, have no demand to hold the domestic currency as an asset.

Capital market equilibrium requires that the quantity of domestic money and the stock of domestic bonds are held willingly by residents and foreigners at the going output and interest rate levels. Since the bond market cannot be in disequilibrium without disturbing the money market, equilibrium in the money market is sufficient to establish that there must also be equilibrium in the bond market.

The demand for real money balances is assumed to depend on the level of real national output and on the domestic interest rate. This is taken, in the absence of inflationary expectations, to be the real rate of interest, i.e.

$$M^d = P f(y, i).^* \tag{8.7}$$

The nominal money supply depends on the quantity of high-powered money, H, and on the parameters which make up the bank multiplier, β.

$$M^s = \beta H. \tag{8.8}$$

High-powered money is issued by the government and comes from two sources:

(1) When the government sells its bonds to the central bank, the latter matches the change in the asset side of its balance sheet with a corresponding change in the debit side by creating public deposits. As the government spends these deposits they accrue in the hands of the private sector, either as commercial bank reserves or as currency in circulation with the public. The total amount of high-powered money from this source is indicated by the total amount of government securities held by the central bank net of public deposits (given the symbol B_G^C).

(2) The second source of H is the accumulation of foreign exchange reserves. A U.K. resident, who has acquired foreign exchange, sells it to the foreign exchange account (known as the exchange-equalisation account in the United Kingdom). In return the resident obtains a claim on the government's bank deposits at the central bank. This accrues either as commercial bank reserves or as currency in circulation.

The two identities associated with H, one relating to its source, equation

---

* The demand for nominal money balances is assumed to be homogeneous of degree one in money prices. Thus $M^d/P = f(y, i)$.

(8.9), and the other relating to the uses of H, equation (8.10), are given below:

$$H = Q + B_G^C \qquad (8.9)$$

$$H = C + R \qquad (8.10)$$

where Q is the foreign exchange reserves, B_G^C is the central bank's net holdings of government debt, C is the currency in circulation and R is the commercial bank reserves. Substituting equation (8.9) into equation (8.8) we derive the money supply function:

$$M^s = \beta(Q + B_G^C). \qquad (8.11)$$

Thus, given β, the domestic money supply will increase if there is a balance-of-payments surplus, if the government fails to finance all of its budget deficit by selling bonds or if the government engages in open-market purchases of its securities.

Foreign Exchange Market (Balance-of-Payments) Equilibrium

This equilibrium requires that the total currency flow is zero (that is the net capital flow equals the current account balance). The net capital flow is assumed to depend on the differential between the domestic and world interest rates, the latter being assumed constant. If there is perfect capital mobility, international capital flows will equalise domestic and world interest rates; the domestic country can only alter its interest rate temporarily, since the country's equilibrium interest rate is necessarily the world interest rate.

The demand functions for exports and imports have been given by equations (8.5) and (8.6). From these we can see that as real output rises, imports rise and so the current account worsens, given a fixed exchange rate and a constant domestic price level. An increasing balance-of-payments deficit as aggregate demand rises can be offset by an increased capital inflow, induced by a higher domestic interest rate (given that capital is not perfectly mobile). Thus there is a locus of income and interest rate levels at which the balance of payments is in equilibrium. This is indicated by schedule B in Figure 8.2.*

In Figure 8.2, given the values of the variables in parentheses and also the other parameters of the model, an overall equilibrium in the three sectors is not possible. When the goods and money markets are in equilibrium and the level of real output is determined as y_0, the balance of payments is in deficit.

* A horizontal B schedule indicates perfect capital mobility, since the equilibrium level of the domestic rate of interest must be the same as the world interest rate. A verticle B schedule indicates complete capital immobility in response to interest-rate differentials. Thus, there is only one level of output consistent with balance-of-payments equilibrium.

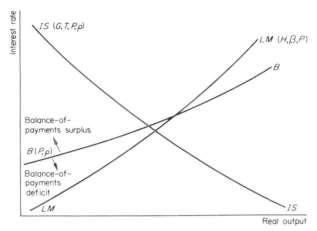

FIGURE 8.2   *The absence of simultaneous equilibrium in the goods, monetary and foreign sectors of the economy*

The question we now have to consider is whether there are forces in the economy and in the rest of the world that will bring about an adjustment to full equilibrium, if the domestic economy is in disequilibrium (see [4]).

8.4   THE KEYNESIAN MODEL (UNEMPLOYMENT AND FIXED DOMESTIC PRICE LEVEL)

The Model with a Flexible Exchange Rate

Since there is disequilibrium on the foreign exchange market as the balance of payments is in deficit, the exchange rate will depreciate. This stimulates aggregate demand for the domestic output by increasing exports and reducing imports. Higher aggregate demand due to the lower exchange rate causes the *IS* schedule in Figure 8.3 to shift up to the left. The *B* schedule moves down because at a lower exchange rate the balance of payments is in equilibrium at a lower interest rate and at a higher level of real output than before. Since this model assumes a perfectly elastic supply of output up to full employment, the domestic price level remains unaltered. The equilibrium solution involves a higher level of real output associated with balance-of-payments equilibrium. At the equilibrium exchange rate, ρ_1, the level of real output has risen to y_1.

If the domestic unemployment is associated with a surplus on the balance of payments, the exchange rate will rise to eliminate that surplus. Since exports will be reduced and imports increased, real output will decline.

Restoring balance-of-payments equilibrium by means of a variable

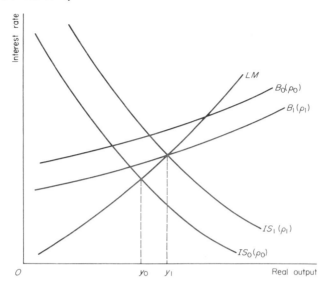

FIGURE 8.3   *Adjustment to overall equilibrium via flexible exchange rates*

exchange rate involves adjustment via a change in relative prices. A depreciation of the exchange rate lowers the domestic price level in terms of the world price level, though the domestic price level itself remains unchanged in terms of sterling. Depreciation of the exchange rate means that U.K. goods become cheaper in terms of foreign goods. An alternative way of expressing this is that the commodity terms of trade, which is the ratio of import prices to export prices, have moved against the United Kingdom. This involves a reduction in welfare for U.K. citizens since they can obtain a smaller quantity of foreign goods for a given amount of domestic goods.*

The Model with a Fixed Exchange Rate

If the exchange rate is fixed and the domestic price level is also rigid, there is no way of automatic adjustment via a change in relative prices. In the case of a deficit on the balance of payments, the authorities can only prevent the exchange rate from falling by intervening in the foreign exchange market. Foreign exchange reserves are reduced in order to buy up the excess supply of sterling. As the foreign exchange reserves fall, high-powered money is contracted and causes a decline in the domestic money supply. As people attempt, unsuccessfully in aggregate, to obtain additional money balances by selling assets the rate of interest rises. This reduces the level of aggregate

---

* This assumes that productivity per man remains constant.

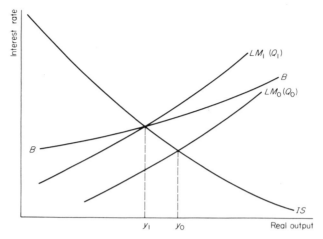

FIGURE 8.4   *Adjustment to overall equilibrium under a regime of fixed exchange rates*

demand and causes additional unemployment. This analysis is illustrated in Figure 8.4. The *LM* function shifts up to the left as the money supply declines until balance-of-payments equilibrium is restored, whereupon the money supply ceases to decline, as foreign exchange reserves are no longer being depleted.

The adjustment that occurs in this case, when both the domestic price level and the exchange rate are fixed, comes about through portfolio adjustment and not via a change in the domestic price level relative to the world price level.

If a balance-of-payments surplus is associated with unemployment and a fixed domestic price level, together with a fixed exchange rate, foreign exchange reserves will be rising. The money supply will expand. Portfolio disequilibrium now exists as the money supply exceeds the demand for money. In an attempt to get rid of excess money balances, residents buy goods and assets. Asset prices rise, and the rate of interest falls. The increase in aggregate demand, together with the reduced capital inflow caused by the fall in the rate of interest, reduce the balance-of-payments surplus to zero.

From this analysis emerge the following conclusions:

(1) If a country is suffering from unemployment and has a balance-of-payments deficit, a policy of allowing the exchange rate to depreciate will correct the deficit and reduce unemployment. In contrast, the maintenance of a fixed exchange rate will increase the level of unemployment if the balance-of-payments deficit is corrected by allowing the money supply to contract.

(2) If a country has unemployment, accompanied by a balance-of-payments surplus, a policy of allowing the exchange rate to appreciate will correct the surplus at the expense of increasing unemployment. In contrast, maintaining a fixed exchange rate and allowing the money supply automatically to increase will reduce unemployment while correcting balance-of-payments disequilibrium.

Sterilisation

If a country operates a fixed exchange rate, its domestic money supply is subject to variation from external causes. A balance-of-payments deficit will reduce the domestic money supply, whilst a surplus will increase it. It has become standard practice for the authorities to offset such variations by neutralising or sterilising the impact of changes in the stock of foreign exchange reserves on the domestic money supply. A deficit involves the central bank in selling foreign exchange and buying sterling to keep up the exchange rate. The proceeds from the sale of foreign exchange are used to buy government bonds from the public, thus preventing the domestic money supply from falling. A surplus country can stop its money supply from rising by selling government bonds to the public. High-powered money is thus kept constant. Any change in foreign reserves is exactly offset by a change in the opposite direction in government net liabilities held by the central bank.

In the case of a deficit accompanied by unemployment, the operation of a fixed exchange rate is not allowed to increase unemployment as the domestic money supply is prevented from contracting. Adjustment to balance-of-payments equilibrium is prevented. The sterilisation programme can only continue so long as the central bank has foreign exchange reserves. Sooner or later a correction of the balance of payments is necessary. This is because of the difficulties of financing the deficit, not because the deficit itself is undesirable. A deficit on the balance of payments enables a country to engage in more investment and consumption than it otherwise could. Reducing the deficit is inevitably painful as it involves a cut in consumption or investment. The consequences are particularly felt in the short run as a cut in living standards if it is consumption that is squeezed.

If the government is committed to keeping the existing exchange rate, the only means of adjusting a current account deficit is to reduce the level of domestic absorption. Given that resources cannot be switched instantaneously from their existing uses into producing additional exports and import substitutes, unemployment will increase. It is in such circumstances that Keynes [3] advocated allowing the exchange rate to be flexible, so that the level of domestic output was not sacrificed to the cause of external equilibrium.

It is easier for a surplus country to continue to sterilise its foreign exchange reserves as these are rising. Nevertheless, it is argued by monetarists that sterilisation cannot continue indefinitely in a world of highly mobile international capital. Take the case of a surplus country. In order to persuade the public to hold an increasing quantity of bonds relative to the constant money stock, interest rates will have to rise. This attracts a capital inflow, increasing the surplus and necessitating yet further sales of bonds in order to keep the money supply constant. For a deficit country a sterilisation policy means falling interest rates and an ever increasing capital outflow involving further purchases of bonds. In either case the situation becomes untenable and adjustment can no longer be prevented. Either the fixed exchange rate policy or the sterilisation policy has to give way.

8.5   THE NEOCLASSICAL MODEL

From the above discussion the existence of two types of adjustment to balance-of-payments disequilibrium has emerged.

(1) The first type is portfolio adjustment which takes place when the demand and supply of money are not in equilibrium.

(2) The second is a change in the relative price of domestic to foreign goods.

So far we have only taken account of a relative price adjustment occurring through a change in the exchange rate. The neoclassical model, which solves for full-employment equilibrium on the basis of flexible prices, can adjust the price level of the domestic country relative to the world price level by domestic price deflation or inflation.

The traditional gold exchange standard was analysed as providing a balance-of-payments adjustment mechanism via changes in the domestic price level. Under the gold standard the domestic money supply had to be directly related to the size of the country's gold reserves. Therefore a surplus country would automatically increase its money supply and a deficit country reduce its money supply. Monetary expansion in a surplus country would cause its price level to rise relative to the world price level. Exports would decline and imports rise, bringing about an elimination of the surplus. Deficit countries would experience a decline in their domestic money supply and a corresponding fall in their price level relative to the rest of the world. As exports rose and imports fell, the deficit would be corrected. This system forced both deficit and surplus countries to adjust to balance-of-payments disequilibrium. Its operation relied on some degree of wage and price flexibility in both surplus and deficit countries.

The operation of the fixed exchange rate system since the Second World War has placed the burden of adjustment on deficit countries. Since the domestic money supply is no longer tied to foreign exchange reserves, governments can neutralise the effect of balance-of-payments disequilibrium upon the domestic money supply. Although such neutralisation may eventually break down, deficit countries can sustain such a policy for a shorter period of time than can surplus countries. Once foreign exchange reserves are exhausted, deficit countries have to adjust. This adjustment is greater when surplus countries are avoiding adjustment.

8.6 A MONETARIST VIEW OF BALANCE-OF-PAYMENTS ADJUSTMENT

Keynesian models in which real output is below its full-employment level can be useful for short-run analysis. Their main drawback for analysing current economic problems is that either the price level (in the two-sector model) or the money wage rate (in the three-sector model) is assumed constant (see Chapter 7).

If real output grows at a reasonably steady rate, deviations from full employment are short-run occurrences which can be neglected for the purposes of long-run analysis. If output is at its full-employment level, then the level of aggregate demand for the domestic output must be at least equal to the amount of output being produced. Therefore a country running a deficit on its current account is absorbing more goods and services than it is producing. The discrepancy between absorption and real domestic output can be viewed as the outcome of portfolio adjustment decisions. If a country's absorption is greater than its output, there is an aggregate decision to run down domestic assets or build up liabilities. This is because a current account deficit is financed by net borrowing from abroad or, if a fixed exchange rate is maintained, by running down official assets. Similarly a decision to absorb less than the domestic output is a decision to add foreign assets or reduce foreign liabilities in the domestic country's portfolio. This way of looking at the balance of payments focuses attention on domestic portfolio disequilibrium as the crux of balance-of-payments disequilibrium.

The model [5] in which the consequences of portfolio disequilibrium are analysed has certain distinct features which are thought to reflect current reality when long-run adjustments are allowed for. Perfect capital mobility is assumed so that the domestic and world level of interest rates will be identical in equilibrium and only diverge in disequilibrium. The domestic price level is assumed fixed in relation to the world price level and will only fall out of line in disequilibrium. This assumption is the consequence of assuming a high elasticity of substitution between U.K. exportable goods (those goods which the United Kingdom produces both for export and home consumption) and importable goods (those goods both imported and produced for home consumption). This means that a rise in the U.K. price level relative to the world price level causes both foreigners and residents to switch from U.K. to foreign produced goods. Given a fixed exchange rate, a deficit on the current account of the balance of payments ensues. If the exchange rate remains fixed, equilibrium can only be restored by a return of the U.K. price level to its equilibrium position *vis-à-vis* the world price level. This can happen via some combination of a decline in the U.K. price level and a rise in the world price level. In this model the United Kingdom cannot affect either its equilibrium interest rate level or, given a fixed exchange rate, its equilibrium price level relative to the rest of the world. In this way the model takes account of the consequences of long-run adjustment that are unaccounted for by models concerned only with short-run adjustment.

Portfolio disequilibrium will manifest itself in the money market. Any discrepancy between the demand and supply of money will result in an adjustment which affects the demand for goods and assets. If the money supply is increased so that it exceeds the demand for money, the excess money balances will be spent on goods and assets.

In a closed, fully employed economy, the additional demand for goods would drive up the price level until equality between the demand and supply of real money balances was restored. In an open economy, with a high degree of substitutability between domestic and foreign goods, the rise in the price of domestic goods switches demand to foreign goods. Thus the excess of absorption over real output manifests itself as a deficit on the current account of the balance of payments. The excess supply of money balances also causes a decline in the domestic interest rate. Because of the high degree of capital mobility there is an increased capital outflow.

Therefore an excess supply of money relative to the demand to hold it causes a deficit both on the current and capital account of the balance of payments. This is the inevitable result of residents being unable to increase their demand for nominal money balances to match the increased supply of money, either by driving down interest rates or by raising the relative domestic price level when the exchange rate is fixed. The only way residents can get rid of their excess cash balances is by spending them on foreign goods and assets. While a balance-of-payments deficit is being run the domestic money supply is declining.

Conversely, an excess demand for money will cause residents to run a balance-of-payments surplus. Given the assumptions of the model, the only way to obtain the desired additional money balances is to obtain an expansion of the money supply by running a balance-of-payments surplus.

Fixed Exchange Rate

If the United Kingdom operates a fixed exchange rate system, its residents can get rid of any excess money balances by passing them on to foreigners. The latter exchange the sterling for foreign exchange which the Bank of England sells in order to prevent a depreciation of the exchange rate. The operation of the fixed exchange rate ensures that the domestic price level remains fixed relative to the world price level, given the high degree of substitutability between domestic and foreign traded goods.

In a closed, fully employed economy an expansion of the money supply relative to the demand for it would result in domestic inflation. The domestic price level would rise until the real value of the stock of money was brought back into equality with the demand for money.

An open economy on a fixed exchange rate can export its inflation to other countries. The inflation is fully exported if the assumptions of this model hold. The excess U.K. money balances swell the foreign exchange reserves of other countries. Given that sterilisation policies fail, foreign countries' money supply is expanded. A stable world price level will only be attained when the world price level has risen sufficiently for the demand and supply of real money balances to be once more in equilibrium. The U.K. price level rises with that of the world, maintaining its relative position. The United Kingdom, in common with all countries, has experienced some inflation. For a given expansion in the U.K. money supply, the United Kingdom experiences a smaller rise in its price level than if it were a closed economy. This is because the rise in the price level has been shared out amongst all the countries rather than occurring only in the United Kingdom.

Flexible Exchange Rate

If the United Kingdom operates a flexible exchange rate system, the portfolio adjustment due to an excess supply of money will depreciate the exchange rate. As the balance of payments remains in equilibrium there is no contraction of the domestic money supply due to dwindling foreign exchange reserves like that which occurs under the fixed exchange rate system. Exchange rate depreciation increases the price of U.K. imports in terms of sterling. At the same time the price of exports falls in terms of foreign exchange. The demand for U.K. goods by foreigners and by import substituting residents increases aggregate demand at home thus causing the domestic price level to rise. Inflation in the United Kingdom will continue until the price level has risen sufficiently to equalise the demand and supply of real money balances.

Policy Conclusions

Several policy conclusions emerge from this analysis.

(1) It is recommended that trading nations should operate a flexible exchange rate system. This would safeguard the rest of the world from suffering the effects of monetary mismanagement in any one country.

(2) From an individual country's point of view it should adopt a fixed exchange rate if it is inflating more rapidly than other countries. Such a policy may not be to the long-term advantage of a country if it promotes world inflation. Therefore a world system of flexible exchange rates is thought to bring net benefits.

(3) A country which grows more rapidly than the average world rate will

experience a consequent growth in the demand for money. If this is not satisfied by domestic credit creation, portfolio adjustment will bring about a balance-of-payments surplus under a regime of fixed exchange rates. To avoid an excessive accumulation of reserves, which earn a low rate of return, the exchange rate would be revalued at discrete intervals. Under a regime of flexible exchange rates the exchange rate of such a country would be appreciating over time.

(4) A country with a slower than average growth rate, which is also allowing its money supply to expand at a faster rate than the demand for money is growing, will experience a deficit under a fixed exchange rate system and exchange rate depreciation under a flexible exchange rate regime. For such a country a regime of flexible exchange rates would not allow its residents to export their excess money balances. In this case the higher growth rate of the money supply relative to the demand for money would cause domestic inflation. Since a deficit cannot be financed indefinitely under a fixed exchange rate and inflation cannot be exported under a flexible exchange rate system, this analysis points to the necessity of controlling the rate of growth of the money supply.

8.7 CONCLUSIONS

General equilibrium requires the simultaneous achievement of both internal and external equilibrium. The automatic adjustment mechanisms whereby a country can attain such an equilibrium are of two types.

(1) The domestic price level changes relative to the rest of the world. This can be brought about in two ways:

    (a) allowing the exchange rate to be flexible, or

    (b) operating a fixed exchange rate and relying on changes in the domestic money supply to bring about changes in the domestic price level.

The classical gold standard, by which the domestic money supply was tied rigidly to the volume of gold reserves, relied upon mechanism (b). The drawback to this method of adjustment is that in the case of a balance-of-payments deficit the downward rigidity of prices forces adjustment to take place through a decline in real output and consequent unemployment. For this reason flexible exchange rates have been advocated by Keynesian economists so that the balance-of-payments equilibrium can be attained at less cost in terms of domestic unemployment.

(2) Balance-of-payments adjustment can also be viewed as occurring through portfolio adjustment. For instance, if a country is running a balance-of-payments deficit under a regime of fixed exchange rates, its money supply will decline if sterilisation is not practised, until equilibrium is restored when the demand and supply of money are once more equal.

Adjustment via changes in the money supply can occur without relying on a change in the domestic price level relative to the world price level.

The monetarist criticism of the fixed exchange rate system as it has operated since the Second World War is that, unlike the gold standard, it did not impose monetary discipline upon governments. Governments, particularly those in surplus countries, have been able to prevent adjustment by sterilisation policies. The system has allowed governments to engage in excessive monetary expansion since the resulting inflation could be exported. This criticism relates particularly to the United States, and to some extent the United Kingdom, who have been able to finance balance-of-payments deficits. This ability stems from the willingness of other countries to hold dollars, and to a lesser extent sterling, as reserve currencies.

Flexible exchange rates are therefore advocated as a means of automatic adjustment in a world where the price level exhibits downward rigidity, and as a way of preventing one country's monetary mismanagement from affecting other countries.

REFERENCES

[1] S. J. Wells, *International Economics* (London: Allen & Unwin, 1969).
[2] C. P. Kindleberger, *International Economics* (London: R. D. Irwin, 1958) chs 2–4.
[3] J. M. Keynes, *A Tract on Monetary Reform* (London: Macmillan, 1923).
[4] R. A. Mundell, 'The Monetary Dynamics of International Adjustment Under Fixed and Flexible Exchange Rates', *Quarterly Journal of Economics* (May 1960).
[5] H. G. Johnson, 'The Monetary Approach to Balance of Payments Theory,' in *International Economics*, ed. M. B. Connolly and A. Swoboda (London: Allen & Unwin, 1972).

9 Inflation

Inflation is a situation of a rising general price level. It is measured as the rate of increase in the general price level over a specified period of time.*

9.1 THE PRICE LEVEL

The price level is measured by taking the weighted average of the prices at a particular moment in time of a large number of commodities. The weight attached to the price of each commodity is the proportion of total expenditure devoted to that good. A price index expresses the price level of each period relative to a base period (usually the beginning of a year) which has its price level fixed at 100. Price indices can cover a group of commodities such as food, housing and capital goods, but price indices which give an idea of the general level of prices are the wholesale price index, the retail price index, the consumer price index and the gross domestic product (G.D.P.) deflator.

The wholesale price index uses the prices quoted by producers for manufactured goods. The consumer price index is weighted according to current expenditure plans and is therefore sensitive not only to movements in individual prices but also to changes in the pattern of expenditure. It covers those goods which make up consumer expenditure in the national income accounts and is used to deflate the money value of consumers' expenditure to arrive at its real value. The retail price index of the Department of Employment is a base weighted index. Its weights, which are constant for each year, are derived from the

* It can be calculated in slightly different ways, as

$$\frac{p_t - p_{t-1}}{p_{t-1}} \quad \text{or} \quad \frac{\frac{1}{2}(p_{t+1} - p_{t-1})}{p_t}.$$

pattern of expenditure over the past three years. This information is obtained from the *Family Expenditure Survey*, which is based on a sample of families excluding high income families.* The G.D.P. price deflator is the most general price index. It is the value of G.D.P. in current year prices divided by G.D.P. measured in base-year prices. This is equivalent to

$$\frac{\text{G.D.P. in current prices}}{\text{G.D.P. price deflator}} = \text{G.D.P. at constant prices.}$$

If the price of one commodity, or a group of commodities, such as imports, increases the general level of prices can remain unchanged if the prices of other commodities fall to reflect the change in the relative prices of individual commodities. Since prices tend to be inflexible downwards, the rise in the price of imports usually causes some increase in the general level of prices.

9.2 THE EFFECT OF A CHANGE IN THE PRICE LEVEL

Comparative Static Analysis

Comparative static analysis only allows us to compare an economy at different price levels, given that no change in the future price level is expected. If one arbitrarily increased the price level in a stationary, fully employed economy prices and wages would rise by the same amount, leaving unchanged people's real incomes and the relative prices of goods and factors of production. The major change caused by the higher price level is that holders of nominally fixed assets are worse off because the real value of their assets has declined, whereas the issuers of nominally fixed liabilities have gained. Analysis often assumes that the gains and losses of private sector debtors and creditors cancel out. As discussed in Chapter 7, it is only when outside money exists that a change in the price level causes a change in the net wealth of the economy.

An increase in the price level, given a nominally fixed stock of money, reduces the supply of real money balances. These are now less than the quantity needed to finance the full-employment level of real output. The reduction in the real value of monetary assets which the rise in the price level causes will result in increased saving in order to restore the equilibrium real value of the stock of monetary assets. In a neoclassical model with flexible prices and wages, the general level of prices must therefore fall until the initial price level is re-established. In the neoclassical model there is thus a unique price level associated with a particular nominal stock of money. Given the parameters of the demand

* See [1], chs 15 and 16 for further details of price indices.

for money function and its arguments, the equilibrium values of the real rate of interest and real output, the quantity of money determines the price level. The solution to the price level is obtained from equation (9.1):

$$M^d = P f(y, i) = M^s \qquad (9.1)$$

$$P = \frac{M^s}{f(y, i)}. \qquad (9.1a)$$

A unique price level is also solved for in the Keynesian static three-sector model of the economy. As discussed in Chapter 8, the fixed money wage level plays an important role in determining the price level. If the money wage rate increases, firms' costs also rise as indicated by an upward shift in the aggregate supply curve of national output. The final outcome is a rise in the price level. In the Keynesian three-sector model, as in the neoclassical model, an increase in the nominal stock of money will, by raising aggregate demand, increase the price level.

Dynamic Analysis

If we wish to study the behaviour of an economy experiencing a continually rising price level, some form of dynamic analysis is required. The most easily analysed inflationary situation is one in which the model is in dynamic equilibrium. This occurs when the actual rate of inflation and the anticipated rate of inflation are equal. In this case the future rate of inflation will have been fully taken into account by lenders and borrowers. Nominally fixed income streams, such as those attached to bonds, will be discounted by the market rate of interest (that is, the expected rate of inflation plus the real rate of interest).* Thus, holders of nominally fixed assets will receive the same rate of return (minus any risk premium) as holders of assets denominated in real terms. So long as the nominal money supply is expanding at the same rate as the rate of inflation, the quantity of real balances is unchanged. Thus a stationary economy will be in a dynamic inflationary equilibrium at the full-employment level of real output. (In a growing economy, the nominal money supply would have to increase at the rate of inflation plus the rate of growth of real output times the income elasticity of the demand for money to maintain the equilibrium rate of inflation.†)

Thus if the expected and actual rates of inflation are equal, the rate of inflation will not change any of the real variables providing all contracts involving the exchange of factors of production, goods or money are

* See Chapter 6, p. 164.
† See Chapter 6, p. 170.

fixed in real terms.* This means revising all nominally fixed contracts, such as money wages and loans, so that their real values are preserved in the face of the anticipated inflation. Such a procedure is termed indexing.

If the actual and expected rate of inflation differ, there is a disequilibrium situation. Decisions are made on the basis of expectations which in the event are not fulfilled. This will cause people to revise their expectations and consequently change their decisions.

9.3 THE COSTS OF INFLATION

Inflation imposes certain costs on society. In order to examine these costs we will distinguish the costs of fully anticipated inflation from those of unanticipated inflation.

The Costs of Fully Anticipated Inflation on the Operation of the Financial System †

A fully anticipated inflation will be reflected in a market rate of interest that exceeds the real rate of interest by the rate of inflation. A higher market rate of interest increases the opportunity cost of holding money, and thus reduces the demand for real money balances. People therefore forgo some of the benefits of the convenience and liquidity derived from holding money.

In Figure 9.1, the demand for real money balances falls from m_0 at a zero expected rate of inflation to m_1 at an x per cent expected rate of

* Comparative dynamic analysis compares an economy at two different fully anticipated rates of inflation. If the actual and fully anticipated rate of inflation increases, there is a reduction in net wealth due to the unexpected decline in the real value of money balances. There follows an increase in saving to rebuild real money balances to their desired level. The increased desire to save reduces the real rate of interest. In a neoclassical growth model this will result in the use of more capital intensive techniques. The capital–output ratio rises to absorb the increased saving, but the equilibrium rate of growth of real output remains unchanged. As real money balances rise, the rate of saving diminishes and the real interest rate begins to rise. Since the rate of inflation is higher, the opportunity cost of holding money, if it pays no interest, is also greater. Therefore people wish to hold a smaller proportion of their total wealth as money. The increased proportion of real capital in relation to total desired wealth holdings means that the equilibrium real rate of interest is lower at the higher rate of inflation. It should be noted that this argument rests on money paying no rate of interest. If money pays a rate of interest, this rises with the anticipated rate of inflation, leaving the opportunity cost of holding money unchanged. In this case a rise in the rate of inflation would not cause any changes in the real variables and would therefore be neutral in its effects.
† See [2].

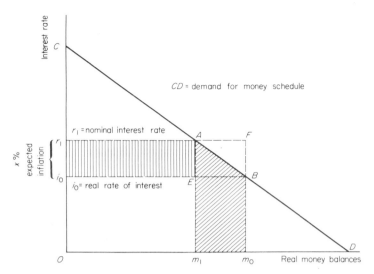

FIGURE 9.1   *The cost of inflation due to the increased cost of operating the payments mechanism, and the inflation tax*

inflation, given the real rate of interest is i_0 per cent and that no interest is paid on money. The total welfare received from holding money balances is given by the area under the demand curve between the origin and the level of real money balances demanded. This area indicates the maximum amount people are prepared to pay, in terms of forgone interest, for the benefits derived from the quantity of real money balances they hold. Thus the loss in welfare for money holders due to their holding m_1 rather than m_0 real balances is given by the area $m_1 A B m_0$. If we assume the marginal cost of supplying real money balances is zero,* then $m_1 A B m_0$ is the net loss in welfare to society as a whole, due to an x per cent expected rate of inflation reducing the volume of real money balances held. A higher expected rate of inflation leads people to spend time and effort in economising on money balances. The welfare loss is the commodities or leisure time thus forgone.

This welfare loss can be avoided by paying the market rate of interest on money (see [3]). Such a policy would lead people to hold the optimal amount of real balances, by equating the marginal benefits from holding money with the marginal cost of supplying it. (The optimal money

* If the marginal cost of supplying money is positive, the total cost of supplying $m_0 - m_1$ real balances is subtracted from $m_1 A B m_0$ to derive the net welfare loss due to inflation.

holdings would be *OD* in Figure 9.1, given a zero marginal cost of supplying money. This gives the maximum area under the demand curve, indicating the maximum attainable social welfare from holding money.) This policy recommendation has certain practical difficulties, such as devising a way to pay interest on notes and coin.

The cost of running the financial system attributable to expected inflation is not serious for mild inflation, but it increases with increases in the rate of price rise. A rough estimate of this cost for the United Kingdom in 1973 has been calculated using Laidler's* estimated long-run demand function for money.† It is assumed that the long-term rate of interest, if no inflation is expected, is 2·5 per cent, whereas the average yield on consols in 1973 was 10·85 per cent. The additional net long-run social cost of running the payments mechanism due to an excess in the market rate of interest of 8·35 per cent over the real rate of 2·5 per cent is estimated to be 1·45 per cent of net national income in 1973. This corresponds to a loss in consumer surplus of £14.50 per person in 1973 prices.

Hyperinflations, unlike mild inflations, can eventually end in a complete breakdown in the monetary system and a return to barter, such as occurred in Hungary and Germany after the Second World War. The most rapid monthly rate of inflation in Germany during this period was $10^{14·6} - 1$ in July 1946. Such crises are resolved by withdrawing the existing currency and issuing a new currency, the supply of which is controlled.

The Costs of Unanticipated Inflation

It is only expected inflation that reduces the demand to hold real money balances and hence decreases the net welfare obtained from the convenience of holding money. When the actual rate of inflation turns out *ex post* to exceed the anticipated rate of inflation, the holders of

* See [17] in Chapter 6.

† The fitted long-run demand for money equation used is $\ln M/P = -1·237 + 0·753 \ln y - 0·569 \ln r$ where M/P and y are real *per capita* money balances and net national income deflated to 1962 prices and r is the market rate of interest. This can be transformed to

$$r = 0·1137 y^{1·3234} (M/P)^{-1·757}.$$

The loss in consumer surplus in 1973 expressed in 1962 pounds *per capita* is A.

$$A = \frac{M/P \text{ at } r = 10·85\%}{M/P \text{ at } r = 2·5\%} \int 0·1137 y^{1·3234} \left(\frac{M}{P}\right)^{-1·757} d\left(\frac{M}{P}\right) = £8.10.$$

A is about 1·45 per cent of y in 1973, as *per capita* net national income was approximately £559 in 1962 prices. This result is in line with U.S. estimates. I am indebted to Alex Rebmann-Huber for this calculation.

money balances experience an unanticipated loss in real purchasing power. Referring again to Figure 9.1, if expected inflation is zero, people hold Om_0 real balances even though the actual rate of inflation is x per cent. They enjoy the extra benefits of the liquidity and convenience of holding $m_1 m_0$ more money than they would have held had they expected an x per cent rate of inflation. Since they judge the additional cost in lost purchasing power, which is $m_1 m_0$ times x (rectangle $AFBE$), as too much to pay for such benefits, they would have only held Om_1 real balances had they been fully informed about the future rate of inflation. Thus, holders of money lose more by unexpected inflation than by fully anticipated inflation. Similarly all holders of nominally fixed assets, such as bonds and building society shares, are made worse off by a rate of inflation which exceeds the rate expected when the assets were acquired.

Unexpected changes in the rate of inflation redistribute wealth and income, so that some gain while others lose. As discussed above, lenders who acquire nominally fixed assets lose while creditors gain from the declining real value of their debt. In contrast, holders of real assets, such as equity, property and works of art, are generally not made worse off by inflation as real asset prices rise secularly with the general price index. Existing holders of real assets will experience an increase in their real wealth that is greater than it would have been without inflation once others, beginning to expect a higher rate of inflation, move into those real assets which are regarded as a good hedge against inflation and bid up these asset prices faster than the rate of inflation.

As well as redistributing wealth, inflation also alters the distribution of incomes. Those living off income from fixed interest securities experience a decline in their real income. The nominal value of welfare benefits needs to be continually raised by the government if their real value is not to fall. More strongly unionised sections are likely to fare better at preserving or even increasing their real incomes. The real incomes of government employees are liable to fall relative to other incomes when the government is reluctant to increase its expenditure. As inflation proceeds, real disposable income declines relative to before-tax income unless the government raises the threshold at which incomes become liable for tax.

Even if everyone fully anticipates the future rate of inflation, redistribution of income and wealth can still occur if people are unable to adjust fully their contracts or if the costs of doing so outweigh the likely benefits. I may fully anticipate that prices will rise by 20 per cent over the next year but be unable to increase my money income by that percentage.

Inflation-borne redistribution arouses resentment, particularly as the gains and losses can be more apparent than real. The nominal profits of firms rise, making their profits appear larger than they are in real terms.

Certain individuals, such as property and commodity speculators, are exaggeratedly seen as the villains of inflation. There is a tendency to be more painfully aware of rising prices than of rising nominal incomes. All these factors are beyond the scope of strict economic analysis, but must be considered in viewing the social and political implications of moderately high rates of inflation by peace-time European standards (that is in excess of 10 per cent).

Before making a rational decision as to whether one should advocate a policy to reduce inflation, one must set the costs of inflation against the costs of reducing inflation. As will be seen in the course of the discussion on the causes of inflation, these costs are likely to take the form of unemployment and the consequent loss of real output.

9.4 INFLATION AS A TAX*

Issuing more money is the means by which the government finances any of its expenditure in excess of revenue obtained by taxation or by borrowing from the public. The government can command resources directly, since people are prepared to sell goods and services to the government in return for the medium of exchange issued by the government. If such government purchases are accompanied by excess demand prices will rise. The people who ultimately pay for the goods and services used by the government, by themselves forgoing real expenditure, are the holders of money balances. The holders of money lose purchasing power as prices rise.

Thus, inflation is a tax (identical to direct and indirect taxes) and is a means of getting the public to transfer goods and services to government use. The tax base of the inflation tax is the quantity of real money balances held. This, times the actual rate of inflation, gives the tax revenue the government collects from inflation and is equal to rectangle AEi_0r_1 in Figure 9.1. The cost of collecting the inflation tax is the net loss in social welfare from the reduction in real money balances caused by anticipated inflation. The longer it takes for the public to adjust their expected rate of inflation to the actual rate of inflation, the larger is the present value of the government's tax revenue from a given rate of inflation. As people come to expect inflation, the quantity of real money balances held falls and the tax base therefore contracts.

Governments are likely to favour the inflation tax if they take a short-run view of the world and rely upon its taking some time for the public to realise that they are being taxed. One cannot say *a priori* that the inflation tax is more costly than direct and indirect fiscal taxes. In undeveloped or dislocated economies the government may be quite unable to raise sufficient revenue by fiscal means or by issuing bonds.

* See [2, 4, 5].

Thus hyperinflations, associated with rapid increases in the supply of money, have been particularly prevalent in economies dislocated by wars or subject to political instability.*

9.5 THE COMPONENTS OF PRICE

In analysing the factors that contribute to inflation it is useful to start by looking at the components of the price of an article. Price is necessarily identical to a cost element plus a profit margin. Profit-maximising behaviour by firms provides a rationale for the relationship between cost and price. Perfectly competitive profit-maximising firms equate price to marginal cost. In long-run equilibrium marginal cost is equal to average total cost, which includes an allowance for a normal or equilibrium rate of profit. There will also be an equality between marginal cost and average variable cost in the short run if these are both constant. In these ways price is related to average variable cost. In addition, oligopolistic firms practise average cost pricing since uncertainty about their demand functions makes it impossible to set marginal revenue equal to short-run marginal cost. Thus it is usual in macro models to equate price to average variable cost plus a profit mark-up.

In short-run analysis average variable cost depends directly on the money wage rate per time period paid to labour, and depends inversely on the average product of labour. Given the money wage rate, the more units of output produced per unit of labour, the lower will be the average variable cost per unit of output. In an economy where output per unit of labour is rising over time the increase in real income can be passed on to the whole population in two ways. The money wage rate can remain fixed so that average variable costs and hence prices fall over time. This is by and large what has occurred in the centrally planned economies behind the 'Iron Curtain'. Alternatively, the money wage rate can rise at the same rate as the increase in productivity, thus leaving average variable costs and hence final goods prices unchanged.

In an open economy the domestic price level is affected by the price, in terms of domestic currency, of imports. If these prices rise, and domestic prices are inflexible downwards, the latter will also rise.

A further factor in the components of price is the profit margin that domestic firms keep between the cost of producing, distributing and retailing goods and the final price. If the profit margin increases, *ceteris paribus*, the price of a commodity will rise, although this is of course a once-and-for-all effect. Finally one has to take into account the effect of taxes and subsidies on prices. The National Institute of Economic and Social Research [6] use the following equation to estimate the consumer

* See [5] for estimates of the tax yield from inflation in several countries which experienced hyperinflation.

price index net of estimated indirect taxes:

$$\text{C.P.I.F.C.}_t = 0\cdot318\,\frac{WS_t}{\text{G.D.P.}} + 0\cdot046MP_t + 0\cdot762\,\text{C.P.I.F.C.}_{t-1}$$

$$(0\cdot094) \qquad (0\cdot021) \quad (0\cdot076) \qquad\qquad (9.2)$$

$$R^2 = 0\cdot999$$

where WS_t is the wage and salary bill in the tth quarter, G.D.P. is at constant prices, MP is the import price index, and standard errors of the estimates are given in parentheses.

9.6 THE ROLE OF A PRICE LEVEL EQUATION IN A MACRO MODEL

A price level equation, such as (9.2), cannot be viewed in isolation from the rest of the equations that constitute a model of the economy. One cannot discuss the determinants of the price level and its rate of change by looking simply at the components of the price equation. This is because these components are not exogenous variables but are influenced by other variables in the system including feedback effects from the price level. This is particularly true of the level of money wages which will be influenced by, among other factors, the state of demand in the labour market. The static three-sector Keynesian model by assuming a fixed, institutionally-determined money wage rate sidesteps this issue. If we are to explain the behaviour of the price level it is not sufficient just to assume that money wages are exogenous. It is also necessary to explain the behaviour of money wages.

We will proceed by examining those theories of inflation which seek to explain the rate of change in money wages. Having done this it is then necessary to consider the extent to which the demand for money function places a limitation on the size of the nominal value of G.D.P. which can be financed by a given stock of nominal money. It should be borne in mind while the discussion temporarily neglects monetary factors, that the price level cannot go on rising indefinitely unless the nominal stock of money is increased.

9.7 THE LABOUR MARKET

Inflation theorists have paid particular attention to labour-market behaviour since this market plays such an important part in the determination of costs. Although one must bear in mind that, while labour-market equations are embedded in a whole model of the economy, the greater simplicity of investigating a single sector has decided advantages. Since the demand for labour is a derived demand for commodities, aggregate demand for output determines the position of the labour-demand schedule in relation to the real wage rate.

A further complication is that at the aggregate level the demand for labour schedule with respect to the real wage rate is not independent of the supply of labour. This is because the supply schedule of labour helps to determine the wage bill, and the wage bill is a determinant of aggregate demand, particularly its consumption component. Thus, if the supply schedule of labour shifts up due to trade union activity the demand for labour will not remain unaffected, as one could assume if one were analysing a small market within the economy. With higher money incomes labour can afford to pay higher prices for goods and services and thus the aggregate demand schedule for labour will also shift up. If money prices and money wage rates rise by the same proportion the real wage rate remains unchanged. Therefore the level of employment and the amount of national output produced can remain constant unless further disturbances occur.

The analysis of the rate of change of money wages and prices requires an investigation of labour-market dynamics. To concentrate on this aspect we will assume a constant level of real output. If real output is growing over time and the marginal productivity of labour is increasing as a result of technical progress and capital accumulation then the demand schedule for labour would be shifting towards the right. The supply curve of labour would also shift to the right over time if the labour force is growing. Thus, if the labour force and real output are growing at the same rate, the real wage rate would remain unchanged. We shall abstact from a growth model and analyse inflation in relation to a constant level of full-employment output.

The equilibrium full-employment level is defined in Chapter 8. It is that rate of employment at which the demand for labour and the supply of labour are equal at the same real wage rate. Both sides of the labour market perceive the money wage rate offered to be the same real wage rate. In other words both sides of the labour market have the same expectations about the future rate of change of prices. For an equilibrium level of full employment these expectations must be fully realised. If actual and expected inflation differ the system cannot be in equilibrium because people will change their behaviour on the realisation that the factors upon which they based decisions have changed.

Frictional Unemployment

In practice labour-market equilibrium will not mean a zero excess supply of labour. At full employment there will still exist unemployed workers looking for jobs and employers with vacancies seeking to hire workers. The equilibrium level of unemployment at which the actual and expected rate of change of prices is zero has been termed the 'natural' rate of unemployment [7]. This type of unemployment is also called frictional unemployment.

The phenomenon of the existence of an unsold quantity of a commodity, which sellers wish to sell and buyers wish to buy at the equilibrium price, arises from the lack of perfect and costless information. Both employers and workers need to search for the information they require for making decisions about offering or accepting employment respectively.

The search for information takes time and this is one element in its cost. Workers seeking new jobs can be divided into two categories; those who are in employment and those who are unemployed. Because the unemployed have more time to look for work they are likely (given they have otherwise the same characteristics as the employed) to find a new job at an acceptable wage rate more quickly than are the employed. Thus it is quite rational for people to quit a job in order to spend time searching if they estimate that this action will increase the present value of their income. Job search theory assumes that workers respond to the real wage rate offered when deciding whether to quit existing employment or to accept or to reject job offers.*

At the beginning of the job search process a worker will base his idea of the real wage he can command on his previous employment experience. As job search proceeds he will revise this estimate according to the money wage offers he receives and the rate of price change that he expects. Thus, an unemployed worker has a reservation real wage and will not accept a job below this wage. As the duration of unemployment persists the reservation wage declines.†

The above discussion points to reasons why a worker aiming to maximise the expected present value of his income may decide to either become unemployed or remain unemployed. These considerations also indicate that measuring unemployment as the number of the labour force not in employment at a particular moment in time gives an incomplete picture of the state of the labour market. The average duration of unemployment is also an important factor. One could have more people unemployed but for a shorter length of time because of factors causing more people to quit employment while job offers are accepted more readily. Such a rise in frictional unemployment would not indicate a decline in economic activity.

On the other side of the labour market are the factors influencing the firm's decisions to hire new workers and retain existing workers. These decisions affect the number of vacancies. A firm gains information about the wage rate it has to offer to attract labour by looking at its quit rate, the quality of its job applicants and the proportion of people offered jobs who accept. The wage rate an individual firm has to offer to maintain a given level of employment and hence vacancies depends on

* See the articles in Phelps [8, 9, 10, 11].
† See [9] for a summary of the empirical evidence in support of this assumption.

the wage rates offered by other firms. Therefore an individual firm will base its wage offer to its existing and prospective employees on the wage rate it expects other firms to offer. This is of course not the only factor, since the labour force the firm wishes to maintain depends upon the demand for its output as well as the wage it needs to pay to attract and retain labour.

Thus, both unemployment and vacancies will exist in markets characterised by imperfect information even if each market is in equilibrium in the sense that the demand for labour at the equilibrium real wage rate equals the quantity of labour willing to work at that real wage rate.

An additional dimension to frictional unemployment and vacancies is provided by the fact that the labour market for the whole economy is an aggregation of many interrelated sub-markets. The micro markets can be distinguished both on an industrial and on a regional basis. As change takes place in the economy some industries and regions decline while others expand. Given that such adjustments take time, unemployment will be higher than average in declining industries and regions, while vacancies will be lower than average. The opposite will occur in expanding industries and regions. The aggregate amount of unemployment therefore depends on its distribution amongst industries and regions. Therefore changes in the industrial structure are a further factor influencing the aggregate volume of vacancies and unemployment.

Relationship Between Vacancies and Unemployment, and the Level of Aggregate Demand

A higher level of aggregate demand will be reflected in a greater demand for labour by firms. Firms make a larger number of acceptable wage offers to unemployed job applicants which reduces the pool of unemployed labour. The greater demand for labour is also reflected in a larger number of vacancies. Thus the quantity of unemployment is inversely related to vacancies.

The relationship between vacancies and unemployment is illustrated in Figure 9.2 [12]. Figure 9.2.a shows that because of frictional unemployment, employment (indicated by the dashed line *EE*) is always less than both the demand for labour and the supply of labour. The distance, such as *ob*, between *EE* and the demand for labour schedule *DD* indicates the number of vacancies. The distance, such as *oc*, between the supply schedule *SS* and the *EE* line gives the volume of unemployment. The lower the real wage rate the greater the number of vacancies relative to the volume of unemployment. This relationship is illustrated in Figure 9.2.b and is derived by plotting unemployment at any given real wage rate in Figure 9.2.a against the vacancies at that real wage rate. The actual position of the *UV* schedule depends on the

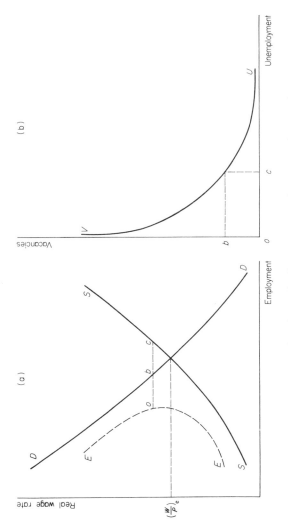

FIGURE 9.2 *The relationship between unemployment and vacancies*

factors determining frictional unemployment and vacancies, other than the level of aggregate demand. The latter variable determines at which point on a given UV schedule the labour market is.

9.8 THE TRADE-OFF BETWEEN UNEMPLOYMENT AND INFLATION

The above discussion has indicated the relationship between aggregate demand in the product market and the level of excess demand in the labour market which, because of imperfect information, is reflected in the rate of unemployment relative to the vacancy rate. The next step is to consider the relationship between unemployment and the rate of change of wages.

The basic hypothesis underlying this relationship is that the rate of change of real wages is proportional to excess demand in the labour market. This is written as

$$\frac{\dot{w}}{w} = f\left(\frac{L^d - L^s}{L^s}\right) \tag{9.3}$$

where $(\dot{w}/w) = (dw/dt)(1/w)$ is the rate of change of the real wage rate, L^d is the demand for labour and L^s is the supply of labour. The demand for labour is made up of those in employment, E, plus vacancies, V. The supply of labour consists of those in employment plus the unemployed, U. Therefore

$$\frac{\dot{w}}{w} = f\left(\frac{V - U}{E + U}\right) = f(U). \tag{9.4}$$

Since vacancies vary inversely with the unemployment rate, the latter variable by itself has been frequently used as a measure of excess demand (see [13, 14]).

Equation (9.3) is deceptively simple as it contains implicitly a larger number of variables. Implicit are those variables, other than the real wage rate, which determine the demand for labour, the most important of these being the productivity of labour and the aggregate demand for output. Also implicit are the variables which determine the supply of labour, namely household preferences and trade union activity. This equation does not establish what the equilibrium real wage is. It only tells us that when the equilibrium real wage rate is established the rate of change of real wages will be zero. The equation implies that when this occurs the level of unemployment will equal the number of vacancies. This is unlikely in practice since labour is not homogeneous. It is most improbable that in the various sub-markets the skills required by employers with vacancies will exactly match the qualifications of the unemployed. Equation (9.3) only specifies an adjustment mechanism. It tells us nothing about whether the disequilibrium which sets off the rate of change in real wages is caused by factors from the demand, or the supply, side, or both sides of the labour market.

The rate of change of real wages equals the rate of change of money wages, $\dot{W}/W$, minus the rate of change of the price level, $\dot{P}/P$:

$$\frac{\dot{w}}{w} = \frac{\dot{W}}{W} - \frac{\dot{P}}{P}. \tag{9.5}$$

In a disequilibrium inflationary situation the actual rate of inflation, $\dot{P}/P$, will not be the same as the expected rate of inflation, $(\dot{P}/P)^e$. In this case the rate of change in the real wage rate anticipated by a worker when he enters into a contract of employment is

$$\frac{\dot{w}}{w} = \frac{\dot{W}}{W} - \left(\frac{\dot{P}}{P}\right)^e. \tag{9.6}$$

If the worker is rational the coefficient relating to the price expectations variable is one. This means that he fully adjusts the increase in money wages for the expected increase in prices to obtain the resulting change in the real wage rate upon which he bases his decision as to whether to remain in his present employment or to continue unemployed as the case may be. If a worker does not fully take into account the inflation that he expects to occur when estimating his real income from his money income, he is said to have 'money illusion'. Behaviour due to money illusion is quite distinct from incorrect expectations. One can overestimate one's future real income because a higher rate of inflation occurs than one expected. This is distinct from money illusion which would cause one not to act in response to one's future real income, even though one is correctly anticipating the rate of inflation that will occur. A coefficient, α, is subsequently attached to the price expectations variable. It will equal one if employees are both rational (that is, they do not suffer from money illusion) and can adjust fully their money wages to compensate for expected price increases.

Equation (9.6) is substituted into equation (9.4) to give

$$\frac{\dot{W}}{W} = f(U) + \alpha\left(\frac{\dot{P}}{P}\right)^e. \tag{9.7}$$

An inverse relationship between the rate of change of money wages and the rate of unemployment is known as a 'Phillips curve' after the original study [13] which purported to show a stable long-run relationship between these two variables (see Table 9.1). The original Phillips function suppressed the expected rate of price change variable by implicitly assuming it to be zero, and was a non-linear relationship between the rate of change of money wages and the percentage of unemployment. Subsequent empirical work by Lipsey [14] modified the Phillips relationship by also including a current rate of price change to

TABLE 9.1 A Summary of Some Econometric Studies on Inflation

Study	Data	Dependent variable	Regression equations	
Phillips [13]	U.K. annual 1861–1957	W_t = rate of change of money wage rates 'hourly)	$-0.900 + 9.638U^{-1.394}$ (fitted for average values 1861–1913)	
Lipsey [14]	U.K. annual 1862–1913, 1923–39, 1948–57	W_r	$-1.21 + 6.45U^{-1} + 2.26U^{-2} - 0.19\,\Delta U + 0.21P$ $0.74 + 0.43U^{-1} + 11.18U^{-4} + 0.34\,\Delta U + 0.69P$ $(2.10)*\phantom{ + 0.43U^{-1}}(6.00)*\phantom{+ 11.18U^{-4}}(0.012)*(0.08)*$	$R^2 = 0.85$ $R_{wU} = 0.38$ $R^2 = 0.91$ $R_{wU} = 0.38$ $R_{wP} = 0.75$
Dicks-Mireaux [17]	U.K. annual 1946–59 (estimated by 2SLS)	W_e = rate of change of earnings, and salaries per person employed per year; P = rate of change of final prices	$3.90 + 0.3P_t + 0.16P_{t-1} + 2.78E_{t-1/4}$ $(0.63)*(0.13)*(0.10)*(0.82)*$ $2.47 + 0.27W_{et} + 0.21M_{t-1/4} - 0.54\,\Delta X_t$ $(1.39)*(0.04)*(0.04)*(0.16)*$	$R^2 = 0.99$
Klein and Ball [18]	U.K. quarterly 1948–56	W_r = annual change in quarterly average weekly wage rates; P = quarterly average of consumer price index	$-0.091U_t + 0.854P_t + 2.90F_t + 10.26$ $(0.013)*(0.092)*(0.40)*$ $35.65 + 0.421W_{et}(\text{level}) + 0.216M_{t-2} + 0.013T_x$ $(13.01)*(0.013)*(0.03)*(0.161)*$	$R^2 = 0.93$ $R^2 = 0.996$
Eckstein and Wilson [19]	U.S. 1948–60, 5 observations of wage round	W_r = rate of increase of average hourly wage rates	$-5.74 + 0.73D_t - 0.56U_t$ $(0.98)*(0.04)*(0.06)*$	$R^2 = 0.998$
Kuh [20]	U.S. quarterly 1950(4)–69(1)	W_e = one-quarter change in log. of average hourly compensation	$-0.1994W_{et-1} + 0.1926\,\Delta X_t + 0.1129P_t + 0.0038U_t$ $(-4.19)(3.806)(2.855)(0.095)$	$R^2 = 0.6412$ $DW = 1.2$

Parkin [21] — U.K. quarterly 1948(3)–69(1)
W_r = rate of change of weekly wage rates

$$W_r = 3.007 + 0.005U + 0.440P^e$$
$$(1.67)* \quad (0.762)* \quad (0.202)*$$
$\lambda = 0.439(0.204)*$
$\rho_1 = 0.483(0.229)*$
$S^2 = 0.701$

Parkin [21] — U.K. quarterly 1948(3)–69(1)
W_r

$$W_r = 3.034 + 0.021E + 0.436P^e$$
$$(0.885)* \quad (0.38)* \quad (0.203)*$$
$\lambda = 0.440(0.204)*$
$\rho_2 = 0.483(0.230)*$
$S^2 = 0.701$

Saunders and Nobay [22] — as [21]

$$3.007 + 0.005U_t + 0.770P^e$$

Solow [23] — U.K. annual 1948–66
P = rate of change of price index for final product

$$0.0618 + 0.575\,\text{u.l.c.} + 0.093M - 0.0453CD - 0.1147LD + 0.2109P^e$$
$$(0.72) \quad (12.623) \quad (13.307) \quad (8.314) \quad (2.062) \quad (3.521)$$
(adaptive expectations coefficients, θ, assumed $= 0.7$)
$R^2 = 0.9808$

U.K. quarterly 1956–66
P = rate of change of price index for final product

$$-0.2325 + 0.0812\,\text{u.l.c.} + 0.00243CU + 0.8085P^e$$
$$(4.77) \quad (1.63) \quad (4.844) \quad (8.113)$$
$\theta = 0.7, \quad R^2 = 0.8443$

Lucas and Rapping [24] — U.S. annual 1930–65 (W = money wage compensation per hour)
U_t = unemployment

$$0.042 - 0.59\,\Delta \ln P_t - 0.41 w_t/w_{t-1} + 0.8U_{t-1}$$
$$(0.01)* \quad (0.08)* \quad (0.24)* \quad (0.05)*$$
$R^2 = 0.925$
$DW = 1.5$

Lucas and Rapping [25] — U.S. annual 1904–65. (W = hourly money wage compensation)
U_t

	const.	$\Delta \ln P_t$	$\Delta \ln P_{t-1}$	$\Delta \ln P_{t-2}$	$\Delta \ln w_t$	$\Delta \ln w_{t-1}$	U_{t-1}	U_{t-2}	R^2	DW
(1904–65)	1.15 (0.63)*	39.16 (6.69)*	35.36 (8.19)*	17.38 (6.84)*	11.86 (9.19)*	26.67 (9.52)*	1.17 (1.13)*	0.322 (0.13)*	0.88	2.01
(1904–29)	insig.	20.09 (8.11)*	30.32 (9.07)*	insig.	34.78 (13.5)*	insig.	0.68 (2.27)*	insig.	0.53	1.91
(1930–45)	insig.	96.87 (15.49)*	insig.	insig.	insig.	insig.	insig.	insig.	0.96	1.37
(1946–65)	insig.	insig.	insig.	insig.	insig.	insig.	insig.	insig.	−0.05	1.54

Godfrey [31] — U.K. quarterly 1957(3)–69(3)
W_r = rate of change of weekly wage rates

$$W_r = 0.6762 + 0.1589P - 0.3536U^{-1.5} + 0.1055N/100 - 0.0736N/100$$
$$(0.238)* \quad (0.1934)* \quad (0.5628)* \quad (0.0534)* \quad (0.1761)*$$
$S^2 = 0.26$

TABLE 9.1 (continued)

Study	Data	Dependent variable	Regression equations
Ward and Zis [32]	U.K. annual 1956–71	W_e = rate of change of hourly earnings	$1.530 - 3.286U_t^{-1} + 1.212N_t + 0.700P_{t-1/4}$ $(0.61)\quad(1.215)\quad\ \ (1.404)\quad\ \ (3.477)$ $R^2 = 0.681\qquad DW = 2.088$
Hines [27]	U.K. annual 1893–1961	W_r = rate of change of money wage rate. (hourly 1921–61)	$-1.9740 + 1.5945\Delta T_t + 0.1282T_t + 0.6804P_t + 0.0812P_{t-1} - 0.0441U_t$ $(0.2418)^*\quad(0.0409)^*\quad(0.1129)^*\quad(0.0276)^*\quad(0.1129)^*$ $R^2 = 0.9953\qquad DW = 1.32$
		P_t = rate of change of price level	$-0.07797 + 0.6924W_{rt} + 0.0396M_{t-1/2} + 0.1346\Delta X_t$ $(0.0348)^*\quad(0.0173)^*\quad\ \ (0.0725)^*$ $R^2 = 0.9834\qquad DW = 0.98$
		T = change in percentage of labour force unionised	$1.4014 - 0.1145T_{t-1} + 0.4664P_t - 0.0978P_{t-1} + 0.0149D_{t-1/2}$ $(0.0083)^*\quad(0.0148)^*\quad(0.0129)^*\quad(0.0048)^*$ $R^2 = 0.98\qquad DW = 1.31$
Hines [28]	U.K. annual 1893–1912	W_r as in [27]	$-1.387 + 0.469\Delta T + 0.068P_{t-1/2} + 6.898U_t^{-1} - 0.011\Delta U_t$ $(0211)^*\quad(0.073)^*\quad\ \ (1.861)^*\quad\ (0.006)^*$ $R^2 = 0.778\qquad DW = 1.8$
	1920–39	W_r as in [27]	$2.004 + 2.080\Delta T + 0.295P_{t-1/2} - 19.317U_t^{-1} + 0.002\Delta U_t$ $(0.312)^*\quad(0.157)^*\quad\ (10.037)^*\quad\ (0.002)^*$ $R^2 = 0.928\qquad DW = 1.224$
	1949–61	W_r as in [27]	$2.390 + 3.134\Delta T + 0.425P_{t-1/2} + 2.259U_t^{-1} - 0.005\Delta U_t$ $(0.808)^*\quad(0.221)^*\quad\ (2.788)^*\quad\ (0.011)^*$ $R^2 = 0.849\qquad DW = 2.926$
Purdy and Zis [30]	U.K. annual 1925–38, 1950–61	W_r as [27]	$0.558 + 0.081T_t^m + 0.474\Delta T_t^m + 0.055P_t + 0.222P_{t-1/2} + 6.368U_t^{-1}$ $(0.36)^*\ (0.054)^*\quad(0.132)^*\quad(0.127)^*\quad(0.118)^*\quad(0.792)^*$ $R^2 = 0.963\qquad DW = 1670$
		P_t as [27]	$-0.232 + 0.063\Delta X_t + 0.239M_{t-1/2} + 0.682W_{rt}$ $(0.318)^*\ (0.148)^*\quad(0.363)^*\quad(0.082)^*$ $R^2 = 0.930\qquad DW = 1.668$
		ΔT_t^m = proxy for trade union militancy	$10.054 - 0.407T_{t-1}^m + 0.355P_{t-1/2} - 0.004D_{t-1}$ $(2.074)^*\ (0.050)^*\quad(0.079)^*\quad(0.0005)^*$ $R^2 = 0.6108\qquad DW = 1.2312$
Harberger [35]	Chile annual 1939–58	P_t = rate of change of the price level	$-1.05 - 1.05y_t + 0.80MS_t + 0.34MS_{t-1}$ $(7.13)^*\ (0.31)^*\quad(0.17)^*\quad(0.16)^*$ $R^2 = 0.84$ $-1.15 - 0.89y_t + 0.7MS_t + 0.29MS_{t-1} + 0.16A_{t-1} + 0.13W_st$ $(9.56)^*\ (0.32)^*\quad(0.18)^*\quad(0.18)^*\quad(0.14)^*\quad(0.22)^*$ $R^2 = 0.87$

| Vogel [36] 16 Latin American countries | P_t | $-0{\cdot}031 - 0{\cdot}298y_t + 0{\cdot}586MS_t + 0{\cdot}407MS_{t-1} + 0{\cdot}014A_{t-1}$
$\qquad\quad (3{\cdot}1)\qquad\;\; (17{\cdot}0)\qquad\;\; (11{\cdot}1)\qquad\;\; (0{\cdot}4)$ | $R = 0{\cdot}82$
$DW = 1{\cdot}88$ |

Key: ( ) indicates statistic; ( )* indicates standard error of estimate; R^2 = coefficient of multiple correlation; S = standard error of regression; DW = Durbin Watson statistic; W_t =rate of change of money wage rate; W_e =rate of change of money earnings; W_s =rate of change of minimum wage paid to Chilean government white-collar workers; w = real wage rate; P = rate of change of the price level; P^e = rate of change of expected price level; A = first difference in the rate of change in the price level; U = per cent of labour force unemployed; E = index of excess demand; CU = capacity utilisation; ΔX = rate of change of labour productivity; u.l.c. = annual proportional change in unit labour costs; D = a profits variable; M = rate of change of import prices; T_x = indirect taxes minus subsidies; ΔT = change in per cent of labour force unionised; ΔT^m = change in per cent of labour force unionised allowing for structural changes; N = number of strikes; MS = rate of change of the money supply; y = rate of change of real national income; λ = coefficient of adjustment lag (Parkin study); ρ_1, ρ_2 = first order autoregressive coefficients (Parkin study); F = political factor; CD = Cripps dummy (Solow study); and LD = Lloyd dummy (Solow study).

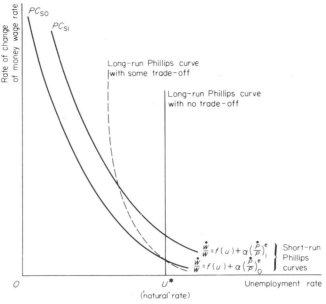

FIGURE 9.3   *The trade-off between unemployment and the rate of change of money wages*

account for cost of living adjustments. (These results are summarised in Table 9.1.)

Given that either the expected rate of price change is constant or α is zero, there will exist a stable Phillips relationship as indicated by PC_{S0} in Figure 9.3.* The relationship between the rate of change of money wages and unemployment can be converted into one between the rate of change of prices and unemployment. This is done by subtracting the rate of increase in labour productivity, $\dot{X}/X$, from the rate of change of wages. Therefore

$$\frac{\dot{P}}{P} = \frac{\dot{W}}{W} - \frac{\dot{X}}{X} = f(U) + \alpha\left(\frac{\dot{P}}{P}\right)^e - \frac{\dot{X}}{X} \qquad \left[\partial\left(\frac{\dot{P}}{P}\right)\Big/\partial U < 0\right]. \qquad (9.8)$$

The rate of change of prices will also be affected by the rate of change of import prices or of the profit mark-up.

Thus, the Phillips relationship appears to offer a trade-off between inflation and unemployment. The theoretical rationale for this trade-off has been established by work on the dynamics of labour market behaviour to which reference has already been made. If the rate of

* The Phillips function is drawn in the positive quadrant since money wage rate changes have not been negative since the Second World War.

inflation is more rapid than that expected by workers, a greater proportion of those seeking jobs will accept wage offers than if the actual and expected rates of inflation are equal. This behaviour arises from workers thinking that the money wage they are being offered is greater in real terms than it actually is. This happens because workers underestimate future inflation.

Thus if the government stimulates aggregate demand, firms start offering higher money wages to attract more labour. Workers respond by accepting these job offers which they think are worth more in real terms than is the case, since they do not anticipate the future increase in prices that will stem from the increase in money wages. One can visualise this as a downward shift in the labour supply curve in relation to the actual real wage as indicated in Figure 9.4. In relation to the expected real wage the supply schedule of labour remains unchanged. There is more labour employed and hence more real output produced while the actual rate of inflation exceeds the rate expected.*

Exactly the reverse occurs when money wages and prices start falling. While labour expects the future price level to be higher than it actually will be they consider the money wage offered to be worth less in real terms than it really is. Thus, a higher proportion of unemployed refuse job offers because they do not come up to their reservation money wage. The duration of unemployment lengthens, and effective aggregate demand declines, exacerbating the degree of unemployment. This pattern of events has already been discussed in Chapter 7 in analysing an economy in depression.

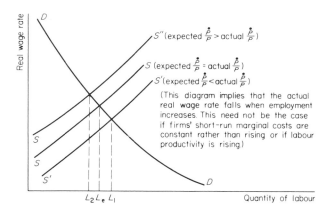

FIGURE 9.4   *The effect of differences between the actual and expected rates of inflation on the supply of labour*

* Students will find a simple exposition of this analysis in [15].

The Long-Run Trade-Off Between Unemployment and Inflation

In the case of actual inflation exceeding expected inflation, unemployment will only remain temporarily below the 'natural' level according to the analysis of Friedman and Phelps [11]. Eventually expectations adjust to the actual level of inflation. Workers no longer over-estimate the real value of the money wage offer they receive. A smaller proportion of money wage offers is therefore accepted and unemployment rises to its 'natural' level. The only difference compared to the previous equilibrium position is that the actual rate of inflation, which is fully anticipated, is higher. This means that there has been an upward shift in the short-run Phillips curve as shown in Figure 9.3. The position of each short-run Phillips curve is determined by a given expected rate of inflation. In the Friedman–Phelps argument the short-run Phillips curve shifts with changes in expected inflation so that the equilibrium level of unemployment always equals the 'natural' rate at every rate of inflation, provided this rate is fully anticipated. In this view there is no long-run trade-off between inflation and unemployment. One can only have less unemployment in the present at the expense of more inflation in the future (see [39]).

Empirical Evidence on the Trade-Off Between Unemployment and Inflation

The existence of a long-run trade-off between unemployment and inflation depends on the value of the coefficient of the price expectations variable. In equilibrium actual and expected inflation are equal and equation (9.8) rearranged becomes

$$f(U) = (1 - \alpha)(\dot{P}/P) + (\dot{X}/X). \qquad (9.10)$$

If α equals one the rate of inflation has no effect at all on the level of unemployment, indicating the absence of any long-run trade-off.

A long-run trade-off will exist if α is less than one. There is an absence of powerful arguments justifying a value of α less than one. This would occur if people are irrational and suffer from money illusion. *Ad hoc* reasons, such as the cost of adjusting money contracts to compensate fully for expected inflation, have been suggested. It is difficult to rationalise why such adjustment costs should persist indefinitely. Rees [16] has also suggested that the lower rate of unemployment brought about by inflation means that workers previously experiencing unemployment acquire skills which increase their productivity and hence the demand for their services, so that they remain in employment even when expected inflation has caught up with the actual rate.

Although the theoretical arguments strongly favour α being equal to one, empirical work has, on the whole, thrown up values of less than one. The earlier U.K. studies (Dicks-Mireaux [17], Klein and Ball [18],

Lipsey [14]) included a current or lagged rate of inflation variable, rather than an expected rate, and obtained coefficients of 0·46, 0·85 and 0·69 respectively (see Table 9.1). Later U.K. studies, such as those of Parkin and Solow [23], used the adaptive-expectations hypothesis to formulate an equation in which the expected rate of change of prices enters as an independent variable. Parkin obtains a coefficient of 0·44 and Solow one of 0·5 for U.S. annual data, 0·2 for U.K. annual data and 0·8 for U.K. quarterly data. Nobay and Saunders [22] point out that use of the adaptive-expectations hypothesis can bias α downwards and, using an alternative structural form, find that the value of α is increased (α equals 0·77 in one form of the model).

To show that a relationship exists between inflation and unemployment it is of course also necessary to establish that unemployment is a significant variable in equations which seek to explain the rate of change of prices or wages.* Furthermore, to support the case that a trade-off exists, which offers policy-makers a choice between unemployment and inflation, it is necessary to show that the rate of change of money wages (or prices) is a stable function of unemployment that does not shift from period to period.

An examination of the empirical evidence reveals that the empirical support for such a stable relationship has never been firmly established. The original Phillips study did not report significance tests on the estimates. A number of observations, such as the 1951 inflation due to the Korean War and the 1949 Cripps wage-restraint policy, lie well off the Phillips curve. In the Lipsey study which purported to support the Phillips relation unemployment was in fact insignificant. Unemployment was found significant in the following studies (summarised in Table 9.1): Eckstein and Wilson [19], Klein and Ball [18], Hines [28] (1893–1912), Dicks-Mireaux [17] and Purdy and Zis [31]. Unemployment is reported as being insignificant in the studies by Lipsey [14], Hines [28, 29] (1920–39, 1949–61), Parkin [21], Ward and Zis [33], Godfrey [31] and Kuh [20]. Lucas and Rapping [24, 25] explicitly test the hypothesis that the relationship between unemployment and the rate of change of money wages is only temporary, by using unemployment as the dependent variable. This contrasts with the other studies mentioned in which the rate of change of money wages or of prices is the dependent variable. The breakdown of the period 1904–65 into three sub-periods reveals the Phillips relationship to be unstable. They test for the absence of a

---

* Econometric studies have used both wage rates and earnings. Weekly wage rates are the minimum rates agreed for a normal working week. Weekly earnings are greater due to piece rates, bonuses and overtime. Earnings can be used on an hourly basis or on a weekly basis, when salaries may be included. Wage drift is used to describe the tendency for earnings to diverge from wage rates. There is some disagreement as to whether or not the difference between earnings and wage rates can be explained by the level of aggregate demand.

long-run trade-off by seeing whether the sum of the price coefficients is insignificantly different from one. This is confirmed for the periods 1904–29 and 1946–65 but not for 1930–45. There is evidence for a short-run Phillips relation in the periods 1904–29 and 1930–45, while the equation completely fails to explain unemployment for 1946–65.*

In conclusion, the theoretical and empirical work indicates that any trade-off between unemployment and a given rate of inflation will be less pronounced as time passes. This prediction is consistent with post-war experience of running economies at low levels of unemployment accompanied by secularly rising inflation.

9.9   STRUCTURALIST THEORIES OF INFLATION

There have been a number of attempts to attribute inflation, particularly the milder forms, to built-in factors in modern market economies.

Sectoral Shift Theories

One group of *ad hoc* explanations sees inflation as the outcome of the reactions in one sector of the economy to events in another. The various sectors of the economy do not develop in step with one another. In sectors which are expanding and experiencing excess demand prices rise. If prices are inflexible downwards they will not decline in contracting sectors, and therefore the general level of prices rises [33].

Some industries experience larger increases in labour productivity than the average. If workers in these industries receive money wage increases equal to the increase in productivity prices can remain constant in these industries. Since one aspect of trade union bargaining involves comparing the pay of their members to that received in other sectors, workers in lower productivity industries also wish to receive similar increases in money wages. The wage round, by which wage increases in one industry trigger off wage increases in another to maintain accepted differentials, causes the average level of money wages to increase by more than the average increase in labour productivity. This puts upward pressure on the price level.†

* A further study by Lucas [26], using data for eighteen countries, directly tests the absence of any long-run trade-off by regressing deviations in real output from trend and the rate of change in prices on the rate of change in aggregate demand measured by nominal expenditure. The absence of a long-run trade-off is supported by the evidence, since in countries with lower and more stable rates of inflation real output responds more to price level changes than it does in countries with more rapid inflation. Theory predicts this difference, as one would expect people in the latter group of countries to have higher expected rates of inflation and to have taken account of the actual rate of inflation when making contracts.

† See [16, 34, 35] for such views.

Trade Union Militancy

The above discussion has touched briefly on the role of trade union bargaining in obtaining wage increases. It has been suggested, notably by Hines [27, 28, 29], that money wage increases can be explained by trade union militancy. The question then arises as to what explains union militancy. One plausible hypothesis is that it is related to previous and expected increases in the price index (or in the cost-of-living index). Others have suggested that it is positively related to firms' profits. It has also been argued that union activity will only succeed in achieving money wage increases when firms are willing to concede these in times when aggregate demand and profits are high. If these factors gave a complete explanation of trade union militancy, the fit of a regression equation for the rate of change of money wages which contained unemployment, the past or expected rate of change of prices and profits would not be improved by the addition of trade union militancy. Hines's empirical work proxies trade union militancy by the rate of change of the proportion of the labour force unionised. This variable is found to be significant and to explain a considerable proportion of the variance of the rate of change of money wage rates in the United Kingdom 1893–1961. Hines's results have been criticised by Purdy and Zis [30] who use different data to measure union militancy by the rate of change of the proportion of the labour force unionised. They find that the militancy variable is only significant when unemployment is included, unlike Hines who found unemployment insignificant. Trade union militancy has also been proxied by strike activity. The number of strikes has been found significant by Godfrey [31], but insignificant by Ward and Zis [32].

There is thus some evidence that trade union activity explains the rate of change of money wage rates and that this activity cannot be entirely attributed to the level of aggregate demand and to changes in the price level. Micro theory of competitive markets would lead one to conclude that a trade union cannot push up real wages without causing more unemployment.* But the wage bargaining situation is one of bilateral monopoly because it largely takes place between oligopolistic firms and trade unions. Such firms can grant wage increases more readily because they anticipate that they can raise their product prices without losing trade as their competitors will follow the same policy. In order to finance the higher money value of transactions that results from this bargaining process, the economy requires an increased stock of nominal money.† If the government, as in the United Kingdom, pursues a policy of

---

* Micro partial equilibrium theory predicts nothing about the nominal level of wages and prices.
† Hines [28], makes this assumption explicit.

stabilising interest rates and maintaining a low level of unemployment, it will respond to the demand for more nominal money balances by increasing the money supply.

9.10   MONETARY THEORIES OF INFLATION

Theories of inflation which stress the role of aggregate demand or structural factors still require an expansion in the money supply to finance the increasing nominal value of national income brought about by rising prices. Monetarists stress that too rapid an expansion in the supply of money relative to the demand for it is the main driving force behind inflation. The resulting excess money balances are spent on assets or goods and services. Investment and consumption demand rise and, if output cannot be expanded, prices rise. Empirical work to support these views has mainly been in the form of relating the level or change in nominal income to the supply of money.* The rate of inflation has been regressed on to changes in the money supply and in the money wage paid to white-collar government employees in Harberger's study [35] of inflation. The role of money is confirmed in this study, money wages adding little to the size of the multiple correlation coefficient. Money is also found to be significant in explaining price changes in Vogel's study [36] of sixteen Latin American countries.

Hyperinflation

Periods of extremely rapid inflation (defined by Cagan [5] to start in the month the price index increases by over 50 per cent a month) have occurred for a few years in countries dislocated by war or political instability, and have been accompanied by large increases in the money supply. As the inflation proceeds the expected rate of inflation increases. The increased opportunity cost of holding real money balances decreases the demand for them. The consequent activity to get rid of excess money balances by spending them adds further fuel to the inflation. Evidence of this process is to be found in Cagan's study of hyperinflation. He shows that velocity increased and that the demand for real money balances can be explained by the expected increase in the rate of inflation. He found the elasticity of the demand for real balances with respect to the expected rate of inflation to be less than one. If the elasticity of the demand for real money balances were greater than one, the demand for money would provide a destabilising factor as each additional one per cent in expected inflation would result in people spending more than one per cent of additional money balances in their attempt to reduce their real money balances. Thus the inflationary process would be self-perpetuating.

* See Chapter 13 for empirical evidence.

9.11 POLICIES TO DEAL WITH INFLATION

Indexing

The welfare cost and redistribution effects of inflation can be prevented by indexing. The income of fixed interest securities can be linked to the price index to prevent the redistribution of purchasing power from lenders to borrowers that otherwise occurs. An interest rate which is adjusted for inflation can be paid on money to prevent the reduction in the demand to hold money and the consequent welfare loss. All wages and salaries can be automatically adjusted to move with the price index.

Fears have been expressed that indexing only makes matters worse by building inflation into the economy. For this criticism to be valid presupposes that money wages would not otherwise have risen by as much as the increase in the price level. In a closed economy this must mean a redistribution of real income away from wage and salary earners to profits and that spending out of profits somehow causes less upward pressure on prices than spending out of wages and salaries.

Indexing has the advantage of lessening the costs, in terms of unemployment, of reducing the rate of inflation. Assume that inflation has been proceeding at a rate of 10 per cent and the government succeeds in reducing inflation to 5 per cent. Indexing is not practised so workers' real wages are not automatically protected. Expectations about inflation take time to adjust, so for a while people expect the rate of inflation to be higher than it actually is. Unemployment increases because a higher proportion of job seekers reject money wage offers as they think these are worth less in real terms than is the case. In other words the economy is moving down a short-run Phillips curve established for 10 per cent expected inflation. It is not until expectations have adjusted to 5 per cent inflation that we move on to a lower short-run Phillips curve so that unemployment falls back to its 'natural' level. Thus in the absence of indexing, trade union activity to increase money wages in accordance with the expected rate of inflation will make it more difficult for a government to reduce the rate of inflation.

If indexing were practised unemployment would not rise so much when the actual rate of inflation is reduced. Also it may be easier to reduce inflation. Money wage offers will not be so frequently rejected because workers know that they will be automatically compensated for any future inflation that occurs. They do not have to ensure this compensation for themselves by insisting on increases in money wages that will compensate for the rate of inflation expected to occur.

Indexing can bring problems for an open economy in which the domestic price level is increased by an increase in the price of imported goods, such as oil. An increase in the price of imported goods relative to domestic goods necessarily involves a reduction in real income. Increasing money wages in an attempt to avoid this type of reduction in real income cannot be successful.

If a government wishes to reduce the rate of inflation two types of policy have been advocated, fiscal and monetary policy or some form of intervention in the process of setting prices and wages.

Fiscal and Monetary Policy

Inflation that results from the government financing its budget deficit by monetary expansion can be tackled by fiscal policy to remove the deficit or by monetary policy to reduce the monetary expansion and finance the deficit by borrowing. The latter course will naturally involve some increase in the rate of interest. Our earlier discussion indicated how a government can run the economy at a lower level of unemployment by incurring inflation. As the trade-off between inflation and unemployment declines with time it becomes necessary to have a higher rate of inflation to achieve a given level of unemployment. The government can reduce inflation by restrictive fiscal and monetary policies. As a result of this unemployment increases above the 'natural' level and remains there until expectations have adjusted to the new, lower rate of inflation. Given the long-run trade-off, the economy only has to be run temporarily at a higher level of unemployment in order to reduce inflation.

Those who favour structuralist explanations of inflation maintain that fiscal and monetary policy cannot tackle this type of inflation since it is not affected by the level of aggregate demand [28]. This view must be moderated by the fact that the price level cannot rise continuously without being financed by increases in the money supply. Once inflation has come to be expected it can continue at rates which are quite unrelated to the current state of aggregate demand. Taking a chronological view of the inflationary process, it can be started up by excess aggregate demand associated with monetary expansion. As inflation proceeds expectations of inflation lead to increases in money wage rates which cause further increases in prices. Thus inflation can occur at a rate which is not associated with the current level of demand. In the monetarist view this inflation can only be reduced by a reduction in the rate of increase of the money supply. This should proceed gradually unless one wants a sharp increase in unemployment. Once inflationary expectations exist any reduction in demand causes a decline in real output as well as an associated decrease in the rate of increase in prices.

Prices and Incomes Policies

The policy recommendations so far discussed offer no painless cure for inflation. This may explain the popularity of the alternative suggested remedy, that of government intervention in the pricing process. Supporters of intervention see it as working by reducing expectations about inflation as well as by holding down wages and prices. Intervention comes in many forms from government exhortation to unions and firms, agencies (such as the Prices and Incomes Board) to monitor wage and price increases, legislation to regulate, freeze or subsidise certain prices, to the full panoply of state controls on prices, wages, production and investment. The latter system is used in centrally-planned socialist economies and has been experienced by capitalist countries in wartime. There is no doubt that complete state control does contain inflation. The Eastern European countries of the Soviet bloc have experienced quite stable price levels in the postwar period, though it should be noted that their money supply has also remained stable. The price level in the United Kingdom rose less in the Second World War than during the First World War due to state price and production controls accompanied by rationing. Germany in the period 1938–44 provides an interesting example of a country experiencing a much less rapid increase in prices than one would have expected from the expansion in its money supply. This can be explained by the extent of government price controls, including a ceiling on stock market prices, and the vigour with which these controls were enforced. (There were cases of individuals executed for selling at above ceiling prices [37].)

The disadvantage of freezing prices is that relative prices can no longer perform their role of allocating resources. Sectors of high demand cannot attract resources from sectors of low demand because the former cannot raise their relative prices. If prices are kept artificially low relative to costs, as in the case of unfurnished accommodation in the United Kingdom, demand is increased while supply is diminished in the absence of a market mechanism to correct this disequilibrium or adequate alternative provision by the government.

If price and wage controls are temporary and piecemeal they are unlikely to succeed in reducing inflation while at the same time incurring costs in the form of inefficient resource allocation. Such controls need extensive state intervention to control inflation which is merely repressed unless its basic causes are also removed.

9.12 REPRESSED INFLATION

Inflation can be repressed by enforcing a ceiling on the price of output, on money wages or on both. In the case of wage controls the repressed inflation will manifest itself as an excess demand for labour by firms who, at the controlled money wage rate, wish to hire more labour than is willing to supply itself. If an effective price ceiling is maintained, demand for final output will be in excess of the quantity supplied. This will cause shortages, associated with lengthening order books and queues in the shops.

Repressed inflation can have an adverse effect on the quantity of real output produced. Money wage controls protect less efficient firms who would not be able to pay the higher money wages that would result from competitive bidding for labour. Thus, decreases in labour productivity have been a feature of repressed inflation [38]. There is an additional tendency for the supply of labour to fall since the opportunity cost of leisure is reduced if people cannot spend their incomes on the goods and services they wish to buy. If this occurs the quantity of goods and services is further reduced, although demand will also fall.

9.13 POLICY CONCLUSIONS

Prices and wage controls do not offer a market economy a permanent solution to the problem of inflation. Repressed inflation still remains and needs to be dealt with by the usual fiscal and monetary methods.

Inflation presents policy-makers with the necessity of comparing the costs of inflation with the costs of anti-inflationary action. This choice must be evaluated over a time horizon. Given the temporary nature of the unemployment–inflation trade-off, the costs of anti-inflationary policy in terms of unemployment occur in the present and near future while the benefits of reduced inflation are not enjoyed until the more distant future. Elected governments and their advisers are reluctant to recognise the unpleasant nature of the choices they face and hesitate to incur present costs for future benefits.

REFERENCES

[1] Freund and Williams, *Modern Business Statistics* (London: Pitman, 1967).
[2] M. J. Bailey, 'The Welfare Effects of Inflationary Finance', *Journal of Political Economy*, 64 (1956).
[3] M. Friedman, *The Optimum Quantity of Money* (London: Macmillan, 1969) ch. 1.
[4] J. M. Keynes, *A Tract on Monetary Reform* (London: Macmillan, 1923) ch. 1.
[5] P. Cagan, 'The Monetary Dynamics of Hyperinflation', in *Studies in the Quantity Theory of Money*, ed. M. Friedman (University of Chicago Press, 1956).
[6] M. J. C. Surrey, *The Analysis and Forecasting of the British Economy* (Cambridge University Press, 1971) ch. 5.
[7] M. Friedman, 'The Role of Monetary Policy', *American Economic Review*, 58 (March 1968).
[8] D. T. Mortensen, 'A Theory of Wage and Employment Dynamics', in *Microeconomic Foundations of Employment and Inflation Theory*, ed. E. Phelps (London: Macmillan, 1970).
[9] C. C. Holt, 'How Can the Phillips Curve Be Moved to Reduce Both Inflation and Unemployment?' in *Microeconomic Foundations*, ed. Phelps.

[10] C. C. Holt, 'Job Search, Phillips Wage Relation and Union Influence: Theory and Evidence', in *Microeconomic Foundations*, ed. Phelps.

[11] E. Phelps, 'Money Wage Dynamics and Labour Market Equilibrium', in *Microeconomic Foundations*, ed. Phelps.

[12] B. Hansen, 'Excess Demand, Unemployment and Vacancies, and Wages', *Quarterly Journal of Economics*, 84 (February 1970).

[13] A. W. Phillips, 'The Relationship Between Unemployment and the Rate of Change of Money Wage Rates in the U.K. 1861–1957', *Economica*, 25 (1957).

[14] R. G. Lipsey, 'The Relationship Between Unemployment and the Rate of Change of Money Wage Rates in the U.K. 1861–1957: A Further Analysis', *Economica*, 27 (1960).

[15] S. Morely, *The Economics of Inflation* (Illinois: The Dryden Press Inc., 1971).

[16] A. Rees, 'The Phillips Curve as a Menu for Policy Choice', *Economica*, n.s., 37 (May 1970).

[17] L. A. Dicks-Mireaux, 'The Interrelationship Between Cost and Price Changes, 1946–59: A Study of Inflation in Post-War Britain', *Oxford Economic Papers*, 13 (1961).

[18] L. R. Klein and R. J. Ball, 'Some Econometrics of the Determination of Absolute Prices and Wages', *Economic Journal*, 69 (1959).

[19] O. Eckstein and T. A. Wilson, 'The Determination of Money Wages in American Industry', *Quarterly Journal of Economics*, 76 (1962).

[20] E. Kuh, 'A Productivity Theory of Wage Levels: An Alternative to the Phillips Curve', *Review of Economic Studies*, 34 (October 1967).

[21] M. Parkin, 'Incomes Policy: Some Further Results on the Rate of Change of Money Wages', *Economica*, n.s., 37 (November 1970).

[22] P. G. Saunders and A. R. Nobay, 'Price Expectations, the Phillips Curve and Incomes Policy', in *Incomes Policy and Inflation*, ed. M. Parkin and M. Sumner (Manchester University Press, 1972).

[23] R. Solow, *Price Expectations and the Behaviour of the Price Level* (Manchester University Press, 1969).

[24] R. E. Lucas and L. A. Rapping, 'Real Wages, Employment and Inflation', in *Microeconomic Foundations*, ed. Phelps.

[25] R. E. Lucas and L. A. Rapping, 'Price Expectations and the Phillips Curve', *American Economic Review*, 54 (1969).

[26] R. E. Lucas, 'Some International Evidence on Output–Inflation Tradeoffs', *American Economic Review*, 63 (June 1973).

[27] A. G. Hines, 'Trade Unions and Wage Inflation in the U.K. 1893–1961', *Review of Economic Studies*, 31 (1964).

[28] A. G. Hines, 'Wage Inflation in the U.K. 1948–62: A Disaggregated Study', *Economic Journal*, 79 (May 1969).

[29] A. G. Hines, 'The Determinants of the Rate of Change of Money Wage Rates and the Effectiveness of Incomes Policy', in *The Current Inflation*, ed. H. G. Johnson and A. R. Nobay (London: Macmillan, 1971).

[30] D. L. Purdy and G. Zis, 'Trade Unions and Wage Inflation in the U.K.: A Reappraisal', in The Proceedings of the Association of University Teachers of Economics Conference, Aberystwyth 1972, *Essays in Modern Economics* (London: Longman, 1973).

[31] L. Godfrey, 'The Phillips Curve: Incomes Policy and Trade Union Effects', in *The Current Inflation*, ed. Johnson and Nobay.

[32] R. Ward and G. Zis, 'Trade Union Militancy as an Explanation of Inflation: An International Comparison', *Manchester School*, 42 (March 1974).

[33] C. L. Schultze, 'Recent Inflation in the U.S.', *Study Paper No. 1*, *Study of Employment, Growth and Price Levels*, Joint Economic Committee, 86th Congress, First Session (1959).

[34] D. Jackson, H. A. Turner and F. Wilkinson, *Do Trade Unions Cause Inflation?* (Cambridge University Press, 1972).

[35] A. C. Harberger, 'The Dynamics of Inflation in Chile', in *Measurement in Economics*, ed. C. Christ (Stanford University Press, 1963).

[36] R. C. Vogel, 'The Dynamics of Inflation in Latin America 1950–69', *American Economic Review* (March 1974).

[37] J. J. Klein, 'German Money and Prices 1932–44', in *Studies in the Quantity Theory of Money*, ed. M. Friedman (University of Chicago Press, 1956).

[38] B. Hansen, *A Study in the Theory of Inflation* (London: Allen & Unwin, 1951).

[39] E. Phelps, 'Phillips Curves, Expectations of Inflation and Optimal Unemployment Over Time', *Economica*, 34 (August 1967).

10 Economic Growth*

The short-run general macro model developed in Chapter 7 and extended to the open economy in Chapter 8 was based on the following three simplifying assumptions.

(1) The time period involved in the analysis was so short that the net investment taking place had no significant effect on the size of the economy's capital stock. This allowed us to concentrate on the effect which that net investment has on the size of aggregate demand while neglecting its effect in increasing the economy's productive capacity.

(2) A constant population. This allowed us to concentrate on the factors underlying the demand and supply of labour from a constant population. However, during the last century and a half the population of almost every country has been increasing at varying geometric rates. This has resulted in an increase in the labour force over time and has been another factor in increasing the productive capacity of the economy.

(3) An unchanging level of technical knowledge. This assumption also needs to be relaxed as increasing technical knowledge has resulted in a continual decrease in the real resources required per unit of output as well as in the introduction of new products. Technical change has been a major historical factor in increasing the economy's productive capacity. It has also stimulated the rate of growth of demand through its impact on the rate of investment.

It is now necessary to extend the earlier analysis in order to examine the effects that capital accumulation, population growth and technical progress have on the equilibrium solution for the economy. The reason for concentrating on equilibrium solutions are as follows.

(a) Equilibrium dynamic solutions are relatively easy to set up and solve, while disequilibrium dynamic systems are much more difficult to

* This chapter has been kindly contributed by Alex Rebmann-Huber.

deal with as their behaviour depends on the error-adjusting mechanisms and lag structures specified.

(b) Neoclassical economists believe that the economy is inherently stable and that it tends to return to some full-employment growth path if it is displaced from this path. On the other hand some Keynesians and neo-Keynesians believe that a capitalist economy is inherently unstable, with such stringent sufficient conditions for equilibrium full-employment growth that it is unlikely to be achieved. In order to throw some light on this difference of opinion it is necessary to examine the conditions necessary for the existence of full-employment equilibrium growth and the stability of this equilibrium growth path.

(c) Whether or not the economy tends automatically towards an equilibrium growth path, one must analyse the necessary and sufficient conditions for the existence of equilibrium growth in order to design government policy measures that aim either to move the economy on to a full-employment equilibrium growth path or to speed its return to such a path.

10.1 THE IMPACT OF CAPITAL ACCUMULATION AND POPULATION GROWTH

We will now consider what impact capital accumulation and population growth have on the economy. For the time being technical knowledge is assumed fixed. It must therefore be kept in mind that the conclusions of this section relate to an economy in which technical change is absent and some would be modified by the presence of technical progress. This is examined later in the chapter.

Capital accumulation and population growth mean that the quantity of available inputs in the aggregate production function increases over time. The concept of an aggregate production function was introduced in Chapter 7 when discussing the supply side of the economy. It is written as

$$y = f(L, K, T) \tag{10.1}$$

where y is the real output per period of time, L is the flow of labour services per period of time, K is the capital stock which yields a proportionate flow of capital services per period of time, and T is the state of technical knowledge which we assume fixed. The law of variable proportions is expected to hold in this economy, so that in the absence of technical change an increase in only one type of input, the other remaining fixed will lead to a less than proportionate change in output and further increases in this input will lead to diminishing increases in output.

For simplicity we assume that the economy as a whole experiences constant returns to scale, so that a given proportionate increase in both capital and labour inputs per period of time will lead to the same proportionate increase in output per period. This implies that in the economy the size of the market for each industry's products is much larger than the capacity output of the plant with the lowest unit costs in the industry. Constant returns to scale for the economy as a whole implies that the aggregate production function is linearly homogeneous in capital and labour inputs. (See the Mathematical Appendix to this chapter, Note 1, for the implications of linear homogeneity in the production function and for the proofs relating to the following discussion.) This means that in the absence of technical change the production function can be written as

$$\frac{y}{L} = F\left(\frac{K}{L}\right) \quad \text{or} \quad y = L\,F\left(\frac{K}{L}\right). \tag{10.2}$$

Thus the average product of labour in the economy, y/L, is an increasing function of the capital–labour ratio, given that factor proportions are variable.

However, the operation of the law of variable proportions allows us to deduce that y/L will increase at a diminishing rate as the capital–labour ratio increases. Therefore a proportionate increase in both labour and capital inputs will keep average output per head constant, while a greater increase in labour inputs to capital inputs will decrease average product per head. This is illustrated in Figure 10.1.

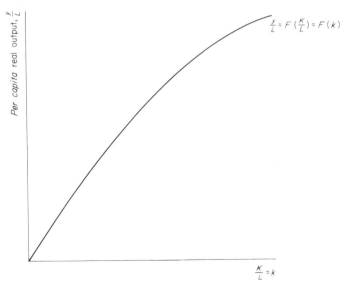

FIGURE 10.1 *Average output per unit of labour input as a function of the capital–labour ratio*

The law of variable proportions implies that the marginal product of a factor decreases as relatively more of that factor is applied to the production of output. This leads to the deduction (see Appendix, Note 1) that the marginal product of capital decreases with increases in the capital–labour ratio, while the marginal product of labour decreases when the capital–labour ratio decreases. Therefore in a competitive economy where profit-maximising entrepreneurs hire factors up to the point where their price is equal to their marginal value product, the equilibrium real wage and real interest rate will change with changes in the capital–labour ratio.

If the capital stock is growing faster than the labour force real interest rates will fall and real wages will rise, while in the case where the labour force is growing faster than the capital stock real interest rates will tend to rise and real wage rates fall. In both cases the increase in inputs into the production process results in a growth in output. However, output only grows at the same rate as any of the inputs if both inputs are growing at the same rate. In this case relative factor prices will remain constant as the capital–labour ratio stays unchanged.

The analysis in earlier chapters concentrated on the impact of net investment on aggregate demand and neglected its effect on the economy's productive capacity. In growth models explicit account is taken of the productive impact of positive net investment which equals the increase in the capital stock. Therefore

$$I = dK/dt. \tag{10.3}$$

A constant labour force in the presence of net investment means that the rate of growth in output capacity will be below the rate of growth of the capital stock because of decreasing marginal returns. If incentives for entrepreneurs to invest are to be maintained the growth in the capacity to produce output must be matched by an increase in aggregate demand. Otherwise the growth of excess capacity will choke off any desire to invest. Therefore as long as net investment is positive any solution for income over time in a macro model must involve some growth (or decay) path for income rather than a stationary long-run equilibrium value. A stationary long-run solution for income can only occur when there is no technical change, a constant labour force, no net investment and zero savings. Any other stationary situation will not persist in the long run.

If we introduce growth in the labour force so that the long-run supply of labour, L, grows at a steady exponential rate of μ, we have

$$L = L_0 e^{\mu t}. \tag{10.4}$$

This growth path in the labour force is depicted in Figure 10.2a. We can also depict it in natural log. form when equation (10.4) becomes

$$\log L = \log L_0 + \mu t. \tag{10.4.a}$$

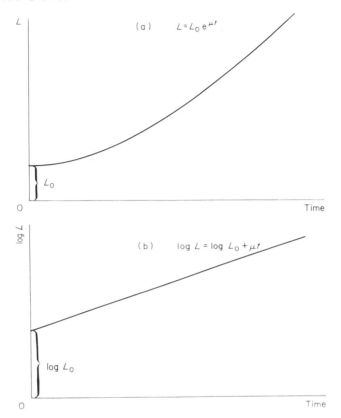

FIGURE 10.2   *The growth path of labour growing at a constant exponential rate,* ρ

This equation, plotted on semi-log. graph paper, is shown in Figure 10.2.b. Here the growth path is a straight line with a positive intercept equal to log L_0 and a positive slope equal to the exponential growth rate, μ.

The continual increase in the labour force will lead to an increase in the economy's productive capacity. Once again it requires an increase in the level of aggregate demand to maintain full employment and long-run equilibrium. If the capital stock increases less rapidly than the labour force, the capital–labour ratio falls. Because of diminishing returns output per head falls so that the rate of growth of output is lower than the rate of growth of the labour force. In this event the real wage rate will have to fall if full employment is to be maintained. Once more equilibrium in the economy, other than in the very short run, will involve some growth path in real national income rather than a constant value of real national income.

When the labour force is growing at some exponential rate μ, income per head, y/L, can only stay constant if the capital stock is also growing at μ and so is aggregate demand. In this situation all the flow variables in the economy must grow through time at the exponential rate μ. The stock of money must also grow at this rate in order to keep the price level constant. Such a rate of growth in all the stock and flow variables would keep the real rate of interest and the real wage rate constant.

The above discussion has shown that any equilibrium solution in a macro model that includes capital accumulation and population growth must necessarily involve finding some growth path for the level of income. An equilibrium solution in a growth context of a macro model with a goods market, a money market and a production sector would involve a growth path in which

(*a*) at every moment in time desired investment and government spending are equal to desired saving plus taxes,

(*b*) the money market is in equilibrium so that $(M/P)^d = (M/P)^s$,

(*c*) full employment or a constant rate of unemployment exists, and

(*d*) there is equality between desired and actual capital stocks.

Growth models without a money market will have an equilibrium growth solution if conditions (*a*), (*c*), (*d*) are fulfilled, while the simplest growth model which concentrates on only the goods market will require (*a*) and (*d*) to be fulfilled. Steady state equilibrium growth is an equilibrium growth rate which occurs at a steady exponential rate. Not all equilibrium growth paths are steady state growth paths. However, most analyses of growth models have been of steady-state solutions.

For policy purposes it would be useful to analyse a macro growth model that includes a monetary sector, such as a growth version of the models developed in Chapters 7 and 8. The dynamic properties of such models are quite complicated [1, 2]. Therefore it is easier to develop the conditions necessary for the existence of an equilibrium growth path and examine the stability properties of such a path in simpler models which exclude the monetary sector. In doing this we will be following the work of the pioneers of growth theory, such as Harrod, Joan Robinson, Solow and Swan.

10.2   THE HARROD GROWTH MODEL

The simplest growth model is that formulated by Harrod [3, 4, 5] which is made up of a goods market and a production sector. The model has the following features.

(1) It neglects the lag structure of the economy as this will have no effect on the steady-state equilibrium solution. This neglect of lag structures is common to many simple growth models as lag structures only have an impact when the economy departs from the equilibrium growth path.

(2) A constant desired capital–output ratio, v. This occurs as Harrod assumes a constant long-run real rate of interest. In the absence of technical change, the assumption of constant relative factor prices will result in constant desired factor input ratios even though the aggregate production function allows factor substitution. It also results in a constant desired capital–output ratio, v, and a constant desired labour–output ratio, u.

(3) Savings are a constant proportion of real income in the economy. This is a simplifying assumption that is consistent with the permanent income hypothesis when measured income is growing at some constant exponential rate.

(4) The labour force is growing at some exogenously determined constant exponential rate, μ.

Goods Market Equilibrium in the Harrod Model

Goods market equilibrium in this model requires that
(*a*) desired savings are equal to desired investment at each moment in time, and
(*b*) the capital equipment in the economy is fully utilised.
If desired investment is not equal to desired savings then the usual multiplier response will occur and will shift the economy away from its current position until desired savings are once more equal to desired investment. If the existing capital stock is not fully utilised there will be a decline in the entrepreneur's incentive to invest and investment will decline in the absence of some great burst of innovations. Given these two requirements for goods market equilibrium, the equations specifying the goods market are

$$\text{equilibrium in the goods market} \quad I = S \quad \quad (10.5)$$

$$\text{desired savings function} \quad S = sy \quad \quad (10.6)$$

$$\text{investment function} \quad I = v(\mathrm{d}y/\mathrm{d}t). \quad \quad (10.7)$$

The investment function (10.7) is derived by assuming that on a growth path with continuous goods market equilibrium expectations are always fulfilled in the aggregate. Therefore entrepreneurs will carry out sufficient investment to achieve the capital stock which will give them the lowest total costs of production for the future expected level of output. This means that in each period entrepreneurs will invest just enough to keep the actual capital stock equal to the desired capital stock. In equation (10.7), v is the desired capital–output ratio given the existence of a fixed real rate of interest, while $\mathrm{d}y/\mathrm{d}t$ is the expected rate of change in income. In equilibrium steady-state growth actual and expected rates of change in income are equal. Therefore equation (10.7) omits specifying that the rate of change in income is the expected rate of change.

For the moment we assume that the economy's labour force is large enough and is growing sufficiently in order to supply any demand for labour from entrepreneurs. Then the economy's equilibrium growth path which maintains equilibrium in the goods market can be determined by simultaneous solution of equations (10.5), (10.6) and (10.7). Substituting for I and S in equation (10.5) gives a first-order differential equation in y and t:

$$v(dy/dt) = sy. \tag{10.8}$$

Dividing through this equation by vy gives

$$\frac{1}{y}\frac{dy}{dt} = \frac{s}{v}. \tag{10.9}$$

Now $(1/y)(dy/dt)$ is the proportional rate of growth of equilibrium real income over time. Therefore equation (10.9) shows that the equilibrium growth rate of income in Harrod's model must be s/v. This equation can be integrated to give a solution for the time path of y in terms of s/v and t (see Appendix, Note 2). Therefore

$$y = y_0 \exp[(s/v)t] \tag{10.10}$$

where y_0 is the value of y at some arbitrary time 0.

The analysis above shows that the growth path of real income y, which maintains equilibrium in the goods market, requires the economy to grow at a steady exponential rate equal to s/v. This rate of growth is called the *warranted rate of growth*. The warranted rate of growth, G_w, is that rate of growth which allows desired savings to be equal to desired investment while maintaining full capacity output at every point in time. It is determined by the parameters s and v so that $G_w = s/v$. This is the only rate of growth which will maintain goods market equilibrium and allow expectations to be completely fulfilled. If at any time the growth rate expected by entrepreneurs is not equal to G_w then the economy will not be on the warranted growth path.

Stability Properties of the Harrod Model

Let the rate of growth of real income expected in the near future by entrepreneurs be j. If the current level of real income is $\bar{y}$ then the level of real income at some time t in the near future that entrepreneurs will expect will be $\bar{y}e^{jt}$. The rate of change with respect to time of this expected real income will be

$$d/dt(\bar{y}e^{jt}) = j\bar{y}e^{jt}. \tag{10.11}$$

Substituting this rate of change of expected real income for dy/dt in equation (10.7) gives the investment function for situations where expected growth in income is different from the actual growth in income. Therefore

$$I = v(\mathrm{d}/\mathrm{d}t)(\bar{y}e^{jt}) = vj\bar{y}e^{jt}. \tag{10.7a}$$

Substituting this value for I into the goods market equilibrium condition $S = I$, and assuming that $S = sy$, gives

$$sy = vj\bar{y}e^{jt} \tag{10.12}$$

where y is the actual value of the real national income at any time t. Rewriting this gives

$$y = (v/s)j\bar{y}e^{jt}. \tag{10.12a}$$

Therefore actual income at time $t = (j/G_w)$ (expected income at time t).

This shows that the expected real income at time t can only equal the actual income at that time if the rate of income growth expected by entrepreneurs, j, is equal to the warranted rate of growth, G_w. When the warranted rate of growth equals the expected rate of growth then aggregate demand at every point in time will be just large enough to keep the economy's capital equipment working at its designed capacity.

If j is below the warranted rate G_w, then actual income at any time t will be below the expected level of income for that period. This shortfall of actual income below expected income will lead to excess capacity in the economy as entrepreneurs had invested in sufficient capacity to meet the expected level of aggregate demand. If this excess capacity leads entrepreneurs to lower their expected rate of growth this will lead to a further decline of the expected and actual growth rates below the warranted growth rate. The opposite situation will occur if j is above the warranted growth rate. This unstable property of the warranted growth path, where deviations off the growth path tend to lead to further movements away from it, is known as the 'knife-edge' property of the Harrod model.

Once the economy is off the warranted path in the Harrod model, whether it eventually moves to some warranted growth path depends on the error-adjustment mechanism adopted by the entrepreneurs to correct their mistaken expectations. Therefore an analysis of the disequilibrium path of the model requires one to specify an error-adjustment mechanism and then carry out a dynamic analysis. Such analyses have been carried out by Jorgenson [6] and by Phillips [7]. These analyses dropped the equilibrium requirement that the desired capital stock is always equal to the actual capital stock and set up error-adjustment functions for investment, so that any excess or short-fall in the desired capital stock over the actual capital stock was only corrected over a number of years, rather than in the immediately following year. These analyses found that unless the error-correcting period was longer than v/s years, once the economy was off the warranted growth path it tended to move further away from this path.

The Natural Rate of Growth in the Harrod Model

The analysis of the Harrod model up to this point has ignored the rate of growth of the labour force and technological change. Assuming that the labour force grows at an exogenous exponential rate μ, the long-run labour supply equation is

$$L = L_0 e^{\mu t}. \tag{10.4}$$

In the absence of technical change the desired labour–output ratio, u, is assumed to be constant and the maximum real output, y, that can be achieved by the economy at any time t is

$$y = (1/u)L_0 e^{\mu t}. \tag{10.13}$$

Therefore the maximum sustainable rate of growth on the supply side of an economy without technical progress is

$$(1/y)(dy/dt) = \mu. \tag{10.14}$$

This is called the natural rate of growth and in the absence of technical progress it is equal to the rate of growth of the labour force, μ.

Technical change can easily be introduced into this model if it is assumed to occur at a steady exponential rate, m, and is of a labour-augmenting type.* This form of technical progress occurs when the labour–income ratio, u, declines at a steady negative exponential rate through time so that

$$u = u_0 e^{-mt}.$$

This means that over time less labour input is required per unit of output and the capital–labour ratio increases. Therefore the maximum real income attainable at any time t becomes

$$y = \frac{1}{u_0 e^{-mt}} L_0 e^{\mu t}$$
$$= \frac{1}{u_0} L_0 e^{(m+\mu)t}. \tag{10.15}$$

Thus with a growing labour force and steady labour-augmenting technical progress, the *maximum sustainable rate of growth on the supply side is the natural rate of growth which is equal to the sum of the rate of technical progress, m, and the rate of growth in the labour force.* Thus

$$(1/y)(dy/dt) = m + \mu. \tag{10.16}$$

* Unless technical progress is of this labour-augmenting or Harrod neutral type there will be no steady-state solution for the model.

Conflicts Between the Warranted and Natural Growth Rates

The earlier analysis of the warranted rate of growth demonstrated that, given s and v, this was the only rate of growth at which the economy could grow if desired savings were to equal desired investment and the actual capital stock was to equal the desired stock of capital. However, the ability of the economy to sustain a particular warranted growth path depends on the warranted growth rate either being equal to or less than the natural rate of growth.

If the warranted rate of growth is equal to the natural rate of growth then it is possible to have a steady-state rate of growth with either full employment (the so-called 'golden age') or a constant rate of unemployment. In this steady-state condition income and capital stock per head will remain constant in the absence of technical change, while it will rise at the same exponential rate, m, as the rate of technical progress if labour-augmenting technical change occurs.

If the warranted rate is below the natural rate of growth then it is possible to maintain steady-state growth at the warranted rate with continually increasing unemployment. Here

$$G_w = s/v < m + \mu.$$

In this situation the standard Keynesian monetary and fiscal policies used to deal with unemployment are totally inappropriate. If $G_w < m + \mu$ and the economy is growing at the warranted rate, G_w, then it is operating at full capacity. Unemployment is growing as investment and saving out of full capacity output is too small to equip all the new arrivals in the labour force, plus those existing workers displaced by technological change, with the quantity of capital necessary for their employment.

Here unemployment is produced by inadequate capital accumulation and saving out of full capacity output, given the desired constant capital output ratio, v. It is not brought about by inadequate aggregate demand, as growth at the warranted rate involves the economy in full utilisation of its capital stock. The Keynesian monetary and fiscal policies to cope with unemployment were designed to deal with deficient aggregate demand. Therefore applying them in this case will only make matters worse by diverting resources away from capital accumulation. This state of affairs makes standard short-run Keynesian analysis inappropriate for many developing countries.

The only sensible way to deal with growing unemployment when the economy is growing at the warranted rate is to increase the warranted rate. This requires either an increase in the rate of savings out of real income so as to increase the rate of capital accumulation out of full capacity real income or a decrease in the desired capital–labour ratio. Both of these may eventually occur under the pressure of economic forces but the process does require a change in relative factor incomes and prices.

If political constraints prevent relative factor prices from changing sufficiently, or if the process of change is slow and difficult, the government could take action to increase the rate of savings. This can take the form of either increasing the incentives for private saving or by directly increasing the rate of public sector savings or pursuing both policies simultaneously. Public sector savings can be increased by raising the rate of taxation and by cutting non-productive government expenditure.

If the warranted rate of growth is above the natural rate of growth the actual rate of growth will be periodically constrained below the warranted rate by a shortage of labour to man the newly produced capital equipment. The analysis in the previous section of the chapter showed that any decline in the expected or actual rates of growth below the warranted rate of growth will lead to excess capacity in the economy. The emergence of excess capacity will diminish the incentive to invest and thus reduce the rate of investment. This will lead to periods of declining aggregate demand and increasing unemployment due to deficient aggregate demand in relation to installed capacity. This is the situation for which traditional Keynesian monetary and fiscal remedies were developed. They have the desired impact on the level and rate of change of unemployment through their effects on aggregate demand. However, as long as the warranted rate of growth remains above the natural rate of growth, the economy will suffer from periodic depressions interspersed by periods of growth.

When the warranted rate of growth exceeds the natural rate of growth the government can reduce the warranted rate through fiscal policy. This is done by changing the proportion of real national income that the government spends on goods and services which do not add to the economy's productive capacity for marketable output and financing this change in expenditure by borrowing from the public.

In the following exposition we assume that the proportion of government expenditure in real national income is γ and that the government finances this expenditure entirely by selling bonds to the private sector. The modified Harrod model in this case is:

$$\text{goods market equilibrium} \qquad I + G = S \qquad (10.5a)$$

$$\text{savings function} \qquad S = sy$$

$$\text{investment function} \qquad I = v(\mathrm{d}y/\mathrm{d}t) \qquad (10.7)$$

$$\text{government expenditure function} \qquad G = \gamma y. \qquad (10.17)$$

Substituting for I, G and S in equation (10.5a) gives

$$v(\mathrm{d}y/\mathrm{d}t) + \gamma y = sy. \qquad (10.18)$$

Manipulating this equation gives

$$\frac{1}{y}\frac{dy}{dt} = \frac{s-\gamma}{v}.$$ (10.19)

This shows that the introduction of government expenditure has lowered the warranted rate of growth which is now $G_w = (s-\gamma)/v$. The warranted rate of growth can now be manipulated by changing the proportion of national income spent on public sector consumption and financing this by an equal change in government borrowing from the public. Therefore the government can lower the warranted rate of growth through changes in fiscal policy at the expense of increasing its fixed interest debt. However, in an exponentially growing economy (unlike the case of a stationary economy) continual deficit financing will not create an insupportable burden of debt. While the government debt will increase absolutely through time, it will tend to some constant ratio with respect to the annual real income [8].

In the absence of government expenditure and taxation the warranted rate of growth is equal to s/v, while the natural rate of growth is equal to $m + \mu$. In the Harrod model s, m and μ are all exogenously determined while v is fixed due to the assumption of a constant real rate of interest. Therefore in the likely event of the warranted rate of growth not being equal to the natural rate of growth (i.e. $s/v \neq m + \mu$) there are no economic forces changing these parameters and thus returning the economy to a long-run full-employment path. Any such path in the Harrod model is either fortuitous or attained through deliberate government policy.

This characteristic of the Harrod model does not seem to be particularly realistic for developed capitalist economies in a long-run growth context. Historically these economies have not experienced prolonged periods of rising unemployment as a result of either deficient demand or insufficient accumulation, although there have been short-run experiences of both phenomena. Therefore much of the work on growth theory in the two decades following the Second World War was a respecification of Harrod's model so that either s, or v, or both, became functions of other economic variables in the models.

Economists belonging to the Cambridge neo-Keynesian school dealt with the problem of differing warranted and natural rates of growth by writing s as a function of income distribution. Due to the retention of profits by firms the marginal propensity to save out of profit income is specified as being higher than the marginal propensity to save out of non-profit incomes. This allows savings as a proportion of income to vary within a band, depending on the distribution of income between profits and non-profits. This allows the warranted rate of growth to take on a range of values. Provided that the natural rate of growth lies within this range, the economy will adjust to a steady-state growth path in the long run [9, 10]. The alternative approach to this problem is the neoclassical approach which concentrates on changes in v, the desired capital–output ratio.

10.3 THE SOLOW NEOCLASSICAL MODEL OF ECONOMIC GROWTH

The neoclassical approach [12, 13, 14] assumes that factor prices are flexible in the long run and respond to excess demand. This allows factor substitution by firms in response to changes in relative factor prices. Aggregating this response by firms across the economy leads to changes in the factor proportions utilised in the aggregate production function, $y = f(L, K, T)$ and this alters the capital–output ratio, v.

The flexibility of factor prices means that in the long run the real rate of interest, ρ, changes to make investment equal to the rate of saving at full capacity output. A fall in the real rate of interest increases the desired capital stock relative to any expected level of income, while a rise in the real rate of interest has the opposite effect. Therefore the long-run neoclassical growth model does not possess an independent investment function. Investment is merely defined as the change in the capital stock, i.e.

$$I = dK/dt. \tag{10.3}$$

The aggregate production function is assumed to be linearly homogeneous in labour and capital inputs and, in the absence of technical change, is written as

$$\frac{y}{L} = F\left(\frac{K}{L}\right). \tag{10.2}$$

This production function is graphed in Figures 10.1 and 10.3, which show a well-behaved production function. Defining $K/L = k$ and substituting for K/L into equation (10.2) this becomes

$$y/L = F(k). \tag{10.2a}$$

The savings function in the model is the proportional savings function used in the Harrod model. This can be written in terms of saving per unit of labour input by dividing through both sides by L so that

$$S/L = s(y/L). \tag{10.6a}$$

The real wage rate in the neoclassical model is also assumed to be flexible in the long run. It adjusts to the level necessary to equate the demand for labour with the available labour force which is growing at an exogenous exponential rate of μ.

It is assumed that the economy is purely competitive* so that profit-maximising firms equate the value of the marginal product of a factor input to its price. Therefore, in equilibrium the real rate of interest, ρ, equals the marginal product of capital and the real wage rate, w, equals the marginal product of labour. This can be expressed as

$$\rho = \frac{\partial y}{\partial K} = \frac{d}{dk}\left[F(k)\right] \tag{10.20}$$

$$w = \frac{\partial y}{\partial L} = F(k) - k\frac{d}{dk}\left[F(k)\right] \tag{10.21}$$

where k is the capital–labour ratio. Equation (10.20) shows the rate of interest in equilibrium as being equal to the rate of change in output per unit of labour input with respect to changes in the capital–labour ratio. Equation (10.21) shows the equilibrium real wage as the difference between total output per unit of labour input and the amount of output per head paid out as profit, where profit is the product of the real rate of interest and the capital–labour ratio. This is shown in Figure 10.3.

The final equation in the Solow model is the equilibrium condition for

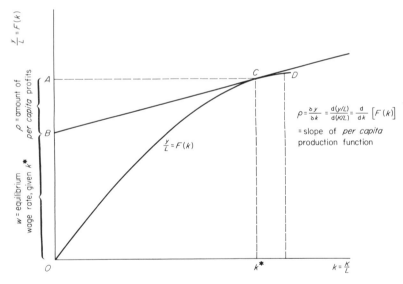

FIGURE 10.3   *The* per capita *production function: wage rate and interest rate in the Solow model*

* The assumption of a purely competitive economy is a simplifying assumption. It is not crucial for the conclusions on the characteristics of the equilibrium steady-state growth path in the neoclassical model.

the product market which is written in terms of investment and savings per unit of labour input:

$$I/L = S/L. \tag{10.5a}$$

The complete Solow neoclassical model expressed in terms of stocks and flows per unit of labour input is:

investment function $\qquad\qquad \dfrac{I}{L} = \dfrac{1}{L}\dfrac{dK}{dt}$ $\qquad$ (10.3a)

savings function $\qquad\qquad\qquad \dfrac{S}{L} = s\dfrac{y}{L}$ $\qquad\qquad$ (10.6a)

equilibrium in goods market $\qquad \dfrac{I}{L} = \dfrac{S}{L}$ $\qquad\qquad$ (10.5a)

aggregate production function $\quad \dfrac{y}{L} = F(k)$ $\qquad\qquad$ (10.2a)

long-run labour supply function $\;\; L = L_0 e^{\mu t}$ $\qquad\qquad$ (10.4)

demand for capital stock $\qquad\quad \rho = \dfrac{d}{dk}F(k)$ $\qquad\qquad$ (10.20)

demand for labour $\qquad\qquad w = F(k) - \dfrac{d}{dk}F(k).$ $\;\;$ (10.21)

This gives a system of seven equations in the seven unknowns of y, I, S, K, L, ρ and w which solves for the values of each of these variables at each point in time. The solution of this model finds the warranted growth rate in income and the capital stock adjusting to the natural growth rate through changes in the desired capital–output ratio. Therefore unless some limit to factor substitution is reached, there is no long-run conflict between the warranted and natural rates of growth. The equilibrium steady-state solution of the model is one where the warranted rate of growth has adjusted to the natural rate of growth. This change in the warranted growth rate requires a change in the rate of return to capital, ρ, and the capital–labour ratio, k. If the warranted rate was originally higher than the natural rate, the adjustment towards the steady-state growth path will require a drop in ρ and a rise in k. This will increase the desired capital–output ratio, v, which lowers the warranted growth rate, s/v. The opposite must happen if the warranted growth path was originally below the natural growth path.

Taking labour inputs as being measured in natural units (i.e. men) the model can be discussed in *per capita* terms such as savings per head, capital per head, etc. The increase in capital per head, dk/dt, can be looked at as the difference between the savings per head, $sF(k)$, and the capital accumulation per head, μk, necessary to equip new entrants to the labour force with the same amount of capital per head as existing workers currently enjoy. The first five equations of the Solow model, equations (10.2a), (10.3a), (10.4), (10.5a) and (10.6a) can be solved in *per capita* terms to give such a relationship:

$$dk/dt = sF(k) - \mu k. \qquad (10.22)$$

This expression, in terms of the capital–labour ratio only, is the fundamental differential equation of the model (it is derived in the Appendix, Note 3). The equation is depicted in Figure 10.4.

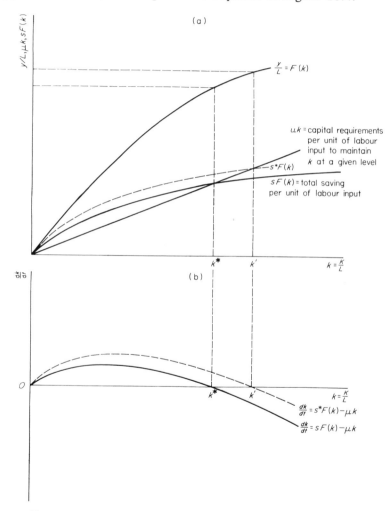

FIGURE 10.4   *The Solow neoclassical model in* per capita *terms*

If dk/dt is positive the capital–labour ratio, k, must be growing through time. Income per head, y/L, must also be growing through time but at a slower rate than k due to the operation of diminishing returns. This can be seen in Figure 10.4a, as a movement in k from k^* to k' causes a less than proportionate increase in y/L. Growth in k leads to an equal rate of growth in μk, the investment necessary to maintain the current level of k with the labour force growing at rate μ, but it leads to a slower rate of growth in savings per head, sy/L. This leads to a decline in dk/dt and the process continues until dk/dt equals zero and $sF(k) = \mu k$. At this point desired saving per head is just equal to the investment per head necessary to maintain the capital–labour ratio at its current value, k^*. This can be seen in Figure 10.4 where $dk/dt = 0$ at k^* which is where $sF(k) = \mu k$. Any point to the left of k^* is one where $sF(k) > \mu k$ so that $dk/dt > 0$ and the capital–labour ratio, k, will be rising over time. Therefore any chance shift to the left of k^* will set up a process of return to that value of the capital–labour ratio.

If dk/dt is negative then the capital–labour ratio, k, must be declining but at a slower rate. The decline in k will produce an equal proportional decline in μk, but a less than proportional decline in saving per head, $sF(k)$. Thus dk/dt moves towards zero and the process continues until $dk/dt = 0$ and $sF(k) = \mu k$. This is illustrated in Figure 10.4. At any point to the right of k^*, $sF(k) < \mu k$ which means that $dk/dt < 0$ and k must be falling through time until k is once more equal to k^*.

The equilibrium solution for the differential equation (10.22) and therefore for the Solow growth model occurs when $dk/dt = 0$. The discussion above shows that this is a stable solution as any displacement from the point $k = k^*$ leads to a return to that value of k. At this point desired saving per head is just equal to the investment per head necessary to keep the capital–labour ratio constant given the rate of growth in the labour force. Therefore, in equilibrium

$$\mu k = sF(k) \tag{10.23}$$

or

$$\mu = \frac{s(y/L)}{k} = \frac{s}{k/(y/L)} = \frac{s}{v}. \tag{10.23a}$$

Thus, in the long-run steady-state equilibrium to which the neoclassical economy tends, the warranted rate of growth, s/v, adjusts to the natural rate of growth. Equation (10.23) can be used to solve directly for y together with the long-run labour supply equation, (10.4). The solution for the equilibrium growth value of y is

$$y = (\mu/s)k^* L_0 e^{\mu t} \tag{10.24}$$

where k^* is the equilibrium capital–labour ratio derived from solving equation (10.23).

Equations (10.23) and (10.24) show that changing the value of the saving ratio, s, does not change the long-run equilibrium growth rate in the model as it does not affect the natural growth rate. However, a rise in the savings ratio will lead to a short-run rise in the rate of growth until the new equilibrium capital–output ratio k' is reached. Once this occurs the economy settles down once more to its natural rate of growth but with a higher income per head and a higher capital–output ratio. This is illustrated in Figure 10.4. An increase in the savings ratio from s to s' leads to a higher level of income per head and a higher capital–labour ratio, k', but the economy returns to equilibrium where income *per capita* and the capital–labour ratio are constant. Thus, in the new equilibrium all stock and flow variables once more grow at the natural rate, μ. The growth paths of income and consumption resulting from a change in the savings ratio is shown in Figure 10.5. Notice that consumption falls at first so that any future rise in consumption is at the expense of forgone current consumption.

The Neoclassical Theorem: the Golden Rule of Accumulation

The end of the last section showed that a rise in the savings ratio would increase incomes per head even though it would not affect the equilibrium long-run rate of growth. However any such rise in saving means an immediate diminution of current consumption which need not be offset by a future increase in consumption. This is because the rise in capital per head increases the rate of investment per head, μk, necessary to keep the capital–output ratio constant. With the law of variable proportions the rise in μk may more than offset the rise in income per head, leaving no room for any rise in *per capita* consumption. Therefore unless one knows of some way of raising the natural rate of growth through investment, an economy can invest far too large a proportion of its current income.

Given the natural rate of growth, the level of investment which will maximise consumption per head in each period along the steady-state growth path will be equal to the level of profits in the economy. This means that along such a steady-state maximal consumption path the rate of return on capital in a competitive economy will be equal to the natural rate of growth, μ (i.e. $\rho = \mu$). Any other rate of investment will lead to a lower level of consumption on the steady-state equilibrium growth path [14].

The proof of the above proposition is as follows. Consumption per head in steady-state equilibrium is the difference between income per head and the necessary investment per head to maintain k, μk. Thus

$$C/L = F(k) - \mu k$$

where C/L is *per capita* consumption in steady state growth as in

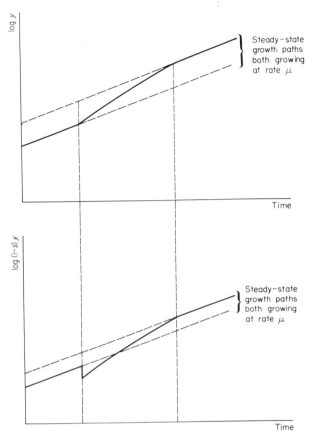

FIGURE 10.5   *Time paths of income and consumption following a rise in the savings ratio*

equilibrium $sF(k) = \mu k$. Now maximum consumption per head occurs when the distance between the production function, $y/L = F(k)$, and the investment requirements per head line, μk, is maximised, as shown in Figure 10.6. This occurs at the capital–labour ratio at which the slope of the production function is equal to the slope of the investment requirements line, μ. The slope of the production function is the marginal product of capital which, in a competitive economy, is equal to the rate of return of capital, ρ. Therefore when the capital stock per head is such that consumption per period on a steady state growth path is maximised, the rate of return on capital is equal to the natural rate of growth.* The

* This result can be achieved by maximising $C/L = F(k) - \mu k$ with respect to k and interpreting the result.

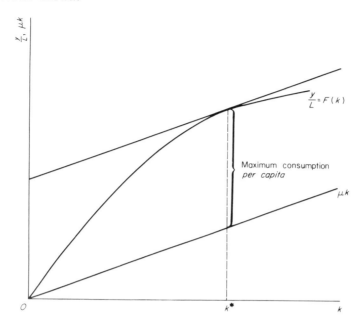

FIGURE 10.6   *The neoclassical theorem: the maximisation of per capita consumption*

rate of saving in this equilibrium state must be large enough to maintain
this level of capital stock per head. Thus the savings ratio must be
adjusted so that $sF(k^*) = \mu k^* = \rho k^*$. Now ρk^* is the amount of profit
per head. Thus maximal consumption along a steady state path is only
attained when saving per head is equal to profits per head. This implies
that along such a growth path investment must equal the level of total
profits.

Short-Run Stability in the Neoclassical Model

In the neoclassical model there is no problem of conflict between the
warranted and natural rates of growth as factor price flexibility allows v
to adjust so that the warranted rate coincides with the natural rate of
growth. The key differences of this model from the Harrod model lie in
the assumptions of
   (1) factor price flexibility, and
   (2) the absence of an independent investment function.
The absence of an independent investment function in the neoclassical
model means that the model neglects the role of entrepreneurial
expectations about the future in affecting the level of investment and

income. This neglect of expectations simplifies the derivation of steady-state solutions which give some insight into the factors underlying the long-run trend growth rate. However, it is misleading to use models that neglect expectations to deal with short-run adjustment paths and fluctuations.

If one introduces an independent investment function, where investment depends on firms' expectations, into the neoclassical growth model, then the instability problem that exists in the Harrod model reappears in the short-run. This is in spite of the possibility of factor substitution. This instability has nothing to do with the difference between the warranted and natural growth paths and will exist when these two paths are identical. The introduction of an independent investment equation over-determines the neoclassical growth model and an equilibrium solution can only be found if either one of the equations becomes dependent or if there is a chance consistency between the equations (i.e. chance dependency of one of the equations). Sen [15] demonstrates this problem using a neoclassical growth model with a Cobb–Douglas production function, $y = A e^{mt} K^{\alpha} L^{1-\alpha}$, together with an independent investment function.

10.4   THE IMPACT OF TECHNICAL CHANGE ON THE NEOCLASSICAL GROWTH MODEL

Technical change can be introduced into the neoclassical growth model in the form of labour-augmenting, or Harrod neutral technical change. In this form of technical change the capital–output ratio, v, does not alter so long as the real rate of interest, ρ, remains unchanged. Labour-augmenting technical progress occurs when machines are redesigned to produce the same output with a smaller labour force or if the labour force becomes more efficient so that fewer workers are needed to man a given machine. This form of technical change has the same impact on the economy's capacity to produce output as an increase in the rate of growth of the labour force. It is the only form of technical progress that is consistent with steady state equilibrium growth in both the Harrod and neoclassical models.

Labour-augmenting technical progress can be handled quite simply in the neoclassical model by dealing with labour in terms of efficiency units rather than in natural units. An efficiency unit can be defined as equal to the productive potential of a natural labour unit (man) at some past date. With a constant capital–output ratio this productive potential can be measured by the output per man at that past date. With labour-augmenting technical progress, which occurs at the rate m, output per unit of labour rises. Thus the number of efficiency units embodied in a natural unit of labour rises at the rate m over time. Therefore the total number of labour efficiency units, L, at time t is

$$\bar{L} = L\,e^{mt} = L_0 \exp[(m + \mu)t].$$

We can now express each equation of the Solow model in terms of income per efficiency unit, capital per efficiency unit, etc. Solving the respecified model gives a differential equation in terms of capital stock per efficiency unit, i.e.

$$\frac{dk}{dt} = sF(k) - (m + \mu)k. \tag{10.25}$$

This has an identical form to the fundamental differential equation, (10.22), except that the coefficient of the last term is now $(m + \mu)$. This gives a stable equilibrium solution in which the warranted rate of growth is equal to the natural rate of growth, $m + \mu$. As the basic equation is identical, all the earlier conclusions relating to the impact of saving on the equilibrium growth rate, on instability and on the neoclassical theorem hold in the presence of labour-augmenting technical change.

The equilibrium state, with labour-augmenting technical change at the rate m, involves output, investment and the capital stock all growing at the rate $m + \mu$. Real wages will increase through time at the rate m while the real rate of interest will remain at ρ^* because the capital stock grows faster than the labour force so that capital per labour efficiency unit stays constant despite the rise in real wages.

The Harrod and Solow models have been criticised for their treatment of technical change. In these models technical change affects the whole capital stock. Both new and old machines are treated alike. Such *disembodied* technical change is similar to a change in plant organisation that increases efficiency. However, in the real world most technical change is *embodied* in new machines while the old machines are not affected. To meet this criticism various neoclassical *vintage* growth models have been constructed [16, 17]. These allow for differences in the efficiency of capital equipment acquired at different dates, each period of acquisition of capital involving a different 'vintage' of capital. All of these models are neoclassical in the sense that they assume factor price flexibility and do not have an independent investment function.

These vintage models differ in that some allow labour to be substituted for capital equipment that is already in existence, while others only allow factor substitution during the planning stage. Here once equipment is produced it has rigid factor proportions. There is also a vintage model which does not allow any factor substitution either in the planning stage or once the capital equipment has been installed. In all of these vintage growth models an increased rate of saving and investment raises the level of income per head but not the steady-state growth rate. This remains equal to the natural growth rate $m + \mu$ when technical change is labour augmenting. This growth path is stable, although the adjustment to equilibrium is not smooth in models that do not allow factor substitution with existing equipment.

10.5 CAMBRIDGE CRITICISMS OF THE AGGREGATE PRODUCTION FUNCTION

Cambridge neo-Keynesians, Joan Robinson [18] in particular, have criticised the use of an aggregate production function in macroeconomic models. The basis of their criticism is that capital goods are produced means of production and that the value of any specific capital good will be affected by changes in income distribution, particularly by changes in the rate of profit (real rate of interest, ρ), as well as by embodied technical change.

The criticism takes two forms. The first attacks the use of marginal productivity theory to determine the real rate of profit in a macro growth model. This, they claim, involves circular reasoning in a world with diverse capital goods. In such a world the aggregate capital stock can only be measured in money terms, by weighting each capital good by its current price, and then using this capital stock to determine the rate of profit via the marginal productivity of capital. If wages and profits enter into the prices of produced capital goods, this implies that the rate of profit must be known in order to determine the size of the capital stock so as to determine the rate of profit! This is why the neo-Keynesians harp on the need for an independent theory that determines the rate of profit [19], even though none of them has provided a consistent theory of the *rate of profit*, as distinct from the level of profit, that is independent of some measure of the capital stock.

To neoclassical economists this seems a mistaken criticism as they see the aggregative approach as just a simplification of a disagrregated general equilibrium system that makes the system amenable to estimation, testing and useful for prediction and policy purposes. In a general equilibrium approach one does not have an explanation based on prior cause and effect, of the rate of profit or of any other price. In a general equilibrium system prices, profits and wages are all determined simultaneously. One does not have to deal with a uni-causal determination of the rate of profit but with a system involving a mutual determination of all prices, including the rate of profit. This system operates in equilibrium and neoclassical economists believe that once out of equilibrium, the system eventually returns to it through some iterative process of adjustment. This adjustment need not be smooth and even in disequilibrium there is a process of mutual interaction amongst the variables.

The Cambridge critique would be much more telling if it could show that there is no theoretical reason for the system, once in disequilibrium, to ever return to some equilibrium set of values. At present this critique seems to be directed against the construction of highly aggregated macro models which aim to give predictions in a disequilibrium situation.

The second form of the Cambridge criticism is theoretically more important although its practical significance may prove to be small. This criticism is directed against the neoclassical concept of a smooth production function where low rates of interest are associated with high capital–labour ratios and *vice versa*.

Capital goods are themselves produced with the aid of capital and labour and their production takes time. This means that the interest component in the price of a capital good in a competitive system will vary, depending on the length of time it takes to produce it. The longer the time necessary to produce the capital good, the larger the impact of interest changes on its competitive long-run market price and the smaller the impact of changes in wages on this long-run price. Therefore as different techniques differ in the length of time necessary to produce their associated capital equipment, changes in the level of interest rates may affect the total costs of using these techniques in different ways. One may find one technique being the lowest cost technique at a very high rate of interest, becoming a high cost technique at a lower rate of interest and reappearing as the lowest cost technique at a very low interest rate.

This phenomenon is called 'reswitching' by the neo-Keynesians. This possibility of a lower capital–labour ratio being used when the rate of interest falls means that there is no *logical necessity* for the neoclassical assumption of an inverse correlation between the capital–labour ratio and the rate of interest to hold and there is a distinct possibility of discontinuities and reversals in the production function. However, there is no logical necessity for the correlation not to hold either.

The demonstration that there is no logical necessity for an assumption to hold does not mean that it is therefore useless and should be discarded. According to the approach of 'positive' economics, assumptions should not be judged on the basis of their logical necessity but rather on whether or not they give useful predictions that allow us to forecast events and thus, to some extent, control them. The Cambridge criticism, although logically impeccable, so far has been entirely negative and has given rise to a joke among some economists: 'there is positive economics and negative economics: the latter is what is taught at Cambridge'. The question of what is a useful theory or simplification cannot be decided on the basis of scholastic reasoning alone. The decision requires empirical testing to refute the theory and its replacement by a theory with a better predictive performance.

10.6 CONCLUSIONS

(1) The long-run steady-state growth rate in the economy is determined by the rate of growth of the labour force and of technical change and not

by the rate of investment. Therefore an increase in the rate of investment will only lead to a short-run increase in the rate of growth, with the economy reverting to the natural rate of growth when it returns to a steady state. The only case where an increase in the rate of investment leads to an increase in the natural rate of growth is when this directly results in an increase in the underlying rate of technical change. This conclusion does not augur well for the comparative growth performance of the United Kingdom, where on both sides of industry there is a basic reluctance to accept change.

(2) The neoclassical theorem shows that a country can invest too much from the point of view of maximising consumption per head on the steady-state growth path.

(3) If either factor prices are rigid for political or institutional reasons, or factor substitutability is restricted, then a situation of full capacity growth with unemployment can only be dealt with by increasing capital accumulation and savings and not by the traditional Keynesian remedies for unemployment.

(4) There is a short-run problem of instability when investment is determined by entrepreneurial expectations.

The growth models considered in this chapter are very simple as they are highly aggregated and exclude a monetary sector. For policy-making purposes it is necessary to develop much more comprehensive disaggregated models which include both government and monetary sectors.

MATHEMATICAL APPENDIX

Note 1

If $y = f(L, K, \bar{T})$ is a linearly homogeneous function in K and L this implies that

$$\lambda y = f(\lambda L, \lambda K, \lambda \bar{T}) \tag{10.1a}$$

which is true for all values of λ. Substituting $\lambda = 1/L$ into the above equation gives

$$\frac{y}{L} = f\left(1, \frac{K}{L}, \bar{T}\right). \tag{10.2}$$

As $\bar{T}$ is assumed constant for the time being we can rewrite this as

$$\frac{y}{L} = F\left(\frac{K}{L}\right). \tag{10.2}$$

Here income per head is a function of only the capital–labour ratio and it is not a function of the absolute size of capital and labour inputs. Writing $K/L = k$, we obtain

$$y/L = F(k). \tag{10.2a}$$

Differentiating y/L with respect to the capital–labour ratio, k, gives

$$\left.\begin{array}{c} \dfrac{d}{dk}\left(\dfrac{y}{L}\right) = \dfrac{d}{dk}[F(k)] \\[2mm] \dfrac{d^2}{dk^2}\left(\dfrac{y}{L}\right) = \dfrac{d^2}{dk^2}[F(k)] \end{array}\right\} \tag{10.20}$$

We will show in equations (10.20) and (10.27) that equilibrium in a competitive economy necessarily implies that

$$\frac{d}{dk}[F(k)] > 0 \quad \text{and} \quad \frac{d^2}{dk^2}[F(k)] < 0.$$

Therefore the two equations in (10.20) show us that increasing the capital–labour ratio, k, increases real income per head, but at a decreasing rate.

We can rewrite the production function for real income as

$$y = L F(k). \tag{10.2}$$

Therefore

$$\frac{y}{L} = F\left(\frac{K}{L}\right). \tag{10.2}$$

$$\frac{\partial y}{\partial K} = \frac{\partial}{\partial K}[LF(k)] = L\frac{d}{dk}[F(k)]\frac{\partial k}{\partial K} \tag{10.20a}$$

$$= \frac{d}{dk}[F(k)] \tag{10.20a}$$

and

$$\frac{\partial y}{\partial L} = \frac{\partial}{\partial L}[LF(k)] = F(k) + L\frac{d}{dk}[F(k)]\frac{dk}{dL}$$

$$= F(k) - k\frac{d}{dk}[F(k)]. \tag{10.21}$$

This shows us that both the marginal product of capital and the marginal product of labour are functions of the capital–labour ratio, k, only and not of the absolute amounts of inputs of capital and labour. Making the usual assumptions that the law of variable proportions holds we know that

$$\frac{\partial^2 y}{\partial K^2} < 0 \quad \text{and} \quad \frac{\partial^2 y}{\partial^2 L} < 0. \tag{10.26}$$

Now

$$\frac{\partial^2 y}{\partial K^2} = \frac{\partial}{\partial K}\left[\frac{\partial y}{\partial K}\right] = \frac{\partial}{\partial K}\left\{\frac{d}{dK}[F(k)]\right\} = \frac{d^2}{dk^2}[F(k)]\frac{\partial k}{\partial K} \tag{10.27}$$

$$= \frac{1}{L}\frac{d^2}{dk^2}[F(k)] < 0. \tag{10.27}$$

As L is always positive this implies that

$$\frac{d^2}{dk^2}[F(k)] < 0. \tag{10.27a}$$

In a competitive economy profit-maximising entrepreneurs hire inputs up to the point at which their marginal value product is equal to their price. Therefore in a competitive economy in equilibrium

$$\rho = \frac{\partial y}{\partial K} = \frac{d}{dk}[F(k)] \geqslant 0 \tag{10.20}$$

$$w = \frac{\partial y}{\partial L} = F(k) - k\frac{d}{dk}[F(k)] > 0 \tag{10.21}$$

where ρ is the interest rate and w is the real wage rate. These must both be greater or equal to zero in any equilibrium solution in the real world. We may assume that $w > 0$ if wage earners are to survive. Now

$$\frac{d\rho}{dk} = \frac{d}{dk}\left\{\frac{d}{dk}[F(k)]\right\} = \frac{d^2}{dk^2}[F(k)] < 0. \tag{10.28}$$

This must be negative using the result in equation (10.27a). Now

$$\frac{dw}{dk} = \frac{d}{dk}\left\{F(k) - k\frac{d}{dk}[F(k)]\right\} = -k\frac{d^2}{dk^2}[F(k)] = -k\frac{\partial\rho}{\partial k} > 0.$$

As $\rho > 0$ and from equation (10.28) we know that $d\rho/dk < 0$. Therefore an increase in the capital–labour ratio will lower the real rate of interest (the real return to capital) and raise the real wage rate. A decrease in the capital–labour ratio will lead to the opposite result.

From equations (10.20) we see that, in the absence of technical change, a constant real rate of interest requires a constant capital–labour ratio, k (and vice versa). Therefore any policy of keeping the real rate of interest constant will lead profit maximising firms to keep the capital–labour ratio constant (i.e. fixed factor proportions). Now

$$\frac{\partial w}{\partial L} = \frac{\partial}{\partial L}\left\{F(k) - k\frac{d}{dk}[F(k)]\right\}$$

$$= \frac{d}{dk}[F(k)]\frac{\partial k}{\partial L} - \frac{d}{dk}[F(k)]\frac{\partial k}{\partial L} - k\frac{d^2}{dk^2}[F(k)]\frac{\partial k}{\partial L}$$

$$= -\frac{k^2}{L}\frac{d^2}{dk^2}[F(k)] < 0.$$

This is negative as $k^2/L > 0$ and $d^2/dk^2[F(k)] < 0$ from equation (10.27a). Therefore the real wage rate decreases as employment increases, the capital stock remaining constant.

Note 2

Equation (10.9) can be rewritten as

$$\frac{1}{y}\,dy = \frac{s}{v}\,dt.$$

Integrating both sides gives

$$\int \frac{1}{y}\,dy = \int \frac{s}{v}\,dt$$

or

$$\ln y = (s/v)t + C.$$

Taking antilogarithms of both sides to the base e gives

$$y = A\,\exp[(s/v)t] \quad \text{where } A = e^{C}.$$

If we are given that $y = y_0$ at $t = 0$, then substituting these values into the equation gives $A = y_0$, i.e.

$$y = y_0\,\exp[(s/v)t]. \tag{10.10}$$

Note 3

Substitute for investment per head and saving per head in equation (10.5) from equations (10.3a) and (10.6a). This gives

$$\frac{1}{L}\frac{dK}{dt} = s\frac{y}{L}. \tag{10.29}$$

Substituting for income per labour input from the aggregate production function, equation (10.2a) gives

$$\frac{1}{L}\frac{dK}{dt} = sF(k). \tag{10.30}$$

Now differentiating both sides of the definition $k = K/L$ with respect to time gives

$$\frac{dk}{dt} = \frac{1}{L}\frac{dK}{dt} - \frac{K}{L}\frac{1}{L}\frac{dL}{dt}. \tag{10.31}$$

The labour supply equation, (10.4), gives the rate of growth of the labour force, $(1/L)(dL/dt)$, as equal to μ. Substituting this into equation (10.31) and re-arranging gives

$$\frac{1}{L}\frac{dK}{dt} = \frac{dk}{dt} + \mu k. \tag{10.32}$$

Substituting for $(1/L)(dK/dt)$ in equation (10.30) gives us the fundamental differential equation of the model in terms of only the capital–labour ratio:

$$\frac{dk}{dt} + \mu k = sF(k) \tag{10.22a}$$

$$\frac{dk}{dt} = sF(k) - \mu k. \tag{10.22}$$

REFERENCES

[1] J. Tobin, 'A Dynamic Aggregative Model', *Journal of Political Economy*, 63 (1955) reprinted in *Growth Economics*, ed. A. K. Sen (Harmondsworth: Penguin, 1970).

[2] H. G. Johnson, 'Money in a Growth Model', in his *Essays in Monetary Economics* (Unwin and Harvard University Press, 1967) reprinted in *Growth Economics*, ed. Sen.

[3] R. F. Harrod, 'An Essay in Dynamic Theory', *Economic Journal*, 49 (1939) reprinted in *Growth Economics*, ed. Sen.

[4] R. F. Harrod, *Towards a Dynamic Economics* (London: Macmillan, 1949).

[5] E. Domar, 'Capital Expansion, Rate of Growth and Unemployment', *Econometrica*, 14 (1946).

[6] D. Jorgenson, 'On Stability in the Sense of Harrod', *Economica*, n.s., 27 (1960).

[7] R. G. D. Allen, *Macroeconomic Theory* (London: Macmillan, 1967) ch. 10.

[8] E. Domar, 'The Burden of Debt and National Income', *American Economic Review*, 34 (1964).

[9] N. Kaldor, 'A Model of Economic Growth', *Economic Journal*, 67 (December 1957).

[10] N. Kaldor and J. A. Mirrlees, 'Growth Model with Induced Technical Progress', *Review of Economic Studies*, 29 (1961–2).

[11] R. M. Solow, 'A Contribution to the Theory of Economic Growth', *Quarterly Journal of Economics*, 70 (1956).

[12] R. M. Solow, *Growth Theory: An Exposition* (Oxford University Press, 1970) chs 1–3.

[13] R. W. Swan, 'Economic Growth and Capital Accumulation', *Economic Record*, 32 (1956).

[14] E. S. Phelps, 'The Golden Rule of Accumulation: A Fable for Growthmen', *American Economic Review*, 51 (1961).

[15] A. K. Sen, 'The Stability of Neoclassical Growth with the Addition of an Investment multiplier', in *The Theory of Interest Rates*, ed. F. Hahn and F. Brechling (London: Macmillan, 1965).

[16] D. Hamberg, *Models of Economic Growth* (New York: Harper & Row, 1971) ch. 5 and appendix.

[17] Solow, *Growth Theory*, ch. 3.

[18] J. Robinson, 'Capital Theory Up To Date', *Canadian Journal of Economics*, 3 (1970).

[19] J. Kregel, *The Theory of Economic Growth* (London: Macmillan, 1972) pp. 23–9.

11 The Trade Cycle

The long-run expansion of industrialised market economies has been accompanied by cyclical fluctuations in economic activity. This type of fluctuation is known as the business or trade cycle. The general feature of the cycle is that an expansion of economic activity is followed by a contraction, which is in turn succeeded by a further expansion. In the expansion phase of the cycle real national output grows, generally at a faster rate when the economy first emerges from a period of depression and then at a slower rate, until the upper turning point of the cycle is reached. The recession phase of the cycle which then follows may involve an absolute decline in real output as was typical of pre-Second World-War depressions or merely a decline below average in the rate of growth of output as in the post-war period.

An essential characteristic of cyclical behaviour is not only that expansion and contraction follow each other, but that each phase of the cycle contains within it the seeds to generate the succeeding phase. It is this aspect of cyclical fluctuations that economic theorists have striven to explain. Although each cycle contains the common elements described above, cycles do differ from one another. The magnitude of the changes in economic variables and the timing of these changes vary. So do particular features of a cycle, for example whether the contraction is accompanied by a financial crisis or the later expansionary phase by a speculative boom.

11.1 MEASURING THE TRADE CYCLE

Cyclical fluctuations in output occur about a long-run rising trend in output. (The following exposition is in terms of output but applies to any other variable which increases secularly.) An empirical measure of what may be presumed to be the equilibrium growth rate is the trend or average rate of growth of output over a period of time. If we have observations of N

years actual annual G.D.P. we can fit a trend equation which estimates the average rate of growth of output:

$$y_t = y_0 e^{gt} e^u \qquad (11.1)$$

where y_t is the output in year t, y_0 is the output in base year 0, g is the trend rate of growth, and u is a random error term. The linearised form of the above equation is

$$\log y_t = \log y_0 + gt + u_t, \qquad (11.1a)$$

We have observations for output for N years and can therefore estimate g. The trend level of output for each year is calculated from equation (11.1a) by substituting g by its estimated value, $\hat{g}$, and giving t its appropriate value.

In Figure 11.1, using equation (11.1a), we plot the log of trend output against time. The slope of the line is the trend rate of growth. The log of actual output is then plotted, the slope of schedule $APTP'F$ being the actual rate of growth at any moment in time.

The peak, or upper turning point, shown at points P and P' in Figure 11.1, occurs at the date when the actual and trend rate of growth of output become equal after a period in which the actual growth rate has been above the trend rate. Similarly the trough, or lower turning point, shown at point T, occurs when the actual growth rate has been below the trend rate.

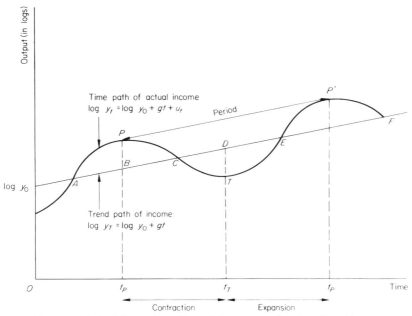

FIGURE 11.1   *The cycle and trend time paths of real national income*

The cycle has two basic dimensions. One is the amplitude which measures the extent of the maximum deviation of the actual growth rate from the trend growth rate. Since the difference between peak and trend may differ from that between trend and trough the amplitude is given by half the distance between peak and trough.

The second dimension to the trade cycle is its time dimension. The period of a cycle is the time it takes to move from a peak (trough) to the next peak (trough). The time path, $PCTEP'$, of a complete cycle can be subdivided into phases. The two major phases are those of contraction and expansion. Contraction is defined as the time period for which the actual rate of growth is less than the trend rate of growth. This is the path PT which is followed during the time period $t_P - t_T$ in Figure 11.1. Conversely expansion occurs when the actual rate of growth exceeds the trend rate of growth, as happens over time period $t_T - t_{P'}$.* The contraction and expansion phases need not last the same length of time. Typically the contraction phase is the shorter. It should also be noted that a longer time than appears to be indicated in Figure 11.1 can be spent growing at the trend rate both at the peak and at the trough.

Reference Cycles

The trade cycle has been defined in general terms as fluctuations in economic activity. This means that it involves a large number of variables and is widely diffused through the economy. The cycling of the time path of an individual variable, such as industrial production, employment or fixed private investment, is known as a specific cycle. The most extensive investigations so far conducted into the cyclical behaviour have been undertaken by the National Bureau of Economic Research in the United States (see [2] and [3]). These researchers have sought an aggregate measure of the United States' cyclical behaviour which can be used to date the phases of past and future trade cycles.

The problem of obtaining such a measure is that the specific cycles move out of phase. For instance movements in output generally precede movements in employment. The N.B.E.R. has obtained an aggregate measure of cyclical behaviour by documenting a large number of specific cycles, comparing their respective phases and dating their turning points.

* These definitions of peak, trough and phase concur with those used by Matthews [1] and are applicable whether the rate of growth in the contraction is negative or positive. Readers may find an alternative measure of the cycle as the deviation of the actual level of output from the trend level. The peaks and troughs of this cycle will concur in time with those of Matthews. If the expansion and contraction phases are defined respectively as occurring when the actual level of output is above or below the trend level of output, their timing can differ from that of Matthews's definition.

They then selected those variables that have cycled reasonably consistently in relation to each other. These were then used to date the reference cycle. The turning points and phases of the reference cycle are dated according to the dates around which the majority of specific cycle turning points and phases have clustered.

Historical Experience of the Cycle

The N.B.E.R. has listed reference cycles for the United States from 1854. The average period of the cycles is just under four years, the expansion phase lasting longer than the contraction phase. Post-war cycles are only slightly shorter, with the contraction phase taking less time than in the pre-war period.

TABLE 11.1 U.K. Cyclical Behaviour of G.D.P. at Market Prices

	Average duration (in years)		Annual growth rates (per cent)		
	Downswing (1)	Upswing (2)	Downswing (3)	Upswing (4)	Difference (4)−(3)
1951–64	2·0	2·3	1·2	4·8	3·6
1920–37	2·0	6·5	−6·6	3·2	9·8
1872–1914	3·8	4·4	−0·4	2·7	3·1

The U.K. experience reveals a sharper contrast between pre-war and post-war cyclical behaviour. This is shown in Table 11.1 taken from Matthews's study[1]. Post-war cycles have been shorter and milder and so far downswings have not been associated with a negative growth rate, except for a very short period of time. The growth rate in the downswings has become lower in recent years. Unemployment has not only been lower throughout the post-war period but has fluctuated much less. A further difference is the greater role of the government. The upswing has typically brought about a balance-of-payments deficit which the government has sought to correct by restrictive monetary and fiscal policy. This action has accentuated, or initiated (interpretations vary), a recession. This has been followed by government action to promote recovery. Some economists maintain that this 'stop–go' policy has been destabilising and thus enhanced rather than reduced cyclical instability. (See Chapter 12 for a further discussion of this problem.) The trend and cycle of real G.D.P. for the United Kingdom 1947–70, derived by the method explained on p. 291, are shown in Figure 11.2. The trend growth rate, estimated by fitting equation (11.1) is 0·0269.

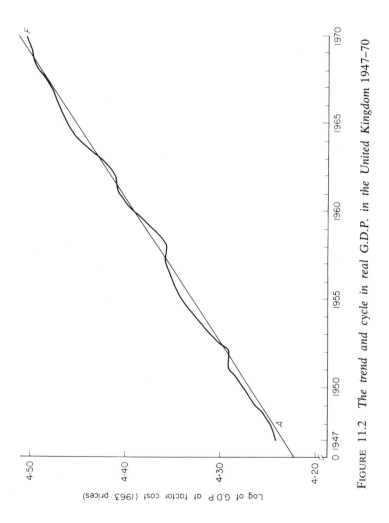

FIGURE 11.2   *The trend and cycle in real G.D.P. in the United Kingdom 1947–70*

11.2 EXPLAINING THE CYCLE

A theory of the trade cycle can explain the general features common to cycles: it cannot provide a blue print for actual cycles that have occurred. Each cycle possesses its own features and requires a more detailed historical explanation assisted by theoretical analysis. We are concerned here to outline theoretical approaches which explain the general configurations of the cycle. The individual characteristics of particular cycles need more detailed empirical analysis.

Trade cycle theorists have sought to explain the central feature of the cyclical behaviour of industrialised, market economies.*This is the regular recurrence of expansion and contraction in the process of long-run economic development. Thus, it appears that expansion generates factors which bring about its own end and induce a period of contraction. Similarly the process of contraction generates the conditions for recovery. These aspects of the cycle have encouraged the development of theories concentrating on factors endogenous to the cycle which will explain the cycle in terms of its internal dynamics.

There is another approach to trade cycle theory which does not rely so strongly on internal factors. It analyses cyclical adjustment paths that are generated by the impact on the economic system of exogenous factors, such as population changes, the accumulation of new inventions [4], the opening up of new territories or changing patterns of international trade. These two approaches are not dissimilar and a very clear classification of endogenous and exogenous factors cannot be made as this distinction depends on what behavioural relationships are included in the model of the economy with which one is working.

A theory of the trade cycle, appealing to either exogenous or endogenous factors, needs to provide answers to the following questions.

(1) What are the impulse factors which start an upward or downward movement?

(2) What propagation mechanisms exist which make an initial movement continue in the same direction?

(3) What brings a cumulative movement to an end?

(4) What causes a reversal in the direction of movement and thus determines the turning point of the cycle?

In answering these questions trade cycle theory is fundamentally concerned with relating cyclical behaviour to a growing economy. Although much of the work on cycles has not been explicitly placed in a growth context, this is nevertheless in the background. One could

---

* The trade cycle as it is known in developed market economies does not appear to exist in centrally planned economies, where investment is centrally controlled and is not subject to fluctuations due to changes in individual decision-makers' expectations. Particular components of national output do fluctuate, sometimes violently, and there is evidence of an inventory cycle (see [5]).

construct models of a stationary economy which would exhibit oscillations when disturbed from equilibrium. Since our historical experience of industrialised economies has been one of growth it is the cyclical behaviour of growing economies that is of interest. Any model which contains net investment is implicitly a dynamic model since the occurrence of net investment means that the capital stock is expanding. A general feature of trade cycle models is the key role played by investment.

11.3 THE ROLE OF INVESTMENT

As we have seen in Chapter 10, a growing economy requires an expanding capital stock. In a steady-state world the labour supply, output, investment and the capital stock would all grow at the equilibrium rate of growth so that the actual capital–output ratio remained equal to the constant optimal capital–output ratio.

Any deviation of the actual from the optimal capital–output ratio will cause the actual rate of growth of investment and hence of capital and output to diverge from the equilibrium rate of growth. If we envisage starting with equal optimal and actual capital–output ratios, they could then diverge either because the actual capital–output ratio moves away from the optimal one or because the optimal capital–output ratio changes. The former may occur because mistaken expectations produce the incorrect amount of investment so that firms find they have too much or too little capital to produce the amount of output that is demanded. Innovations and changes in available techniques cause the replacement of existing types of capital with new kinds of capital goods. The optimal capital–output ratio may change as a result of a change in the relative availability and hence in the relative price of labour and capital. This can be brought about by changes either in the structure of the population and the labour force or by an alteration in the aggregate propensity to save.

We can distinguish two situations when the economy is off its steady-state growth path.

(1) When the optimal capital–output ratio exceeds the actual capital–output ratio so that the actual capital stock is less than the desired stock. Firms therefore wish to invest more rapidly than they would in long-run growth equilibrium in order to adjust the capital stock to its desired level. While this is occurring the economy is in the expansion phase of the cycle since it is growing at a faster rate than its trend rate.

(2) When the actual capital–output ratio exceeds the optimal capital–output ratio, firms are in general holding more capital than is currently required in relation to the flow of output. Investment is thus reduced below its long-run equilibrium rate of growth. The actual rate of growth

of output also lies below trend and the economy experiences contraction.

Thus, a divergence between the actual and optimal capital–output ratios, which can be due to a variety of causes, acts as an impulse factor in initiating contraction and expansion.

11.4 THE MULTIPLIER–ACCELERATOR INTERACTION [6]

The accelerator theory of investment, which is derived from the capital stock adjustment principle, when combined with the multiplier, generates cumulative upward movements in output. As discussed in Chapter 10, it provides the mechanism for generating continual increases in aggregate demand to absorb the increased supply of output in a growing economy. An initial increase in aggregate demand is propagated by the multiplier–accelerator interaction into further increases in income.

The First Order Multiplier–Accelerator Interaction

The simplest specification of the accelerator function for net investment is

$$I^n_t = v(y_t - y_{t-1}). \tag{11.2}$$

In this version the capital stock is fully adjusted to its desired level at the end of each period. When firms enter the current period their capital stock is not optimally related to current output as it was adjusted to last period's output. Investment (or disinvestment) therefore takes place but not until the end of the period. Consumption is assumed to depend proportionately on the current level of income:

$$C_t = (1-s)y_t \tag{11.3}$$

where s is the marginal propensity to save. The model is solved by assuming short-run equilibrium is achieved in each period whereby aggregate demand equals national output:

$$y_t = C_t + I_t + A_t \tag{11.4}$$

where A is the autonomous expenditure. Therefore for short-run equilibrium we must have

$$y_t = (1-s)y_t + v(y_t - y_{t-1}) + A_t. \tag{11.5}$$

Output and demand vary from one period to another because aggregate demand depends on last period's income as well as on current income. When last period's income differs from this period's income aggregate demand changes from period to period. Solving equation (11.5) for y_t we obtain

$$y_t = \left(1 + \frac{s}{v-s}\right) y_{t-1} - \frac{A_t}{v-s} \qquad (11.6)$$

Equation (11.6) is an example of a first order linear difference equation as it is lagged just one period. Using equation (11.6) we can derive the time path of income. We start from a static equilibrium level of income which equals A/s. (This is derived from equation (11.5) by setting $y_t = y_{t-1}$ and solving for the static equilibrium level of income.) Income then diverges from its static equilibrium level. In the initial period 0 income is y_0, thus the initial divergence is $y_0 - A/s$. From equation (11.6) we obtain therefore that income in period 1 is

$$y_1 = \left(1 + \frac{s}{v-s}\right) y_0 - \frac{A}{v-s}$$

$$y_2 = \left(1 + \frac{s}{v-s}\right) y_1 - \frac{A}{v-s} \qquad (11.6b)$$

$$= \left(1 + \frac{s}{v-s}\right)\left[\left(1 + \frac{s}{v-s}\right) y_0 - \frac{A}{v-s}\right] - \frac{A}{v-s}$$

$$= \left(1 + \frac{s}{v-s}\right)^2 y_0 - \frac{A}{v-s}\left[1 + \left(1 + \frac{s}{v-s}\right)\right].$$

Therefore continuing on for y_3, y_4, etc. by substituting into equation (11.6) we obtain

$$y_t = \left(1 + \frac{s}{v-s}\right)^t y_0 - \frac{A}{v-s}\left[1 + \left(1 + \frac{s}{v-s}\right)\right.$$

$$\left. + \left(1 + \frac{s}{v-s}\right)^2 + \cdots + \left(1 + \frac{s}{v-s}\right)^{t-1}\right]$$

$$= \left(1 + \frac{s}{v-s}\right)^t y_0 - \frac{A}{s}\left[1 - \left(1 + \frac{s}{v-s}\right)^t\right]$$

$$= \left(1 + \frac{s}{v-s}\right)^t \left(y_0 - \frac{A}{s}\right) + \frac{A}{s} \qquad (11.7)$$

$$= (1+g)^t \left(y_0 - \frac{A}{s}\right) + \frac{A}{s} \qquad (11.8)$$

where $g = s/(v-s) =$ warranted rate of growth in this discrete period case.

Thus, given $s/(v-s)$ is positive, any initial divergence from static equilibrium is continuously magnified, the rate of increase in income proceeding at the warranted rate of growth, $g = s/(v-s)$. Therefore a first order multiplier–accelerator interaction will not generate cycles but will produce a continual expansion in output because s and v must be specified as positive.

There are four basic types of adjustment path that a variable can follow. The adjustment path can converge towards equilibrium, in which case the model is stable, or diverge from equilibrium, in which event the model is unstable or explosive. The adjustment path is further characterised as oscillating or monotonic. The latter path always moves in the same direction. The four kinds of adjustment path are shown in Figure 11.3 and illustrated using the general form of equation (11.7) which is

$$y_t = \alpha^t \left(y_0 - \frac{A}{s} \right) + \frac{A}{s} \, . \tag{11.7a}$$

The four types of adjustment path are

(A) Stable and monotonic when α lies between zero and plus one. α^t gets steadily smaller as t increases so that the divergence of income from equilibrium eventually becomes negligibly small.

(B) Stable and oscillating when α lies between minus one and zero. As t tends to infinity α^t tends to zero but in doing so alternates between being positive when t is an even number and being negative when t is an odd number. The adjustment path oscillates around the equilibrium value of income, which is therefore overshot a number of times. As the oscillations gradually die away the cyclical path is said to be damped.

(C) Explosive and monotonic if α is greater than one. As time progresses α^t gets larger. In the model discussed above the adjustment path is explosive because s and v are positive, hence α is greater than one. Whether income is continually rising or falling is determined by the direction of the initiating movement away from equilibrium.

(D) Explosive and oscillating. If α is less than minus one, α^t again tends to infinity as time passes. Since α is a negative number, α^t is

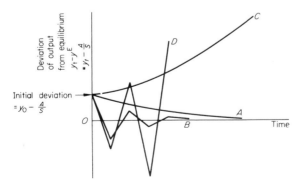

FIGURE 11.3 *The four types of adjustment path*

alternatively positive and negative depending on whether t is an even or an odd number. Because α^t gets absolutely larger as time passes, equilibrium is overshot by ever increasing amounts. Cycles of ever increasing amplitude are said to be anti-damped.

Second Order Multiplier–Accelerator Interaction

Given the values of s and v that occur, we require income to be lagged by more than one time period if the multiplier–accelerator relationship is to generate cycles. A second order multiplier–accelerator interaction contains both current income and income lagged by one and two periods. A number of models of this type, based on varying assumptions, can be set up. In the model outlined below consumption is assumed to be a function of income lagged one period. The accelerator equation assumes that because of lags net investment makes good last period's discrepancy between the desired and actual capital stock. This means that current investment is related to last period's change in output and not this period's. It is this factor that causes cyclical fluctuations.

$$C_t = (1 - s)y_{t-1} \qquad (11.9)$$

$$I_t^n = v(y_{t-1} - y_{t-2}). \qquad (11.10)$$

Substituting equations (11.9) and (11.10) into (11.4) we obtain

$$y_t = (1 - s + v)y_{t-1} - vy_{t-2} + A. \qquad (11.11)$$

This of course has the same static equilibrium solution as equation (11.5), namely that income equals A/s. Equation (11.11) is a second order difference equation because it has two lags.*

The type of adjustment path followed by output in this model depends on the numerical values of v and s. Figure 11.4 shows the various combinations of values for v and s which will give the four types of adjustment path. Cycles will occur if v and s lie within the areas B or D. For example. if $s = 0 \cdot 3$, v must lie between $0 \cdot 31$ and $2 \cdot 37$ for the adjustment path to exhibit oscillations. For this particular model (though not for some others: see Samuelson's model [6] for a different result) a capital–output ratio of less than one produces convergence while a v greater than one causes divergence, irrespective of the size of the marginal propensity to save. In general a small capital–output ratio is required to produce antidamped cycles.

Table 11.2 presents numerical examples which illustrate the four types of adjustment path by taking pairs of values for s and v from each of the areas A, B, C and D of Figure 11.4. The marginal propensity to

* Readers who wish to look up the method of solving second order difference equations are advised to consult other sources, e.g. [7, 8, 9].

TABLE 11.2 Adjustment path of national income following a one period change in autonomous expenditure of 30

Period	A: $s=0.3$ $v=0.2$			B: $s=0.3$ $v=0.8$			C: $s=0.3$ $v=3$			D: $s=0.3$ $v=1.5$		
	y_t	$y_{t-1}-y_{t-2}$	I_t^n	y_t	$y_{t-1}-y_{t-2}$	I_t^n	y_t	$y_{t-1}-y_{t-2}$	I_t^n	y_t	$y_{t-1}-y_{t-2}$	I_t^n
1	1030	0	0	1030	0	0	1030	0	0	1030	0	0
2	1027	30	6	1045	30	24·0	1111	30	90	1066	30	45
3	1018·3	−3	−0·6	1043·5	15	12·0	1321	81	243	1100·2	36	54
4	1011·5	−8·7	−1·74	1029·3	−1·5	−1·2	1854	210	630	1121·4	34·2	51·3
5	1006·7	−6·83	−1·4	1009·1	−14·3	−11·4	3196	533	1599	1116·9	21·2	31±
6	1003·7	−4·8	−0·9	990·2	−20·2	−16·2	7686	1342	4026	1074·9	−4·6	−6·9
7	1002	−2·9	−0·6	978·0	−18·9	−15·1				989·6	−41·9	−62·9
8	1001·1	−0·9	−0·18	914·9	−12·5	−10·0				854·7	−85·4	−128·1
9	1000·6	−0·5	−0·11	979·9	−3·1	−2·5				807·9	−124·9	−187·4
10	1000·4	−0·2	−0·03	990·0	5·0	4·0				780·3	−56·8	−85·2
11				1001·1	10·1	8·0				804·9	−27·6	−41·3
12				1010·3	11·5	9·2				900·3	24·6	36·9
13				1014·5	9·2	7·4				1073·3	95·5	143·2
14				1013·6	4·3	3·4				1310·8	173·0	259·5

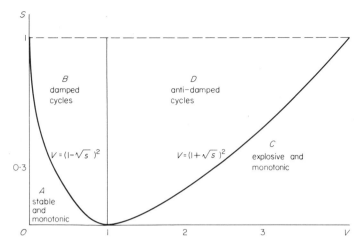

FIGURE 11.4   *The combinations of v and s which give the four types of adjustment path*

save is taken to be 0.3 in all four cases and v is varied to give different adjustment paths. Autonomous expenditure is assumed to be equal to 300 which gives an equilibrium level of output of 1000. The difference between 1000 and income in period t gives the divergence from equilibrium.

The initial deviation from equilibrium is caused by an increase in period 1 of 30 in autonomous expenditure which returns to 300 in all subsequent periods. In the divergent monotonic case income moves steadily away from equilibrium. Cycles occur in cases B and D. After the initial shock, equilibrium is approached but is overshot. Income falls below equilibrium and returns, again overshooting. The cycles in case B diminish with time and there is convergence towards equilibrium, unlike case D.

The lagged capital-stock adjustment mechanism, linked with particular values of v and s is responsible for this cyclical behaviour. When income rises so does the desired capital stock, but the actual capital stock is not increased until the next period. Take case B. Income rises by 30 in period 1 but net investment does not rise (by 24) until the next period. This increase in investment demand stimulates an increase in income but, because autonomous expenditure falls back to 300, income rises less in period 2 than in period 1. Consequently net investment is lower in period 3 than in period 2. The fall in net investment causes income to descend from its peak level of 1045. Since income has fallen, firms wish to hold less capital stock than actually exists. This is indicated by a desired disinvestment of -1.2. The fall in investment promotes a further fall in output which is carried below its equilibrium level. As income falls its rate of decline diminishes and disinvestment eventually reduces the actual capital stock below its desired level. Net investment becomes positive in period 10 and as a consequence output rises.

11.5 NON-LINEAR MULTIPLIER–ACCELERATOR MODELS

The multiplier–accelerator is a simple mechanism which gives some insight into the processes that can generate cycles. The relationship requires modification if it is to be a more adequate reflection of economic reality. We single out four aspects of actual trade cycle experience which the multiplier–accelerator mechanism outlined above does not explain.

(1) The accelerator theory of net investment does not behave in the same way for falling income as it does for rising income. The change in output times the optimal capital–output ratio indicates the desired change in the capital stock. This is not the same as the actual change in the capital stock which is actual net investment or disinvestment. When output is rising firms undertake net investment to remove the discrepancy between the desired and actual capital stock. The rate of actual net investment is then determined by the accelerator relationship, though this rate may be modified by lags and by capacity limitations in the capital-goods-supplying industries.

When the actual capital stock exceeds its desired level, the accelerator relationship only determines the *desired* rate of net disinvestment. It does not determine the *actual* rate of net disinvestment. This depends on the rate at which the capital stock depreciates. Thus, in the contraction the multiplier–accelerator interaction illustrated in Table 11.2 is inadequate because it assumes that the actual rate of disinvestment equals the desired rate lagged one period. We know that this cannot be so, given the nature of the capital stock.

(2) Positive net investment, let alone gross investment, has not ceased entirely during depressions as occurs in the multiplier–accelerator model outlined above. Even in the very severe depression of 1929–33, when U.S. G.N.P. fell by 30 per cent, real gross private investment fell by 90 and not by 100 per cent.

(3) The cycles generated by an unmodified multiplier–accelerator relationship produce booms and slumps of the same duration, whereas contractions have lasted for a shorter period of time than expansions.

(4) The cycles generated by the multiplier–accelerator interaction are either damped or explosive. Only if v and s have particular values is a regular cycle of constant amplitude produced. To achieve this in the model developed here, v must equal one for all values of s. Such stringent requirements are unlikely to be fulfilled in practice, yet actual

cycles have been fairly regular and have displayed no tendency to either die out or become explosive.

In order to accommodate these factors into models of the trade cycle, the multiplier–accelerator relationship is made non-linear, either by the values of the coefficients s and v, which determine short-run consumption and investment, being variable or by placing limitations on the multiplier–accelerator to make its behaviour in the boom differ from that in the depression. We will now examine several different suggestions for such models.

Goodwin's Non-Linear Accelerator Model

Goodwin's model is built upon the asymmetric behaviour of investment discussed in point (1). In the boom the desired capital stock exceeds the actual stock and net investment occurs at a constant rate, $\dot{k}^*$, which is determined by the capacity of the capital-goods-producing industry. Once the desired capital stock is achieved, the rate of investment falls. The resultant decline in output reduces the desired capital stock below its actual level. Net disinvestment occurs at the depreciation rate of $\dot{k}^{**}$ until the actual capital stock declines to its desired level whereupon the economy again enters its expansion phase.

In this model the cycle is self-perpetuating and regular and thus accommodates point (4). The model also takes account of long-run growth by postulating that the desired capital stock grows continually at the natural rate of growth due to technical progress. This provides a rationalisation for longer booms and shorter slumps. In the expansion the duration of the gap between the desired and actual capital stock is lengthened and in the contraction it is shortened by the continued growth of the desired capital stock at the natural growth rate. This process is illustrated in Figure 11.5.

Explosive Cycles: Ceilings and Floors

If the underlying adjustment path is explosive, as would be indicated by a capital–output ratio greater than one, checks on the expansion and contraction of aggregate demand are required to produce models which exhibit regular cycles. This type of trade cycle model was suggested by Hicks [11]. The trade cycle is generated within a growing economy. Thus investment is classified as induced if it depends primarily on the rate of increase of income and as autonomous if it depends primarily on other factors. Hicks also postulates that the accelerator only operates in the expansion and not in the contraction when the actual rate of disinvestment depends on the rate of depreciation.

Autonomous investment continues to exist in the depression and thus provides a floor to the trade cycle by setting a level below which national

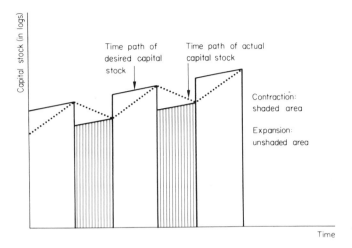

Capital stock (in logs)

Time path of desired capital stock

Time path of actual capital stock

Contraction: shaded area

Expansion: unshaded area

Time

FIGURE 11.5   *Goodwin's model of the trade cycle*

output will not fall. Since autonomous expenditure is growing over time this floor will be rising so that output in one depression is likely to stop falling before it reaches the lowest level attained in the previous slump (see Figure 11.6).

The fact that net investment has continued to remain positive in the depression has cast some doubt on a capital-stock adjustment process which involves disinvestment. This phenomenon is not so puzzling when viewed in the context of a dynamic economy. In such an economy some industries are expanding and others contracting for reasons, such as changes in factor availability and technical knowledge, which occur independently of the trade cycle. Also in a growing economy some firms will have long-term expectations of increased demand and in a depression will still wish to replace old equipment with new types of equipment or even to expand their capital stock. In a highly aggregated model all such forms of investment which do not depend primarily on short-run changes in national income are lumped together by Hicks and called autonomous investment. So long as autonomous investment is positive the aggregate capital stock must be decreasing at a rate less than its rate of depreciation. If autonomous investment is sufficiently large the total capital stock will be increasing despite the fact that some firms are not replacing their capital stock during the contraction.

The floor level of output, determined by autonomous investment, sets a limit to which the capital stock can fall in industries which engage in induced investment. Once the capital stock has reached this level, firms need to replace capital equipment. Investment and hence output rise,

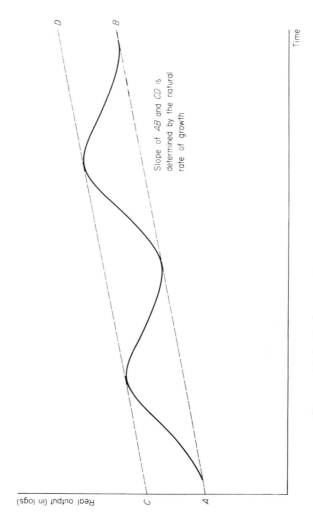

FIGURE 11.6 *Explosive cycle contained by floors and ceilings*

the accelerator mechanism is set in motion and the economy moves into its expansion phase.

During expansion the actual rate of growth exceeds the steady-state rate of growth. This is achieved by a combination of an increase in the marginal propensity to save and a reduction in the capital–output ratio. Thus the actual growth rate, which equals the short-run marginal propensity to save, s, divided by the actual incremental capital–output ratio, v^a, rises. The rise of the M.P.S. in the upswing is predicted by both the relative income and permanent income hypotheses of consumption. The actual capital–output ratio falls because the excess of the desired over the actual capital stock causes firms to utilise their existing capital equipment more intensively. The actual growth rate cannot continue indefinitely above the natural growth rate because labour-augmenting technical progress and the labour force are growing too slowly to provide enough labour to maintain this rate of growth of the capital stock.

The growing scarcity of labour relative to capital provides a rationale for the existence of the ceiling. Since capital is becoming excessive in relation to labour, firms reduce their rate of net investment in order to prevent the actual capital–output ratio from exceeding the optimal capital–output ratio. Thus, the actual rate of growth of investment and output falls towards the steady-state rate of growth. This is illustrated in Figure 11.5 where one can see the two rates of growth converging at the peak. The natural rate of growth provides a ceiling by preventing the actual growth rate from exceeding the natural growth rate for more than a limited time. Thus the ceiling prevents an explosive upward movement in the rate of growth of output.

For the model to generate a downturn endogenously, rather than continuing to grow at the natural rate, we require the reduction in the rate of growth that occurs as the peak is approached to be destabilising. The reduction in the rate of growth of output caused by the decrease in the rate of investment then leads to a further reduction in investment and a further divergence of the actual from the desired capital–output ratio. If output then falls absolutely, induced investment ceases during the contraction until the lower turning point is reached.

Hicks's theory has been criticised on three main grounds (see [12, 13]). The existence of an effective ceiling which does bring about the downturn has been questioned. The reliance on autonomous investment to provide a floor is felt to be unsatisfactory. The increase in the marginal propensity to consume in the downturn has been alternatively suggested as a factor preventing the continued decline in output and thus setting the floor. Since consumption is based on past income, this floor is rising in a growing economy. The multiplier–accelerator relationship can generate an upper turning point before the ceiling is reached; even if unmodified it would produce explosive cycles. The existence of a floor is sufficient to put an end to an explosive adjustment path. The floor only allows the cycle one full period before it is brought to an end and a new set of initial conditions starts off another cycle.

Damped Cycles: Random Shocks

An alternative explanation of a regular cyclical pattern, first put forward by Frisch [14], is provided by those who believe that the underlying adjustment path converges towards equilibrium. Long-term progress along the equilibrium time path is prevented by the repeated occurrence of shocks, such as investment booms, monetary crises, wars or rapid population changes. Such an event jolts the economy off its equilibrium path. A cyclical adjustment path is set up by the response of the system to such a shock. Before the cycle dies away it is subjected to another disturbance so that a regular cyclical pattern persists.

Empirical work supports the hypothesis of converging adjustment paths. Although the size of the average capital–output ratio would generate anti-damped cycles, the size of the short-run incremental capital–output ratio is much smaller. As shown in Chapter 4, the assumption of a distributed lag investment function produces a smaller marginal capital–output ratio of $v(1-\mu)$, where μ is the lag coefficient. Hickman's comparison of econometric models of ten countries shows that for eight countries the accelerator coefficient in the investment function is considerably less than one. Consistent with this finding is the result that all these models are dynamically stable and only some of them behave cyclically. Stimulations with a monotonically converging model of the U.S. economy, which subjected it to random disturbances, generate cycles which correspond quite closely to those charted by the N.B.E.R. [16].*

Inventory Cycles

The accelerator mechanism provides a more plausible theory of the cyclical behaviour of inventory investment than it does of fixed capital formation. This is because stockbuilding is closely related to expected demand, given that stocks are held as a buffer between the production and sale of output. The capital-stock adjustment principle has been applied to the analysis of inventory cycles, notably by Metzler [19].

If output rises less rapidly than expected, excess inventories are acquired. Inventory orders are cut and so is production. As sales out of stock continue at a greater rate than new additions to stock the desired

* Theoretical [16] and empirical [17, 18] work suggest that cycles are generated in stochastic models by the existence of random disturbances. In models which are stable and monotonically converging, or do not contain an accelerator (Chow [16]) oscillations are produced by random shocks.

inventory level is attained. Orders must then be increased to prevent actual stocks falling below their desired level. The accelerator applies to the downturn of the inventory cycle because the rate of inventory disinvestment is determined by the rate of change of sales and not to any extent by depreciation. The inventory cycle is shorter than the general trade cycle. It can occur as a mild cycle or it can aggravate a more widespread cycle in economic activity.

To explain the cycle by means of the multiplier–accelerator mechanism alone requires the assumption that monetary factors behave in an entirely accommodating way so that they have no effect on real aggregate demand. This is an extreme assumption. Monetary factors do play some part in producing and modifying cyclical behaviour.

11.6 THE INFLUENCE OF MONETARY FACTORS

There are differences of opinion regarding the importance of monetary factors in explaining cyclical behaviour. Some theorists give only a secondary role to monetary influences while others see monetary factors as having either major or even primary significance.

A Secondary Role for Monetary Factors

Keynesian theories of the trade cycle invoke monetary factors to provide a fuller explanation of the trade cycle, particularly in relation to the turning points (see Hicks [11] and Duesenberry [12, 13] for examples). As the expansion proceeds, the demand for money rises in order to finance the increasing value of transactions. If the supply of money increases less rapidly, interest rates rise and help to check the rate of growth of investment. The resulting reduction in the rate of growth of output is carried below the equilibrium rate of growth so that contraction sets in.

In the depression the demand for money decreases, bringing down interest rates. Low interest rates help to stimulate investment, once it receives a boost, and the high ratio of bank reserves to deposits allows bank credit to expand rapidly once confidence is restored. Thus monetary factors contribute to raising the actual growth rate above its trend value.

A Primary Role for Monetary Factors

The monetarist view, which stretches back to classical writings, holds that money has no long-run effect on the rate of change of real national output but that in the short run monetary disturbances can exert powerful independent influences on real output.* The relationship

* The theoretical basis for the short- and long-run influence of money has already been discussed; see particularly Chapters 6 and 7.

between money and income in the United States has been thoroughly documented by Friedman and Schwartz [20]. They support the monetarist hypothesis regarding the long-run influence of money by singling out four periods of economic stability, 1882–92, 1903–13, 1923–9 and 1948–60, during which real income grew at similar rates but the rate of change of the price level varied between minus 1 per cent and plus 2 per cent. The variation in the rate of change of the price level is explained by differences in the rate of growth of the money supply. They consider that the long-run rate of growth of real output and the money supply are largely independent.

Short-run monetary fluctuations are associated with similar fluctuations in real output. Friedman and Schwartz consider that the primary causal link goes from monetary changes to variations in real output. They believe this is particularly important in the explanation of severe contractions. Six of the contractions are classified as severe: (1873–9, 1892–4, 1907–8, 1921–2, 1929–33 and 1937–8). In the severe contractions the money supply decreased and four of them were accompanied by a banking crisis.

Since the money supply has generally continued to increase during less severe recessions, Friedman and Schwarz relate fluctuations in the rate of change of the money supply to variations in economic activity. One such exercise involves comparing the reference cycle with a step function in the rate of change of the money supply. Each step occurs when the rate of change of the money supply passes from a high to a low rate and vice versa. On average decreases in the rate of change of the money supply precede the reference peak by seven months, while increases in the rate of change of the money supply lead the reference cycle trough by four months. The standard deviation of the lead in the money supply series is eight months at the peak and six months at the trough.

From this and other evidence Friedman and Schwartz conclude that changes in the rate of growth of the money supply cause changes in the same direction in real output which occur after quite a long and variable lag. It is this type of evidence which leads Friedman to eschew the use of discretionary monetary policy since it is likely in these conditions to be unsuccessful.*

The arguments supporting the Friedman position have been the subject of controversy, particularly relating to whether changes in the money supply primarily depend on national income or occur independently. Another issue concerns the timing evidence. Friedman himself recognises that the timing of a relationship whereby variable X leads variable Y by no means justifies the conclusion that X causes Y. Tobin [23] and others have devised models in which income is the causal factor

---

* The following two chapters discuss this in greater detail.

but money leads income, or in which money is the prime mover but income leads money. Although Friedman's theoretical underpinning of a causal and timing relationship that goes from money to income is not fully worked out, the alternative possibilities, such as an increase in output inducing a rise in the money supply several months before the increase in output actually occurs [25], seem less plausible.

In support of his contention that money supply changes occur independently of output and produce disturbances in output, Friedman cites three occasions (January to June 1920, October 1931, and July 1936 to January 1937), when the Federal Reserve System* deliberately followed a restrictionary policy. This led to a sharp contraction in the money supply to be followed by a severe contraction in industrial output.

Cagan provides further detailed evidence for the United States of the cyclical behaviour of the determinants of the money stock. He estimates that about one-half the variation of the money supply about its trend is accounted for by the currency–money supply ratio, one-quarter by the reserve ratio and one-fifth by 'high-powered' money. The latter variable has become more important in recent cycles. Since 'high-powered' money is subject to government control it can vary independently of income, unless the government chooses to allow it to vary with income. This leaves us with the currency and reserve ratios as variables which could depend on income and thus cause money to dance to the tune played by income.

As the demand for money grows more (less) rapidly in relation to its supply, the rate of interest is predicted to rise (fall). If a rise (fall) in the interest rate decreases (increases) the currency or reserve ratio the money supply will expand (contract), given a constant 'high-powered' money base (see Chapter 5). In this event the direction of causality is from income to the money supply so that the latter is endogenous.

Cagan considers the evidence to support the interest rate mechanism outlined above to be weak but finds other ways in which the state of business activity influences the currency and reserve ratios. As the expansion approaches the peak the currency ratio tends to rise. (The reasons for this are not clear.) The rate of growth of the money supply falls and checks the growth of output. Once the contraction sets in both ratios rise. Banks become more cautious about lending and wish to strengthen their liquid assets position. The public, experiencing similar uncertainties, raise their desired currency ratio. Both these factors lower the money supply (or alternatively its rate of growth) and strengthen the forces of contraction. This process may become self-generating, as the attempt by banks and the public to make their asset portfolios more liquid drains banks of cash reserves. Banks then need to liquidate more

* The central bank of the United States.

assets and the public, losing confidence in the banks, draw out more cash. A full-scale bank panic can be triggered off which exacerbates the contraction. Monetary factors can therefore contribute to cyclical disturbances in economic activity, both by occurring independently and by being related to changes in national income.

There are two aspects to the neo-Keynesian case that money is of little importance in influencing the level of economic activity in the short run. One, which we have just discussed, is that the money supply should be determined endogenously by national income. The other is that national income should be unresponsive to changes in the money supply. This necessitates velocity changing so that money supply changes are rendered ineffective (see Chapter 6). An increase in the money demand, accompanied by a reduction in the rate of growth of the money supply such as might occur at the peak, causes higher interest rates which drive up velocity. This means people are financing each pound's worth of annual income with less money. If money is to have little influence, the changing demand for money with respect to output that occurs over the trade cycle must be accompanied by large pro-cyclical variations in velocity. Also, the change in interest rates which accompanies the change in velocity should have little effect on expenditure.

The observation that velocity rises in the upswing and falls in the downswing therefore weakens the case for the powerful influence of money. Friedman [27] distinguishes between measured velocity, the usual calculation of velocity, which is current income divided by the stock of money, and desired velocity which is permanent income divided by the money stock. Since permanent income changes less over the cycle than measured income, desired velocity will vary less than it appears to do when measured inappropriately.

Monetary factors are a necessary feature of cyclical behaviour. One would not expect every cycle to be explained by the same combination of real and monetary factors. Thus monetary disturbances can be the main instigators of some cycles while being only contributory factors to others.

11.7 THE CYCLICAL BEHAVIOUR OF THE PRICE LEVEL

While the price level tended to vary pro-cyclically during the pre-war period this is no longer true of post-war cycles. In the United Kingdom not only has the price level continued to rise throughout the period but there has been an inverse relationship between the rate of change of prices and the rate of growth of output. One possible explanation is that during the recession average costs rise because firms operate capital equipment at below full capacity and reduce employment less than output. This hypothesis is not supported by Neild's single-equation regressions [28]. This study suggests that firms base their pricing decisions on long-run not short-term productivity changes. Prices are also determined, with a lag, by money wages. The fact that changes in money wages lag employment changes and that these lag output changes can account for the observation that the price cycle lags the output cycle by about two years. Since the period of the cycle is about four years this gives us the trough in the output cycle coinciding with the peak in the price cycle.

The existence of expectations of future inflation explains the persistence of inflation during periods of growing unemployment and thus explains the lag between increased unemployment and a reduction in the rate of inflation (see Chapter 9). If the recovery occurs quickly, say prompted by government intervention, the reduced rate of inflation and expansion in output and employment will occur simultaneously. Therefore the observation of a short-run inverse movement of the rate of inflation and the rate of growth of output does not justify the conclusion that reducing aggregate demand will have no effect on the rate of inflation. Such a proposition ignores the time lags involved.*

11.8 INTERNATIONAL PROPAGATION OF TRADE CYCLES

Fluctuations of business activity in one country both affect, and are affected by, economic events in other countries. The links between countries in the form of trade and capital flows can be stabilising as well as destabilising.

Exports and imports can act as stabilisers for a country experiencing an internally generated cycle. Exports, if determined mainly by foreign countries' national income, are little affected by changes in domestic income, while the marginal propensity to import contributes to a smaller expenditure multiplier.† Lending and borrowing abroad may also be stabilising. For instance, capital shortages which occur in the boom can be relieved by borrowing from abroad.

On the other hand disturbances in one country can be transmitted to another. A country suffering from recession cuts its imports. The

* See Laidler [29] for a trade cycle model incorporating expected inflation. This can generate inflation in all phases of the cycle. This model predicts that the rate of change of inflation should be directly related to that of output. The model excludes government intervention.

† The basic foreign trade multiplier is derived using the following symbols.
$C = (1-s)y$, $M = my$, where $M =$ imports.
$y = E = C + A - M = (1-s)y + A - my$
$y = A/(s+m)$ where $1/(s+m)$ is known as a foreign trade multiplier.
More complex foreign trade multipliers take account of the effect of changes in the domestic country's imports and exports on foreign countries and the repercussions back to the domestic country.

consequent reduction in exports for other countries depresses their level of economic activity, This can feed back to the domestic country via reductions in its exports. Similarly a country experiencing a recession and an accompanying liquidity crisis is likely to cut back its foreign lending and sell foreign assets. This spreads the financial crisis to other countries. This is illustrated by the withdrawal of U.S. funds from Europe following the collapse of the stock exchange boom in 1929. There is also the danger that during a world-wide recession, as occurred in the 1930s, countries take steps to protect their individual interests by pursuing policies, such as protecting domestic industries from foreign competition or subsidising exports, which induce retaliatory measures from other countries. As a result total world trade declines further and production falls to even lower levels.

11.9 CONCLUSION

The basic mechanism for generating cyclical fluctuations is the same whether viewed in a single country or world-wide context, and both real and financial factors are inextricably linked. An individual country can experience a cyclical fluctuation independently of world conditions. Even when countries are experiencing similar conditions, the cycle in each economy tends to move out of phase because of transmission lags and differential responses to similar stimuli.

Trade cycle theory has provided quite a comprehensive analysis of the general elements of cyclical behaviour, although pronounced differences remain in the emphasis given to various factors. Past cycles have been extensively documented and analysed. The outstanding problem remains the analysis of the current state of the economy, in judging what is the present phase of the cycle and in short-run forecasting. This type of analysis is made particularly difficult if the lags between changes in variables are both long and variable.

REFERENCES

[1] R. C. O. Matthews, 'Postwar Business Cycles in the United Kingdom', in *Is The Business Cycle Obsolete?* ed. M. Bronfrenbrenner (New York: Wiley, 1969).
[2] A. F. Burns and W. C. Mitchell, *Measuring Business Cycles* (New York: N.B.E.R., Studies in Business Cycles, no. 2, 1946).
[3] M. K. Evans, *Macroeconomic Activity* (New York: Harper & Row, 1969) ch. 16.
[4] J. Schumpeter, *Business Cycles* (New York: McGraw-Hill, 1939).
[5] M. Bronfrenbrenner, ed., *Is The Business Cycle Obsolete?*, Part III. 'Economic Fluctuations Under Socialism'.
[6] P. Samuelson, 'Interactions Between the Multiplier Analysis and

the Principle of Acceleration', *Review of Economics and Statistics*, 21 (1939).

[7] W. Baumol, *Economic Dynamics* (New York: Macmillan, 1959) Part IV, 'Single Equation Models'.

[8] R. G. D. Allen, *Mathematical Economics* (London: Macmillan, 1956) chs 3–8.

[9] M. K. Evans, *Macroeconomic Activity*, appendix to ch. 13.

[10] R. M. Goodwin, 'The Non-Linear Accelerator and the Persistence of Business Cycles', *Econometrica*, 19, 1 (January 1951).

[11] J. R. Hicks, *A Contribution to the Theory of the Trade Cycle* (Oxford University Press, 1950).

[12] J. Duesenberry, 'Hicks on the Trade Cycle', *Quarterly Journal of Economics*, 64, 3 (August 1950).

[13] J. Duesenberry, *Business Cycles and Economic Growth* (New York: McGraw-Hill, 1958).

[14] R. Frisch, 'Propagation Problems and Impulse Problems in Dynamic Economics', in *Readings in Business Cycles*, ed. R. A. Gordon and L. R. Klein (London: Allen & Unwin, 1966).

[15] B. G. Hickman, 'Dynamic Properties of Macroeconomic Models: An International Comparison; in *Is The Business Cycle Obsolete?* ed. Bronfenbrenner.

[16] G. C. Chow, 'The Acceleration Principle and the Nature of Business Cycles', *Quarterly Journal of Economics*, 82, 3 (1968).

[17] I. and A. F. Adelman, 'The Dynamic Properties of the Klein–Goldberger Model', *Econometrica*, 27 (October 1959).

[18] I. Adelman, 'Business Cycles: Endogenous or Stochastic?', *Economic Journal*, 70 (December 1960).

[19] L. A. Metzler, 'The Nature and Stability of Inventory Cycles', *Review of Economics and Statistics* (1941); reprinted in *Readings in Business Cycles*, ed. Gordon and Klein.

[20] M. Friedman and A. J. Schwartz, *A Monetary History of the United States 1867–1960* (Princeton University Press, 1963).

[21] M. Friedman and A. J. Schwartz, 'Money and Business Cycles', *Review of Economics and Statistics*, 45, 1, 2 Supplement (February 1963).

[22] J. Tobin, 'The Monetary Interpretation of History', *American Economic Review*, 55 (June 1965).

[23] J. Tobin, 'Money and Income: Post Hoc Ergo Propter Hoc', and M. Friedman, 'Comment on Tobin', *Quarterly Journal of Economics*, 84 (May 1970).

[24] P. Cagan, *Determinants and Effects of Changes in the Stock of Money, 1875–1960*, National Bureau of Economic Research (1965).

[25] N. Kaldor, 'The New Monetarism', *Lloyds Bank Review* (July 1970).

[26] F. Glahe, *Macroeconomics, Theory and Policy* (New York: Harcourt Brace Jovanovich, 1973) chs 13–14.

[27] M. Friedman, 'The Demand for Money: Some Theoretical and Empirical Results', *Journal of Political Economy*, 66 (1958).

[28] R. R. Neild, *Pricing and Employment in the Trade Cycle: A Study of British Manufacturing Industry 1950–61* (Cambridge University Press, 1963).

[29] D. Laidler, 'Simultaneous Fluctuations in Prices and Output: A Business Cycle Approach', *Economica*, n.s., 40 (February 1973).

12 The Theory of Economic Policy

Economic policy refers to the action taken by government agencies to achieve particular objectives. This definition delineates two sets of variables, target variables and instrumental variables.

Target variables are those for which the government seeks desirable values and are the immediate goals of economic policy. The major target variables are full employment, a stable price level, a satisfactory rate of economic growth, an equitable distribution of income and balance-of-payments equilibrium. The last named objective is not so much desired in itself, since running a balance-of-payments deficit allows a country to enjoy a higher standard of living by consuming a larger volume of goods and services than it would if the balance of payments were in equilibrium. As deficits cannot be financed indefinitely, balance-of-payments equilibrium has to be sought and its requirement sets a constraint upon the other objectives.

The other objectives, apart from an equitable income distribution, are not desired directly for themselves but for the benefits they bring in terms of living standards. The quantification of these objectives is not usually precise, unless the economy is a planned one, and will vary from country to country and from one period of time to another. For example full employment in the United Kingdom was defined by the 1944 Beveridge Report on *Full Employment in a Free Society* as 3 per cent unemployment. From the end of the Second World War to the late 1960s full employment turned out to mean about 1·1–1·5 per cent unemployment. This has probably now increased and it has become more acceptable to run the economy at a slightly higher average rate of unemployment. Ideas as to what is the desirable value for a target variable are generally constrained by knowledge of what is feasible. The pursuit of unrealistic targets will inevitably result in failure, as in the case of the U.K.'s ill-fated 1965 National Plan which assumed a steady 4 per cent rate of growth, significantly higher than that achieved in the past.

12.1 RELATING INSTRUMENTAL VARIABLES TO TARGET VARIABLES

In order to achieve the desired values of the target variables the determinants of the target variables must take on appropriate values. Instrumental variables are those variables that the government can manipulate to achieve its economic objectives. Instrumental variables are necessarily exogenous variables as the government must be able to determine their values independently of the other variables in the system. For instance tax rates are an instrumental variable, whereas tax revenues are not since their value is determined not only by the tax rates set by the government but also by the level of national income. Similarly 'high-powered' money is, in principle, an instrumental variable, whereas the money supply is not. The quantity of money depends not only on the volume of 'high-powered' money but also on the volume of bank lending which is not directly under government control.

The instrumental variables need to be set at values which will give the desired values of the target variables. Since the economy is made up of interdependent behavioural relationships one cannot in general set one instrumental variable to determine one target. The whole set of target and instrumental variables have to be looked at as a whole. Take the case of the *ISLM* model of an open economy. An increase in government expenditure, undertaken to reduce unemployment, would also worsen the balance-of-payments position. A reduction in the money supply accompanied by higher interest rates, which increase the net capital inflow, would adversely affect the unemployment rate. Given interdependencies between variables, it is essential to co-ordinate all the instrumental variables and relate them to all the target variables.

As well as co-ordinating the instrumental variables it is also necessary to have a sufficient number of them relative to the number of independent objectives. If the number of independent targets which are set at specific values exceeds the number of instrumental variables, it will not be possible to achieve all the targets simultaneously.

This point is illustrated by considering the reduced form of an *ISLM* model of an open economy. There are assumed to be two targets, balance-of-payments equilibrium combined with a desired level of unemployment. The first case considered is a model in which the quantity of money has no effect on the level of either of the target variables. The reduced form of the model therefore gives both the balance of payments and unemployment as functions of the level of government expenditure,

$$U = a_0 - a_1 G \qquad (12.1)$$

$$B = b_0 - b_1 G \qquad (12.2)$$

where U is unemployment, B is the balance of payments ($B > 0$ denotes a surplus), G is government expenditure and U^*, B^* indicate target values.

This gives us two equations in one unknown, G, which can only give a consistent solution if the equations are dependent. This will only occur when

$$U^* = \frac{a_1}{b_1} B^* + \frac{a_0 b_1 - a_1 b_0}{b_1}. \qquad (12.3)$$

This can only occur by chance. If U^* and B^* deviate from this relationship, dictated by the parameters of the economy, then only one of the targets can be achieved. The other target variable will adjust to the equilibrium value dictated by the parameters of the economy and the size of government expenditure necessary to achieve the pre-set target variable.

If the model is altered by specifying that both U and B depend also on the supply of money which is a function of the instrumental variable, 'high-powered' money, the reduced form of the *ISLM* model then becomes

$$U = a_0 - a_1 G - a_2 H \qquad (12.4)$$

$$B = b_0 - b_1 G - b_2 H. \qquad (12.5)$$

There are now two instrumental variables to play with in order to achieve the desired values for the two target variables. This gives us two equations in two unknowns, which can be solved if the equations are independent. Equations (12.4) and (12.5) are solved simultaneously to determine the values of government expenditure, $\hat{G}$, and 'high-powered' money, $\hat{H}$, necessary to attain the target values for U and B.

$$\hat{H} = \frac{b_1 U^* - a_1 B^* + a_1 b_0 - a_0 b_1}{a_1 b_2 - a_2 b_1} \qquad (12.6)$$

$$\hat{G} = \frac{a_2 B^* - b_2 U^* + b_2 a_0 - a_2 b_0}{a_1 b_2 - a_2 b_1}. \qquad (12.7)$$

The unique solution for government expenditure, $\hat{G}$, and the 'high-powered' money supply, $\hat{H}$, which give the desired values for both target variables is illustrated in Figure 12.1. Schedule U^* is derived from equation (12.4) for a given target value of U. It shows the different combinations of government expenditure and 'high-powered' money which give the desired level of unemployment, U^*. Similarly schedule B^* shows the combinations of government expenditure and 'high-powered' money that give balance-of-payments equilibrium. Where the two schedules intersect is determined that combination of G and H that will give balance-of-payments equilibrium and the target level of unemployment.

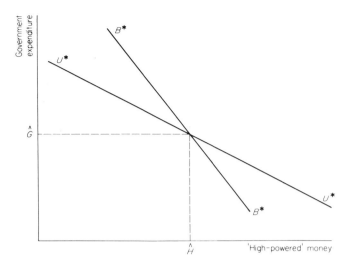

FIGURE 12.1   *Policy solution with two targets and two instruments*

The introduction of a third instrumental variable, such as a flexible exchange rate, provides us with one degree of freedom. For each value of the exchange rate there will be a combination of government expenditure and 'high-powered' money compatible with the desired values of the two target variables. This is illustrated in Figure 12.2. If the exchange rate is lowered the balance-of-payments position will be

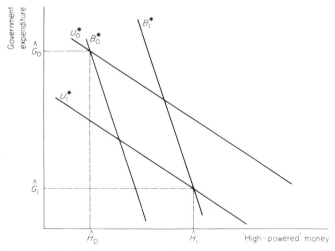

FIGURE 12.2   *Policy solutions with two targets and three instruments*

improved for a given volume of 'high-powered' money and government expenditure. This is shown by schedule B_0^* shifting up to B_1^*. The U_0^* schedule shifts down to U_1^* since lowering the exchange rate increases aggregate demand. Therefore one can achieve the target level of unemployment at a lower level of government expenditure and 'high-powered' money. The diagram shows two possible combinations of fiscal and monetary policy, $\hat{G}_0$, $\hat{H}_0$ and $\hat{G}_1$, $\hat{H}_1$, that will result in the simultaneous attainment of both targets, providing the exchange rate is set at the appropriate level in each case.

This analysis shows that if the government sets n independent target variables at specific values it must have at least n effective instrumental variables. Because of the interdependent relationships amongst variables, the government must co-ordinate the instrumental variables. The value set for each instrument must take into account the desired values of all the target variables and how these target variables are affected by the other instrumental variables. In general it is not possible to set one instrumental variable to achieve one target in isolation from the other instrumental and target variables.*

Conflicts in Policy Objectives

It is frequently pointed out that policy objectives may be in conflict; for instance that price stability or balance-of-payments equilibrium can only be obtained at the cost of a higher level of unemployment. The above analysis indicates that these conflicts arise from an insufficient number of effective instrumental variables relative to the number of targets. They can also be due to the policy-makers' lack of knowledge about the coefficients of the reduced form of the model of the economy.

* If $y_j = j$th target variable, $x_i = i$th instrumental variable and $k = n$,

$$
\begin{bmatrix} a_{11} & \cdots & a_{1n} \\ a_{n1} & \cdots & a_{nn} \end{bmatrix}
\begin{bmatrix} x_i \\ \cdot \\ \cdot \\ \cdot \\ x_k \end{bmatrix}
=
\begin{bmatrix} y_j \\ \cdot \\ \cdot \\ \cdot \\ y_n \end{bmatrix}
$$

is the reduced form of a model where all the instrumental variables have to be related to all the target variables. If the model is such that each instrumental variable is related to just one target variable, the reduced form will be

$$
\begin{bmatrix} a_{11} & 0 & \cdots & 0 \\ 0 & a_{22} & \cdots & 0 \\ 0 & & \cdots & 0 \\ 0 & & \cdots & a_{nn} \end{bmatrix}
\begin{bmatrix} x_i \\ \cdot \\ \cdot \\ \cdot \\ x_k \end{bmatrix}
=
\begin{bmatrix} y_j \\ \cdot \\ \cdot \\ \cdot \\ y_n \end{bmatrix}.
$$

If any non-zero elements appear in the cells off the principal diagonal, one must then set the related instrumental variables with regard to more than one target.

The state of economic knowledge is such that governments do not know precisely at what values to set the instrumental variables in order to achieve the desired targets. The lack of such information combined with insufficient co-ordination of instrumental and target variables make it difficult for the authorities to achieve simultaneously all their targets so that some objectives are attained at the expense of others.

The management of the U.K. economy in the post-war period illustrates the difficulties of achieving simultaneously all targets when there is an insufficient number of effective instrumental variables. From 1947 to 1967 fiscal and monetary policy, with greater emphasis on the former, were the major instrumental variables used by governments striving for full employment, price stability, balance-of-payments equilibrium and a faster rate of growth. The actual economic record is characterised by successive balance-of-payments crises, when the government corrected the deficit by reducing domestic aggregate demand, thus increasing unemployment. Once a surplus on the balance of payments had been achieved, aggregate demand was stimulated and unemployment reduced until another balance-of-payments crisis forced the government to re-adopt restrictive measures. Not until 1967 did the government allow itself to use a third instrumental variable, that of lowering the exchange rate. Since June 1972 the exchange rate has been allowed some degree of fluctuation, thus providing an additional means of adjustment.

This period has also been characterised by attempts to find additional instrumental variables. Since the 1960s successive governments have hoped that a prices-and-incomes policy would provide an additional instrumental variable which would enable the economy to run at a lower level of unemployment without having to pay the price of a higher rate of inflation. There has been a distinct tendency to set the fiscal and monetary instrumental variables at levels which are based on the presumption that the prices-and-incomes policy variable will be more effective in the future than past experience would indicate. The search for new instrumental variables is an attempt to avoid the unpleasantness of accepting that some trade-off will have to be made amongst the target variables, given that there are at present an insufficient number of instrumental variables.

12.2   THE TRADE-OFF AMONGST TARGET VARIABLES

The Tinbergen [1] approach to planning economic policy, which has just been discussed, takes as a starting point a set of values that each target variable is required to attain. The instrumental variables are then solved so as to simultaneously achieve all the targets. An alternative approach, developed primarily by Theil [2], has the advantage of being able to provide a solution to the policy planning problem even when the number of targets exceeds the number of instrumental variables.

The policy-maker is ascribed a utility function in which the target variables enter as arguments. This utility function is then maximised subject to the constraints of the economic system. These constraints are contained in the economic model of the economy. This approach is illustrated using the reduced form of the *ISLM* model given by equations (12.1) and (12.2). The policy-maker's utility function is

$$S = f(U, B) \quad \text{where } S = \text{utility} \quad \frac{\partial S}{\partial U} < 0, \qquad \frac{\partial S}{\partial B} > 0. \quad (12.8)$$

This is maximised subject to the restrictions of equations (12.1) and (12.2). The constraints can alternatively be expressed in the form of a trade-off function between unemployment and the balance-of-payments position by solving equations (12.1) and (12.2) for unemployment as a function of the balance of payments.

Equation (12.9) shows the levels of unemployment and the corresponding balance-of-payments position brought about by various levels of government expenditure. A rise in government expenditure will lower unemployment and worsen the balance of payments. The trade-off function between U and B is*

$$U = \frac{b_1 a_0 - a_1 b_0}{b_1} + \frac{a_1 B}{b_1} \quad (12.9)$$

and is the equation of schedule AC in Figure 12.3.

The policy-maker's indifference curves are shown as S_0, S_1 and S_2. These indicate that an improved balance of payments is traded-off against a higher level of unemployment and that a diminishing marginal rate of substitution between the two objectives is assumed. The highest attainable level of utility, given the constraint of the trade-off function, is S_1 so that a balance-of-payments surplus of B_1 combined with an unemployment rate of U_1 is selected. The level of government expenditure which will achieve this combination of objectives is determined from equations (12.1) and (12.2).

An alternative formulation of a policy-maker's utility function is the loss function which depends on the difference between the target value of the objective and the value actually attained. For the model discussed above such a loss function could be expressed as†

$$L = f[(U - U^*)^2 + (B - B^*)^2]. \quad (12.10)$$

---

* Multiply equation (12.1) by b_1, equation (12.2) by a_1, subtract (12.1) from (12.2) and rearrange.

† The deviations are squared so that positive and negative deviations do not cancel each other out.

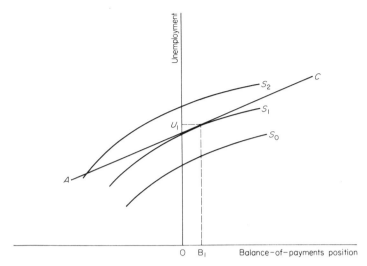

FIGURE 12.3   *The trade-off between two targets*

The objective is then the minimisation of the loss function subject to the constraints provided by the economic system.

Intertemporal Choice

An important aspect of policy-makers' decision-taking is trading-off present against future utility. Present benefits can be obtained at the expense of future costs and vice versa. For example, unemployment can be reduced in the present by increasing the rate of inflation. The future cost of this is higher rates of inflation and the cost of future unemployment for a time if the rate of inflation is reduced.* Thus the present benefits of a lower current unemployment rate are only obtained at the expense of future costs. The opposite case is illustrated by the situation where the growth rate of the economy is increased for a time by a greater rate of current investment. This involves forgoing some current consumption for the sake of future consumption. Therefore current costs and benefits must be weighed against future costs and benefits.

12.3   DYNAMIC ANALYSIS OF ECONOMIC POLICY: STABILISATION

Our previous discussion on the selection of instrumental variables which would produce the desired values for the target variables was in

* See [39] in Chapter 9.

comparative static terms. As the economy does not adjust instantaneously, economic policy has not only to be concerned with the determination of a desirable equilibrium state but also with how to move the economic system to such a situation and how to keep it there.

Economic policy considered in this dynamic context is referred to as stabilisation policy. The objective of stabilisation policy is to keep the economy on a desired path through time. It is presumed that the desired path is a steady-state path, such as a balanced growth path. The objective of stabilisation policy is usually defined in terms of a steady rate of growth of real G.D.P., accompanied by the full utilisation of capital and labour resources, and a stable price level. An alternative to a stable price level would be a constant rate of inflation equal to the expected rate of inflation.

Once more than one variable is taken account of a precise definition of stabilisation policy becomes more difficult. For instance, given that exogenous disturbances do occur, a policy aimed at stabilising interest rates would cause fluctuations in aggregate demand and hence G.D.P. An exogenous contraction in investment would be magnified if the rate of interest were kept constant instead of being allowed to fall.

There is a presumption underlying stabilisation policy that stability is desirable. This can be attributed to a human dislike of uncertainty, to the proposition that greater certainty promotes economic growth and that full utilisation of resources eliminates a source of economic waste. On the other hand stability, in the sense of remaining stationary, implies an economy with little growth or change. Such a state of affairs does not as yet appear to be generally desired. The objective of stabilisation policy therefore appears to be the desire to promote a smooth rate of economic change which reduces dislocations in production and employment patterns. This type of stability may involve a cost in terms of economic dynamism and the rate of growth. This discussion reveals the difficulties inherent in establishing what precisely are the goals of society and the trade-offs that exist amongst these goals. The analysis of stabilisation policy will be limited to the objective of maintaining the economy on a steady-state growth path for G.D.P.

Measuring the Impact of Stabilisation Policy

In order to measure the impact of stabilisation policy it is necessary to refer to the characteristics of the adjustment path through time of a variable which, for the purposes of discussion, we take to be real G.D.P. The adjustment path describes how a variable behaves over time when disturbed from equilibrium compared to its equilibrium path. The characteristics of the adjustment path are as follows.

(a) The path is stable or unstable, depending upon whether or not there is convergence to equilibrium.

(*b*) The path may or may not oscillate.

(*c*) The distance G.D.P. is from its equilibrium value at every point in time. For a cyclical adjustment path the maximum attained by this distance is known as the amplitude of the cycle.

(*d*) The length of time spent away from equilibrium.* Combining characteristics (*c*) and (*d*) provides the variance exhibited by the variable, which is the sum of the squared deviations of the actual value of G.D.P., y_t, from its equilibrium value, y_t^E:

$$\text{variance of } y = \frac{1}{T} \sum_{t=1}^{T} (y_t - y_t^E)^2. \tag{12.11}$$

Variance gives a composite measure of characteristics (*c*) and (*d*) and does not distinguish between them. A large divergence of y_t from y_t^E that takes place over a short period of time can give the same variance over a given time period as a smaller divergence of y_t from y_t^E that lasts longer.

(*e*) A further characteristic is the speed of adjustment. This needs to be defined as the time taken for G.D.P. to get within *x* per cent of its equilibrium value and to remain within that range. Thus an oscillating adjustment path could reach equilibrium before a monotonic adjustment path but overshoot equilibrium, not reaching permanently within *x* per cent of equilibrium G.D.P. until after the monotonic adjustment path does. This is illustrated in Figure 12.4.

Given a tendency for the economy to fluctuate around its equilibrium path due to its reaction to exogenous shocks, stabilisation policy aims to counteract such fluctuations. To do this counter-cyclical policy needs to

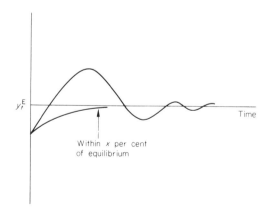

FIGURE 12.4   *The speed of adjustment*

* These points were raised in Chapter 1, p.12 and Chapter 11, p. 299.

produce effects on G.D.P. which are, at any moment in time, in the opposite direction to the deviation of G.D.P. from its equilibrium that is being caused by other factors. It is possible that counter-cyclical policy may fail to do this and even make matters worse by reinforcing existing cyclical forces and thus enlarging the deviation of G.D.P. from equilibrium.

Counter-Cyclical Policy: Stabilising or Destabilising?

The possibility that counter-cyclical policy may not be successful makes it particularly important to evaluate its impact. To do this we need to compare the adjustment path of output in the presence of stabilisation policy with its behaviour if the policy measure is not enacted. The precise nature of such a comparison depends on the model used and on the characteristics of the adjustment path chosen for measuring the effect of stabilisation policy.

Milton Friedman's model [4] provides a useful starting point for evaluating the problems faced by stabilisation policy. He uses a variance measure of stabilisation in the context of a simple, statistical model, defining the following symbols: X_t is the income at time t in the absence of counter-cyclical policy. This is also known as the 'pure cycle' value of income. Z_t is the income at time t in the presence of counter-cyclical policy. U_t equals $Z_t - X_t$. It is the amount added to or subtracted from X_t due to the combined effects of all past and present counter-cyclical policies which are felt at time t.

Because of lags the effects on income of a counter-cyclical policy measure taken in period 0 will be spread out over a number of time periods. Thus income in any one period of time will be feeling the impact of counter-cyclical policies taken in previous time periods. The net effect on income of these past and present policies may be positive or negative depending both on the size and timing of each policy measure and on the basic structure of the economic system which determines how the changes in the instrumental variables are channelled over time to affect other variables.

The statistical model is based on the definition

$$Z_t = X_t + U_t. \tag{12.12}$$

Friedman uses variance to measure the impact of counter-cyclical policy. Such policy is stabilising if the variance of income with the policy, σ_z^2, is less than the variance of income without the policy, σ_x^2. To obtain a sample of observations for Z_t which would enable one to estimate the variance of income with and without policy one would need the following information which is depicted in Figure 12.5.

(a) Observations of the actual value of G.D.P. in T time periods,

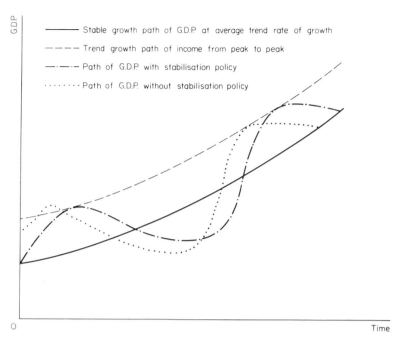

FIGURE 12.5 *Comparing the path of G.D.P. with and without stabilisation policy*

given that some stabilisation policy has been in operation. This is indicated by the hatched line.

(b) The stable growth path that income would have followed in the absence of fluctuations. This can be estimated by fitting a trend equation of the form $Y = Y_0 e^{gt}$ and estimating the average rate of growth achieved. This is indicated by the solid line. An alternative equilibrium path used for making comparisons is to estimate that rate of growth G.D.P. would have attained had the economy always operated at the level of capacity achieved at cyclical peaks. This is indicated by the dashed growth path.

(c) An estimate of the pure cycle income, that is what income would have been in each period in the absence of stabilisation policy. This is indicated by the dotted line. This is a particularly difficult part of any empirical evaluation of stabilisation policy. Defining a 'neutral' policy cannot be done satisfactorily when there are so many economic variables that are to some extent affected by what the government does. Empirical studies that have been done have inevitably defined a neutral policy in a very restrictive way. Generally neutrality is defined as the absence of certain tax and government expenditure changes that did take place.*

Having defined neutrality, the next problem is that of estimating what G.D.P. would have been in the absence of the specified policy changes. To do this requires specifying a particular economic model. One method of investigation is to carry out simulations with large-scale econometric models. These are disaggregated versions of the Keynesian three-sector macro model containing up to 300 endogenous variables and equations. The model can be run with and without a given policy measure and the time paths of the endogenous variables compared. So far most empirical investigations of stabilisation policy have not had access to large-scale econometric models and have fallen back on one-sector static or dynamic Keynesian models of varying degrees of disaggregation.

Having obtained observations over time of income without policy, X_t, and income with policy, Z_t, and income growing at its trend rate of growth, y_t^E, the variance of income without and with policy could be estimated, i.e.

$$\sigma_x^2 = \frac{1}{T} \sum_{t=1}^{T} (X_t - y_t^E)^2$$

$$\sigma_z^2 = \frac{1}{T} \sum_{t=1}^{T} (Z_t - y_t^E)^2.$$

Friedman uses the theoretical properties of this statistical measurement of stabilisation to establish the conditions necessary for a successful stabilisation policy. Applying the formula for the variance of a sum of two variables one obtains†

$$\sigma_z^2 = \sigma_{(x+u)}^2 = \sigma_x^2 + \sigma_u^2 + 2r_{xu}\sigma_x\sigma_u \qquad (12.13)$$

* Examples of attempts at the quantitative assessment of stabilisation policy can be found in [5, 6, 7, 8]. These take the basic form of $y = C + I + G$, where $C = b(1-t)y$ and $t = $ tax rate.

$$\text{G.D.P. without policy is } X = \frac{I+G}{1-b}.$$

$$\text{G.D.P. with policy is } Z = \frac{I+G}{1-b(1-t)}.$$

†
$$\begin{aligned}
\text{var } Z &= E(Z - \bar{Z})^2 = E(X + U - \bar{X} - \bar{U})^2 = E[(X - \bar{X}) + (U - \bar{U})]^2 \\
&= E[(X - \bar{X})^2 + 2(X - \bar{X})(U - \bar{U}) + (U - \bar{U})^2] \\
&= E(X - \bar{X})^2 + E(U - \bar{U})^2 + 2E(X - \bar{X})(U - \bar{U}) \\
&= \text{var } X + \text{var } U + 2 \text{ cov } XU \\
&= \text{var } X + \text{var } U + 2r_{xu} \sqrt{(\text{var } X)} \sqrt{(\text{var } U)}
\end{aligned}$$

since
$$r_{xu} = \frac{\text{cov } XU}{\sqrt{\text{var } X} \sqrt{\text{var } U}}.$$

(Bar indicates expected value of a variable.)

where r_{xu} is the correlation between X_t and U_t, and σ_x, σ_u, are respectively the standard deviations of X_t and U_t. Dividing both sides by σ_x^2 gives a measure of the success of stabilisation policy in terms of the proportion of the pure cycle fluctuations in G.D.P. that is not removed by the policy, i.e.

$$\frac{\sigma_z^2}{\sigma_x^2} = 1 + \frac{\sigma_u^2}{\sigma_x^2} + 2r_{xu}\frac{\sigma_u}{\sigma_x}. \tag{12.14}$$

Since perfect stabilisation requires that there be no fluctuations whatever in income, σ_z^2 of zero indicates perfect stabilisation. This requires that the correlation between X_t and U_t, r_{xu}, is minus one and that σ_x^2 equals σ_u^2. Some degree of stabilisation is achieved if σ_z^2/σ_x^2 lies between zero and one, while the policy is destabilising if σ_z^2/σ_x^2 exceeds one. If σ_z^2/σ_x^2 lies between zero and one it must be the case that

$$-1 < r_{xu} < -(\sigma_u/2\sigma_x). \tag{12.15}$$

A perfectly stabilising counter-cyclical policy requires that in every time period the pure cycle deviation of G.D.P. should be exactly offset by the counter-cyclical policy causing an equal-sized deviation in G.D.P. in the opposite direction. The pure cycle deviation is $(X_t - y_t^E)$; therefore perfect stabilisation requires that the offsetting policy deviation, U_t, should equal $-(X_t - y_t^E)$. Since $Z_t = X_t + U_t$ we have

$$Z_t = y_t^E + (X_t - y_t^E) + U_t.$$

Therefore when policy is perfectly stabilising

$$Z_t = y_t^E + (X_t - y_t^E) - (X_t - y_t^E) = y_t^E.$$

This is illustrated in Figure 12.6 where, superimposing the pure cycle deviation of G.D.P. upon the deviations from trend caused by policy, gives a time path of G.D.P. which is the same as the steady-state path and thus exhibits no fluctuations.

A correlation of minus one between X_t and U_t* means that the two cycles are exactly in opposite phase, but this is not sufficient for policy to be perfectly stabilising. As shown above not only must the two deviations $(X_t - y_t^E)$ and U_t, have opposite signs, they must also be of equal absolute size. The latter condition requires that the standard deviations of X_t and U_t are equal. Thus we get Friedman's condition for perfect stabilisation that equation (12.4) should equal zero.

If one of the conditions but not the other is satisfied policy fails to be perfectly stabilising. An example of this is shown in Figure 12.7. The time

---

* Since we are calculating var X_t as deviations from trend, y_t^E, it will be the same as the variance of $(X_t - y_t^E)$ since the latter variance is calculated as deviations about zero. Thus the correlation of X_t and U_t will be the same as the correlation between $(X_t - y_t^E)$ and U_t.

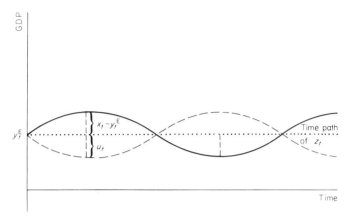

FIGURE 12.6   *Perfectly stabilising policy*

paths of $(X_t - y_t^E)$ and U_t have a minus one correlation but the standard deviation of $(X_t - y_t^E)$ is larger than that of U_t. In this situation only a proportion of the pure cycle deviation in G.D.P. is removed since a positive pure cycle deviation, such as ab, is offset by a smaller negative deviation in G.D.P. of bc due to counter-cyclical policy.

If the correlation between $(X_t - y_t^E)$ and U_t lies between minus one and zero, the two cycles are no longer in exactly opposite phase. The

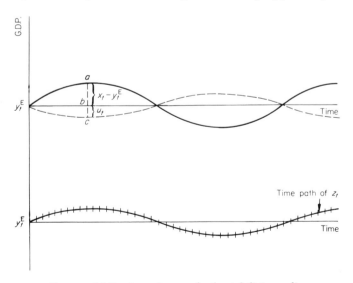

FIGURE 12.7   *Less than perfectly stabilising policy*

peak in the $(X_t - y_t^E)$ cycle does not match the trough in the U_t cycle. This is illustrated in Figure 12.8, where the trough of the U_t cycle lags the peak of the $(X_t - y_t^E)$ cycle by a quarter of the length of the cycle. The two cycles have the same amplitude and frequency so the standard deviation of X_t equals the standard deviation of U_t. Superimposing the $(X_t - y_t^E)$ cycle on to the U_t cycle gives the time path of Z_t. In this example counter-cyclical policy is destabilising since the variance of income with policy exceeds the variance of the pure cycled G.D.P. This result is due to the magnitude of counter-vailing policy, which is measured by σ_u, being too large in relation to the amount of negative correlation achieved between $(X_t - y_t^E)$ and U_t.

The optimal value for σ_u can be obtained by differentiating equation (12.14) with respect to σ_u.

$$\frac{\mathrm{d}}{\mathrm{d}\sigma_u}\left(\frac{\sigma_z^2}{\sigma_x^2}\right) = 2\frac{\sigma_u}{\sigma_x^2} + 2\frac{r_{xu}}{\sigma_x} = 0. \tag{12.16}$$

Therefore the optimal value for σ_u is

$$\sigma_u = -r_{xu}\sigma_x. \tag{12.17}$$

Equation (12.17) shows that the strength of counter-cyclical policy must be related positively to the magnitude of both the pure cycle deviations in G.D.P. and the absolute size of the correlation between X_t and U_t which must be negative if any stabilisation is to take place at all. For example, if $r_{xu} = -0.5$, σ_u should be set equal to $0.5\ \sigma_x$ and, using

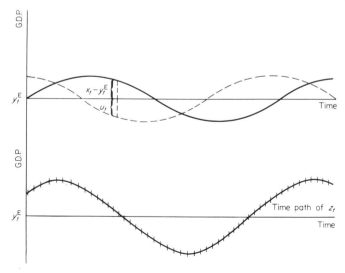

FIGURE 12.8   *Destabilising counter-cyclical policy*

equation (12.14), one can calculate that 25 per cent of the variance in the pure cycle G.D.P. will be eliminated. But if σ_u were increased to $0 \cdot 75 \, \sigma_x$, given the same correlation coefficient, the proportion of the variance reduced would fall to $18 \cdot 75$ per cent.

The Effect of Lags on the Operation of Counter-Cyclical Policy

This analysis indicates that an important requirement for successful counter-cyclical policy is a good inverse correlation between the pure cycle deviations of G.D.P. and the response of G.D.P. to policy measures. It is difficult to achieve this degree of correlation because of lags in the system which prevent the policy induced response in G.D.P. from cycling in exactly the reverse phase to the pure cycle deviations.

The policy lag can be split into two types. The inside lag is the time taken between the deviations of actual G.D.P. from its desired path and the implementation of counter-cyclical policy. First, it takes time for policy-makers to recognise that a deviation of G.D.P. from its desired time path has occurred. This lag can be reduced by increasing the speed with which statistics are gathered and improving forecasting techniques. The second component of the inside lag is due to institutional and political factors which cause delay in the implementation of policy. The outside lag refers to the time taken for the target variables to be affected by the policy measure, once this has been implemented. This type of lag has already been examined with respect to consumption, investment and the demand for money functions.

The longer is the lag the greater is the period of time over which the effects of a policy change on G.D.P. are extended. The shorter are the pure cyclical fluctuations, the more likely it is that the policy-induced deviations in G.D.P., implemented to counteract a negative (positive) pure cycle deviation, will still be in existence when the pure cycle in income turns upwards (downwards) (see Figure 12.8). In this event the correlation between pure cycle and policy-induced deviations in G.D.P. will be low in absolute terms and may even be positive.

The values of r_{xu} corresponding to different lengths for the complete cycle and for the policy lag (defined as the time taken for a policy to achieve 50 per cent of its effect) have been calculated by Wittes [9]. Negative values for r_{xu} only appear when the policy lag is not more than three-quarters and the cycle is quite long. Given the shortness of post-war cycles, which have averaged four years in the United Kingdom the results indicate the likelihood of counter-cyclical policy being destabilising, particularly if the policy reaction is large.

Further Theoretical Work on Stabilisation Policy

The analytical framework for the theoretical study of stabilisation policy is the construction of a dynamic model in which the target variables are lagged dependent functions of the instrumental variables. Thus one can construct time paths for G.D.P. with and without given policy measures. The time paths are generated by subjecting the model to a single or recurring random exogenous disturbances. Conclusions are reached either by looking at the time paths of G.D.P. [11] or by minimising policy-makers' loss functions. Much of this type of work is concerned with devising optimal control policies. This involves devising ways for the economic system to respond automatically to certain signals so that these responses act in a stabilising manner. An example of such an automatic response would be a rule which changed government expenditure in the opposite direction to and by a given proportion of the pure cycle deviation in G.D.P.

In most of these models stability is promoted by the use of optimal policy controls as compared to a passive response by the authorities. The precise nature of the passive response varies from model to model but it precludes any deliberate policy to counter deviations in G.D.P. Long lags in the response of G.D.P. to policy changes do not render an optimal counter-cyclical policy destabilising. So long as these lags are known the required amount of corrective action can be calculated. The important element in making counter-cyclical policy ineffective is uncertainty. When the exact response over time of G.D.P. to a change in an instrumental variable is unknown, there is some probability that counter-cyclical policy will be destabilising [13].

No firm conclusions, which can be applied to the real world, about the relationship between the length of the policy lag and the likelihood of successful stabilisation policy have yet emerged from the theoretical literature. Tentative conclusions are that long and uncertain lag structures, combined with large counter-cyclical action, promote instability.*

Automatic Stabilisers

Given that long policy lags hinder the operation of stabilisation policy, ways have been suggested for reducing lags. The inside lag can be eliminated for policy instruments which respond automatically to changes in G.D.P. and do not therefore require deliberate government action. The government budget provides such an automatic stabiliser since tax revenues, with a given structure of tax rates, move in the same direction as national income. Similarly government expenditure on unemployment benefits moves counter-cyclically. The money supply also acts as a stabiliser by reducing the size of the expenditure multiplier. Empirical studies indicate that automatic stabilisers reduce the fluctuations in G.D.P. by 20–40 per cent [14, 15, 16, 17].

* For further details consult [10, 11, 12, 13, 14].

12.4 THE POLICY DEBATE: RULES VERSUS DISCRETION [18]

There is a difference of opinion amongst economists as to the extent to which governments should operate discretionary policies. Deliberate intervention to keep the time path of G.D.P. on course has been termed 'fine-tuning'. The debate revolves round two main issues.

(1) The extent to which the economy is self-regulating. Orthodox Keynesian thought emphasises the inability of the economy to remain in equilibrium without government action. Neoclassical economists are more optimistic about the equilibrating properties of the economy and advocate changes to improve the economy's self-correcting mechanisms, as opposed to the discretionary interventions by government which are favoured by Keynesians.

(2) Keynesians are more optimistic about the ability of goverments to operate appropriate stabilising discretionary policies. Opponents of this view consider that the degree of economic knowledge, both empirical and theoretical, is insufficient to ensure that governments will follow appropriate discretionary policies. It is thought that the adherence of governments to specific policy rules would reduce the risks of incorrect action, arising from incomplete knowledge of the workings of the economy or from the pursuit of short-term goals which are in conflict with long-run objectives.

Milton Friedman, an advocate of policy rules, has proposed two types of policy rule. The first [19] involves running a balanced government budget taking the cycle as a whole. The budget would be allowed to go into deficit in the recession and the deficit would be financed by increasing the rate of growth of the money supply. This would be offset by a budget surplus, accompanied by a contraction in the rate of growth of the money supply in the expansionary phase of the trade cycle. Latterly [20], because of the long and variable lag he believes exists for monetary policy, he favours expanding the money supply at a constant rate and eschewing the use of discretionary monetary policy.

12.5 CONCLUSION

The resolution of the debate between proponents of discretionary government action and those who favour policy rules requires further research into the following areas.

(*a*) The form of the main macro functions in the economy, especially with regard to their lag structure.

(*b*) Theoretical and empirical work on how policy lags, especially those of uncertain length, affect the probability of implementing successful stabilisation policies. So far theoretical work does not show conclusively that long adjustment lags make counter-cyclical policy less stabilising than a passive response by the authorities. Optimal control policies can be devised if there is exact knowledge of the way the economy behaves. Long lags by themselves are not destabilising if their size and distribution is known. The major difficulty in operating stabilisation policy is that the economy's responses are uncertain so that the correct timing and magnitude of counter-cyclical policy is not known. Theoretical work does suggest that the risks of inappropriate policy action can be diminished if policy lags are reduced.

(c) Empirical work on the performance of stabilisation policies that have actually been implemented. Assessments of post-war U.K. demand-management policies reveal a tendency for delayed action, followed by an excessively strong policy response when the effects of the inital action were slow in coming through. Theoretical work, such as that by Friedman [4] and Phillips [10, 11], indicate that this type of policy reaction is likely to be destabilising.

REFERENCES

[1] J. Tinbergen, *Economic Policy: Principles and Design* (Amsterdam: North-Holland, 1956).

[2] H. Theil, *Optimal Decision Rules for Government and Industry* (Amsterdam: North-Holland, 1964).

[3] W. J. Baumol, 'Pitfalls in Countercyclical Policy; Some Tools and Results', *Review of Economics and Statistics* (February 1962).

[4] M. Friedman, 'The Effects of a Full-Employment Policy on Economic Stability, A Formal Analysis', in his *Essays in Positive Economics*.

[5] B. Hansen and W. Snyder, *Fiscal Policy in Seven Countries, 1955–65,* (Paris: O.E.E.C., 1969).

[6] W. Snyder, 'Measuring Economic Stabilisation, 1955–65', *American Economic Review* (December 1970).

[7] J. A. Bristow, 'Taxation and Income Stabilisation', *Economic Journal* (1964).

[8] M. Artis, 'Fiscal Policy for Stabilisation', in *The Labour Government's Economic Record 1964–70*, ed. W. Beckerman (London: Duckworth, 1972).

[9] M. H. Wittes, 'The Scope of Counter-cyclical Monetary Policy', *Journal of Money, Banking and Credit*, 3, 3 (August 1971).

[10] A. W. Phillips, 'Stabilisation Policy in a Closed Economy', *Economic Journal* (June 1954).

[11] A. W. Phillips, 'Stabilisation Policy and the Time-Forms of Lagged Responses', *Economic Journal*, 68 (June 1957).

[12] W. Poole, 'Optimal Choice of Monetary Policy Instruments in a Simple Stochastic Macro Model', *Quarterly Journal of Economics*, 84 (May 1970).

[13] S. Fischer and J. P. Cooper, 'Stabilisation Policy and Lags', *Journal of Political Economy*, 81, 4 (July–August 1973).

[14] R. A. Musgrave and M. H. Miller, 'Built in Flexibility', *American Economic Review* (March 1948).

[15] P. Eilbott, 'The Effectiveness of Automatic Stabilisers', *American Economic Review*, 56 (1966).

[16] P. H. Pease, 'Automatic Stabilisation and the British Taxes on Income', *Review of Economic Studies*, 29 (February 1962).

[17] D. C. Smyth, 'Built in Flexibility of Taxation and Automatic Stabilisation', *Journal of Political Economy*, 74 (1966).

[18] M. Friedman and W. W. Heller, *Monetary vs. Fiscal Policy*, (New York: Norton, 1969).

[19] M. Friedman, 'A Monetary and Fiscal Framework for Economic Stability', in his *Essays in Positive Economics*.

[20] M. Friedman, *A Programme for Monetary Stability* (New York: Fordham University Press, 1960).

13 Monetary and Fiscal Policy

Monetary and fiscal policy form the two main instruments for aggregate demand management in the United Kingdom. However, it should be borne in mind that these policies also relate to other objectives. Government budgetary policy affects the distribution of income and wealth and the allocation of resources, including their allocation between the private and public sectors. Similarly monetary policy has distributional and allocative effects and can be used to promote a more efficient allocation of liquid capital. An attempt to do this by promoting competition between banks was made in the United Kingdom by the introduction of Competition and Credit Control in 1971. The following discussion is restricted to the role of monetary and fiscal policy in demand management.

13.1 THE RELATIVE EFFECTIVENESS OF MONETARY AND FISCAL POLICY IN AN OPEN ECONOMY[1, 2, 3, 4, 5, 6]

Much hot air has been spent debating the relative effectiveness of monetary and fiscal policy. We need to pause to consider what is meant by 'relative effectiveness'. A straightforward comparison of the effect on the equilibrium level of aggregate demand of a £1 million increase in the supply of money with that of a £1 million increase in government spending is not meaningful as one is not comparing like quantities. One policy involves increasing a stock while the other involves increasing a flow. One can make an unambiguous comparison of the effect of fiscal (or monetary) policy on the equilibrium level of aggregate demand under varying economic circumstances, for instance different values for the elasticity of the demand for money with respect to the rate of interest. This exercise has already been carried out for a closed economy in Chapter 2 and is now undertaken for an open economy.

To avoid confusion monetary policy is determined as referring to deliberate actions taken to change the domestic stock of money, fiscal variables remaining unchanged. Fiscal policy concerns alterations in government spending and in the tax rate structure which are financed by selling government bonds.* Thus, an increase in government expenditure which is financed by increasing the supply of money is both a fiscal and a monetary measure. The following comparative static analysis only looks at the effects of changes in fiscal and monetary policy on the static equilibrium level of aggregate demand.

An Open Economy With Perfect Capital Mobility

If perfect capital mobility exists the domestic and world rates of interest are equal in equilibrium. The domestic country, the United Kingdom, cannot permanently alter its rate of interest relative to the rest of the world. The effects on aggregate demand of fiscal and monetary policy are compared under regimes of fixed and flexible exchange rates. An expansionary fiscal policy, shown in Figure 13.1 by a shift in the IS schedule from IS_0 to IS_1, will increase aggregate demand and initially

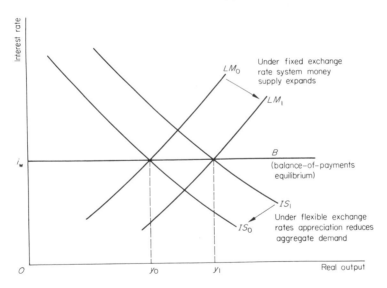

FIGURE 13.1 *Fiscal policy when capital is perfectly mobile*

* See Chapter 2. Note that changes in the tax revenue (or government expenditure on transfer payments) that are due only to changes in national income are endogenous and are not changes in fiscal policy instrumental variables.

raise the interest rate. The higher domestic rate attracts a larger net inflow of foreign funds.

Case 1: *fiscal policy, fixed exchange rate.* If the exchange rate is fixed the balance-of-payments surplus brought about by the net capital inflow continues so long as the U.K. rate of interest exceeds the world level. This causes the money supply to expand and is indicated in Figure 13.1 by a shift in the *LM* function from LM_0 to LM_1. Since there is perfect capital mobility the equilibrium U.K. interest rate cannot increase because so long as it is above the world rate of interest foreign capital flows into the country. This means that ultimately the government finances its increased expenditure by selling bonds to foreigners. Under a fixed exchange rate system this leads eventually to an increase in the money supply as sterilisation of the foreign exchange inflow cannot be carried out if international capital is perfectly mobile.

Because the equilibrium level of the domestic interest rate does not rise, fiscal policy has a greater impact on real aggregate demand than it would have in a closed economy. With no foreign sector the government has to finance its expenditure by selling bonds to the domestic private sector. This, plus the increased demand for money arising from the higher G.D.P. due to the fiscal policy, drive up the interest rate and investment is adversely affected. The fiscal policy multiplier in an open economy with perfect capital mobility is the same size as in a one-sector Keynesian model because it is not constrained by any negative feedback effects from the money supply. It should be noted that the impact on aggregate demand of the fiscal policy is not entirely attributable to fiscal policy. The expansion of the money supply that is brought about by the effects of fiscal policy also contributes.

Once the U.K. and world interest rates are again equal the balance-of-payments surplus disappears. The increased flow of imports caused by the higher level of aggregate demand is just matched by an increased capital inflow to give balance-of-payments equilibrium.

Case 2: *fiscal policy, flexible exchange rates.* If the exchange rate is flexible the balance-of-payments surplus due to the increased capital inflow which follows an expansionary fiscal policy is eliminated by an appreciation of the exchange rate. The money supply therefore remains unchanged. The higher exchange rate reduces the aggregate demand for the national output by reducing exports and increasing imports and shifts the *IS* function back towards its original position. Equilibrium is once more attained when the *IS* function has regained its original position. Thus, fiscal policy has no lasting effect on the level of aggregate demand.

Case 3: *monetary policy, fixed exchange rates.* The same comparison for monetary policy yields the reverse results. An expansion of the money supply under a fixed exchange rate system can have no lasting effect on aggregate demand. As the domestic rate of interest falls a net capital outflow occurs, thus reducing the domestic supply until it has returned to its original level. As shown in Figure 13.2, there is no effect at all on the equilibrium level of aggregate demand. Any attempt to sterilise the money supply merely prolongs the process until foreign exchange reserves and borrowing powers are exhausted.

Case 4: monetary policy, flexible exchange rates. Under a flexible exchange rate system the balance-of-payments deficit caused by the net capital outflow is corrected by a depreciation of the exchange rate. This allows the domestic money supply to remain unchanged at its new level. Exchange rate depreciation increases aggregate demand by reducing imports and increasing exports. This is shown in Figure 13.2 by an upward shift in the *IS* schedule. Thus aggregate demand is increased from y_0 to y_2 at which level the demand for money equals the increased money stock.

Summary. If there is perfect capital mobility then under a fixed exchange rate system fiscal policy is very effective and monetary policy completely ineffective. If the exchange rate is flexible then fiscal policy becomes completely ineffective, whereas monetary policy is very effective at changing aggregate demand.

An Open Economy With Less Than Perfect Capital Mobility

In an economy with less than perfect capital mobility the balance of payments is affected by the response of the net capital flow because of

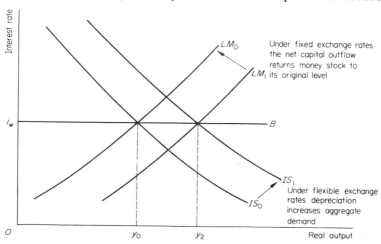

FIGURE 13.2 *Monetary policy when capital is perfectly mobile*

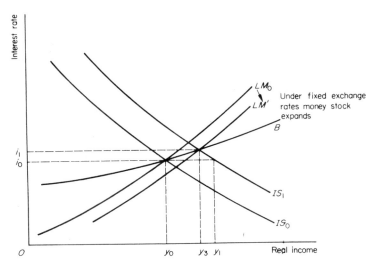

FIGURE 13.3   *Fiscal policy under fixed exchange rates: imperfect capital mobility*

interest rate changes but the domestic interest rate can be kept
permanently at a different level to the world interest rate. This model
was used in Chapter 11.

Case 1: fiscal policy, fixed exchange rates. The effectiveness of fiscal
policy under a regime of fixed exchange rates is now less than it was in
the case of perfect capital mobility. When capital mobility is not perfect
the net capital inflow that results from the increased domestic interest
rate stops short of completely returning the domestic interest rate to its
original level. As shown in Figure 13.3, balance-of-payments equilibrium is regained at an interest rate of i_1 and a level of aggregate demand
of y_3. Because the new equilibrium rate of interest is higher than in the
case of perfect capital mobility the level of aggregate demand is
correspondingly less.

Case 2: fiscal policy, flexible exchange rates. Under flexible exchange
rates the effect of a change in fiscal policy depends on whether it causes
the exchange rate to appreciate or depreciate. Take the example of the
government increasing the budget deficit and financing it with bond
sales. The resulting increase in the rate of interest brings in additional
capital from abroad. Meanwhile the expansion of aggregate demand
increases the flow of imports. If the increased value of imports is less
than the increased net capital inflow there will initially be a balance-of-
payments surplus. The exchange rate will appreciate and cause some

reduction in aggregate demand. In this event fiscal policy will be less effective under a flexible exchange rate, given imperfect capital mobility, than under a fixed exchange rate.

This result will not hold if the increased budget deficit initially causes an increase in imports that exceeds the increased net capital inflow. In this event the exchange rate will depreciate, giving an additional stimulus to aggregate demand. Thus, fiscal policy would be more effective under a flexible exchange rate than under a fixed exchange rate system.

Case 3: monetary policy, fixed exchange rates. Under fixed exchange rates monetary policy will still have no permanent effect on the level of aggregate demand. If we start from a position of balance-of-payments equilibrium, an increase in the money supply can only be temporary. The initial increase in aggregate demand and the reduction in the domestic interest rate will cause a balance-of-payments deficit. The resulting foreign exchange reserve drain reduces the domestic money supply until, as depicted in Figure 13.4, the initial equilibrium position is regained. The expansionary effect on domestic aggregate demand can only continue so long as sterilisation prevents the money supply contracting to its original level.

Case 4: monetary policy, flexible exchange rates. Under a flexible exchange rate system an increase in the money supply can now

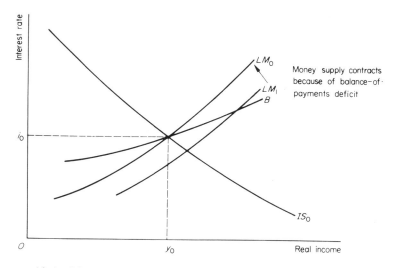

FIGURE 13.4 *Monetary policy under fixed exchange rates: imperfect capital mobility*

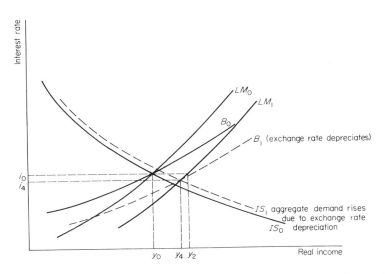

FIGURE 13.5   *Monetary policy under flexible exchange rates: imperfect capital
mobility*

permanently lower the domestic rate of interest. Since balance-of-
payments equilibrium will be achieved at a lower rate of interest
compared to the case of perfect capital mobility, the exchange rate will
depreciate less. This means that there will be a smaller stimulus to
aggregate demand from this source. As indicated in Figure 13.5, the
depreciation of the exchange rate increases aggregate demand, shifting
the IS function from IS_0 to IS_1, and improves the balance-of-payments
trade-off (B_0 shifts to B_1). Therefore aggregate demand rises to y_4 as
compared to the larger increase to y_2 that occurs with perfect capital
mobility.

Summary.   Given less than perfect capital mobility, monetary policy will
again be more effective under a flexible exchange rate system than
under a fixed exchange rate system. Fiscal policy will also be more
effective with a flexible exchange rate than with a fixed exchange rate if
fiscal expansion (contraction) initially causes a deficit (surplus) on the
balance of payments.

Simplifications Made in the Analysis Above

In studying monetary and fiscal policy in the United Kingdom one
cannot ignore the open nature of the economy. The analysis we have
just conducted made a number of simplifying assumptions.

   One particularly vital assumption was the constancy of the domestic price level. This assumption is made because of the absence of simple theory in *ISLM* analysis of how both the price level and real output can be determined endogenously. The neoclassical model with its assumption of price flexibility solves for full employment equilibrium real output. Comparative static analysis with this model is therefore unsuitable for short-term policy analysis. On the other hand use of the two-sector Keynesian model, with its assumption of price level constancy, is also unsuitable for policy analysis in an economy that is reasonably fully employed.

With these points in mind one should modify the above analysis. Expansionary fiscal and monetary policy will cause some rise in the domestic price level relative to the world price level which will have negative feedback effects on aggregate demand via reductions in exports and increases in imports.

Another simplification is the neglect of feedback effects to the U.K. economy resulting from the impact of U.K. policy measures on foreign economies. For instance, an increase in imports in the United Kingdom, which raises national incomes abroad, can feed back to the United Kingdom in the form of increased demand for U.K. exports. Similar feedback effects can be transmitted through interest rates.

A third simplification is that a basically short-run analysis has been conducted and thus the distinction between the requirements of flow and stock equilibrium is not brought out clearly. For short-run equilibrium, balance-of-payments equilibrium is established when the current account deficit (surplus), which is a flow concept, is exactly offset by a net capital inflow (outflow), which is a change in stock variables. If we have an unbalanced current account, stock equilibrium is not achieved because residents are engaged in either continual net lending or borrowing abroad. Therefore in this case domestic residents' portfolios are not in equilibrium in a model in which national income is stationary.

A continual net accumulation of assets or liabilities, which is consistent with portfolio equilibrium is only feasible in the context of growing economies. Therefore to deal properly with the requirements of stock equilibrium on the balance of payments we need to conduct a long-run analysis of growing economies. The static equilibrium analysis conducted in Section 13.1 solves for short-run equilibrium on the assumption that no repercussions due to stock disequilibrium have yet occurred.*

Monetary Policy in an Open Economy

A model of an open economy with something less than perfect capital mobility is the most applicable to the United Kingdom. The analysis indicated that under fixed exchange rate, which the United Kingdom

* See [8] for a fuller discussion of this point.

operated until June 1972, monetary policy is ineffective in affecting the equilibrium level of real output. This is true even under the simplified Keynesian assumption of a less than full-employment equilibrium level of real output. The ineffectiveness of monetary policy stems from the inability of a country on a fixed exchange rate to determine its equilibrium stock of money. There are two important points to bear in mind with respect to the ineffectiveness of monetary policy in these circumstances.

(1) Fiscal policy is necessarily accompanied by monetary changes over which the authorities ultimately have no control. As we have seen, a policy of fiscal expansion raises the domestic rate of interest and thus increases the money supply via an inflow of foreign short-term capital. Attempts to prevent the money supply from rising by engaging in the open-market sale of bonds must ultimately fail as they only attract further inflows of capital. To attribute the effects of fiscal policy changes which inevitably bring about monetary changes solely to fiscal policy would be incorrect.

(2) The conduct of monetary policy does have important short-run disequilibrium effects, even if the equilibrium stock of money cannot be changed and therefore cannot affect the equilibrium level of real output. To deduce that monetary policy will have no effect on the equilibrium level of real national output because the equilibrium stock of money cannot be affected is not to deny its importance in disequilibrium.

Inappropriate monetary policy can cause disequilibrium, while the proper use of monetary policy can promote adjustment to equilibrium. For instance, increasing the stock of money more rapidly than it is absorbed by a rising demand for money by U.K. residents induces a portfolio disequilibrium which is eventually adjusted by the purchase of foreign goods and assets. This brings about a balance-of-payments deficit as a result of the increase in demand for foreign currency by holders of sterling. This implies that a balance-of-payments deficit under a fixed exchange rate system can be corrected by deliberate monetary policy measures as opposed to relying on the automatic mechanism of a diminishing money supply.

13.2 DYNAMIC ANALYSIS OF FISCAL AND MONETARY POLICY

The analysis of the impact of a policy measure can be subdivided into two components.

(1) Comparative static and comparative dynamic analysis, which deduce the effect on the steady-state equilibrium value of the target variables of changes in the instrumental variables.

(2) Dynamic analysis of the time path of adjustment of the target variables gives measures of the effectiveness of an instrumental variable

in terms of its speed of adjustment and stabilising properties (see Chapter 12).

The basic *ISLM* model can be made dynamic by the inclusion of lagged behavioural functions. These lags fall into two categories.

(1) *The expectations lag.* There is usually a lag in the response of the expected value of a variable to changes in its current value. One way of coping with this lag in economic models is via the adaptive expectations hypothesis which has already been used in explaining the adjustment of permanent income to changes in current income (see Chapter 3). In the permanent income hypothesis the expectations lag determines the proportion of any change in current income in period t that is transmitted to a change in permanent income in periods $t, t+1, \ldots, t+n$. A knowledge of the adaptive expectations lag, λ, is sufficient to work out the time pattern of response for a geometric distributed lag function. The *lower* is the value of λ in the consumption function derived from the permanent income hypothesis,

$$C_t = a + k\lambda y_t + (1-\lambda)C_{t-1} \tag{13.1}$$

the *smaller* is the influence of a change in current disposable income on current consumption and thus the *longer* is the lag.

Because of its lag structure the permanent income hypothesis of consumption has important implications for fiscal policy. Tax changes work by changing the level of disposable income and thus affecting consumption. The second and subsequent multiplier effects of changes in government spending on goods and services also depend for their effectiveness on changing consumption. The long-run multiplier can be the same for the absolute income hypothesis as for the permanent income hypothesis but the time taken for consumption to respond fully to a change in current income will be longer for the latter hypothesis. The smaller is the change in permanent income in response to a change in current income the longer it will take for the full impact of a fiscal policy measure on aggregate demand to be felt via the consumption function mechanism. If tax changes are thought to be temporary then there would be very little change in permanent income, making the fiscal policy multiplier small [7].

Adaptive expectations lags are introduced into other functions, such as the demand for money function, whenever permanent income enters as a determinant. Expectations about changes in the price level are an important element of the analysis of any inflationary economy. Such expectations will be influenced by current and past price level changes and will influence the rate of change of money wages and of market interest rates.

(2) *Adjustment lags.* Adjustment lags form a second class of lags. These measure the time taken by the dependent variable to adjust to a change in the value of its determinants, as opposed to the expectations lag which concerns the time taken for the value of the determinant itself to change. When adjustment lags are postulated one specifies both the long-run desired function for a variable, such as investment or the demand for money, and a short-run adjustment function. The latter specifies what proportion of the adjustment between the actual and desired value of the dependent variable occurs in each period.

A stock adjustment lag is postulated for the investment function. The capital stock is assumed to be related to past levels of output by means of a geometrically declining lag function, where γ is the lag coefficient. The net investment equation thus derived is

$$I_t^n = v\gamma y_t - \gamma K_{t-1}. \tag{13.2}$$

The *smaller* is γ the more slowly the capital stock adjusts to changes in output and hence the *longer* the lag. The rationale underlying the lag is that adjustment involves costs as well as benefits so that maximising the present value of net benefits leads to gradual adjustment.*

13.3   DYNAMIC MODELS OF THE ECONOMY

The implications for fiscal and monetary policy of various specifications for expectations and adjustment lags in the major behavioural functions have been analysed using the framework of the *ISLM* model. One particular model, that of Laidler [9], is discussed in order to give an example of this type of analysis. It must be borne in mind that the conclusions are specific to this model.

This model specifies that consumption and the demand for money are functions of permanent income. As permanent income is only partially adjusted to a change in current income, different lag structures produce different income adjustment paths in response to fiscal and monetary policy changes. The basic model is set out below.

$$C_t = ky_{pt} \tag{13.3}$$

$$I_t = I_0 - ai_t \tag{13.4}$$

$$G_t \text{ is exogenous} = G_0 \tag{13.5}$$

$$y_t = C_t + I_t + G_t \tag{13.6}$$

$$M_t^d = my_{pt} - li_t \tag{13.7}$$

$$y_{pt} = \lambda y_t + (1 - \lambda)y_{pt-1} \tag{13.8}$$

$$M_t^d = M_t \tag{13.9}$$

* See Chapter 4 pp 102–3, see also reference [6] related to Chapter 4.

where C is consumption, I is investment, G is government expenditure, y_p is permanent income, y is current income, i is the rate of interest, M^d is the demand for money, and M is the supply of money.

In long-run equilibrium current and permanent income are equal and the steady-state reduced form equations for permanent income and the rate of interest are

$$y_P = \frac{I_0 + G_0}{1 - z} + \frac{M}{(l/a)(1 - z)} \qquad (13.10)$$

$$i = \frac{I_0 + G_0}{(l/m)(1 - z)} - \frac{(1 - k)M}{l(1 - z)} \qquad (13.11)$$

where $z = k - (am/l)$.

Permanent income and the interest rate are shown as dependent on two exogenous instrumental variables, namely government expenditure and the money supply. From equations (13.10) and (13.11) we can obtain the long-run government expenditure and money multipliers

$$\frac{\partial y_P}{\partial G} = \frac{1}{(1 - z)}, \qquad \frac{\partial i}{\partial G} = \frac{1}{(l/m)(1 - z)}$$

$$\frac{\partial y_P}{\partial M} = \frac{1}{(l/a)(1 - z)}, \qquad \frac{\partial i}{\partial M} = -\frac{(1 - k)}{l(1 - z)}.$$

The long-run multipliers tell us what will be the steady-state equilibrium value of permanent income and the interest rate following a change in government expenditure or the money supply. This is all the information one can glean from comparative static analysis.

To plot the adjustment paths of income and the rate of interest we need to calculate their values in each period from the date of the policy change to the time of their convergence to equilibrium. Thus, the speed of adjustment is measured as the time taken to get within a given range (0·05) of steady-state equilibrium. The adjustment path is therefore a succession of short-run equilibria for income and the interest rate obtained by requiring the goods and money markets to be cleared in each period.

The short-run consumption and demand for money functions are

$$C_t = k\lambda y_t + k(1 - \lambda)y_{pt-1} \qquad (13.3a)$$

$$M_t^d = m\lambda y_t + m(1 - \lambda)y_{pt-1} - li_t \qquad (13.7a)$$

The short-run reduced form equations for income and the interest rate are

$$y_t = \frac{I_0 + G_0}{(1 - \lambda z)} + \frac{M}{(l/a)(1 - \lambda z)} + \frac{(1 - \lambda)z}{(1 - \lambda z)} y_{pt-1} \qquad (13.10a)$$

$$i_t = \frac{\lambda(I_0 + G_0)}{(l/m)(1 - \lambda z)} - \frac{(1 - \lambda k)M}{l(1 - \lambda z)} + \frac{(1 - \lambda)}{(l/m)(1 - \lambda z)} y_{pt-1}. \qquad (13.11a)$$

In long-run equilibrium $\lambda = 1$ and equations (13.10a) and (13.11a) reduce to equations (13.10) and (13.11). From equations (13.10a) and (13.11a) one can derive the impact multipliers. These give the change in income and interest rates in the first period after a change in monetary or fiscal policy.

$$\frac{\partial y_t}{\partial G_t} = \frac{1}{1 - \lambda z}, \qquad\qquad \frac{\partial i_t}{\partial G_t} = \frac{\lambda}{(l/m)(1 - \lambda z)}$$

$$\frac{\partial y_t}{\partial M_t} = \frac{1}{(l/a)(1 - \lambda z)}, \qquad \frac{\partial i_t}{\partial M_t} = \frac{-(1 - \lambda k)}{l(1 - \lambda z)}.$$

If the impact multiplier is larger than the long-run multiplier there will be an initial overshooting of equilibrium. In the second period income and the interest rate then reverse direction and move steadily towards equilibrium. Overshooting will occur if the z coefficient is negative. Model B in Figures 13.6 and 13.7 is characterised by a negative z. Given the value of k, since $z = k - am/l$, z is more likely to be negative the more interest responsive is investment, the more income responsive is the demand for money and the less interest responsive is the demand for money. These are all so-called neoclassical features. Monetary and fiscal policy both lead to overshooting under the same conditions but this is a feature of this particular model. In model A, characterised by a positive z, there will be monotonic convergence to equilibrium for both changes in government expenditure and the money supply.

As shown in Figures 13.6 and 13.7, the size of the expectations lag coefficient λ affects the speed of adjustment in both model A and B. The speed with which income adjusts increases as the length of the lag diminishes (i.e. λ gets larger).

To understand the different adjustment paths that are generated in these models one needs an appreciation of the positive and negative feedbacks on income which exist within the model. These are illustrated in Figure 13.8 for the case of expansionary fiscal and monetary policies. The expenditure multiplier, by which an increase in income increases consumption which increases income, provides a positive feedback mechanism. Negative feedback arises from the increase in output increasing the demand for money which causes the interest rate to rise and investment to be adversely affected.

In the case of monetary policy the initial fall in the rate of interest stimulates investment. In both model A and B the interest rate falls initially below its equilibrium level. It starts rising towards equilibrium once the increased income caused by the response of investment to the initial fall in the interest rate begins to raise the demand for money. The negative feedback effects are then in operation. Both positive and negative feedback effects work simultaneously. The direction in which

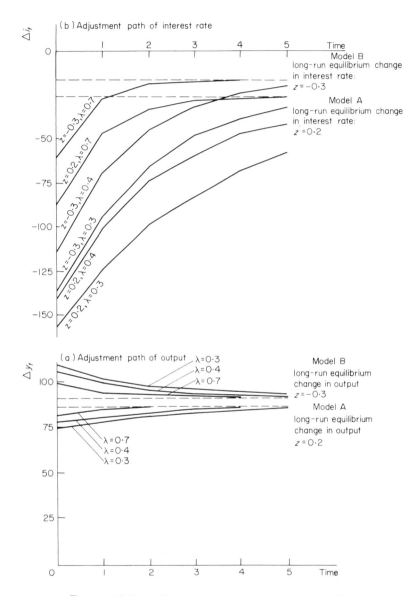

FIGURE 13.6   Adjustment to a change in monetary policy

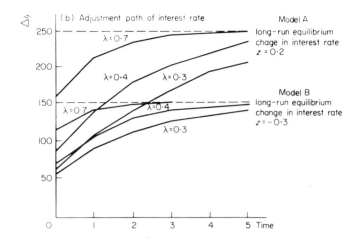

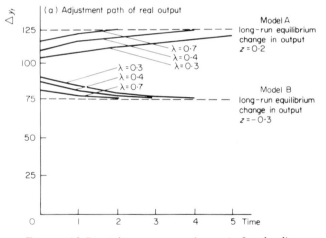

FIGURE 13.7   *Adjustment to a change in fiscal policy*

output actually moves in any one time period depends on whether the positive feedback effects are stronger or weaker than the negative feedback effects.

The reasons for models *A* and *B* producing different adjustment paths and the impact of the expectations lag are now examined.

Model A. In model *A* a positive *z* coefficient means that investment responds less to interest changes either because investment is interest

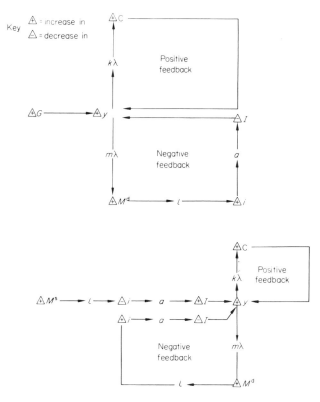

FIGURE 13.8   *Positive and negative feedback*

inelastic or because the interest rate is relatively unresponsive to changes in the demand for money. This means that the negative feedback effects from investment to output which are due to the upward pressure on interest rates brought about by rising national income are not particularly strong. At no time do the negative feedback effects outweigh the positive feedback effects so that output increases steadily towards equilibrium along a monotonic adjustment path. Adjustment proceeds more slowly the smaller the lag coefficient, λ, as consumption responds more slowly to increases in income thus prolonging the process of expanding output.

Model B. In model *B* a negative *z* means that investment is quite responsive to interest changes, either because investment is interest elastic or because the interest rate responds strongly to changes in the demand for money. The overshooting of equilibrium occurs because the negative feedback effects from investment, as in model *A*, do not have their full impact immediately but, unlike model *A*, have a stronger total impact. Because the negative feedback effects are delayed output initially rises above its equilibrium level. Output starts returning to equilibrium once the negative feedback effects come into operation and outweigh the positive feedback effects. In the case of fiscal policy the rise in the interest rate is delayed and hence the fall in investment is postponed. In the case of monetary policy the interest rate falls further below its equilibrium level in model *B* and thus gives a greater stimulus to investment than in model *A*. Therefore output overshoots equilibrium for both monetary and fiscal policy measures.

The overshooting is greater the smaller is λ. This is because the response of consumption and hence of income takes longer the smaller is λ. Thus, the rise in the demand for money and the consequent upward pressure on the interest rate are delayed. Therefore the negative feedback effects of the rising interest rate which come via investment are retarded, causing a greater initial overshooting of output. The greater the initial overshooting the further there is to travel back to equilibrium. Hence adjustment takes longer the smaller the lag coefficient, λ.

The analysis also indicates that longer lags can make the system more unstable as shown by the size of the initial overshooting in model *B*. Associated with this behaviour is the problem of inferring from the current movements in variables the direction in which the economy is moving and what effect policy measures are having. The behaviour of the interest rate shows that after the initial reaction income may still rise in response to monetary expansion although the interest rate is also rising. This points to the difficulty of using the interest rate as an indicator of whether monetary policy is having a restrictionary or expansionary impact on the economy.

13.4 EMPIRICAL EVIDENCE

The theoretical work on fiscal and monetary policy poses two sets of questions that require empirical investigation.

(1) How large are the long-run fiscal and monetary policy multipliers?

(2) How quickly does the system respond to monetary and fiscal policy changes?

The deductions of economic theory show the implications that different values of the steady-state and lag coefficients have for the answers to the above questions. The dynamic analysis we have just done was limited to a model containing only an expectations lag. The analysis of models containing adjustment lags indicates that it is important to distinguish expectations lags from adjustment lags, as they have differing effects. This presents problems as it is difficult to differentiate between the two types of lag in empirical work (see [10, 11, 12, 13]).

Econometric studies of individual behavioural equations yield probable values for the steady-state and lag coefficients. A number of these behavioural relationships have been examined in earlier chapters and their relevance to determining the impact of monetary and fiscal policy should be kept in mind.

Interest Rate Behaviour

Investigations of interest rate behaviour indicate that there is some evidence supporting the theoretical deductions of the dynamic *ISLM* model that expansionary (restrictive) monetary policy initially causes interest rates to fall (rise) by more in the short run than in the long run. These tests regress changes in the interest rate on lagged changes in the money supply.* Cagan and Gandolphi [14] carried out such a test on U.S. monthly data 1910–65. They report that a 1 per cent increase in the rate of change of the money supply causes the short-term rate of interest to decline for seven months till it is 2·6 basis points† below its starting level. It then rises, passing its starting level after fifteen months and reaches a peak of 3·6 basis points above after twenty-five months. Gibson [15] obtains shorter lags so that the initial negative effect on the rate of interest is offset after six to nine months following a rise in M_2. (He uses monthly observations for the United States in the period 1947–66 and a number of the coefficients are insignificant.) Regressions using quarterly data for the United Kingdom in the period 1955–66 give similar adjustment paths for interest rates though the evidence is less clear cut as some coefficients are insignificant and the pattern of negative signs followed by positive signs is less evident. Examples are given below [16]:

$$i_t = 1·55 y_t - 6·09 m_t + 4·99 m_{t-1} + 0·96$$
$$(0·48) \quad (2·71) \quad (2·21)$$

$$\Delta i_t = 0·268 \Delta y_t - 1·26 \Delta m_t + 0·743 \Delta m_{t-1}$$
$$(0·903) \quad (1·63) \quad (0·883)$$

where m are real money balances and Δ indicates first differences.

As well as investigating individual economic relationships one can also estimate models of the economy to obtain evidence on the impacts of monetary and fiscal policy. In this area investigators have differed over the appropriate methodology.

The Structural Approach

Large-scale econometric models containing up to 300 equations are constructed by disaggregating the major macro relationships. These

---

* These tests have the usual problems of bias if the money supply itself is related to the rate of interest.
† 100 basis points = 1 percentage point of the interest rate.

models are dynamic as they contain lagged dependent variables. Simulation exercises with these models involve changing the values of the instrumental variables and comparing the time paths of the endogenous variables with and without the policy changes. The chief merit of this approach is that it enables one to see the interrelationships between variables and the transmission channels through which one variable exerts its influence over others. This increases one's knowledge not only of how the economic system responds but also why it behaves in certain ways.

The advocates of this approach attempt to understand a complex world by building complex models. Econometric model-building is more advanced in the United States than in the United Kingdom. Early models were basically disaggregated Keynesian income–expenditure models. Recently greater attention has been paid to specifying a more fully developed monetary sector as in the F.R.B.–M.I.T. [17, 18] model. Simulations with this model show that monetary policy has a more important impact than indicated by earlier models (see Table 13.1). Introducing the monetary sector reduces the size of the fiscal policy multiplier, as one would expect from *ISLM* analysis, but fiscal policy is estimated to be quicker acting than monetary policy. One difficulty with the use of econometric models is that their ability to show the effectiveness of various policy measures depends on the specification of channels through which these policy influences can be felt. If it is the case that monetary policy effects are very diffuse, the full impact will not be picked up by an econometric model.

The 'Reduced Form' Approach

The 'reduced form' approach is advocated on the grounds of simplicity. Since the world is complex one can best attempt to understand it by searching for theories which can explain much with relatively few variables. This approach does not strictly derive reduced forms, as the relationship tested is not derived from the structural equations of a model. Instead the dependent variable is assumed to be a function of exogenously determined variables.

The use of the 'reduced form' approach in monetary research originated in the Friedman–Meiselman [20] study of the relative ability of autonomous spending and the money supply to explain changes in consumption. The results of this work and the critical replies to it are shown in Table 13.1 in the form of long-run multipliers. Another example of the 'reduced form' approach is the St Louis equation of Andersen and Jordan [23]. This equation specifies that G.N.P. depends on certain monetary and fiscal policy variables. As no underlying structural model is explicitly stated one cannot glean from this model any information about the structural relationships or about the transmission mechanisms. The main difficulty with this approach is that the

TABLE 13.1 Estimates of Monetary and Fiscal Policy Multipliers: Response of G.N.P. to a Unit Change in the Policy Variable

Study	Sample	Multiplier re monetary variable	Elasticity re monetary variable	Multiplier for exogenous spending	Multiplier for taxes
Friedman–Meiselman [20]	annual, 1948–57	2·58 (for M2)	1·22	1·71	–1·71
	quarterly, 1945–58	2·94	1·39	1·06	–1·06
Ando–Modigliani [21]	annual, 1929–58 excluding war	0·26 (for M*)	0·09	1·62	–1·98
DePrano–Mayer [22]	annual, 1929–63 first differences	1·05 (for M2)	0·50	1·51	n.c.
Andersen–Jordan [23]	quarterly, 1952–68 first differences	16·01 (for adjusted monetary base)	1·67	–0·54	0·51
deLeeuw–Kalchbrenner [24]	quarterly, 1952–68 first differences	11·6 (for adjusted unborrowed reserves)	0·55	2·5	–2·8
Wharton School model	quarterly postwar	2·9 (for unborrowed reserves)	0·11	2·9	–2·4
Brookings model	quarterly postwar	8·2 (for unborrowed reserves)	0·31	2·7	–1·2
Ando–Goldfeld model	quarterly postwar	3·4 (for reserve base)	0·31	3·3	–2·2
F.R.B.–M.I.T. model [18]	quarterly postwar	20·6 (for unborrowed reserves)	0·55	2·7	–2·5

Source: [19].

determinants of the dependent variable must be truly exogenous or the estimated coefficients in the regression equation will be biased. Much of the debate over the 'reduced form' approach has revolved around the selection of exogenous explanatory variables.

The original St Louis model regressed quarterly changes in G.N.P. in current prices both upon lagged quarterly changes in the money stock or alternatively on the money reserve base, and upon fiscal policy changes as measured by changes in either government expenditure or full-employment tax receipts or the full-employment budget surplus* (U.S. data 1952–68). Only the sum of the coefficients of the monetary variables was significant. The model found that the major impact of both policy variables occurred within four quarters. Andersen and Jordan claimed on the basis of this evidence that monetary policy has a larger impact, is more predictable and is quicker acting than fiscal policy. Therefore they advocate the use of discretionary monetary policy. A similar study by Keran [26], using U.S. quarterly data for the period 1919–69 produced results in the same vein.

The St Louis work has not gone unchallenged [24, 25]. The chief area of contention is the direction of causation between G.N.P. and the money supply. Although it is agreed that the money supply itself is not entirely exogenous, the monetarist view requires that the 'high-powered' money base is determined independently of G.N.P. This makes the money–income causal link dominant, and the income–money causal link much less important.

The St Louis equation has been tested using alternative specifications of the policy variables in order to improve their degree of exogeneity. The modified St Louis equation of de Leeuw and Kalchenbrenner [24] uses unborrowed reserves† which can more readily be accepted as being exogenous than can the money supply. This gives results similar to those of the F.R.B.–M.I.T. econometric model of the U.S. economy, as is shown in Figure 13.9.

It would appear that the empirical results are more sensitive to alternative specifications of the monetary policy variable than to the type of statistical model used. As the money supply variable is peeled down to more exogenous elements, the lag in the response of G.N.P. increases (see Figure 13.10). Hamburger [28] concludes his survey of the empirical evidence relating to the monetary policy lag in the United States thus:

Use of unborrowed reserves suggests that less than forty per cent of the

* These are the values estimated to exist if the economy were at full employment given the existing fiscal structure.
† That proportion of commercial bank reserves which has not been borrowed from the central bank. In the United States, unlike the United Kingdom, banks borrow directly from the Central Bank.

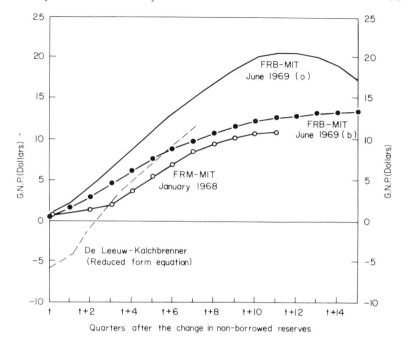

FIGURE 13.9 *Cumulative effects of a one-dollar change in non-borrowed reserves on G.N.P.*

impact of a monetary action occurs within five quarters and that the full effect is distributed over two and a half years. On the other hand use of the money supply, the monetary base or total reserves suggests that most of the effect occurs within four or five quarters.

U.K. Evidence

The quantity and quality of empirical evidence for the United Kingdom is substantially lower than that for the United States. Walters and Barrett [29] have repeated the Friedman–Meiselman tests for the U.K. economy using annual data for the period 1878–1963 (excluding war years). The results are presented below.

ΔA_t is the annual change in autonomous expenditure defined as gross private domestic investment plus government expenditure plus exports minus imports.

ΔM_t is the annual change in the money supply defined as notes, coin and bank deposits of joint stock banks.

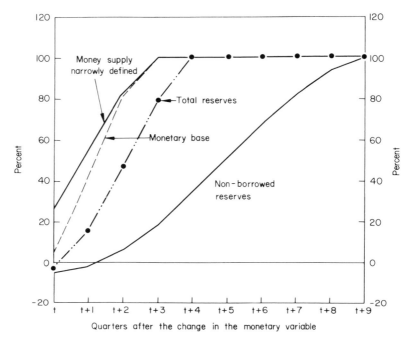

Figure 13.10   *Cumulative percentage distributions of the effects of various monetary aggregates on G.N.P.*

ΔC_t is the change in consumers' expenditure.

The equations are in logarithmic form. The standard deviation of the estimate is given in brackets. DW indicates the Durbin–Watson statistic.

1878–1914, 1920–38, 1948–63:

$$C_t = 2 \cdot 16 + 0 \cdot 486\,M_{t-1} + 0 \cdot 328\,A_t$$
$$\quad\;\; (0 \cdot 08)\;(0 \cdot 037)\qquad (0 \cdot 032)$$

$$\bar{R}^2 = 0 \cdot 995, \quad DW = 0 \cdot 39$$

partial correlation of C and $M = r_{12 \cdot 3}^2 = 0 \cdot 714$

partial correlation of C and $A = r_{13 \cdot 2}^2 = 0 \cdot 607$

$$\Delta C_t = 0 \cdot 0053 + 0 \cdot 406\,\Delta M_{t-1} + 0 \cdot 204 A_t$$
$$\quad\;\; (0 \cdot 0022)\;(0 \cdot 106)\qquad (0 \cdot 033)$$

$$\bar{R}^2 = 0 \cdot 442, \qquad DW = 1 \cdot 45$$

$$r_{12 \cdot 3}^2 = 0 \cdot 181, \qquad r_{13 \cdot 2}^2 = 0 \cdot 361.$$

1878–1914:

$$\Delta C_t = 0\cdot0031 + 0\cdot576\ \Delta M_{t-1} + 0\cdot187\ \Delta A_t$$
$$(0\cdot002)\quad(0\cdot088)\qquad\quad(0\cdot031)$$

$$\bar{R}^2 = 0\cdot579,\qquad DW = 1\cdot87$$
$$r^2_{12\cdot3} = 0\cdot564,\qquad r^2_{13\cdot2} = 0\cdot197.$$

1921–38:

$$\Delta C_t = -0\cdot0027 + 0\cdot25\ \Delta M_{t-1} + 0\cdot194\ \Delta A_t$$
$$(0\cdot0012)\ (0\cdot133)\qquad\quad(0\cdot038)$$
$$\bar{R}^2 = 0\cdot678,\qquad DW = 1\cdot89$$
$$r^2_{12\cdot3} = 0\cdot202,\qquad r^2_{13\cdot2} = 0\cdot65.$$

1948–63 (first differences for this period gave insignificant results):

$$C_t = -2\cdot12 + 0\cdot763\ M_{t-1} + 0\cdot523\ A_t$$
$$(0\cdot93)\ (0\cdot137)\qquad\quad(0\cdot041)$$
$$\bar{R}^2 = 0\cdot996,\qquad DW = 1\cdot21$$
$$r^2_{12\cdot3} = 0\cdot700,\qquad r^2_{13\cdot2} = 0\cdot925.$$

These results indicate that both autonomous expenditure and the stock of money contribute to determining consumption. The findings do not support the conclusion of Friedman and Meiselman that the money multiplier is more stable than the autonomous expenditure multiplier. The money supply appears to have been more important before 1914, whereas autonomous expenditure correlates more closely with consumption in the later periods.

The St Louis tests are replicated for the U.K. economy by Artis and Nobay [31], with reservations about the statistical reliability of these tests. Quarterly data for the period 1958 to the third quarter of 1967 were used and the results are reproduced in Table 13.2. Government fiscal measures are estimated as the first round multiplier effects of certain tax changes and changes in hire-purchase terms on G.D.P. Government fiscal measures and the broad money supply, M_3, minus deposits held by the government and by financial institutions, appeared to be the best representative variables for fiscal and monetary policy respectively. The monetary policy variables operate with a greater lag, the average lag of broad money supply changes being 3·2 quarters compared with 0·2 quarters for fiscal policy measures. Thus, the St Louis results are reversed. One similarity that does exist is the tendency for fiscal policy measures lagged two or more periods to possess negative signs indicating an initial overshooting of G.D.P. Further tests, using the same method of estimating lags as the St Louis study, gave insignificant results.

Although little confidence can be attached to the estimates, it is interesting to note that a measure of the lagged responses of G.D.P. to

TABLE 13.2 Effects of fiscal and monetary policy changes upon G.D.P. in the United Kingdom [31]

Step-wise regression results[a]

Equation (1)
$$\Delta G.D.P. = 122 \cdot 0 - 0 \cdot 7\,(\Delta G.D.P._{-1}) + 11 \cdot 6\,(\Delta G.F.M._{-1}) + 0 \cdot 5\,(\Delta ADV._{-5}) + 0 \cdot 8\,(\Delta F.E.R.) - 0 \cdot 5\,(\Delta G.D.P._{-2})\ 0 \cdot 2\,(\Delta B.M.S._{-4})$$
$$(5 \cdot 9) \qquad (6 \cdot 1) \qquad\qquad (4 \cdot 7) \qquad\qquad (5 \cdot 1) \qquad\qquad (3 \cdot 8) \qquad\qquad (2 \cdot 6)$$
$$R^2 = 0 \cdot 73 \qquad S.E. = 47 \cdot 1 \qquad DW = 1 \cdot 8$$

Equation (2)
$$\Delta G.D.P. = 161 \cdot 1 - 0 \cdot 7\,(\Delta G.D.P._{-1}) + 8 \cdot 3\,(\Delta G.F.M._{-1}) + 0 \cdot 4\,(\Delta ADV._{-5}) - 0 \cdot 3\,(\Delta G.D.P._{-2}) - 0 \cdot 01\,(\Delta B.M.S._{-4})$$
$$(4 \cdot 1) \qquad\qquad (3 \cdot 4) \qquad\qquad (2 \cdot 8) \qquad\qquad (2 \cdot 0) \qquad\qquad (0 \cdot 3)$$
$$R^2 = 0 \cdot 48 \qquad S.E. = 64 \cdot 1 \qquad DW = 1 \cdot 5$$

Equation (3)
$$\Delta G.D.P. = 160 \cdot 6 - 0 \cdot 7\,(\Delta G.D.P._{-1}) + 8 \cdot 3\,(\Delta G.F.M._{-1}) + 0 \cdot 4\,(\Delta ADV._{-5}) - 0 \cdot 3\,(\Delta G.D.P._{-2})$$
$$(4 \cdot 4) \qquad\qquad (3 \cdot 6) \qquad\qquad (2 \cdot 8) \qquad\qquad (2 \cdot 1)$$
$$R^2 = 0 \cdot 48 \qquad S.E. = 63 \qquad DW = 1 \cdot 5$$

Equation (4)
$$\Delta G.D.P. = 97 \cdot 0 + 9 \cdot 3\,(\Delta G.F.M._{-1}) - 7 \cdot 0\,(\Delta G.F.M._{-2})$$
$$(3 \cdot 0) \qquad\qquad (2 \cdot 3)$$
$$R^2 = 0 \cdot 23 \qquad S.E. = 73 \cdot 9$$

Equation (5)
$$\Delta G.D.P. = 77 \cdot 6 + 10 \cdot 8\,(\Delta G.F.M._{-1}) - 8 \cdot 3\,(\Delta G.F.M._{-2}) + 0 \cdot 2\,(\Delta ADV._{-4})$$
$$(3 \cdot 6) \qquad\qquad (2 \cdot 8) \qquad\qquad (1 \cdot 9)$$
$$R^2 = 0 \cdot 31 \qquad S.E. = 70 \cdot 9$$

(a) The symbols have the following meanings: G.D.P. = gross domestic product; G.F.M. = government fiscal measures; ADV. = advances; F.E.R. = full-employment budget receipts; B.M.S. = broad money supply. Other symbols have their usual meaning. For further explanations, see text.

Quarterly changes are indicated by the symbol Δ; *t*-ratios are shown in parentheses below the coefficients.

fiscal and monetary policy changes indicate non-monotonic adjustment paths. This reinforces the message of theoretical analysis that one should not necessarily expect a steady approach to equilibrium. Artis and Nobay's results show fiscal policy causing an initial overshooting of equilibrium for two quarters, whereas monetary policy produces an initial movement in the opposite direction to equilibrium.

13.5 CONCLUSION

The early post-Keynesian confidence that Keynesian economics had provided the means of regulating a market economy by the judicious use of fiscal policy has evaporated (or should have!). This change has been brought about by a combination of experience with demand-management policies and the increasing recognition in theoretical and empirical work of the importance of dynamic analysis. In order to apply appropriate policies one has to know initially what is the current state of the economy and the direction in which it is moving. One then needs knowledge of the magnitude and timing of the economic system's responses to given stimuli. Dynamic analysis indicates the difficulties of inferring from the current movement of variables the direction and strength of future movements. It is thus difficult to know precisely when and how to act.

Because of these problems some economists have eschewed the use of discretionary policy in favour of set policy rules. The lack of widespread support for such views is no doubt partly due to its conflicting with the self-interest of economists and politicians who like to feel that they are capable of beneficially influencing the economy.

The debate over discretion versus rules is partly founded on value judgements about the desirability of government intervention and the capacity of governments to act intelligently. It also concerns disagreement over empirical facts. These concern first the degree of automatic stability in the economy, which determines the necessity for government intervention. The second issue concerns the means of control and establishing the economic system's dynamic responses to fiscal and monetary variables. Here the disagreement concerns the way available data are interpreted. The major post-war academic development has been a renewed awareness of the importance of monetary variables. This is not yet reflected in U.K. economic policy which remains firmly wedded to fiscal measures, reinforced with intermittent credit restraint, while little prominence has been given to the behaviour of the money supply.

This book has stressed the importance of lags in economic analysis. A backward glance at economic history indicates a lag between economic events and changes in economic theory, followed by a further lag in the application of economic theory by policy-makers. *The General Theory* evolved as a response to the inappropriate policy recommendations provided by economic theory to deal with chronic depression. Post-war economic policy has continued to apply theories derived on the basis of assumptions relevant to depressed economies to entirely different economic conditions. Leafing through the *National Institute Economic Review* [32] one will find U.K. policy advisers are still working with one-sector Keynesian income–expenditure models in the 1960s.

The standard macro models are ill-suited to explain short-run behaviour in the current circumstances. The Keynesian model determines real income on the basis of an assumed money wage level, which is an appropriate simplification for a depressed economy. The neoclassical model explains long-run real income determination and price level determination on the basis of a given quantity of real income. We require a model which will explain the short-run behaviour of an economy experiencing inflation and operating at a reasonably full level of capacity utilisation. Elements of such a model are appearing in current work on inflation and the labour market and in the monetarist attempt to provide a theoretical structure for the short-run influence of money on real variables.

REFERENCES

[1] R. A. Mundell, 'Capital Mobility and Stabilisation Policy Under Fixed and Flexible Exchange Rates', *Canadian Journal of Economic and Political Science*, 34, 4 (November 1963) and in his *International Economics* (London: Macmillan, 1968) ch. 18.

[2] R. A. Mundell, 'The Monetary Dynamics of International Adjustment Under Fixed and Flexible Exchange Rates', *Quarterly Journal of Economics*, 74 (May 1960); also in *International Economics*.

[3] A. O. Krueger, 'The Impact of Alternative Government Policies Under Varying Exchange Systems', *Quarterly Journal of Economics*, 79 (1965).

[4] J. M. Fleming, 'Domestic Financial Policies Under Fixed and Floating Exchange Rates', *International Monetary Fund Staff Papers*, 9, 3 (1962).

[5] H. G. Johnson, 'Some Aspects of the Theory of Economic Policy in a World of Capital Mobility', in *Further Essays in Monetary Economics* (London: Allen & Unwin, 1972).

[6] H. G. Johnson, 'Theoretical Problems of the International Monetary System', in *Further Essays in Monetary Economics*.

[7] R. Eisner, 'Fiscal and Monetary Policy Reconsidered', *American Economic Review*, 59, 1 (1969).

[8] H. G. Johnson, 'Towards a General Theory of the Balance of Payments', in *International Trade and Economic Growth* (London: Allen & Unwin, 1958).

[9] D. Laidler, 'The Permanent Income Concept in a Macroeconomic Model', *Oxford Economic Papers*, n.s., 20 (March 1968).

[10] D. Tucker, 'Dynamic Income Adjustment to Money Supply Changes', *American Economic Review*, 56 (June 1966).

[11] D. Tucker, 'Credit Rationing, Interest Rate Lags and Monetary Policy Speed', *Quarterly Journal of Economics*, 82 (1968).

[12] E. Feige, 'Expectations and Adjustments in the Monetary Sector', *American Economic Review*, 57 (May, 1967).

[13] G. R. Fisher and D. K. Sheppard, 'Interrelationships Between Real and Monetary Variables: Some Evidence from Recent U.S. Empirical Studies', in *Issues in Monetary Economics*, ed. H. G. Johnson and A. R. Nobay (Oxford University Press, 1974).

[14] P. Cagan and A. Gandolphi, 'The Lag in Monetary Policy as Implied by the Time Pattern of Monetary Effects on Interest Rates', *American Economic Review*, 59 (May 1969).

[15] W. E. Gibson, 'The Lag in the Effect of Monetary Policy on Income and Interest Rates', *Quarterly Journal of Economics*, 84 (May 1970).

[16] A. A. Walters, 'Money Multipliers in the U.K. 1880–1962', *Oxford Economic Papers*, n.s., 18 (1966).

[17] F. de Leeuw and E. M. Gramlich, 'Channels of Monetary Policy', *Federal Reserve Bulletin*, 55 (June 1969) reprinted in *Monetary Economics: Readings on Current Issues*, ed. W. E. Gibson and G. G. Kaufman (New York: McGraw-Hill, 1971).

[18] A. Ando and F. Modigliani, 'Econometric Analysis of Stabilisation Policies', *American Economic Review*, 59 (1969).

[19] E. M. Gramlich, 'The Usefulness of Monetary and Fiscal Policy as Discretionary Stabilisation Tools', *Journal of Money, Credit and Banking*, 4, Part 2 (May 1972).

[20] M. Friedman and D. Meiselman, 'The Relative Stability of Monetary Velocity and the Investment Multiplier in the U.S.', *Impacts of Monetary Policy*, Commission on Money and Credit (Englewood Cliffs, N.J.: Prentice-Hall, 1963).

[21] A. Ando and F. Modigliani, 'The Relative Stability of Monetary Velocity and the Investment Multiplier, *American Economic Review*, 55 (1965).

[22] M. De Prano and T. Mayer, 'Autonomous Expenditures and Money', *American Economic Review*, 55 (1965).

[23] L. C. Andersen and J. L. Jordan, 'Monetary and Fiscal Actions: A Test of their Relative Importance in Economic Stabilisation', *Federal Reserve Bank of St Louis Monthly Review*, 50, 11 (November 1966) reprinted in *Monetary Economics*, ed. Gibson and Kaufman.

[24] F. de Leeuw and J. Kalchenbrenner, 'Monetary and Fiscal Actions: A Test of their Relative Importance in Economic

Stabilisation – Comment', *F.R.B. St Louis Monthly Review*, 51, 4 (April 1969).

[25] R. G. Davis, 'How Much Does Money Matter? A Look at Some of the Recent Evidence', *F.R.B. of New York Monthly Review*, 51 (June 1969) reprinted in *Monetary Economics*, ed. Gibson and **Kaufman**.

[26] M. W. Keran, 'Monetary and Fiscal Influences on Economic Activity: The Historical Evidence', *F.R.B. St Louis Monthly Review*, 51 (November 1969).

[27] L. C. Anderson and K. M. Carlson, 'A Monetarist Model for Economic Stabilisation', *F.R.B. St Louis Monthly Review*, 52 (1970).

[28] M. J. Hamburger, 'The Lag in the Effect of Monetary Policy: A. Survey of Recent Literature', *F.R.B. of New York Monthly Review* (December 1972).

[29] C. R. Barrett and A. A. Walters, 'The Stability of the Keynesian and Monetary Multipliers in the U.K.', *Review of Economics and Statistics*, 48, 4 (November 1966) reprinted in *Readings in British Monetary Economics*, ed. Johnson.

[30] A. A. Walters, 'The Radcliffe Report – Ten Years After: A Survey of Empirical Evidence', in *Money in Britain, 1959–69* ed. H. G. Johnson and D. R. Croome (Oxford University Press, 1970).

[31] M. Artis and A. R. Nobay, 'Two Aspects of the Monetary Debate', *National Institute Economic Review* (August 1969) reprinted in *Readings in British Monetary Economics*, ed. Johnson.

[32] B. Hopkin and W. Godley, 'An Analysis of Tax Changes', *National Institute Economic Review*, 32 (May 1965).

Author Index

Subject Index